Oxford AQA GCSE History

Thematic Studies

c790-Present Day

AUTHORS
Lindsay Bruce
J. A. Cloake
Kevin Newman
Aaron Wilkes

SERIES EDITOR
Aaron Wilkes

CONSULTANT
J. A. Cloake

OXFORD

OXFORD
UNIVERSITY PRESS

Great Clarendon Street, Oxford, OX2 6DP, United Kingdom

Oxford University Press is a department of the University of Oxford. It furthers the University's objective of excellence in research, scholarship, and education by publishing worldwide. Oxford is a registered trade mark of Oxford University Press in the UK and in certain other countries

© Oxford University Press 2016

The moral rights of the authors have been asserted

First published in 2016

All rights reserved. No part of this publication may be reproduced, stored in a retrieval system, or transmitted, in any form or by any means, without the prior permission in writing of Oxford University Press, or as expressly permitted by law, by licence or under terms agreed with the appropriate reprographics rights organization. Enquiries concerning reproduction outside the scope of the above should be sent to the Rights Department, Oxford University Press, at the address above.

You must not circulate this work in any other form and you must impose this same condition on any acquirer

British Library Cataloguing in Publication Data

Data available

978-0-19-837013-0

Kerboodle Book 978-0-19-837017-8

10 9 8 7 6 5 4

Paper used in the production of this book is a natural, recyclable product made from wood grown in sustainable forests. The manufacturing process conforms to the environmental regulations of the country of origin.

Printed in India by Manipal Technologies Limited

Approval message from AQA

This textbook has been approved by AQA for use with our qualification. This means that we have checked that it broadly covers the specification and we are satisfied with the overall quality. Full details of our approval process can be found on our website.

We approve textbooks because we know how important it is for teachers and students to have the right resources to support their teaching and learning. However, the publisher is ultimately responsible for the editorial control and quality of this book.

Please note that when teaching the AQA GCSE History course, you must refer to AQA's specification as your definitive source of information. While this book has been written to match the specification, it cannot provide complete coverage of every aspect of the course.

A wide range of other useful resources can be found on the relevant subject pages of our website: www.aqa.org.uk.

Links to third party websites are provided by Oxford in good faith and for information only. Oxford disclaims any responsibility for the materials contained in any third party website referenced in this work.

From the authors:
Lindsay Bruce: Firstly, I would like to thank my family for being so encouraging and proud of me. Also, my friends who didn't complain that I had no time for them. Laura and Theo, thank you for keeping everything going at work. Finally, my wonderful partner Chris for being there every day to proofread, make cups of tea and tell me I could do it when I wanted to give up. I love you.

Kevin Newman: For Laura, Seth and Eddie. Thanks also to Sarah Flynn and Janice Chan for all the help, encouragement and being great to work with. Massive thanks also, for all their support and guidance, to Aaron Wilkes and Jon Cloake.

Aaron Wilkes: I would like to acknowledge the brilliant team at OUP, including Janice Chan, Rebecca DeLozier and Sarah Flynn, and also Melanie Waldron and Jon Cloake, who have contributed to this project in all sorts of invaluable ways. I also thank the people at home – Emma, Eleanor and Hannah – who put up with me opening my laptop in all sorts of places, at all sorts of times, and without whom I wouldn't have been able to help produce this series.

The publisher would like to thank the following people for offering their contribution in the development of this book:
J.A. Cloake, Fred Batchelor, Ed Hutchinson, Aaron Wilkes, Helen Reilly and Indexing Specialists (UK) Ltd.

Contents

Thematic Studies c790-Present Day

Introduction to the Oxford AQA GCSE History series 4

Britain: Health and the people

Timeline 6

Part one: Medicine stands still
Chapter 1: Medieval medicine — 8
Chapter 2: Medical progress — 10
Chapter 3: Public health in the Middle Ages — 16

Part two: The beginnings of change
Chapter 4: The impact of the Renaissance on Britain — 24
Chapter 5: Dealing with disease — 32
Chapter 6: Prevention of disease — 40

Part three: A revolution in medicine
Chapter 7: Advances in medical science in nineteenth-century Britain — 42
Chapter 8: Further impact of Germ Theory in Britain — 50
Chapter 9: Improvements in public health — 54

Part four: Modern medicine
Chapter 10: Modern treatment of disease — 62
Chapter 11: The impact of war and technology on surgery — 72
Chapter 12: Modern public health — 76
How to … analyse significance 84
How to … analyse sources 86
How to … compare similarities 88

Britain: Power and the people

Timeline 90

Part one: Challenging authority and feudalism
Chapter 1: Constraints on kingship — 92
Chapter 2: The origins of parliament — 98
Chapter 3: Medieval revolt and royal authority — 104

Part two: Challenging royal authority
Chapter 4: Popular uprisings against the Crown — 110
Chapter 5: Divine right and parliamentary authority — 116
Chapter 6: Royal authority and the right to representation — 126

Part three: Reform and reformers
Chapter 7: The extension of the franchise — 130
Chapter 8: Protest and change — 138
Chapter 9: Workers' movements — 148

Part four: Equality and rights
Chapter 10: Women's rights and the campaign for the vote — 154
Chapter 11: Workers' rights — 160
Chapter 12: Minority rights — 166
How to … analyse significance 172
How to … analyse sources 174
How to … compare similarities 176
How to … evaluate main factors 177

Britain: Migration, empires and the people

Timeline 178

Part one: Conquered and conquerors
Chapter 1: Invasion — 180
Chapter 2: A Norman Kingdom and 'Angevin' Empire — 188
Chapter 3: The birth of English identity — 194

Part two: Looking west
Chapter 4: Sugar and the Caribbean — 200
Chapter 5: Colonisation in North America — 206
Chapter 6: Migrants to and from Britain — 214

Part three: Expansion and empire
Chapter 7: Expansion in India — 218
Chapter 8: Expansion in Africa — 230
Chapter 9: Migrants to, from and within Britain — 242

Part four: Britain in the twentieth century
Chapter 10: The end of the British Empire — 250
Chapter 11: The legacy of the British Empire — 254
Chapter 12: Britain's relationship with Europe — 262
How to … analyse significance 266
How to … analyse sources 268
How to … compare similarities 270
How to … evaluate main factors 271
Practice Questions for Paper 2: Thematic Studies 272
Glossary 278
Index 284

Introduction to the Oxford AQA GCSE History series

The Oxford AQA GCSE History series has been specially written by an expert team of teachers and historians with examining experience to match each part of your AQA course. The chapters which follow are laid out according to the content of the AQA specification. Written in an interesting and engaging style, each of the eye-catching double-pages is clearly organised to provide you with a logical route through the historical content.

There is a lively mix of visual **Sources** and **Interpretations** to enhance and challenge your learning and understanding of the history. Extensive use of photographs, diagrams, cartoons, charts and maps allows you to practise using a variety of sources as evidence.

The **Work** activities and **Practice Questions** have been written to help you check your understanding of the content, develop your skills as a historian, and help you prepare not just for GCSE examinations, but for any future studies. You can develop your knowledge and practise examination skills further through the interactive activities, history skills animations, practice questions, revision checklists and more on *Kerboodle**.

Thematic Studies

Thematic Studies focus on key developments in the history of Britain over a long period of time. You will study in detail one of the following periods: Health and the people (c1000 to the present day); Power and the people (c1170 to the present day); or Migration, empires and the people (c790 to the present day). You will look at the importance of factors such as war, religion, government and the role of the individual, and how these factors impact upon society.

Understanding history requires not just knowledge, but also a good grasp of concepts such as causation, consequence and change. This book is designed to help you think historically, and features primary sources: these sources will help you to think about how historians base their understanding on the careful evaluation of evidence from the past.

We hope you'll enjoy exploring these Thematic Studies –

Jon Cloake
Series Consultant

Aaron Wilkes
Series Editor

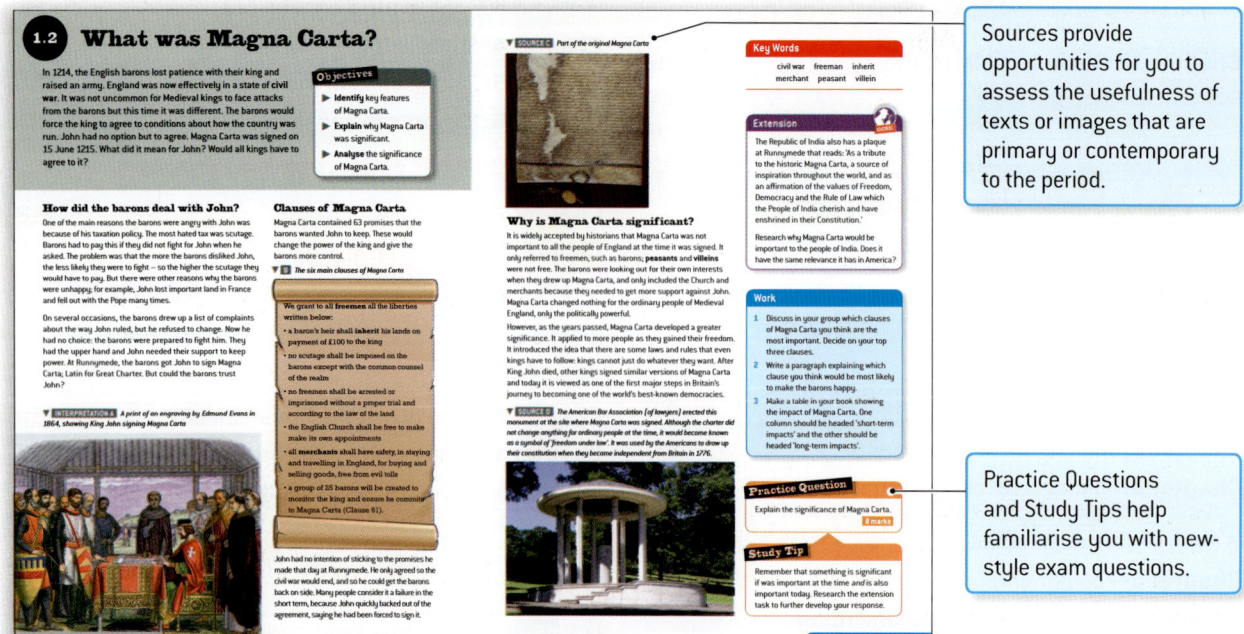

Britain: Power and the people

*Kerboodle is not approved by AQA.

How to use this book

Written for the new AQA specification, the features in this book include:

Objectives
At the beginning of the sections, you will find a list of learning objectives. These are based on the requirements of the course.

▼ SOURCE ▼ INTERPRETATION
Sources introduce you to material that is primary or contemporary to the period, and **Interpretations** provide you with various people's different perspectives on the past.

Practice Question
These are focused questions to help you practise your history skills, including evaluating sources and essay writing. They give you an idea of the types of questions you might get in an examination.

Study Tip
These are hints to highlight key parts of **Practice Questions** and will help you answer the questions.

Fact
Fascinating references, facts or anecdotes that will make you think and add to your knowledge and understanding.

Work
The activities and questions aim to develop your knowledge, understanding and key history skills. They are designed to be progressive in terms of difficulty, and to get you to think about the topic, become familiar with the history, and apply what you have learned.

Extension

This is an opportunity to challenge you to investigate the history more deeply through independent research and reflection.

Key Words
The important phrases and terms are highlighted and are also defined in the glossary. Learn what they mean – and how to spell and use them correctly.

Timeline

A short list of dates identifying key events to help you understand chronological developments.

Key Biography
Details of a key person to help you understand the individuals who have helped shape history.

Thematic Studies c790–Present Day 5

Timeline

Britain: Health and the people

This thematic study covers over 1000 years in the history of medicine and public health in Britain. You will explore how medicine and public health changed, why change happened when it did, whether change brought progress, and the significance of the changes. You will also consider how factors – such as war, chance, religion, science and technology – sometimes worked together to bring about particular developments at a particular time; and what their impact upon society was. And although the focus of this study is the development of medicine and public health in Britain, it will draw on wider world ideas and events to show how they affected medicine and public health in Britain over this long sweep of history.

Fact

Historians sometimes add a 'c' before dates. This stands for 'circa', which means 'around' or 'approximately'.

c1230
Compendium Medicine is written by Gilbert Eagle – a comprehensive English medical textbook blending European and Arab knowledge of medicine

1628
William Harvey proves the circulation of the blood

1724
Guy's Hospital is founded in London

1200 — 1300 — 1600 — 1700

1250
This illustration shows a Medieval doctor checking the patient's urine and pulse
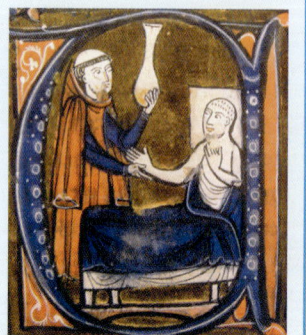

1348
Black Death arrives in England

1882
Robert Koch's work on the identification of tuberculosis is publicised in Britain

1928
Alexander Fleming discovers that penicillin kills bacteria

1978
First 'test-tube' baby is born

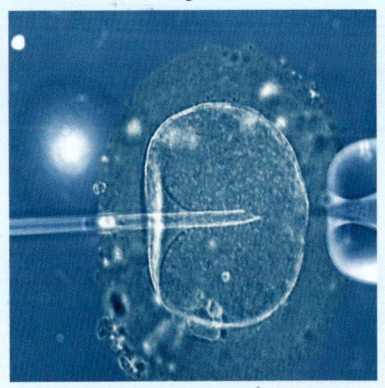

1858
Joseph Bazalgette begins building a network of sewers under London's streets

1847
James Simpson uses chloroform as an anaesthetic

1848
First Public Health Act is introduced

1953
Francis Crick and James Watson publish their research on the structure of DNA

2000

1900

1800

1798
Edward Jenner develops cowpox as a protection against smallpox

1867
Joseph Lister publishes a description of carbolic antiseptic in surgery

1948
NHS comes into operation

1963
First liver transplant is carried out in America

1906
First of the Liberal social reforms – including free school meals for the poorest children, free medical checks and free treatment – is introduced

2003
Human Genome Project is declared complete with the final sequencing of the entire human genome; this is a huge breakthrough in understanding how genes help determine who a person is

Britain: Health and the people

1.1 What did a Medieval doctor know?

This book focuses on the development of medicine and public health in Britain from Medieval times (also known as the Middle Ages, c1000–1500), to the present day. Of course, even before the Medieval period in Europe, people had tried to cure illness in the **Ancient World**. The ideas of famous Greek doctors like Hippocrates and Galen had been passed on and became an essential part of the treatments used by a Medieval doctor. To understand this history, and the importance of medical ideas from the Ancient World, you will need to understand where Medieval people went for medical advice.

Objectives

- **Outline** what a Medieval doctor knew, including natural, supernatural, Hippocratic and Galenic ideas.
- **Explain** what training Medieval doctors received.
- **Examine** the medical options for a poor or rich person in the Medieval period.

Fact

The Medieval period, AD 500–1500, can be divided into the Early Middle Ages, the High Middle Ages and the Late Middle Ages. This book starts in the High Middle Ages. Medical ideas from the Ancient World were lost in the Early Middle Ages because of wars, but by the High Middle Ages Europe had become more peaceful and stable, so medical knowledge found its way back into Europe from the Islamic world.

If you were ill in Medieval England, there were many people to go to for treatment. It was a medical marketplace, from the local wise woman to the **barber-surgeon** in the town, and – if you could afford it – a university-trained doctor.

What could a Medieval doctor do?

Medieval doctors followed the ancient Greek method of 'clinical observation', or bedside observation of the patient, to produce a **diagnosis** of the disease. By the Medieval period, rather than noting all the symptoms, doctors tended to concentrate on just two indicators: they only took the pulse and noted the colour, smell, and taste of the urine. From this, the doctor might prescribe natural medicines made from plants, animal products, spices, oils, wines, and rocks.

A common treatment was **bloodletting** (or 'purging'), which was when blood was removed by opening a vein or using **leeches** to suck it out. The cure didn't often work, because the blood had to be taken from exactly the right spot on the body. Other treatments might involve giving you something to make you vomit or go to the toilet. Remedies often combined natural with supernatural approaches, such as prayers, charms and **astrology**.

▲ SOURCE A *An illustration from a book published in 1250 showing a Medieval doctor examining a patient's urine and checking his pulse*

The four humours: beliefs about the cause of illness

Medieval doctors based their natural cures on the Ancient Greek theory of illness, which involved the equal balance of four '**humours**' within the body. They believed that a person became ill when the humours were out of balance, and the doctor's job was to restore this balance. If there was too much blood, then the patient would be bled; if there was not enough they might be advised to drink more red wine. The theory of the four humours fitted what the Medieval doctor could observe.

8 Chapter 1 Medieval medicine

▼ **B** *According to the theory of the four humours, each element was strongest in a specific season, with specific qualities. The element showed itself in the corresponding bodily liquid or humour.*

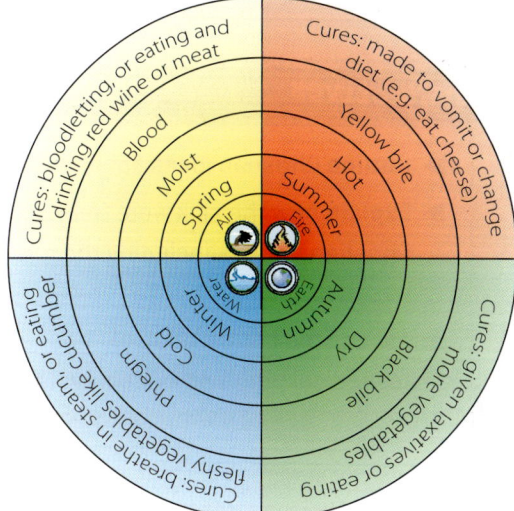

A Medieval doctor's training

To qualify as a doctor in the Middle Ages could take at least seven years of study at a university like Oxford or Cambridge. The doctors learned mainly by listening to lectures and debating what they had read about in books. It was possible for a fully qualified doctor to leave university without having seen an actual patient.

Doctors in Britain learned the treatments of Hippocrates and Galen, together with the medical knowledge from the Muslim, Indian and Chinese worlds. They studied British medical textbooks, such as Gilbert Eagle's *Compendium Medicine* (c1230), which were based on Greek knowledge: they dealt with each part of the body working from the head downwards, and brought together medical theory, recipes, charms and Christian prayers.

Who did ordinary people turn to?

There were few university-trained doctors in Medieval England, and they were expensive. Less respected but more common were the barber-surgeons in towns. For most people who lived in small villages there would be a wise woman or man who offered traditional remedies for illness. The wise people used a mixture of natural herbal remedies, first aid and supernatural cures. Their knowledge would be passed down by word-of-mouth, but some was written down. One of the earliest remedy books was the Anglo-Saxon manuscript *Leech Book of Bald* (950). In markets and fairs there would be many people offering herbal potions; some would pull teeth, mend dislocated limbs or perhaps even set a fracture in splints.

Christianity was very central to Medieval people's lives, so sick people might also turn to the local monastery or the parish priest for medical help. People at the time believed that God could send illness as a punishment for wickedness and crimes, so prayers and charms were often used as remedies. Prayers were often made to Christian saints who were said to cure specific ailments.

Key Words

Ancient World   barber-surgeon   diagnosis
bloodletting   leech   astrology   humours

▼ **SOURCE C** *An illustration from 1450, showing a treatment using the four humours theory*

Work

1. Where could you find medical advice in the Medieval period if you were a) poor or b) rich?
2. Where did a Medieval doctor's knowledge come from?
3. List at least two ways in which medical knowledge was passed on in the Medieval period.
4. Study **Source C**. What do you think this treatment is trying to cure?
5. In your own words, explain how a patient could be treated using the theory of the four humours.
6. Discuss with a partner: what are the obvious differences between Medieval doctors and modern doctors today?

Extension

Research some of the Medieval saints that people prayed to in order to make them better or to protect them from illness. You could start with Saint Lucy, Saint Anthony or Saint John of Bridlington.

Britain: Health and the people

2.1 How did Christianity affect Medieval medicine?

Throughout the Medieval period, Christianity was the only main religion in Western Europe. The Christian Church was a powerful organisation that influenced the decisions of kings and emperors, and possessed great wealth. It advised both ordinary and great people about how they should live their lives. What were Christian attitudes towards the sick? And did the Church help or hinder medical progress in the Medieval period?

Objectives

▶ **Outline** Christian ideas about medicine.

▶ **Explain** how the sick were treated by the Christian Church, including the role of hospitals.

▶ **Assess** the contribution of Christianity to medical progress in Medieval Britain.

What were Christian ideas about health and medicine?

The Christian Church believed in following the example of Jesus, who healed the sick. For this reason, Christians believed that it was good to look after the sick, and so they founded many hospitals. However, there was a strong belief that illnesses came from God, and curing an illness would be a challenge to God who had sent it as a punishment or a test of faith. So, it was important to care for the patient, not necessarily cure them.

Prayers to God were therefore the most important treatment: 'To buy drugs or to consult with physicians doesn't fit with religion,' said Saint Bernard, a famous twelfth-century Christian monk. The Church also encouraged the belief in miraculous healing. There were many shrines filled with relics of the bones, hair and other body parts of a holy person. These shrines were places that people made **pilgrimage** to, for help with their illnesses, such as the shrine of Saint Thomas Becket at Canterbury.

While the Church valued prayers, it also respected the traditional medical knowledge of the Ancient World because it thought Hippocratic and Galenic ideas were correct. Monks preserved and studied these ideas: they copied out the books by hand, as well as traditional medical books like Pliny's *Natural History*, which was an encyclopaedia of everyday family remedies.

How did Christians treat the sick?

Between 1000 and 1500, more than 700 hospitals were started in England. Many hospitals were centres of rest where sick people might recover in quiet and clean surroundings. Some were small, with enough space for only 12 patients (the same number as Jesus had disciples). Many hospitals did not have doctors but a chaplain (a priest), and were run by monks or nuns to a strict pattern of diet and prayer.

Hospitals depended on charity for money, and were mainly financed by the Christian Church or by a wealthy **patron**. There were several different types of hospitals: for example, there were hospitals or asylums for the mentally ill, such as Bedlam in London. Monasteries had infirmaries (small dormitory wards) that could provide free treatment to the sick and the poor. There were a few large hospitals, such as St Leonard's in York.

▼ **SOURCE A** *An illustration, from c1500, of the Hotel Dieu in Paris, a late Medieval hospital; the French king's doctors worked there*

10 Chapter 2 Medical progress

Key Words				
pilgrimage	patron	leprosy	contagious	crusading order

Fact

St Leonard's Hospital was built during the reign of the Norman King Stephen (1135–54). By 1370, St Leonard's could look after over 200 sick people. From the time of the Normans, the hospital enjoyed the patronage of kings and the right to collect special taxes from the surrounding area.

There were also special hospitals called 'Lazar houses' that dealt with people who had **leprosy**. The disease was **contagious**, so to prevent people catching it, leprosy hospitals were set up outside towns. In England these 'houses' were often started by the **crusading orders** such as the Knights Templar in the twelfth century, because many crusaders caught the disease, which was widespread in the Middle East at the time.

Did Christianity help or hinder medical progress in the Medieval period?

In Europe, the training of doctors began after 1200, when the continent became more peaceful and prosperous. The Christian Church controlled the universities because that was where religion was studied and where Church leaders were trained; medicine was usually the second subject studied after religion. In Britain, the Church controlled the training of doctors in the universities of Oxford and Cambridge. There they taught the medical ideas of the ancient Greeks and Romans. The training was to make the old knowledge clear and understandable; it was not to discover new ideas.

The Christian Church approved of Galen's books because he believed in a single God: this fitted with Christian ideas. However this meant that it was difficult to challenge anything that Galen wrote, as it would be seen as a criticism of the Church. Church attitudes to new ideas was shown by what happened to the thirteenth-century English monk, Roger Bacon: he was arrested for suggesting that doctors should do original research and should not trust the old books.

Ultimately, the Church saw the role of the doctor not as a healer, but as someone who could predict the symptoms and duration of an illness, and provide the reasons for why God might inflict the illness on the person. This gave people comfort, and allowed patients and their families to put their affairs in order and die in peace. As Faritius, the famous eleventh-century doctor and abbot of Abingdon, said to the family of a little boy who died under his care, 'there is no medicine for death.'

▼ **SOURCE B** A sixteenth-century painting showing Saint Elizabeth of Hungary (tending to the patient, bottom left), who was famous in the thirteenth century for helping the poor and the sick

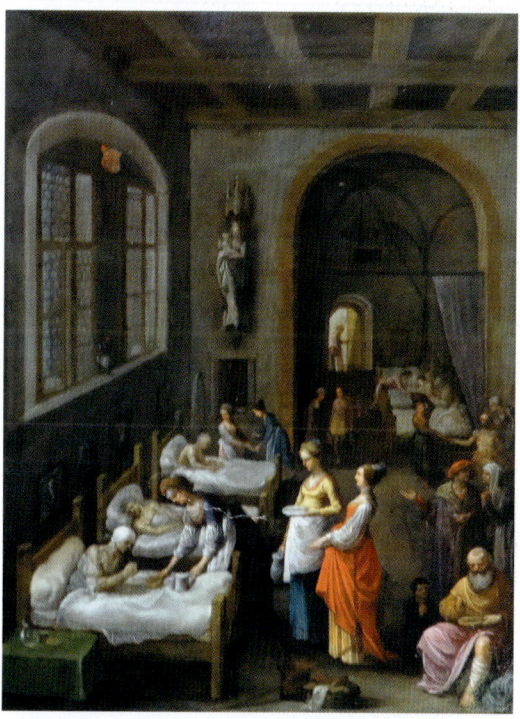

Work
1. What did Medieval Christians think caused illnesses?
2. How did Christians treat sick people in Medieval times? Try to identify three points.
3. Study **Source A**. Describe what you can see in the hospital. How does it support what you have read about Medieval hospitals?
4. Do you agree or disagree that the Christian Church held back medical progress? Explain your answer.

Practice Question
How useful is **Source B** for understanding Christian ideas about illness? **8 marks**

Study Tip
In a 'how useful' type of question about a visual source, remember to consider what the provenance tells you as well as what you can learn from the image.

2.2 How did Islam affect Medieval medicine?

Western Europe entered a period known as the Early Medieval period when the Roman Empire lost its power. At this time, Islam became the main religion in the Middle East and North Africa. Led by its Prophet, Muhammad, the followers of Islam established an enormous and unified Islamic Empire. During the height of Islam's culture and learning from c750–1050, Islamic doctors made great contributions to medical knowledge. What did they contribute to medical science? And why were they able to do so?

Objectives

- **Outline** Islamic ideas about medicine.
- **Explain** why Medieval Islamic doctors made medical progress.
- **Assess** the contribution of Medieval Islamic medicine to medical progress.

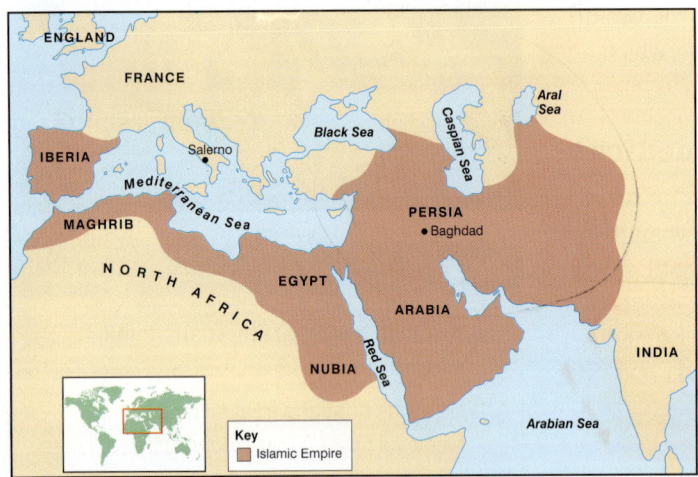

A A map showing the extent of the Islamic Empire by 750

The Islamic Empire was a single state ruled by one man, known as the **Caliph**. Caliphs provided the peace and order needed for medical progress. Moreover, many Caliphs were interested in science and supported Islamic medicine. During the reign of Caliph Harun al-Rashid (786–809), the capital city of Baghdad became a centre for the translation of Greek manuscripts into the language of Islam: Arabic. The Caliph's library preserved hundreds of ancient Greek medical books by Hippocrates and Galen, which were lost to Western Europe during the Early Middle Ages. Al-Rashid's son, Caliph al-Mamun (813–33), developed his father's library into 'The House of Wisdom', which was the world's largest library at the time, and a study centre for scholars. The Islamic religion itself encouraged medical learning: Prophet Muhammad inspired people to 'seek learning even as far as China' and said, 'For every disease, Allah has given a cure.' So, scientists were encouraged to discover those cures.

What were Islamic ideas on health and medicine?

In the Islamic Empire the first hospitals were set up for people with mental illnesses. These people were treated with compassion as victims of an unfortunate illness. This was very different from how Christian doctors thought of them – as being punished by God.

In 805, Caliph al-Rashid set up a major new hospital in Baghdad with a medical school and a library. Unlike Medieval Christian hospitals, this was intended to treat the patients, and not simply care for them. Hospitals called bimaristans were built in many Islamic cities to provide medical care for everyone: men and women, rich and poor, Muslim and non-Muslim. Doctors were permanently present and medical students trained alongside them.

Did Islam help or hinder medical progress in the Medieval period?

Two Muslim doctors in particular, Rhazes and Avicenna, had a great influence on medicine in Western Europe. Their discoveries, along with the old medical knowledge of the ancient Greeks, first found their way to Western Europe in the Middle Ages. This was through the Latin translations of a merchant named Constantine the African, who arrived in Italy around 1065. Gerard of Cremona, an Italian translator, continued this work in the twelfth century with the first Latin translation of Avicenna's book, *Canon of Medicine*. The universities in Padua and Bologna in Italy soon became the best places to study medicine in Europe. These medical ideas reached England through trade, as merchants brought new equipment, drugs and books.

Chapter 2   Medical progress

Key Biography

Al-Razi (c865–c925)
Known in Western Europe as Rhazes, he stressed the need for careful observation of the patient, and distinguished measles from smallpox for the first time. He wrote over 150 books. Although a follower of Galen, he thought that all students should improve on the work of their teacher. One of his books was called *Doubts about Galen*.

Ibn Sina (980–1037)
Also known as Avicenna, he wrote a great encyclopaedia of medicine known as *Canon of Medicine*. Comprising over a million words, it covered the whole of ancient Greek and Islamic medical knowledge at the time. It listed the medical properties of 760 different drugs, and contained chapters on medical problems such as anorexia and obesity. It became the standard European medical textbook used to teach doctors in the West until the seventeenth century.

Key Words

Caliph   dissection

Extension

As well as preserving the writings of the ancient Greeks and Romans, Islamic doctors added their own, new knowledge. Research some of the new drugs from the Islamic world such as camphor, laudanum, naphtha and senna.

SOURCE B *From the front cover of a fourteenth-century Italian copy of Avicenna's* Canon of Medicine

Fact

Although Islam did not allow human **dissection**, the thirteenth-century Islamic doctor, Ibn al-Nafis, concluded that Galen was wrong about how the heart worked. He said that the blood circulated round the body via the lungs. Unfortunately his books were not read in the West, and Europeans continued to accept Galen's mistake until the seventeenth century.

Work

1. Identify three things that Islam believed about medicine and illness.
2. Study the provenance of **Source B** and what is happening in the picture. How does it link to what you have learned?
3. Did Islam help or hinder medical progress? Explain your answer using the following factors: government, ideas, science, communication, individuals.

Practice Question

Was the preservation of the writings of the ancient Greeks and Romans the most important contribution that Islam made to medical progress?

16 marks
SPaG: 4 marks

Study Tip

What do you think were the different contributions that Islam made to medical progress? You might consider the scientific approach, the new drugs, the books, the discoveries, or the hospitals. Write about several contributions and then explain which one you think was the most important.

Britain: Health and the people   13

2.3 How good was Medieval surgery?

Surgery in the Medieval period was a risky business. Surgeons had no idea that dirt carried disease. Some believed it was good to cause pus in wounds, and operations were done without effective painkillers. Surgery was limited, since surgeons could not help patients with deep wounds to the body: these patients would die from bleeding, shock and infection. What kind of surgery occurred then? Did any surgeons make progress during the Medieval period?

Objectives

- **Describe** who did surgery in Western Europe and the Islamic Empire during the Medieval period.
- **Explain** what types of surgery could be done at the time.
- **Evaluate** the medical progress achieved in surgery.

Who practised surgery?

Many Medieval surgeons were not surgeons in the modern sense. Most were barbers who combined hair cutting with small surgical operations such as bloodletting and tooth extraction. Compared with doctors, barber-surgeons were lower class medical tradesmen. Surgeons learned their skill by being apprenticed to another surgeon, watching and copying them; or they learned on the battlefield since wars were frequent in the Medieval period.

▼ **SOURCE A** *A fourteenth-century illustration of trepanning*

What could a Medieval surgeon do?

The most common surgical procedure was bloodletting, which was done to restore the balance of humours in the body. It was performed by making a small cut on the inside of the arm, from which the blood was allowed to run out. Amputation, or the cutting off of a painful or damaged part of the body, was another common treatment. It was known to be successful in cases of breast cancer, bladder stones, and haemorrhoids. In Medieval times, it was thought that epilepsy was caused by demons inside the brain – so a surgeon might cure an epileptic patient by drilling a hole into the skull to let the demon out!

Most surgery took place on battlefields. In everyday life, surgery was performed as a last resort. Patients faced the problem of pain and shock in operations. Some attempts were made to put the patient to sleep, but more often than not the patient had to be held or tied down. Surgeons used natural substances such as mandrake root, opium and hemlock as **anaesthetics** for their operations, but too strong a dose might kill the patient. **Cauterisation** was a very common method of burning the wound to stop the flow of blood: it was usually done with a heated iron and was immensely painful. A surgeon would have many different tools: saws for amputation, arrow pullers, cautery irons and bloodletting knives.

Who made progress in surgery during the Medieval period?

The science of surgery in Western Europe and in the Islamic Empire was advanced during the Medieval period by surgical pioneers who tried new methods. Their books were read in Latin by educated and religious men in Europe; in England, they were translated into English. By the end of the fourteenth century, English doctors and surgeons could read about the ideas of many surgeons. Some examples follow.

Abulcasis

Abulcasis, a Muslim surgeon considered the 'father of modern surgery', wrote a 30-volume medical book, *Al Tasrif*, in 1000. He invented 26 new surgical instruments and described many new procedures, including using ligatures for tying off blood vessels. He made cauterisation popular.

▶ **SOURCE B**
A fifteenth-century illustration of the surgeon Abulcasis and his assistant cauterising a mouth wound

Frugardi

Roger Frugardi of Salerno, Italy, wrote a textbook on surgery called *The Practice of Surgery* in 1180. It was widely used in Europe. Frugardi warned against trepanning, tried ambitious operations on the chest, and attempted to remove bladder stones.

Hugh of Lucca and his son Theodoric

Hugh of Lucca and his son Theodoric were famous surgeons who worked at Bologna University, Italy. They wrote a book in 1267 criticising the common view that pus was needed for a wound to heal. They used wine on wounds to reduce the chances of infection and had new methods of removing arrows. Despite being ahead of their time, their ideas about preventing infection went against Hippocratic advice and did not become popular.

Mondino

There was a new interest in **anatomy** in the fourteenth century. In 1315, a public dissection was allowed in Bologna, supervised by Mondino de Luzzi, a famous professor. In 1316, Mondino wrote the book *Anathomia*, which became the standard dissection manual for over 200 years. Dissections were introduced in most European universities to train doctors and to show them that Galen was correct. Even if the body did not fit Galen's description, they did not doubt Galen: people believed that the body must be wrong!

Key Words

trepanning   anaesthetic   cauterisation   anatomy

De Chauliac

One of the most famous surgeons of the Medieval period was the French surgeon, Guy De Chauliac. His famous textbook *Great Surgery* (1363) dominated English and French surgical knowledge for 200 years. The textbook contains references to Greek and Islamic writers like Avicenna; he quoted Galen about 890 times. He did not like Theodoric of Lucca's ideas about preventing infection and he wrote about his opinion in detail in his book, which was the main reason that Lucca's ideas did not catch on.

John of Arderne

John of Arderne was the most famous surgeon in Medieval England. His surgical manual, *Practica* (1376), contained illustrations of his operations and instruments. It was based on Greek and Arab knowledge and his experience in the Hundred Years War between England and France. He used opium and henbane to dull pain. He charged a large fee for an operation he developed to treat an anal abscess (swelling with pus), a condition common in knights who spent long periods on horseback. In 1368, he tried to separate the surgeons from lower-class barbers by forming a work association called The Guild of Surgeons within the City of London.

Work

1. a Who carried out most surgery in the Medieval period?
   b How did they learn their trade?
2. What were the two most common surgical procedures?
3. Three problems for the surgeon are to take away pain, prevent infection and stop bleeding. Discuss in pairs or in groups: what were the traditional solutions of most Medieval surgeons to these three surgical problems?

Extension

Do you think there was any progress in surgery during the Medieval period? Explain your answer.

Britain: Health and the people

3.1 Where was public health worse in the Medieval period?

Public health refers to the health and well being of the population as a whole, in a particular place and at a particular time. People often assume that conditions in Medieval towns were awful. They were certainly poor by modern standards, but the levels of cleanliness and hygiene were rising in some places during the Medieval period. How were these improvements made? Why were there problems with public health? To what extent did people care about cleanliness?

Objectives

- **Describe** the public health conditions in Medieval towns.
- **Explain** attitudes to public health in Medieval England.
- **Assess** the quality of public health in Medieval towns.

What was public health like?

Medieval towns were built near rivers or other bodies of water, because they needed easy access to water; rivers also provided a means of transport. There were various systems of water supply in Medieval towns. Most people got their water from local springs, wells or rivers. Some towns had elaborate systems built by the Romans to supply water, which still worked well. However, as towns grew, the existing systems could not cope with the increased demand for water. So, Medieval towns such as Exeter and London used new technology with pipes made of wood or lead.

Many town dwellers also used rivers and streams to remove their sewage and other waste. Sometimes, however, people just threw their toilet waste onto the street, along with other household rubbish.

Most towns and some private houses had **privies** (a toilet located in a small shed outside a house or building), with **cesspits** underneath where the sewage was collected. In some towns, people left money in their wills so that public privies for the town's citizens could be built and maintained. Cesspits would be dug out annually by **gong farmers**, and like dung heaps, they were a valuable source of manure. If they were not emptied regularly, the sewage from these cesspits easily seeped into and polluted rivers and wells.

Towns were generally dirty places. There were some paved streets, but in small towns, streets became muddy when it rained. In addition, the open drains that ran down street centres to carry away water and waste would often overflow. In a downpour, privy cesspits might also overflow, leaving excrement spread over the road. Streets outside the houses of wealthier citizens were swept by their servants and were therefore cleaner, but in poorer areas the streets stank and were often littered with waste.

▼ **INTERPRETATION A** A Medieval street scene, drawn by an artist in 1962

Keeping towns clean

Between 1250 and 1530, the number of towns in England grew as the population rose, which put pressure on public health facilities. Mayors and councillors knew that improvements would be expensive, but they did not want to become unpopular by increasing local taxes to fund these improvements.

Also, the lack of sanitation was partly because people had no knowledge of germs

16 Chapter 3 Public health in the Middle Ages

and their link to disease and infection. They did think, however, that disease was spread by 'bad air', so they were keen to remove unpleasant smells.

Rivers provided water to businesses such as bakeries and breweries, which also used the rivers to remove their waste. Town councils tried to stop businesses from polluting rivers in this way, but this was difficult. In towns, people lived side-by-side with businesses. Leather tanners, for example, used dangerous chemicals and smelled awful, while meat butchers created waste products such as blood and guts, which were then dumped into rivers. Local craft guilds tried to restrict the skilled workers' activities to certain areas, and to regulate the nuisances that their tradesmen caused. In Worcester, for example, a law of 1466 said that the entrails and blood of butchered animals had to be carried away that same night.

What did town councils do?

Some Medieval town councils in England tried to keep the environment clean and healthy. They passed various local laws encouraging people to keep the streets in front of their houses clean and to remove their rubbish, but it was not easy to maintain cleanliness.

so where throw rubbish??

▼ **SOURCE B** *From the records of a London Court case in 1321:*

> The jury decided that Ebbegate Lane used to be a public passage. Master Thomas Wytte and William de Hockele built privies projecting out from the walls of their houses. From the privies human filth falls onto the heads of the passers-by and blocks the passageway.

Key Words

public health   privy   cesspit   gong farmer

Work

1. What were the most important sources of water in a Medieval town?
2. a Identify three things in Medieval towns that were a threat to people's health.
   b Identify three things in Medieval towns that might have kept people healthy.
3. Study **Interpretation A**. What can you see in it that you have learned about from these two pages?
4. Read **Source B** carefully. What offence has been committed here?

Practice Question

Compare public health in a Medieval town with public health in a Medieval monastery. In what ways were they different?   **8 marks**

Study Tip

In your answer refer to the water supply, dealing with sewage, and attitudes to cleanliness in each place.

Timeline

1298	1330	1371	1374	1388
King Edward I complains that unhygienic conditions in York are a danger to his soldiers preparing for invasion, so the council orders the building of public latrines in the city	Glamorgan council passes laws to stop butchers throwing animal remains into the High Street, and orders that no one should throw waste onto the streets or close to the town gates	The London mayors and councillors try to make the city healthier by prohibiting the killing of large animals within the city walls	The London local council gives up trying to control building and sewage disposal over the Walbrook stream. Instead they make householders who use the stream pay a fee to have it cleaned each year	Parliament passes a law which fines people £20 for throwing 'dung garbage and entrails' into ditches, ponds, and rivers. However, it is not easy to make people obey the laws nor to catch those who disobey them

Britain: Health and the people   17

3.2 Where was public health better in the Medieval period?

There were some places where public health was much better than in the dirty towns and cities of Medieval England. The houses of wealthy families and religious buildings such as monasteries, abbeys and nunneries, for example, had good health conditions. What facilities did they have, and why did they choose to have them?

Objectives

▶ **Discuss** the public health conditions and facilities in Medieval abbeys and monasteries.

▶ **Analyse** why conditions were better in religious sites.

Monasteries and abbeys

Christian monasteries and abbeys were often situated in isolated, out of the way places, but still near to rivers. Water was such an important resource for the monks that they would even redirect a river to ensure a reliable supply, as they did at Rievaulx Abbey in Yorkshire. They did this to supply their mills as well as to deliver pure water to kitchens, bakeries and brew houses.

Monasteries had elaborate systems of pipes to deliver the water to wash basins (or lavers). Filtering systems were also installed to remove impurities by allowing dirt to settle out of the water.

Most monasteries had excellent facilities for washing, which was done in a room called a **lavatorium**, where waste water could be emptied into a river. They had toilets, or privies, and these sometimes contained potties to collect urine (which was valuable for tanning and bleaching cloth in the monks' wool trade). The toilets were then emptied into a pit, from which the waste could be dug out and carted away as manure. The privies and cesspits could be flushed clear from time to time by diverting local river water through them, such as at Westminster Abbey in London.

Monks' routines

Monks had religious routines of cleanliness which helped to keep them healthy. Baths were rare luxuries for the rich, but monks were ordered to use them, as cleanliness was a sign of piety and celibacy (abstaining from marriage). Some monks had a bath once a month; the Benedictine monks were allowed two a year – one at Christmas and one at Easter. Monasteries had bathhouses, which were connected to the drainage systems. The Benedictine monks washed their clothes regularly, as well as their

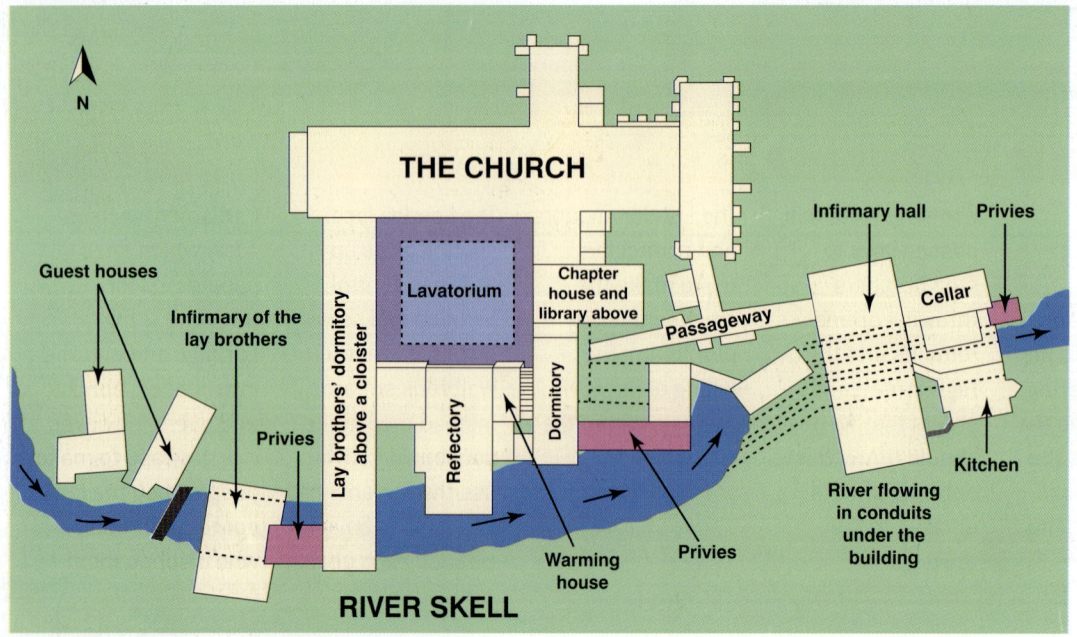

▼ **A** The layout of Fountains Abbey in Yorkshire. The river flows from west to east, and took dirty water away from the toilets. Freshwater was provided from a number of local wells.

heads and faces, and feet were washed in a religious ceremony twice a week. Monasteries also had infirmaries with a good supply of water; a few had leeching houses where patients could be bled.

Why were conditions better?

Monasteries and abbeys were very wealthy in the Medieval ages: many people gave money, valuables and lands to these religious institutions in return for prayers to be said for them and their loved ones when they died. In England, monks also made a lot of money from the production of wool, and in order to keep sheep, they needed large areas for grazing. Land like this was usually far away from towns. All this wealth allowed the monks to build good sanitation facilities.

Monks were educated and very disciplined. They had access to medical books and manuscripts in their monastic libraries, as well as infirmaries, where monks were trained in the use of herbs for healing. Many of the medical books explained the ancient Roman idea of a simple routine or regimen for life: this involved moderation in diet, sleep and exercise to balance the humours. Under the strict guidance of the abbot in charge of the monasteries, obedient monks would try to lead simple lives with these routines; an early thirteenth-century guide to monastic life stated 'Filth was never dear to God.' Monks also learned from the Ancient World that a basic principle of good sanitation was to separate the supply of clean water from the wastewater that came from the toilets and wash places.

In general then, conditions were better in monasteries and abbeys because of their good health facilities, their

▼ **INTERPRETATION B** *A painting showing monks looking after their herbal garden; it was painted in 1952 by Robert Thom, who carried out careful research into the medicinal plants used in Medieval times for this painting*

Key Words

lavatorium   lay people   epidemic

isolation, and the monks' knowledge and discipline. The Christian Church believed that **lay people** were sinful, and this is partly the reason why monasteries were built a long distance away from towns. The isolation helped to protect the monks from the worst of **epidemics** such as the plague.

▼ **SOURCE C** *A thirteenth-century poem called* The Salerno Regimen of Health; *this was popular in Europe, and would have been found in medical books in monastic libraries:*

> The Salerno school does by these lines impart,
> All health to England's King, and does advise
> From care his head to keep, from wrath his heart,
> Drink not much wine, sup light, and soon arise,
> When meat is gone, long sitting breedeth smart:
> And after noon still waking keep your eyes.

Extension

Can you summarise what the medical advice is for the king in **Source C**?

Work

1. Discuss with a partner: what can you identify in Medieval monastic life that we would expect for good hygiene today?
2. Study diagram **A**. Can you identify how the locations of the different facilities in the abbey might help to keep the monks clean and healthy?

Practice Question

Was the wealth of a monastery the main factor in keeping monks healthy in Medieval England?

16 marks
SPaG: 4 marks

Study Tip

Consider all the factors that affected the health of Medieval monks, including the isolation of religious sites, the facilities and their knowledge. Write about all the factors and say which one you think was the most important.

Britain: Health and the people   19

3.3A Consequences of poor public health: the Black Death

The Black Death was an epidemic disease in the Medieval period; it began in Asia and travelled rapidly along the trade routes to Western Europe. It reached Constantinople (in modern day Turkey) in 1347 and arrived in England in 1348. The Black Death killed nearly half of Europe's population. In Britain, at least 1.5 million people died. What caused it, and why did it spread? Why were people so terrified of catching it?

Objectives
- Describe the main symptoms of the Black Death disease.
- Explain beliefs about its causes, treatment and prevention.
- Evaluate the impact of the disease.

The Black Death

Historians believe that the Black Death was a combination of both the **bubonic** and the **pneumonic plagues**. The bubonic plague was spread by fleas: buboes or lumps were found on a person's groin, neck and armpits. The lumps oozed pus and bled when opened, then a high fever and vomiting of blood would follow. The pneumonic plague was a more deadly form of disease: it infected the lungs, causing fever and coughing, and was spread by contact with a victim's breath or blood.

▼ **A** *The spread of Black Death across Europe; the plague reached England in 1348*

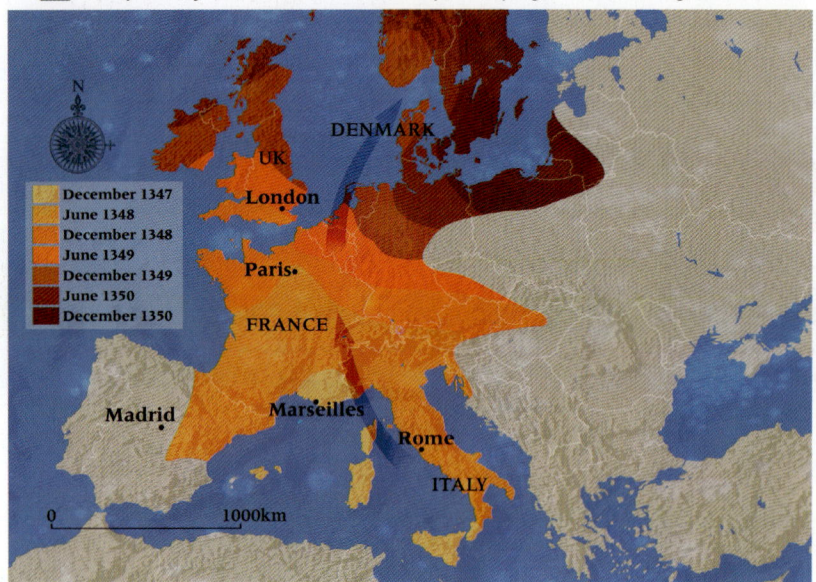

▼ **SOURCE B** *The Italian writer Boccaccio describes the symptoms of Black Death in 1348:*

> The first signs of the plague were lumps in the groin or armpits. After this, livid black spots appeared on the arms and thighs and other parts of the body. Few recovered. Almost all died within three days, usually without any fever.

▼ **SOURCE C** *Robert of Avesbury, a chronicler at the Archbishop of Canterbury's court, wrote in 1349:*

> The pestilence, which had first broken out in the land of the Saracens (the Middle East), became much stronger; it visited all the kingdoms with the scourge of sudden death. It began in England in Dorset, and immediately advancing from place to place attacked men without warning. Very many of those attacked in the morning were dead before noon. And no one it touched lived longer than three or four days. And reaching London, it deprived many of their life every day, and increased so greatly from February till April 1349 that there were more than 200 dead bodies a day buried in the new Smithfield cemetery. The grace of the Holy Spirit finally intervening, about May, 1349, it ceased in London.

20 | Chapter 3 | Public health in the Middle Ages

What did people think caused the Black Death?

European doctors in the fourteenth century did not understand infections or how diseases were transmitted, and so they were at a loss to explain the cause of the Black Death. They blamed it on the position of stars and planets, on bad air, or even on the poisoning of wells by Jews (none of these was true). Blaming the plague on Jews led to many attacks against Jewish communities in Europe, but this did not happen within England since most Jews had been expelled 50 years earlier by King Edward I. Many people were very religious, and they believed that God was punishing them for their sins: they thought that only God's anger could produce so many horrific deaths.

▼ **SOURCE D** *A fifteenth-century French painting showing Saint Sebastian praying on behalf of plague victims*

What really caused the Black Death?

The Black Death was thought to have been an outbreak of mainly bubonic plague caused by the **bacteria** *Yersinia pestis*. This bacteria thrived in the stomachs of fleas that lived on the blood of rats. When rats died of the plague, the fleas had to find a new host and moved on to humans. Death

Key Words

bubonic plague   pneumonic plague   bacteria   quarantine

could be very quick for weaker victims, such as those with malnutrition. In the Medieval period, food shortages were common, and the resulting high food prices meant people didn't eat well, which weakened people's immunity (their ability to fight infection).

The Black Death spread quickly due to several reasons: one was that in crowded ports and towns, people lived close together and knew nothing about contagious diseases. If the bubonic plague reached the lungs of the victim, then they could spread the pneumonic form of the plague to others, through the air, by coughing. The disposal of bodies was crude and helped to spread the disease still further, as those who handled the dead bodies did not protect themselves in any way. In villages, bodies that were hastily buried in shallow pits could be dug up by wild animals at night; the body parts would be spread around. The filth that littered streets gave rats the perfect environment to breed and increase in number.

Authorities had no idea what caused the plague. They had simple laws about keeping streets clean, but there was little enforcement of the laws, and few effective regular ways of cleaning the streets. People did not always practise cleanliness, and it was common to throw rubbish and human waste into the streets and rivers.

How did people try to deal with the plague?

No medical knowledge existed in Medieval England to cope with the disease. People tried anything to escape it, including drinking mercury, or shaving a chicken and strapping it to the buboes. Understandably, peasants were terrified at the news that the Black Death might be approaching their village or town. Some fled to other towns and villages. Most avoided contact with other people; local councils also tried to **quarantine** infected places.

Fact

One of the more extreme actions taken in Europe to prevent Black Death was flagellation: some people wanted to show their love of God by whipping themselves, hoping that God would forgive them their sins and that they would be spared. Flagellation was not welcomed in England.

Work

1. What was the main characteristic of the bubonic plague?
2. According to **Source C**, what made the Black Death a terrifying disease?
3. Identify two things that might have helped people avoid the plague, and two that would not.
4. What do you think is the reason why there were so many different incorrect explanations of the causes of Black Death at the time?

Britain: Health and the people   21

3.3B Consequences of poor public health: the Black Death

By the end of 1350, the Black Death had subsided, but it never really died out in England over the next few hundred years. There were further outbreaks in 1361–62, 1369, 1379–83, 1389–93, and throughout the first half of the fifteenth century. The plague is thought to have returned at intervals with varying degrees of deadliness until the eighteenth century. On its return in 1603, for example, the plague killed 38,000 Londoners, and it came again in the Great Plague of 1665. By the early nineteenth century, the threat of plague had diminished, but it was quickly replaced by a new disease – **cholera**.

The impact of the Black Death

The Black Death had a huge impact on society. In Medieval England, it killed at least a third of the population between 1348 and 1350. Older age groups were more easily affected, and experienced a higher number of deaths.

The Black Death had enormous economic and social consequences. Fields went unploughed as the peasants who usually did the farming became victims of the disease. Food was not harvested and it rotted in the fields; village farm animals were untended and escaped into forests. Whole villages were often wiped out by the plague, but those who survived often faced starvation.

Food shortages

Towns and cities too faced food shortages, as the nearby villages could not provide them with enough food. The Medieval lords (noble landowners) who lost their farmer peasants to the disease changed to sheep farming, since this required fewer workers. This change to sheep farming in turn reduced the supply of basic foods such as bread. As a result of the Black Death, inflation occurred: the price of food went up (because there was less of it around), creating more hardship for the poor. In some parts of England, food prices quadrupled, and became unaffordable.

Peasant wages

Laws at the time stated that peasants could only leave their village if they had their lord's permission. After the Black Death, many lords were desperately short of workers for their land, so they actively encouraged peasants to leave the village where they lived to come to work for them. When peasants did this, their new lord refused to return them to their original village. On the other hand, some of the peasants who survived the Black Death believed that God had specially protected them. Therefore, they took the opportunity to improve their lifestyle by demanding higher

▼ **SOURCE E** *Illustration in a fourteenth-century history book written by an abbot, recording the impact of the Black Death; it shows people carrying coffins*

wages: they knew that lords were desperate to get their harvests in. All of this began to upset the idea of the **feudal system**, a form of Medieval land ownership that tied peasants to the land. So, an indirect consequence of the Black Death was that new laws were introduced, which caused anger and revolt among peasants. To curb peasants roaming around the countryside looking for better pay, the government introduced the Statute of Labourers in 1351.

▼ **SOURCE F** Adapted from the Statute of Labourers, 1351:

> No peasants could be paid more than the wages paid in 1346. No lord or master should offer more wages than paid in 1346. No peasants could leave the village they belonged to.

Fact

Though some peasants ignored the Statute of Labourers, many knew that disobedience would lead to serious punishment. This created great anger, which was to boil over eventually in the Peasants' Revolt of 1381. A long-term cause of the revolt was that after the Black Death, the vastly reduced number of peasants found it harder to pay (and more bitterly resented) the new taxes that the king demanded to fund his wars abroad.

Another impact of the Black Death was that opinions about the Catholic Church changed: some of the churchmen were criticised for cowardice when they deserted their villages. However, this was balanced out by the vast number of priests who died. So, while the reputation of the Church was damaged, it also lost a great number of experienced clergy. It was a serious blow to the Catholic Church. Due to the misunderstanding of the causes of Black Death, there was also widespread persecution of minorities such as foreigners, beggars and lepers.

Fact

Can you catch the plague today?
From 1944–93, 362 cases of human plague were reported in the USA. The plague could become a major health threat again, but so far, only one case of drug-resistant plague has occurred (in Madagascar in 2014).

Key Words

cholera   feudal system

Work

1 When were there other outbreaks of plague in England?
2 In what ways did the plague affect the Catholic Church?
3 Create a mind-map showing the short-term and long-term consequences of the deaths of so many farmer peasants. You could also organise your consequences under headings, such as economic, social, cultural, and political.
4 'The number of people who died was the most important consequence of the Black Death.' Work with a partner to discuss this view. Do you agree with it? Why or why not? You could use your mind-map from Question 3 to help you answer this question.

Practice Question

How useful is **Source E** to a historian studying the impact of the Black Death in England? **8 marks**

Study Tip

To answer this question, try to use the caption (provenance), and also describe what you can see is happening in the image.

Extension

In 2013, the tunnelling for London's new Crossrail station at Farringdon uncovered a plague pit belonging to the Charterhouse monastery. Scientists believe that so many bodies buried in such a short space of time must have meant the deaths were caused by pneumonic plague (with death rates of 90 to 100 per cent) rather than bubonic plague (with date rates of 50 per cent). Look up the research findings: in what ways did the discoveries add to or change historians' understanding of the Black Death and its impact?

Britain: Health and the people

4.1 What was the Renaissance?

Look carefully at Sources A and B. Source A is a drawing of the human body, from the Middle Ages. Source B is a drawing of the human body, made during the **Renaissance**. What are the differences between the two pictures? It seems obvious that the person who drew Source B knew more about the human body than the artist of Source A. Why was the artist able to create a more accurate picture? What has this to do with the Renaissance?

Objectives

- **Define** the term Renaissance.
- **Examine** the causes of the Renaissance.
- **Assess** the impact of the Renaissance on medicine.

Defining the Renaissance

The Renaissance is a term that describes a period in history that flourished in the late 1400s. It bridged the era between the Late Middle Ages and the Early Modern time, and began in Italy. At that time Italy was divided into a number of rich, powerful, independent city-states, one of which was Florence. In Florence, wealthy businessmen and traders were interested in the world of the ancient Greeks and Romans, and they paid educated scholars and artists to investigate it and translate it for them. The discoveries made by studying these ancient books both delighted and inspired the people who read them, but they also became critical of the many versions of the old texts. They wanted their knowledge to be based on an accurate, original version. This approach applied not only to old texts, but also to other aspects of their lives. People did not just accept what they were told, but began to ask questions, find evidence themselves and experiment with new ideas. Throughout Italy, people started to believe that being educated in art, music, science and literature could make life better for everyone. In fact, as people's interest in the ancient knowledge grew, many said the experience was a 'rebirth' of learning (the word 'renaissance' means 'rebirth' in Italian). The Renaissance changed the way people viewed their lives.

▼ **SOURCE A** *A Medieval drawing of the human body*

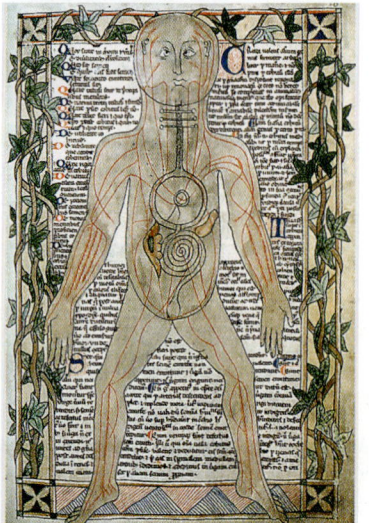

▼ **SOURCE B** *Sketches of the human body, by Leonardo da Vinci; he was a Renaissance scientist, inventor, and painter who made over 30 human dissections*

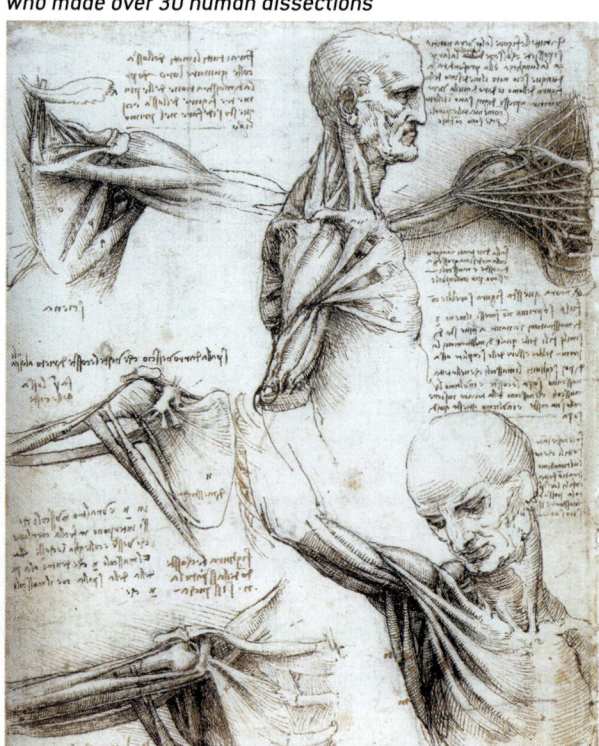

The Renaissance takes hold

The Renaissance was a cultural movement where people questioned accepted truths, searched for evidence, and experimented with new ideas. For centuries, people had accepted that the Church had all the answers to their questions. Now, many educated people wanted to find out for themselves and work out what the right answers were. Scientists experimented; traders explored new lands and made more accurate maps; doctors tried different treatments; and artists began using new methods to make their paintings more lifelike than ever.

How did the Renaissance spread?

Before the Renaissance, books were rare and expensive because they had to be copied out slowly by hand. This meant that knowledge was restricted to a few people who could afford or had access to books. As more people read about the Ancient World and experimented, they wanted to share their discoveries. A new invention made in 1451, the printing press, allowed them to do this: it printed pages far more quickly and accurately than before. As a result of the printing press, more people could read the ancient books as well as books about new discoveries.

Extension

One of the most difficult things historians have to do is to understand the way ideas affect events. Medicine is only one area of human knowledge you will learn about that was affected by the Renaissance. Find out how some other areas of knowledge, such as art, music, science or literature, developed because of the Renaissance. For example, you could look up the contributions of these Renaissance figures: Leonardo da Vinci, Thomas More, Erasmus or Copernicus.

Work

1. In your own words, state what was 'reborn' in the Renaissance.
2. How did the invention of the printing press affect the spread of Renaissance thinking?
3. How did Renaissance artists help progress in medicine?
4. Which of the consequences of the Renaissance would have the biggest impact on medical progress? Explain your answer.

Key Words

Renaissance

▼ **SOURCE C** *A printing press, c1500; the invention of the printing press can be compared to the invention of the Internet, as both allowed ideas and information to spread far more quickly than before*

New lands

Explorers, sailors and merchants used more accurate maps. The discovery of the Americas in the late 1400s showed the value of finding new things and making discoveries, rather than sticking to old ideas. New foods and medicines were also brought back from this 'new world'.

New inventions

New technology such as gunpowder meant injured soldiers got new types of wounds. As a result, doctors had to find new ways to deal with these wounds. Some used new scientific methods of learning to find out better ways to treat injuries.

New learning

A scientific method of learning began, which involved observation, hypothesis and experimentation. Much of this started with doctors and scientists reading books from ancient Greece and Rome. Soon scholars began to question old established beliefs.

Consequences of the Renaissance

New ideas spread quickly

The printing press allowed new ideas to spread quickly around Europe, and old and new books to be studied.

New style of art

A new desire to show the human form in more realistic detail led artists to study the body more carefully.

Britain: Health and the people   25

4.2 The impact of the Renaissance on Britain: the work of Vesalius

In 1537, a young Belgian medical student called Andreas Vesalius published a book which completely supported the centuries-old views of the ancient Greek physician Galen about human anatomy. By 1543, the same student was a Professor of Anatomy, and published a revolutionary textbook which showed the many mistakes that Galen had made. What made Vesalius change his mind about Galen? The textbook transformed the teaching of anatomy. What was so revolutionary about his new book? How did Vesalius contribute to medical progress?

Objectives

- **Consider** anatomical knowledge before Vesalius and the challenge his work posed.
- **Explain** the methods of and opposition to Vesalius.
- **Examine** Vesalius' achievement and contribution to medical progress in England.

Andreas Vesalius (1514–64) was born in Belgium. His studies led him to the University of Paris, where he was taught by Jacob Sylvius, a professor who was a fanatical follower of Galen's teaching of anatomy (and who later became a fierce opponent of Vesalius' discoveries). Vesalius was a gifted student, and it was no surprise when he became Professor of Surgery at the University of Padua in Italy.

Unusually for the time, Vesalius did the dissections of the human body himself, rather than leaving it to an assistant. He carried out his own research to locate the best places for bloodletting. From his dissections, he began to realise that there were many mistakes in Galen's writing when compared with his own observations of the human body.

Until this time, doctors had believed Galen had given a correct description of anatomy. Dissections had been carried out to prove Galen was right, not to check or challenge him. When other doctors observed the same differences that Vesalius noticed, they blamed either the particular body they were dissecting, or said that human anatomy had changed since Galen's times.

Fact

Galen (AD 131–201) was a famous Greek physician. His books showed important and often accurate observations on the human anatomy, including the heart, kidney and nerve functions. Galen's views dominated medical practice and how medicine was taught in universities for 1400 years.

▼ **INTERPRETATION A** *A 1962 painting, by Robert Thom, of Vesalius dissecting. He explains his observations, rather than simply reading Galen's descriptions aloud: his students found this a fascinating new way to learn.*

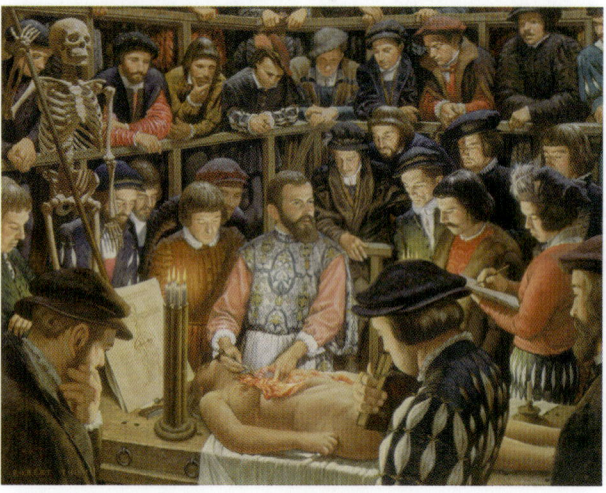

Vesalius and anatomy

Through careful observation, Vesalius realised that sometimes Galen's findings were wrong, because they were based on animal dissections rather than human ones. Vesalius also dissected animals to show how Galen had gained his knowledge: the breastbone in a human being has three parts, not seven as in an ape, for example. Vesalius' lectures were very popular. He promoted dissection as a way to discover more about the body, and as a way that students could learn about the body.

The knowledge that Vesalius gained from dissection was made available to everyone through his beautifully

26 Chapter 4 The impact of the Renaissance on Britain

illustrated textbook *The Fabric of the Human Body* (1543). The illustrations were startlingly precise. Unlike previous anatomy books, which focussed on individual organs of the body, the textbook was organised differently to explain how the different systems within the body worked, such as the skeleton, the muscles, the nerves, the veins, digestion and reproduction. However, Vesalius faced heavy criticism for daring to say that Galen was wrong. He had to leave his job in Padua and later became a doctor for the Emperor Charles V.

Vesalius' contribution to medical progress in England

Vesalius' work soon found an appreciative audience in England. Within two years of publication, an Italian printer, Thomas Geminus, published *Compendiosa*, a book which copied all of Vesalius' illustrations. For the text, Geminus used the famous French surgeon, Henri de Mondeville's, 1312 book *Surgery*. Geminus sold his book to be used as a manual for barber-surgeons in London to learn their trade. *Compendiosa* was very popular in England, and three editions were published between 1545 and 1559. In the latter half of the sixteenth century, many copies of Vesalius' original book came to England, where they influenced and inspired English surgeons.

Vesalius' work overturned centuries of belief that Galen's study of anatomy was correct. He used the Renaissance approach because he based his work and writings on questioning and research on the human body itself. Through dissection and through his book, Vesalius shared new knowledge with the world. And although Vesalius' work did not lead to any medical cures, it was the basis for better treatments in the future. Vesalius showed others how to do proper dissections, and famous sixteenth-century anatomists who followed his approach, such as Fabricius, Realdo Columbo and Fallopius, used dissection to find out more about specific parts of the body.

Fact

Henry VIII gave barber-surgeons a charter in 1540 to form the Company of Barber-Surgeons, making it a respectable and regulated profession. Through the charter, barber-surgeons were granted the corpses of four criminals every year for public dissection.

▼ **SOURCE B** *An illustration of the skeletal system in Vesalius' textbook; a copy of this rare and important work can be viewed in the British Library in London*

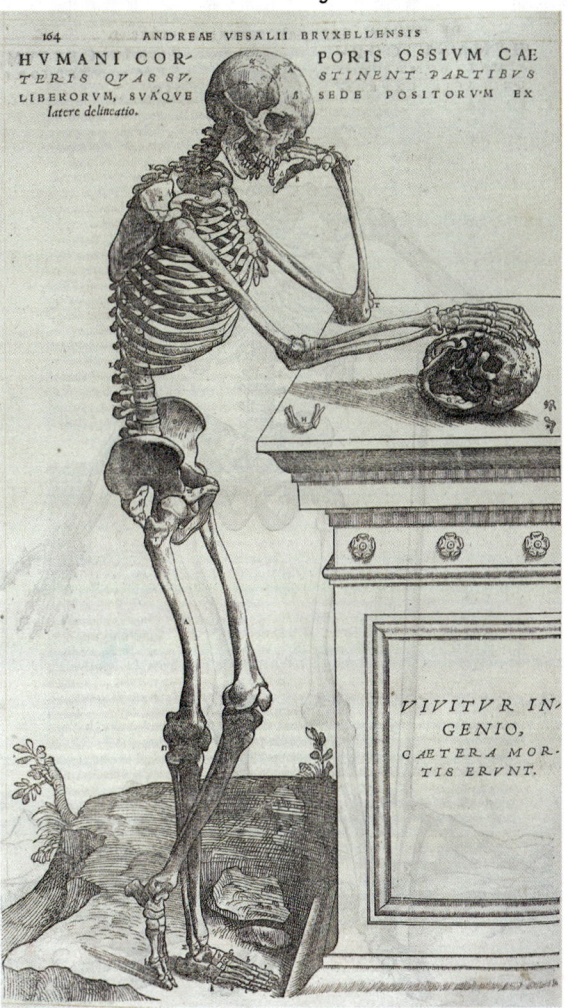

Work

1. What did Vesalius find out about Galen's work? Explain your answer carefully.
2. How does **Interpretation A** show what was new about Vesalius' approach to anatomy?
3. Why was Vesalius' textbook so revolutionary?
4. How did Vesalius have an immediate impact in England?

Practice Question

Compare Medieval anatomy with Renaissance anatomy. In what ways were they different?

8 marks

Study Tip

Review what you have learned about Medieval anatomy from pages 14–15. You could refer to the knowledge they each had and the attitudes to dissection in both periods.

Britain: Health and the people   27

4.3 How important were Paré's discoveries?

In 1536, during the Battle of Milan, two injured soldiers were brought to the young French surgeon, Ambroise Paré. Their faces were disfigured and their clothes still smouldered from the gunpowder that had scorched them. Another soldier asked Paré if they could be helped. Sadly, Paré said they could not, because they were too badly wounded. The soldier went over to the wounded men and calmly slit their throats. Paré shouted at him but the soldier said, 'I pray that if I was ever in such a state someone would do the same for me so that I would not suffer as they did.'

Objectives

- **Consider** surgical knowledge before Paré and the challenge his work posed.
- **Describe** the methods and discoveries of Paré.
- **Examine** Paré's achievement and contribution to medical progress in England.

Ambroise Paré (1510–90) went on to be surgeon to four French kings, became the most famous surgeon in Europe, and published several books about his work. Paré had first learned surgery as an apprentice to his brother, who worked at a hospital in Paris. He then became a French army surgeon. How did Paré's experiences inspire him to make his discoveries?

Treating gunshot wounds and bleeding

In Paré's time, guns were fairly new inventions, so surgeons were not used to treating gunshot wounds. At first, surgeons thought gunshot wounds were poisonous, and the standard way of dealing with them was described in the influential book *Of Wounds in General* (1525) by Jean de Vigo. This stated that the wounds had to be burned out using boiling oil. On top of the pain of the wound, this treatment was agonising for the patient. Paré observed this and was upset by the suffering. During a French battle in 1537, when he ran out of hot oil, he improvised. Vigo recommended a cream of rose oil, egg white and turpentine be smeared over the wounds after cauterising with the burning oil. Without the oil, Paré used just the cream to soothe the patients. Despite his worries, Paré's patients slept well and their wounds healed quickly. Paré challenged accepted practice based on observation and experimentation, and wrote a book about treating wounds in new and better ways in 1545.

Another method Paré promoted was the use of ligatures (strings or threads) in amputations (cutting off a limb). The usual way of stopping bleeding was by cauterising a wound – putting a red-hot iron, called a cautery, on it.

INTERPRETATION A Paré treating a wounded soldier, in a picture drawn in 1962 by Robert Thom. It shows the moment when Paré's hot oil ran out.

Paré revived an old method to stop bleeding, by tying ligatures around individual blood vessels, recommended by Galen. This was very effective compared with cauterising, which he called the 'too cruel way of healing'. Paré also designed the *bec de corbin* or 'crow's beak clamp' to halt bleeding while the blood vessel was being tied off with a ligature. However, ligatures could introduce infection to a wound; they also took longer to implement than cauterising: speed was crucial during battle surgery. Due to the number of amputations that Paré had to do, he quickly moved on to designing and making false limbs for wounded soldiers, and included drawings of them in his writings.

Chapter 4 The impact of the Renaissance on Britain

▼ **SOURCE B** *An illustration from Paré's book showing the artificial limbs he designed for patients after amputations*

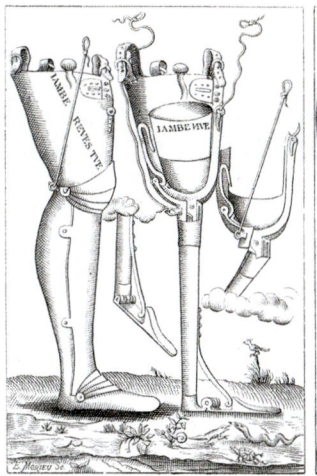
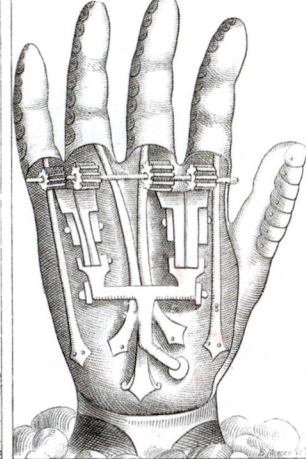

▼ **SOURCE C** *A picture from William Clowes' book, Proved Practice, showing the many chemical potions, mixtures and lotions in his medicine chest. He advised the Elizabethan navy surgeons on what to carry in their surgical chests, and is also credited with inventing a new paste that stopped the bleeding of wounds.*

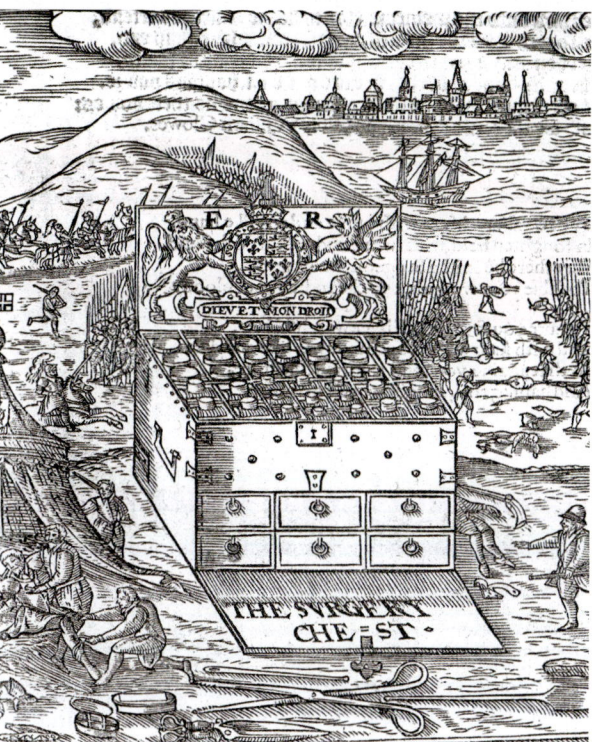

What was Paré's contribution to medical progress in England?

Paré admired, read and learned from the work of Andreas Vesalius. In his 1561 book *Anatomie Universelle* and his famous *Works on Surgery* (1575), Paré included large sections of Vesalius' work on anatomy. By translating Vesalius' writings from the original Latin into French, Paré greatly increased surgeons' understanding of anatomy, since most surgeons were not taught Latin. Paré's books soon circulated throughout Europe.

Paré's *Works on Surgery* was widely read by English surgeons in the original French, and an English handwritten translation of the book was given to the library of the Barber-Surgeons of London in 1591. This was long before it was printed in English in 1634.

In sixteenth-century England, there were a number of surgeons who followed Paré's Renaissance approach to surgery: these surgeons observed, questioned and experimented with new ideas. The most famous was William Clowes (1544–1604), surgeon to Queen Elizabeth I. He greatly admired Paré as the 'famous surgeon master', and like Paré, gained most of his medical experience on the battlefield. He was talented at stopping bleeding from wounds, and carried a vast number of healing potions in his medicine chest. He agreed with Paré that gunshot wounds were not poisonous. In 1588, he published his book *Proved Practice*, which shared his own knowledge about how to deal with battlefield wounds, especially those caused by gunpowder. Clowes also acknowledged Paré as the source for his treatments of burns using onions in 1596.

Work

1. Describe in your own words the moment that the artist has captured in **Interpretation A**. What point do you think the artist is making?
2. Consider the statement: 'Paré was compassionate, resourceful, and skilled.'
    a. How might his work show this?
    b. Do you agree with the statement?
3. The spirit of the Renaissance was to do with observation, questioning and experimentation. In what ways did Paré's work show this?
4. Explain how each of the following factors contributed to the progress of medicine: chance; war; individual brilliance; technology; communication.
5. What was the impact of Paré's work in England?
6. Study **Source C**. How does it confirm what you know about William Clowes?

4.4 What was Harvey's contribution to medical progress?

William Harvey (1578–1657) was an English doctor who had studied medicine at Cambridge and Padua. Harvey began work at St Bartholomew's Hospital in London in 1609, and became doctor to King Charles I in 1632. By 1616, he was able to comment in a lecture to medical students: 'The blood must move in a constant circle and is driven by the heart's power.' This was a new theory, different from what doctors had thought for a long time. Yet it was another 12 years before Harvey felt confident enough to publish this theory in his famous book *De Motu Cordis* (On the Motion of the Heart). Why did he take so long to let the world know of his discovery?

Objectives

- **Consider** the state of medical knowledge before Harvey's work and the challenge it posed.
- **Explain** the methods of and opposition to Harvey.
- **Examine** Harvey's achievement and contribution to medical progress in England.

Galen's ideas under attack

According to Galen, new blood was constantly made in the liver, and used as a fuel that was burned up in the body. Galen said that blood passed from one side of the heart to the other through invisible holes. Although this had been challenged by influential doctors such as Ibn al-Nafis and Vesalius, they were not believed. In the sixteenth century, other doctors had made important discoveries to do with blood: Realdo Columbo said that blood moved along the veins and arteries, and Fabricius proved there were valves in the veins. William Harvey read what these anatomists at Padua had discovered and built upon their work, but his own theory of the blood directly contradicted the view of the widely respected Galen.

Harvey's theory of the blood

Harvey was a rigorous scientist who had read widely what other doctors before him had written about the heart. From 1616, he set about the exploration of his ideas about blood circulation: he took what he had read as his starting point, then built up his knowledge of the heart through dissection. Harvey studied human hearts, and also observed the slow-beating hearts of cold-blooded animals to understand how the muscles worked. He experimented by trying to pump liquid the wrong way through valves in the veins, proving that blood could only go round one way. He worked out mathematically how much blood would have to be produced if, as Galen said, it was a fuel for the body. Harvey was a careful scientist who drew conclusions from methodical observations and experimentations.

▼ **INTERPRETATION A** *A 1962 painting by Robert Thom, showing Harvey demonstrating how the blood flows one way through the blood vessels of the arm*

Harvey probably took 12 years from first having the idea of the circulation of the blood to publishing it, because of the revolutionary nature of his theory and also because he did not understand every aspect of how blood works in the body. Even when he published *De Motu Cordis* in 1628, there were still things that he did not know. For example, although he was sure the blood circulated, he did not know why, and he knew that his critics would expect an answer. Neither could Harvey explain why blood in the arteries was a different colour from blood in the veins. He could not tell other doctors how the blood moved from the arteries to the veins, but he suggested that it was absorbed by the veins. Lastly, he knew that if he were right, he would be challenging many of the contemporary medical ideas based upon balancing the four humours, especially the concept of bloodletting.

Fact

In Harvey's lifetime, there was no microscope good enough to see the tiny capillaries that connect the veins to the arteries. In 1661, four years after Harvey died, Professor Marcello Malpighi used one of the first effective microscopes to discover the capillaries. This was proof that what Harvey suggested must be true, and is an example of how technology helped medical progress.

Reactions to Harvey's discovery

When Harvey published his findings in 1628, his critics said he was mad to suggest blood circulated; others ignored his ideas. Some doctors rejected his theory because he was contradicting Galen, who had long been the authoritative voice on how blood worked. They thought that it was impossible that Harvey was correct. Others were very hostile, such as the French anatomist Jean Riolan, at the University of Paris, who called Harvey a 'circulator': this was slang for a travelling **quack** (an unqualified, often useless, doctor). In 1636 in Germany, Professor Caspar Hofmann watched Harvey demonstrate his theory, but then dismissed his calculations about the body's amount of blood as 'the mere trick of an accountant'. Despite all the criticism, Harvey's theory was accepted by many within his lifetime, but it took another 50 years before the University of Paris taught it to medical students.

SOURCE B The title page of Harvey's book, published in 1628

Harvey's discovery was not immediately useful, and further scientific discovery was needed. Doctors would not be able to replace or transfuse blood until 1901, when they knew about blood groups. However, understanding the circulation of the blood was a vital stage in the development of surgery and in the diagnosis of illness. Many modern medical treatments would not work unless blood circulation was understood: for example, blood tests (which help diagnose diabetes or heart, kidney or liver disease), blood transfusions and heart transplants.

Key Word

quack

INTERPRETATION C A nineteenth-century painting showing Harvey explaining to King Charles I the circulation of blood, using the heart of a deer from the royal parks

Work

1. What did Galen think blood was for?
2. Describe at least three methods Harvey used in his discovery of how blood works.
3. In pairs or in groups, discuss:
   a. Why did people at the time reject Harvey's theory?
   b. How did Harvey's theories start to be recognised as true?

Practice Question

Explain the significance of the work of William Harvey for the development of surgery.

8 marks

Study Tip

Try to explain whether Harvey's discovery had an impact at the time, and whether it continued to be important later on and to us today.

Britain: Health and the people 31

5.1 How scientific was seventeenth- and eighteenth-century medicine?

Although some doctors and surgeons engaged with the Renaissance approach to science and applied lots of rigorous testing in the sixteenth century, many more doctors did not do this. Even in the seventeenth century, ancient unscientific beliefs such as the four humours were still used to treat everyone, from ordinary people to Charles II, the King of England. What kinds of treatments were available at the time? How effective were they?

Objectives

- **Describe** traditional and new methods of treating disease in the seventeenth and eighteenth centuries.
- **Explain** the ideas behind the traditional or quack treatments.
- **Assess** how far the measures were effective.

Treatments fit for a king

At 7:00am on 2 February 1685, King Charles II's excellent health deserted him. One of his doctors, Sir Charles Scarburgh, recorded the detail that the king collapsed with a 'disturbance in his brain'. The royal medical team swung into action. These people were the best that money could buy.

The king received in total some 58 drugs, and he was purged, bled, blistered and cauterised. None of these treatments helped the chronic kidney disease that killed him; furthermore, the kidney disease may have been brought about by the poisonous mercury treatments that the king had taken for 'curing' syphilis.

▼ **SOURCE A** Excerpts from Scarburgh's medical records of King Charles II in February 1685:

> We opened a vein in his right arm and drew off 16 ounces (425 ml) of blood, then another 8 ounces (212 ml). To free his stomach of all impurities we gave him an **emetic** and then a **purgative** to drain away the humours; to accelerate the purgative we gave him an **enema** and applied blistering agents to his shaved head. (2 February)
>
> We gave him a purgative and drew off 10 ounces (300 ml) of blood from both jugular veins. (3 February)
>
> Alas his Majesty's strength seemed exhausted: he was seized by a mortal distress in breathing, and died. (6 February)

What treatments were available for ordinary people?

Medical treatments available to ordinary people in the seventeenth and eighteenth centuries still depended on what they could afford. They could get medical advice from different people:

- **Barber-surgeons:** poorly trained people who would give you a haircut and perhaps perform a small operation like bloodletting or tooth pulling.
- **Apothecaries:** they had little or no medical training, but sold medicines and potions.
- **Wise women:** their treatments often relied on superstition. However, they often had extensive knowledge of plants and herbs.
- **Quacks:** showy, travelling salesmen who sold all sorts of medicines and 'cure-alls'.

▼ **SOURCE B** A seventeenth-century painting of a quack salesman selling medical 'cures' to the sick

Chapter 5 Dealing with disease

As the treatment of Charles II shows, bloodletting continued to be a common treatment. It was even done regularly to prevent illness. People still had a lot of faith in the royal touch to cure the disease scrofula, or 'king's evil': an average of 3000 people a year arrived in London hoping to be cured by the king's touch. There were many homely herbal remedies that were passed down from generation to generation. Some worked, for example honey can kill bacteria and the willow tree contains aspirin, which dulls pain.

The introduction of the printing press helped ordinary people collect books on herbal remedies, such as the English doctor Nicholas Culpeper's *The complete herbal* (1653). Culpeper used plants and astrology in his treatments. Unusually for the time, Culpeper was highly critical of bloodletting and purging. Along with traditional herbal remedies quack medicine flourished.

New lands, new medicines

Explorers on voyages of discovery brought back new natural medicines:

- The bark of the Cinchona tree from South America contained quinine, which helped treat malaria.
- Opium from Turkey was used as an anaesthetic.
- The military surgeon, John Woodall, began using lemons and limes to treat scurvy in 1617.
- Tobacco from North America was wrongly said to cure many conditions, from toothache to plague.

▼ **SOURCE C** *In 1659, one of Culpepper's students, William Ryves, published a biography of his master in which he reported Culpeper's view of the Royal College of Physicians:*

> Bloodsuckers, true vampires, who have learned little since Hippocrates, they use bloodletting for illnesses above the waist and purging for those below it. They evacuate and revulse their patients until they faint.

Key Words

emetic   purgative   enema

▼ **SOURCE D** *A page from* The complete herbal; *according to Culpeper, the herb lovage (middle left) was 'a herb of the sun, under the sign of Taurus' which strengthened the throat and dried up phlegm*

Key Biography

Thomas Sydenham (1624–89)

Sydenham was an English doctor who was famous for recognising the symptoms of epidemic diseases such as scarlet fever, and for classifying illnesses and medicines correctly (such as iron for anaemia). He was critical of quack medicine, and he also stressed the careful observation of symptoms. However, he dismissed the value of dissections and ignored Harvey's discovery because it did not help in treating patients. Sydenham still used all of the usual bleeding methods for treatment, but he often advocated doing nothing and letting nature take its course. His book *Medical Observations* (1676) became a standard textbook.

Work

1. What was the theory behind the types of treatment that Charles II received? Explain your answer.
2. Study **Source B**. How did a quack convince people that he or she was to be believed?
3. Make a table of natural and supernatural treatments and remedies used at this time. Highlight the ones that were new.
4. Thomas Sydenham was both innovative and traditional. Do you agree? Why or why not?

How did doctors deal with the Great Plague?

The plague was a devastating disease that hit Britain many times. The best known outbreak was the Black Death in the fourteenth century. There were further, smaller outbreaks of plague over the next few hundred years, and in 1665, it returned once more and killed about 100,000 people in London (around a quarter of the city's population). This time it was known as the Great Plague. It also killed thousands more in the rest of the country. Did people learn anything to help them deal with the latest epidemic of plague?

Objectives

- **Explain** how the Great Plague affected people at the time.
- **Summarise** the measures taken against the plague.
- **Evaluate** how far the measures were scientific.

What did people think caused the Great Plague of 1665?

Many people still believed that the plague was a punishment from God for their sins; other people blamed the movement of planets or 'poisonous' air. The real cause of the plague was again the fleas that lived on rats, which were attracted to the rubbish that was mostly in the poorer parts of the city.

Remedies and treatments at the time had no effect: some patients were bled with leeches. People smoked to keep away the 'poisoned' air, or sniffed a sponge soaked in vinegar. Many strange Medieval remedies that were still used involved using animals such as frogs, snakes and scorpions to 'draw out the poison'. Chickens and pigeons were also used. Treatments that seem odd now were shared as sound medical advice: for example, the apothecary William Boghurst recommended that when close to death from the plague, the remedy to try was: 'You may cut up a puppy dog alive and apply in warm to the sores.'

How did people try to cure the Great Plague?

Doctors still had no cure for the plague. If you were rich enough, one of the simplest remedies was to move to the countryside to avoid catching it. For example, King Charles II and his court left London and moved to Oxford.

There was some evidence that people were beginning to make a strong connection between dirt and the disease. From studying the Bills of Mortality, people realised that most deaths occurred in the poorest, dirtiest parts of the city where people lived in the worst housing.

There was a more organised approach to dealing with the plague this time. Mayors and councillors issued orders to try to halt the spread of the disease. The authorities were concerned with identifying people with the plague, and they paid 'women searchers' who would examine the sick and note those with plague symptoms. Then, the plague victims were quarantined (locked up) in their houses; watchmen stood on guard to make sure that they did not leave and spread the disease. Those houses with plague victims had a red cross painted on the door and the words, 'Lord have mercy on us'.

▼ **SOURCE A** A Bill of Mortality showing a list of all the causes of death within London in one week in 1665

Extension

Study **Source A** carefully. What are the top three causes of death? What percentage of deaths were due to plague? What do some of the causes of death tell us about medical knowledge at this time?

The bodies of those who had died from the plague were brought out at night when fewer people were about, when the orders to 'bring out your dead' were heard. Bodies were then thrown into carts to be buried in mass plague pits. Fires were

▲ **INTERPRETATION B** *A view of the Great Plague in seventeenth-century London, drawn in 1864*

Work

1. Identify three things in **Interpretation B** that show the impact of the plague.
2. Study **Source C**. Write a description of what you think is happening in each picture.
3. Discuss with a partner: do you agree that the outbreak of the Great Plague was dealt with more effectively than the Black Death? Explain your answer.

lit to try to remove the poisons that were thought to be in the air. Homeowners were ordered to sweep the streets in front of their houses, and pigs, dogs and cats were not allowed in the streets where there was plague. Plays or games that would bring together large crowds were banned. Furthermore, trade between towns with the infection was stopped, and the border with Scotland was closed.

How did the plague end?

It has often been written that the Great Fire of London in 1666 ended the plague because it burned down the poor housing and sterilised the streets by burning the waste. This was not true. The fire destroyed houses within the city walls and by the River Thames. The poorest areas were outside the city walls, where most of the plague deaths happened. The plague actually declined because the rats developed a greater resistance to the disease, and so their fleas did not need to find human hosts. After 1666, quarantine laws prevented epidemic diseases coming into the country on ships.

Practice Question

Compare the Black Death in the fourteenth century with the Great Plague in the seventeenth century. In what ways were they similar? **8 marks**

Study Tip

Compare aspects that are the same, such as knowledge of the cause of the epidemic, measures taken, and the impact at the time.

▼ **SOURCE C** *A broadsheet (news leaflet) from 1665 showing the effects of the Great Plague in a city*

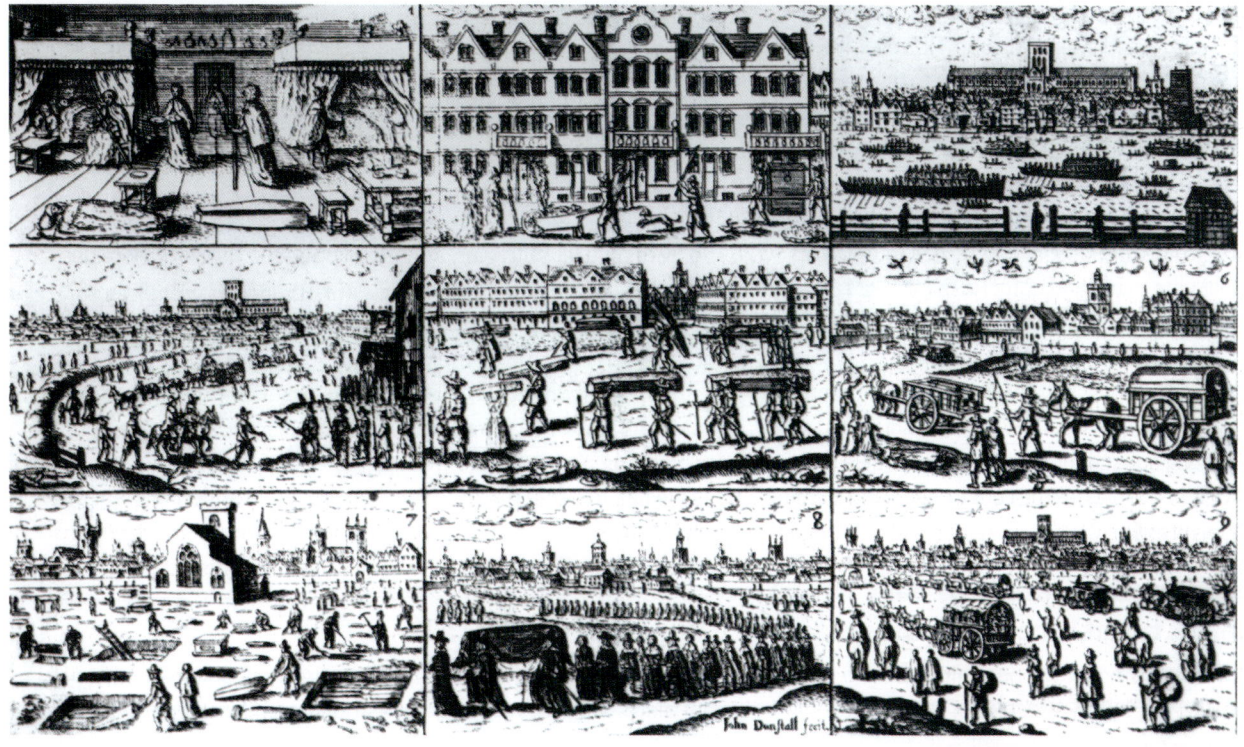

Britain: Health and the people 35

5.3 How did hospitals change in the eighteenth century?

We have seen that Medieval infirmaries or hospitals in England were small and run by the Christian Church: these were places where people came to be cared for rather than to be cured. Many of these early hospitals were funded by rich men donating money to Church causes. However, when King Henry VIII turned England from Catholic to Protestant in the 1530s, his actions affected hospitals. What were hospitals like after the Medieval period? How were they different?

Objectives

- **Describe** the changes to the training and status of surgeons and doctors.
- **Explain** the growth of new hospitals, and how they were different from Medieval hospitals.
- **Assess** the contribution that eighteenth-century hospitals made to medical care.

As part of the religious conflict between Henry VIII and the Catholic Church, the king seized the wealth of rich Catholic monasteries and closed them down (through a process called the dissolution of the monasteries). The king gave money to start hospitals such as St Bartholomew's and St Thomas' in London; it was at St Bartholomew's that William Harvey investigated the circulation of the blood in the seventeenth century.

Who built hospitals in the eighteenth century?

Up to the seventeenth century, hospitals were still places for the sick to rest, to receive simple remedies, and to pray. However, it was in the early eighteenth century that the idea of modern hospitals using modern methods to cure patients began. These hospitals were different because they were founded and supported by the charitable gifts of private people. In London, Westminster Hospital (1719) was founded by a private bank, and Guy's Hospital (1724) was founded by a merchant called Thomas Guy. Guy was a businessman who had initially supported St Thomas' Hospital, but then gave the money to build Guy's. Hospitals were also built by 'private subscription', where local people clubbed together to pay for the construction and running of a hospital.

What happened in an eighteenth-century hospital?

In the new hospitals not only were the sick cared for, but the doctors of the future

SOURCE A *A drawing of Guy's Hospital from a London guidebook published in 1755*

received training, as medical schools were often attached to hospitals. Individual wards were developed for different types of disease. Although doctors learned mainly through lectures and reading in medical schools, new charity hospitals like the one in Edinburgh gave final-year students the opportunity to gain experience by following the medical professor through the wards.

Doctors also liked to gain an official post at a hospital, because it gave them a better reputation and attracted wealthy private patients. While the doctor attended the ordinary people in the hospital for free, it was the fees paid by private patients which were a doctor's main source of income. The types of treatment given in hospitals were still primarily based on the four humours approach of bleeding and purging. Towards the end of the eighteenth century, as well as treating patients for free, hospitals added dispensaries where the poor would be given medicines without any charge, such as the public dispensary of Edinburgh, which started in 1776.

Types of hospitals

The eighteenth century saw not only general hospitals for the sick, but also specialist types. St Luke's Hospital in London in 1751

B *A list of notable hospitals founded during the eighteenth century*

Hospital	Founded	Paid for by
Royal Infirmary of Edinburgh	1729	Local churches and wealthy citizens
Bristol Royal Infirmary	1735	Wealthy merchant, Paul Fisher
York County Hospital	1740	Gifts from wealthy local people
Middlesex Hospital	1745	Private subscriptions
Manchester Royal infirmary	1752	Local factory owner, Joseph Bancroft
Addenbrooke's Hospital in Cambridge	1766	Bequest (inheritance) from Dr J. Addenbrooke, and local subscriptions
Leeds General Infirmary	1771	Five local doctors
Birmingham General Hospital	1779	Local businessmen, doctors and landowners

became the second large public hospital, after Bethlem, for the mentally ill. London's Lock Hospital for venereal (sexually transmitted) disease opened in 1746. Another new type of hospital was the maternity hospital. For example, wards were set aside in Middlesex Hospital for pregnant women in 1747, and what became known as the British Hospital for Mothers and Babies was set up in 1749.

One particular social problem became more noticeable in the early eighteenth century: high child mortality rates. In the 1720s and 1730s, there were severe epidemics of typhus and influenza, and the death rate among children was alarming. There were poor provisions for babies and children to be given medical treatment. This upset a retired ship's captain, Thomas Coram, who gathered enough public support to build a hospital for sickly or poor children that he 'found' abandoned on the streets. He started the Foundling Hospital in 1741: it cared for orphaned children by giving them a clean environment, clothing and some simple education up to the age of 15. It became one of London's most popular charities.

Hospital boom

Between 1720 and 1750, five new general hospitals were added to London's two ancient hospitals and nine more throughout the country. By 1800, London's hospitals alone were handling over 20,000 patients a year. Compared to 1400, when each of the 470 hospitals in the whole of England had room for only ten patients at most, this was a huge increase. There was a religious motive behind this change in hospital numbers and the focus on patient care and cure. As seventeenth-century conflicts were often based around religion, in the eighteenth century there were some Christians who wanted to include as many different opinions as possible within the Church of England. They downplayed the importance of religious beliefs and styles of church services, and instead stressed that good Christians did more than go to church – they showed their faith by trying to do good deeds in the community.

Attitudes to diseases were changing too. People began to abandon the idea that illness was a punishment for sin; they began thinking that illness could be dealt with from a more evidence-based, scientific point of view. For example, St Luke's Hospital's senior doctor at the time, William Battie, advocated that mental illness was no less curable than any other disease.

SOURCE C *A painting of Thomas Coram, by the famous artist William Hogarth, 1740*

Work

1. What types of people founded hospitals in the eighteenth century?
2. Other than caring for the sick, what else did eighteenth-century hospitals do?
3. What was new about hospitals at this time?
4. Discuss in pairs or in a group: why had attitudes to hospitals changed? In what ways did religion affect hospitals?

5.4 Why should we remember John Hunter?

John Hunter was born into a farming family in East Kilbride, near Glasgow, in 1728. At the age of 20, he joined his elder brother William in London, who had started an anatomy school there and was a popular doctor who specialised in childbirth. William's profitable practice meant he had little interest in research but his younger brother John, on the other hand, soon showed a great talent for precise dissection and anatomical research. John's other job was to rob graves at night to supply bodies for his brother's anatomy school! With these diverse talents, how did John Hunter go on to make great changes in the field of anatomy?

Objectives

- **Outline** the work of John Hunter.
- **Examine** John Hunter's approach to surgery and anatomical knowledge.
- **Evaluate** John Hunter's contribution to medical progress.

Look through the following diagram carefully and read about John Hunter in the Key Biography. You can then evaluate his contribution to medical progress.

Key Biography

John Hunter (1728–93)

INTERPRETATION A *John Hunter*

While working for his brother, John Hunter studied with two of England's most famous surgeons: William Cheselden and Percivall Potts. Hunter became an army surgeon in 1760; after three years he left the army to set up a surgical practice in London. In 1768, he became a surgeon at St George's Hospital. He was appointed Surgeon to King George III in 1776, and Surgeon-General to the army in 1790. Although he earned large amounts of money during his life, he used most of it for research and for his specimen collection. He died in debt and in poverty in 1793.

Teaching

Hunter was admitted to the Company of Surgeons in 1768, after which he set up a large practice and trained hundreds of other surgeons in his scientific approach. Many young surgeons that Hunter trained and inspired became great medical teachers and professors, and helped to bring about famous teaching hospitals in nineteenth-century Britain and America. For example, Edward Jenner (see pages 40–41), trained with him and became a firm friend.

Books

Hunter's writings on his scientific research were widely read, and were a major contribution to surgical knowledge. His books helped the surgical profession by showing the theoretical knowledge about anatomy that every surgeon needed. His writings were all based upon his observations, his practical skill as a dissector, and his willingness to experiment. In 1771, he published *The Natural History of the Teeth*, which made use of the dentistry he had learned. His book *On Venereal Disease* (1786) was partly based upon his own self-experimentation; it was translated into several European languages and was widely read. His experience in the army contributed to his book *Blood inflammation and gunshot wounds*: although this was published after his death, it finally put to rest the idea that gunshot wounds were poisoned and therefore that the area around the wound needed to be cut out. Hunter further explained his new idea that the wound should not be made larger, but treated as any other wound. From dissecting many human bodies, Hunter was able to make discoveries about the nature of disease, infections, cancer, and the circulation of the blood.

Scientific method

John Hunter was an early promoter of careful observation and the use of the scientific method in surgeries. He even went so far as to experiment on himself in 1767. There was a debate in his time about whether gonorrhoea and syphilis were the same venereal disease (they are actually different diseases). It was thought that two diseases could not exist together in the same organ of a body. So, Hunter injected himself with pus from the sores of a gonorrhoea patient. Unfortunately, and unknown to Hunter, the gonorrhoea patient also had syphilis. It took him three years to recover using the standard mercury treatment.

Hunter's willingness to try radical approaches was also shown in 1785 when a man was admitted to St George's Hospital with a throbbing lump (aneurysm) on his knee joint. The usual treatment would be to amputate the leg above the throbbing tumour. Hunter's dissections led him to think that if the blood supply were restricted above the aneurysm, then it would encourage new blood vessels to develop and bypass the damaged area. Hunter first tested his theory by experimenting on animals. He then conducted surgery on the patient: he cut into the man's leg and at several points tied off the artery to restrict the blood flow above the aneurysm. Six weeks later the man walked out of hospital: Hunter had saved the man's leg.

What were John Hunter's contributions to medical progress?

Specimens

Hunter collected a huge selection of anatomical specimens. In his collection he preserved 3000 stuffed or dried animals, plants, fossils, diseased organs, embryos, and other body parts. Hunter experimented with inflating narrow blood vessels with wax to study blood flow. A famous item in Hunter's collection was the skeleton of a 2.3-metre-tall (7-feet-7-inches-tall) Irish giant, Charles Byrne, which he acquired in 1783. His collection, including Byrne's skeleton, was later given to the Royal College of Surgeons in England.

Fact

Royal College of Surgeons

Henry VIII allowed the Company of Barber-Surgeons to be formed in 1540, which maintained barber-surgeon standards and controlled qualifications to the trade. By 1745, surgeons were anxious to have their skills recognised as superior to that of barbers, and an Act of Parliament created a separate Company of Surgeons, with a base near to Newgate gaol (to allow the continuous supply of executed prisoners for dissections). The king named the Company of Surgeons as the Royal College of Surgeons in 1800; it still exists to this day to oversee surgeons' training, and to advise the government.

Practice Question

Compare the work of Andreas Vesalius and John Hunter. In what ways were they similar? **8 marks**

Study Tip

Consider whether Vesalius produced work in the same four areas as John Hunter. Who had to overcome the greater opposition to his work?

Work

1. Study **Interpretation A**. In what ways did the artist try to show the different achievements of John Hunter's life?
2. a Draw a simple timeline of Hunter's life, and label key events.
   b Using your timeline, explain how each aspect of Hunter's work was linked to the others. For example, how were his books related to his scientific investigations?
3. Do you think we should remember John Hunter? What was the most important aspect of his work?

6.1 How did Edward Jenner help defeat smallpox?

One of the biggest killer diseases in the eighteenth century was smallpox. It was a highly infectious **virus** that passed from one person to another by coughing, sneezing or touching, and it killed 30 per cent of those who caught it. The first symptoms were fever, headache and a rash, followed by pus-filled blisters covering the entire body. Even if you survived, you could be left blind or with deep scars. Doctors at the time tried to prevent smallpox by using **inoculation**, but it was controversial and didn't always work. However, a country doctor named Edward Jenner found a better way to prevent smallpox. How did people react to his discovery?

Objectives

- **Describe** smallpox and its treatment using inoculation.
- **Explain** how Edward Jenner made his discovery, and the opposition he faced.
- **Evaluate** the impact of vaccination.

What was inoculation?

In Medieval China and other parts of Asia, people had been using a basic form of inoculation to prevent smallpox. They scratched pus or scabs from a smallpox victim onto healthy people's skin: they didn't realise it but it gave them a mild dose of the disease, which allowed them to build up resistance against attacks of the full, killer form of the disease. In 1721, smallpox inoculation was in demand in Britain when a fashionable aristocrat named Lady Mary Wortley Montagu had her children inoculated. She had seen it done in Turkey.

Inoculation became very profitable. For example, in the 1760s, a father and son surgeon team, Robert and Daniel Sutton, devised an easier way of inoculation and earned a fortune. Only the rich could afford the treatment though. By the end of the 1770s, more and more doctors used the 'Sutton' method, and it became the normal practice for preventing smallpox. However, there were problems with inoculation:

- There were strong religious objections: some people still argued that God sent illness to test people's faith or to punish them for their sin, so preventing sickness with inoculation was wrong.
- As germs and infection were not understood well at the time, it was hard for people to accept the idea of giving a small amount of disease to prevent a bigger disease. Doctors argued about the risk of dying from smallpox compared with that of dying after inoculation.
- Sometimes inoculation gave people a strong (instead of mild) dose of smallpox, which could kill them.
- Any inoculated person could still pass smallpox to others.
- The poorest people could not afford inoculation, so they were not protected.

However, the practice of inoculation slowly became more common in the 1740s and 1750s.

▼ **SOURCE A** *A painting, from 1823, of a man being shown his face affected by smallpox*

Key Biography

Edward Jenner (1749–1823)

Jenner was an apprentice to a country surgeon from age 13 to 19, then went on to study in London with the renowned John Hunter (see pages 38–39). Hunter encouraged him to conduct experiments and test theories. He returned to Gloucestershire as a country doctor in 1772. In 1798, he published a book on **vaccination**. He was honoured by being appointed physician extraordinary to King George IV in 1821.

40 Chapter 6 Prevention of disease

Jenner's discovery of vaccination

Smallpox inoculation was a well-known treatment before Edward Jenner became a surgeon. Jenner may have heard stories that milkmaids who caught cowpox (a similar, but milder version of smallpox that commonly affected cows) were protected against smallpox, and he decided to test this theory out.

In Gloucestershire in 1796, Jenner carried out an experiment: he inserted cowpox into a poor eight-year-old boy. If the cowpox worked, then the child would not react to the follow-up smallpox inoculation; if it failed, then he would develop smallpox scabs in the normal way. Six weeks later, he gave the boy smallpox inoculation: no disease followed.

Jenner called his cowpox inoculation technique vaccination, based on the Latin word for cow (*vacca*). To prove that vaccination against smallpox worked without the need for someone to catch cowpox directly from a cow, Jenner gave cowpox to another patient, and then took cowpox pus from that patient to vaccinate a new patient. He tested this 16 times over several weeks. None of the patients reacted to smallpox inoculation, which allowed Jenner to conclude that cowpox protected humans from smallpox.

Opposition to change

Jenner published his vaccination findings in 1798, but he could not explain how vaccination worked, which made it difficult for others to accept it. Many doctors profited from smallpox inoculation, so they disliked his findings. In the London Smallpox Hospital, William Woodville and George Pearson carried out tests using cowpox, but their equipment was contaminated and one of their patients died, so they concluded that Jenner was wrong, and that there was little difference between smallpox inoculation and vaccination. Also, Jenner was not a fashionable city doctor, so there was snobbery against him. Despite criticisms Jenner had powerful supporters, especially when members of the royal family were vaccinated, and parliament agreed to give Jenner £10,000 for his research in 1802.

Impact of Jenner's discovery

Attitudes changed as people eventually realised that vaccination was more effective and less dangerous than inoculation. Although a few other people had used cowpox to prevent smallpox before Jenner, he had a greater impact because he proved his theories using scientific methods and carefully identified the cowpox disease. Jenner may not have discovered vaccination, but he made others notice it. By the 1800s, doctors were using his technique in America and Europe, and in 1853, the British government made smallpox vaccination compulsory.

Key Words

virus   inoculation   vaccination

Fact

Jenner didn't make the connection between cowpox and smallpox until he attended a local medical society in 1768. A surgeon called John Fewster reported there that when he tried to give smallpox inoculation to farmers who had had cowpox before, there was no effect on them. Although Fewster did not carry out any further research, this failure of inoculation inspired Jenner to experiment with cowpox.

Work

1. In your own words, explain the difference between inoculation and vaccination.
2. What were the objections to inoculation and vaccination?
3. Prepare an essay plan for the question: 'Explain the significance of vaccination in the development of medicine.'

Practice Question

Has the role of the individual been the main factor in the development of medicine in Britain since Medieval times?

16 marks
SPaG: 4 marks

Study Tip

You could refer to Jenner and his vaccination, but there are other people that you could mention. What were these people's special talents? Don't forget you need to consider other factors as well.

7.1 How was pain conquered?

By 1800, the status of surgeons had improved, thanks to men like John Hunter (see pages 38–39). However the experience of surgery for the patient was still terrifying. This was because surgeons had no effective way of controlling and stopping pain during an operation. Surgeons managed to solve this problem in the nineteenth century. How did they do it, and did it revolutionise surgery?

Objectives

▶ **Explore** the development of anaesthetics, including the role of James Simpson and chloroform.

▶ **Explain** the opposition to anaesthetics and how it was overcome.

▶ **Assess** the impact of anaesthetics on surgery.

SOURCE A *A painting from the seventeenth century showing a foot operation being carried out before anaesthetics were available*

Pain relief was not new: pain-deadening substances were used in the Medieval period. The most important of these were hashish, mandrake, and opium: while these chemicals (made from plant extracts) did dull the pain, it was difficult to judge an effective dose from a lethal one. There was, of course, alcohol, but this made the heart beat faster and the bleeding more difficult for surgeons to control. Some patients had religious objections to alcohol and preferred to sing hymns and suffer the pain. The result was that before surgeons had an effective and safe anaesthetic, they had to operate quickly to spare the patient pain, and they could not carry out complicated, internal surgery.

Nitrous oxide

As scientific knowledge developed in the eighteenth century, chemists found new anaesthetic substances. The first of these was nitrous oxide. In 1795, the Bristol physician Thomas Beddoes and his young assistant, Humphry Davy, experimented with inhaling nitrous oxide. Davy published an account in 1800: he described how the gas made him laugh, and feel giddy and relaxed, but he did not recognise its medical value. It became a fairground novelty: people paid to inhale it and then fell about, laughing hysterically, much to the amusement of the crowd. It was not until 1844 that an American dentist, Horace Wells, saw fairground laughing gas as an anaesthetic possibility and used it in the removal of one of his own teeth. However, his demonstration failed to convince doctors.

Ether

Around the same time William Clark, another American dentist, experimented with a different chemical: ether. In January 1842, he used it in a tooth extraction. This time doctors took notice. In March, an American country doctor, Crawford Long, used ether to remove a neck growth from a patient. On 16 October 1846, William Morton helped give a public demonstration in a Boston hospital. News of the American anaesthetic experiments quickly spread to Europe. Britain's most acclaimed surgeon, Robert Liston, was keen to be the first to try ether as an anaesthetic. He called it a 'Yankee Dodge' and used it in a leg amputation leg in December. An effective anaesthetic had arrived.

But ether had its drawbacks: it was difficult to inhale, it caused vomiting, and it was highly flammable. For convenience, and to avoid hospital infection, many patients chose to have their operations at home in front of an open fire: using ether in these circumstances could be disastrous.

Chloroform

There was still a need for a safe and effective anaesthetic. The breakthrough came in 1847 when a Scottish doctor, James Simpson, discovered chloroform. The story goes that Simpson and friends had been testing a number of different substances when somebody knocked over a bottle of chloroform. Simpson's wife brought them dinner but found them all sleeping peacefully.

Why was there opposition to anaesthetics?

It seems strange today that doctors should object to using anaesthetics, but surgeons were used to operating quickly and on a conscious patient. A few army surgeons during the Crimean War (1853–56) thought that soldiers should dutifully put up with the pain. In the early days of using chloroform, some patients died. This was because men and women of different sizes needed different amounts of chloroform. The most famous case was Hannah Greener, who died in 1848 during an operation to remove her toenail. There were also religious objections to removing the pain of childbirth with anaesthetics, as it was thought to be God's will and a punishment for sin.

However, these objections were quickly overcome by a royal example. By 1850, Queen Victoria had had many difficult labours. Dr John Snow convinced her husband, Prince Albert, that anaesthetics were safe. On 7 April 1853, Snow used chloroform to help Queen Victoria give birth to Prince Leopold. The Queen was in no doubt when she wrote, 'the effect was soothing, quieting and delightful beyond measure'.

For the patient, the conquest of pain was a major step forward, but in itself the introduction of anaesthetics did not revolutionise surgery. This was because there was still a severe death rate from infection (known at the time as 'hospital fever' or 'hospitalism') after the operation. It would take another decade before hospital infections were defeated.

▼ **INTERPRETATION C** *A drawing from the 1860s of Hannah Greener's death from a chloroform overdose during an operation*

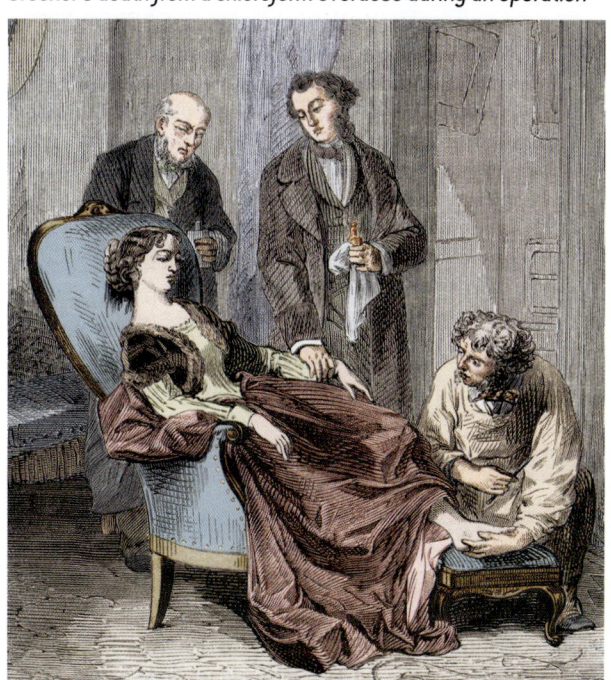

Work

1. **a** Draw a mind-map to show the different reasons why some people objected to using anaesthetics.
   b Why were the objections overcome?
2. Explain why the development of anaesthetics did not completely revolutionise surgery in the 1840s and 1850s.
3. Write a paragraph of no more than 250 words to explain the contribution of the following individuals to the development of anaesthetics: Humphrey Davy, James Simpson, John Snow, Robert Liston.

Fact

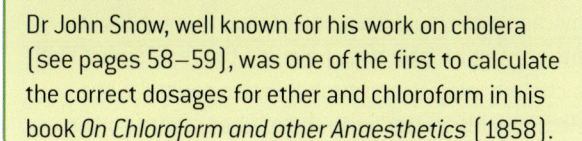

Dr John Snow, well known for his work on cholera (see pages 58–59), was one of the first to calculate the correct dosages for ether and chloroform in his book *On Chloroform and other Anaesthetics* (1858).

Practice Question

How useful is **Source A** to a historian studying the development of surgery?   **8 marks**

Study Tip

You could first consider what you can see in the picture. Try to organise your thoughts around the following four headings: pain, infection, bleeding, and operating theatre.

7.2 How did doctors in Britain find out that germs caused diseases?

Hospital infections made surgery highly dangerous, but in the 1860s, the new science of bacteriology (study of **microbes**) helped scientists to understand the real causes of infection. How did scientists in Europe and Britain discover that germs caused diseases? Did this discovery help to revolutionise surgery?

Objectives

- **Explain** beliefs about causes of infection before the 1860s.
- **Describe** the wider public health debate in early nineteenth-century Britain.
- **Summarise** Pasteur's experiment and theory.

We now know that an infection is the invasion of the body by microbes (very tiny organisms which include bacteria); different microbes can cause different diseases. But long before scientists made the connection that microbes were actually germs, surgeons believed that when a person was weak, sepsis (or 'poison') began inside the wound and caused it to be infected. They mistook infections for chemical reactions, and didn't realise that they were actually caused by living organisms. They were puzzled about why some deep wounds could heal quickly, while other surface scratches proved to be fatal. Surgeons would initially try to keep the patient healthy and let them heal naturally; then they tried to reduce inflammation with bandages and cleanliness. If the wound became infected, they used cauterising or acids to burn away the affected tissues.

What did people think caused infections?

In 1677, the first basic microscope was invented, which allowed scientists to see the tiny organisms moving about in water droplets, food, and animal and human body parts. Scientists even identified microbes in the blood of sick people, but no link was made between microbes and diseases then. Scientists carried out more experiments, but it did not make things any clearer. For example, in 1699 Francesco Redi boiled up a liquid and sealed it against the air. No microbes appeared, so he concluded that infection came from the outside. However, in 1748 John Needham repeated Redi's experiment and found microbes. People did not realise that the results depended on how clean the equipment was and how careful the scientist was.

In the eighteenth century, scientists had all sorts of ideas about how diseases came about. One theory was **spontaneous generation**: the idea that microbes could appear as if by magic when something rotted. They thought the disease caused the microbes, not the other way round. There was also an assumption that all microbes were much the same.

In the nineteenth century, some people began to question these theories. They believed in **specificity**: that microbes were not all the same, and that certain ones (bacteria or germs) actually caused specific diseases. Scientists found evidence for this. For example, in 1835 Agostino Bassi linked a specific microbe (a fungus) to a silkworm disease called muscarine. In 1840, a Swiss Professor of Anatomy, Friedrich Henle, was the first person to challenge spontaneous generation and suggest microbes were the cause of infection. Henle based his work on Bassi. At the time this new theory was dismissed.

Public health debate about epidemics

In early nineteenth-century Britain, there was increased concern about infection and disease as a result of the surge in epidemic diseases in the fast-growing, dirty, overcrowded industrial towns (see Chapter 9). Public health reformers like William Farr and Florence Nightingale argued that cleaning up the environment would stop epidemics. These people were **anti-contagionists**: they believed that epidemics such as cholera, plague and typhoid were caused when infections interacted with the environment (soil or water) and created the disease that would then attack the weak. Their solution was to clean up an area.

The same ideas were applied by doctors like James Simpson, who wanted hospitals relocated or rebuilt. For example, there were public campaigns to move hospitals such as Manchester Royal infirmary or St Thomas' in London into the countryside. Linked to this debate, many people believed in the popular theory of **miasma**, or 'infectious mist': the idea that there was 'bad air', and that disease was spread by this air.

Set against them were the views of **contagionists**, such as John Simon, who believed that infection was spread by contact with an infected person or bacteria. Contagionists thought that epidemics could be controlled by quarantine or preventing contact. Even though contagionists were correct, the problem for them was that some people who came into contact with a diseased person did not become sick.

The first surgeon in Britain to suggest a non-chemical cause of infection was Thomas Wells in 1864. He referred to the French scientist, Professor Louis Pasteur's recent discoveries, and to the idea of using **antiseptic** substances to destroy microbes.

Who was Louis Pasteur?

The biggest challenge to the theory of spontaneous generation and miasma in Europe came from Pasteur. From 1857 to 1860 he investigated why wine and beer often went sour. He designed a clever series of experiments to show that if air was kept out of the swan neck of a flask, the liquid inside it would not go off. Pasteur identified the specific microbe responsible for souring wine, and showed that heating it to the right temperature could kill all the microbes. He proved that germs did not come alive on their own, that they could be found in places they could reach easily, and that they infected things and turned them bad. Pasteur concluded that bacteria, or germs, were the real cause and that it was a biological, not a chemical, process. This was Pasteur's **Germ Theory**.

In the late 1860s, largely through the work of the surgeon Joseph Lister, Pasteur's Germ Theory came to the attention of British doctors.

Key Words

microbe   spontaneous generation   specificity
anti-contagionism   miasma   contagionism
antiseptic   Germ Theory

A *Pasteur's swan-necked flask experiments*

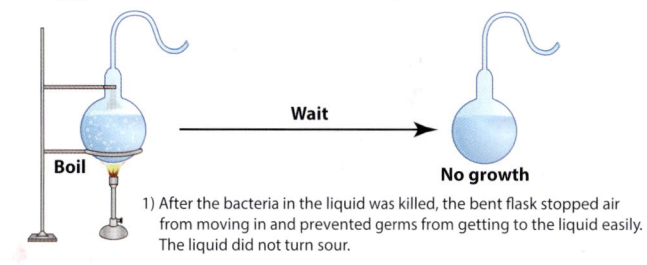

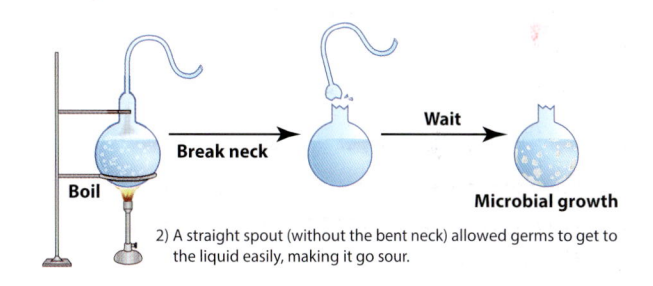

1) After the bacteria in the liquid was killed, the bent flask stopped air from moving in and prevented germs from getting to the liquid easily. The liquid did not turn sour.

2) A straight spout (without the bent neck) allowed germs to get to the liquid easily, making it go sour.

Key Biography

Louis Pasteur (1822–95)

Pasteur was a French chemist and biologist best known for his new discoveries on the causes and preventions of diseases. In 1861, he published his Germ Theory of diseases. He also made important contributions to advances in vaccination, fermentation and pasteurisation (the process of killing bacteria in liquid food such as milk or wine).

Work

1. How did surgeons deal with infection before the 1860s?
2. What were the two main points of view on the public health debate in nineteenth-century Britain?
3. In your own words, describe:
   a. Pasteur's swan-necked flask experiment
   b. Germ Theory.

Britain: Health and the people

7.3 How important was Joseph Lister?

Joseph Lister is credited with helping to bring Pasteur's Germ Theory to acceptance in Britain. He also made use of the Germ Theory in his discovery of antiseptic surgery. What was Lister's contribution to medical science?

Objectives

- **Describe** Joseph Lister's antiseptic ideas and techniques.
- **Assess** why there was opposition to Lister's antiseptic approach in Britain.

Key Biography

Joseph Lister (1827–1912)
Born in Essex, Lister studied surgery and became a fellow of the Royal College of Surgeons in 1852. In 1860, he moved to Glasgow to become a Professor of Surgery. He introduced new principles of cleanliness in surgery.

In Glasgow, 1860, Joseph Lister realised that operations went well as long as the wound was kept free from infection. A Professor of Chemistry, Thomas Anderson, then suggested to Lister that he might be interested in a report by the French scientist Louis Pasteur. Lister thought that Pasteur's Germ Theory might explain the problems of infection he encountered. He asked Anderson if there was a chemical that could kill bacteria; Anderson recommended the use of carbolic acid.

Lister and the antiseptic approach

Lister believed that infections only happened when the skin was broken, and microbes could get in and start an infection. In place of the skin, Lister decided to put a chemical barrier. His first experiment with an antiseptic method was in August 1865. A young boy, Jamie Greenlees, had been run over by cart, which had fractured his leg. The bones were sticking through the skin of Jamie's leg. The traditional surgical procedure would be to amputate above the fracture. Instead, Lister set the bones and used dressings that had been soaked in carbolic acid. The dressings stayed in place for four days, after which time Jamie complained of irritation. Lister feared the worst and expected to find an infection when he took off the dressings. He was impressed to see instead that the fracture and the skin were healing well; the irritation was because of the strength of the carbolic acid. The dressings were replaced and the wound stayed infection-free. After six weeks, Jamie walked out of hospital.

Lister began to test this antiseptic approach out on other surgeries: his method was to spray carbolic acid to coat the surgeon's hands, the wound and the instruments used in an operation. He also soaked the bandages, ligatures and dressings to be applied to the wound in diluted carbolic acid.

▼ **SOURCE A** *An operation in Edinburgh, 1871, where Lister's methods are being used*

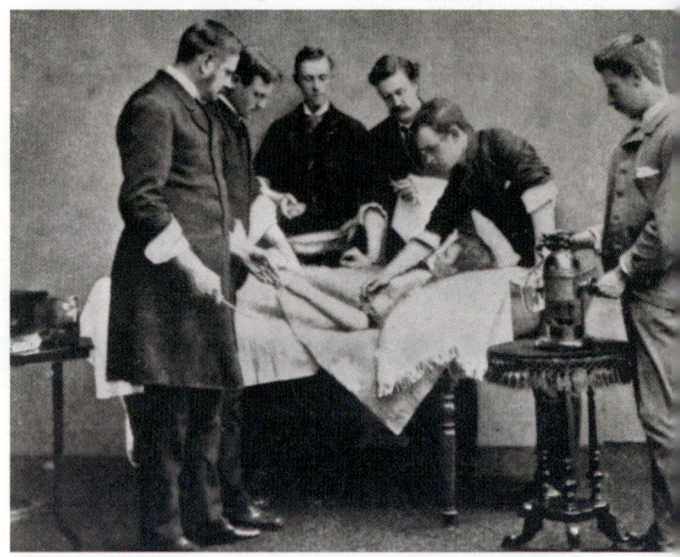

▼ **B** *The number of patients dying after Lister used his antiseptic method fell dramatically, as his own records show*

Years	Total amputations	Lived	Died	Mortality (%)
1864–66 (without antiseptics)	35	19	16	46
1867–70 (with antiseptics)	40	34	6	15

Chapter 7 Advances in medical science in nineteenth-century Britain

Reactions to Lister's work in Britain

Lister published his results in March 1867, giving details of 11 patients with compound fractures, none of whom died of infection. He also publicised Pasteur's Germ Theory through his explanation of the antiseptic technique. In August 1867, Lister lectured doctors about his techniques for using carbolic acid dressings in compound fractures. What was controversial was that he said that infection in wounds was caused by microbes in the air. Surgeons had long debated whether to leave wounds open to the air or to cover them with bandages. Lister argued that the oxygen in the air was irrelevant: it was the microbes in the air that were important. He said that the cause of sepsis came from outside the body and not from spontaneous generation, and recommended his form of antiseptic surgery, which people nicknamed 'Listerism'.

But Lister's ideas were criticised. In 1860s Britain, when people were still not very familiar with Germ Theory, Lister's biologically-based theory of infection was not seen to be the correct view. The wider public health debate was still focused on various chemical theories about causes of infection. Many British surgeons were coming up with new theories: for example, in 1868, Professor John Bennett argued that as cells died, they spontaneously generated infection.

The most influential writer on surgical infection was Charlton Bastian, who strongly championed spontaneous generation. He wrote and lectured widely against Listerism in the late 1860s to the early 1870s. And although Lister clearly linked his techniques with Pasteur's proven new ideas, he retreated from these wider discussions about infection theories, and focussed his research on surgery itself.

Reasons for opposition to antiseptic surgery

- Doctors at the time did not accept Pasteur's Germ Theory and there were many opinions in Britain about the role of microbes in surgery and the causes of infected wounds.
- In the late 1860s, antiseptic chemicals had been widely used, and what Lister was proposing was not revolutionary.
- Lister claimed that his methods of dealing with wound infections were superior to others, but some surgeons thought that their existing methods worked perfectly well.
- His methods were often difficult or unpleasant to use. Carbolic acid made people's hands dry up and crack, and breathing it irritated their lungs. It took a long time for the nurses to prepare his carbolic methods. Lister tried to improve his techniques and made changes. Some surgeons pointed to this as a weakness and suggested that Lister did not know what he was doing.

Although Lister gave advice to prevent hospital infections, he still did not fully understand microbes. In the early 1870s, he believed that microbes were very simple things and incorrectly thought that there might be only one type that caused disease. He also did not scrub his hands before surgery, but merely rinsed them in carbolic acid, and he continued to operate in his street clothes.

SOURCE C *Due to Listerism, carbolic acid became associated with a germ-free environment, as this 1910 soap advertisement shows*

Work

1. Describe Lister's antiseptic techniques in surgery.
2. Explain how Lister applied Pasteur's Germ Theory to his own discoveries.
3. Why was there opposition to Lister's antiseptic ideas?

Practice Question

Explain the significance of Lister's work for the development of medicine. **8 marks**

Study Tip

Consider the impact of Lister's work at the time in saving lives and changing the way surgeons and doctors thought about their work. Mention the use of antiseptics in medicine today.

7.4 The debate continues in Britain: accepting Pasteur's Germ Theory

By the 1890s, surgeons in Britain had moved away from antiseptic methods of surgery to **aseptic** ones. So, surgical practices became safer, but doctors were still unsure how people got infections. Various infection theories were still hotly debated, despite Lister's attempts to share Pasteur's Germ Theory with the British audience. Why did it take so long for Pasteur's work to be accepted in Britain? What were the steps towards the acceptance of Germ Theory in Britain?

Objectives
- **Explore** why Pasteur's theory took so long to be accepted in Britain.
- **Examine** the contribution of British scientists and doctors to the acceptance of Pasteur's Germ Theory.

Aseptic surgery

By the 1890s, surgeons in Europe and North America went beyond Lister's antiseptic methods and developed aseptic surgery. Operating theatres were no longer to be soaked in carbolic acid in order to kill microbes; rather, microbes were to be excluded from the start. Surgeons had to be well-scrubbed, wearing gowns and new, thin flexible gloves, and using well-sterilised instruments. The first British surgeon to use rubber gloves was Berkeley Moynihan in the 1890s. Facemasks, rubber gloves, surgical gowns, and replacing huge public operating theatres with smaller rooms dramatically reduced infections. Aseptic surgery depended on accepting Pasteur's theory. When did this begin to happen in Britain?

The evidence for Germ Theory

Louis Pasteur understood from his experiments that specific germs might turn liquid foods – such as milk – sour, or give diseases to animals. However, his ideas were not immediately accepted in Britain. Also, most doctors at the time still did not believe that microscopic germs could harm something as large and advanced as a human. Instead, the idea that specific germs might cause diseases was first noted in Britain not by doctors, but by vets.

The cattle plague of 1866

During the cattle plague of 1866, it was assumed that the disease had started spontaneously. Farmers were reluctant to kill cattle, so the disease quickly spread nationwide. It was soon realised that the outbreak could only be controlled by the quarantining and slaughtering of cattle. As a result of this, there were food shortages and prices rose.

The government appointed the leading scientific user of the microscope, Professor Lionel Beale, to investigate the crisis. In June 1866, Beale's findings not only recognised the specific microbe responsible, 'a living particle of extremely minute size', but also demonstrated how the microscope could help with

▼ **SOURCE A** *A public notice in 1867 in Eccles, Berwickshire showing the use of quarantine to control the cattle plague*

CATTLE PLAGUE.
NOTICE.

NOTICE IS HEREBY GIVEN, That persons who are not employed on the Farm of LANGRIG, in the Parish of Eccles and County of Berwick, are prohibited from entering any Building or Enclosed Place on said Farm, without my permission in writing.

JOHN DOVE.
LANGRIG,
19th November, 1867.

NOTICE IS FURTHER GIVEN, That any person contravening this Order is liable, under the Act of Parliament 29 Vic. cap. 15, to a Penalty of £5, or imprisonment for each offence, and the Police are authorised to apprehend offenders, or report them for prosecution.

GEORGE H. LIST,
Chief Constable.
COUNTY POLICE OFFICE,
Dunse, 19th November, 1867.

J. M. WILKIE, PRINTER DUNSE.

complex medical research. The cattle plague was clearly identified as an example of a contagious disease.

Bastian versus Tyndall

Despite Beale's findings, the dominant view in Britain about infection was still that it occurred spontaneously, and that it was a chemical action that produced poisons. The views of Charlton Bastian, Professor of Anatomy at University College London, dominated debate and he had written many articles in the late 1860s that supported spontaneous generation.

However, in January 1870, Bastian came up against the arguments of the physicist John Tyndall. Tyndall very publicly defended Pasteur's Germ Theory, and argued against Bastian. Tyndall lectured on both dust and disease, bringing together Pasteur and Lister's work with experiments on light that showed the tiny microbes in ordinary air.

> **Key Word**
>
> aseptic

SOURCE B *John Tyndall, painted c1890*

Typhoid fever

Many British doctors' views about Germ Theory finally changed due to public health debates about the disease typhoid fever. Typhoid fever was an infectious bacterial fever, and symptoms included red spots and severe intestinal irritation. It was common throughout Britain, but public awareness was raised in 1861 when it was said to be the cause of Prince Albert's death. Anti-contagionists had always said that typhoid fever was the disease that clearly proved they were right about cleaning up urban areas. Therefore it was important news when, in 1874, the scientist Emanuel Klein announced that he had identified the typhoid microbe. Immediately, Tyndall criticised spontaneous generation and said that Germ Theory explained typhoid fever. Unfortunately, Klein was mistaken: he had not found the typhoid microbe.

However, within two years, the work of Robert Koch and others after him proved to doctors that Germ Theory could explain human diseases such as typhoid fever.

> **Fact**
>
> ### Natural remedies
>
> While debates raged about whether illnesses were caused by biological or chemical processes, many doctors continued to use natural drugs, such as herbs, to heal people and prevent sickness. For example, it had been known since the seventeenth century that Peruvian bark could prevent malaria.

> **Extension**
>
> You will find that John Tyndall (1820–93) is an important figure in public health debates in Britain in the nineteenth century. Research his contributions to nineteenth-century science.

> **Work**
>
> 1. How does aseptic surgery differ from antiseptic surgery?
> 2. a How did the 1866 cattle plague contribute to people's acceptance of Pasteur's Germ Theory in Britain?
>   b What about typhoid fever? How did that contribute to the acceptance of the theory?
> 3. It took a long time for Germ Theory to be accepted in Britain. Create a timeline or a chart to explain the contribution of all the individuals who helped in its acceptance, and the opposition they faced at the time. Make sure you include: Lionel Beale, John Tyndall, Joseph Lister.

Britain: Health and the people

8.1 How did scientists discover that germs caused human diseases?

Louis Pasteur made a momentous breakthrough in 1861 with the publication of his Germ Theory. He had proven that germs were all around, and some of them could cause disease – but he was a chemist, not a doctor. He wasn't able to link his Germ Theory to humans. Many doctors did not realise that germs could harm humans too. It took a German doctor, Robert Koch, to apply Pasteur's theories to human diseases. How did Koch's work impact on medical progress in Britain?

Objectives

- **Describe** Robert Koch's methods and discoveries on microbes.
- **Evaluate** the contribution of Koch to medical progress.
- **Explain** Koch's impact in Britain.

Key Biography

Robert Koch (1843–1910)

Dr Robert Koch was born in Germany. He studied to be a doctor, and was a brilliant student under Professor Frederick Henle (the first person to challenge spontaneous generation and suggest that microbes caused infection). Koch worked as a surgeon in the Franco-Prussian War; from 1872 to 1880 he was German Medical Officer. He was a pioneering microbiologist, and he was appointed to the Imperial German Health Bureau in Berlin. Koch is known as the founder of modern bacteriology (study of bacteria), and made key discoveries in public health, including identifying the specific bacteria that caused anthrax, cholera, and tuberculosis. He was awarded the Nobel Prize in 1905.

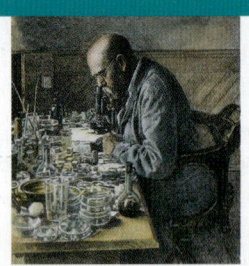

Koch and Pasteur's Germ Theory

Koch first became famous in 1876 for his work on anthrax microbes. Anthrax is a disease that causes sores on the lungs, and can kill both humans and animals. Koch found a way of staining and growing the particular germ he thought was responsible for anthrax. He then proved that it was this bacterium that caused the disease by injecting mice and making them ill. For the first time, he was able to apply Pasteur's theory to prove that germs caused diseases in humans.

Later on, using similar methods, Koch was able to identify the germs that caused the deadly diseases of cholera and tuberculosis. Although Koch was very much inspired by Pasteur, they saw each other as rivals: through their new scientific discoveries, they competed in honour of their respective countries.

Robert Koch's methods

Koch not only made improvements, but also changed the study of bacteria. Previously it was believed that most germs were the same. His methods and findings allowed other scientists to locate specific germs that might cause specific human diseases. Some of his main principles of studying bacteriology follow.

- To prove a specific bacterium was responsible for a specific disease, Koch said the bacterium had to be present in successive experimental animals that were infected with it. The bacterium could be retrieved from each dead animal and cultured (grown) again.
- Koch developed the technique of growing microbes on a plate made of solidified agar (a seaweed extract), which encourages microbes to grow.
- He found ways of using dyes to stain specific microbes under the microscope so that they would stand out among all the other germs.
- He also developed ways of photographing microbes so that other scientists could study them in detail, and find them in samples.

Koch turned bacteriology into a science. He perfected the methods that allowed scientists to hunt specific disease-causing microbes.

A *Robert Koch's laboratory method of identifying specific disease-causing microbes*

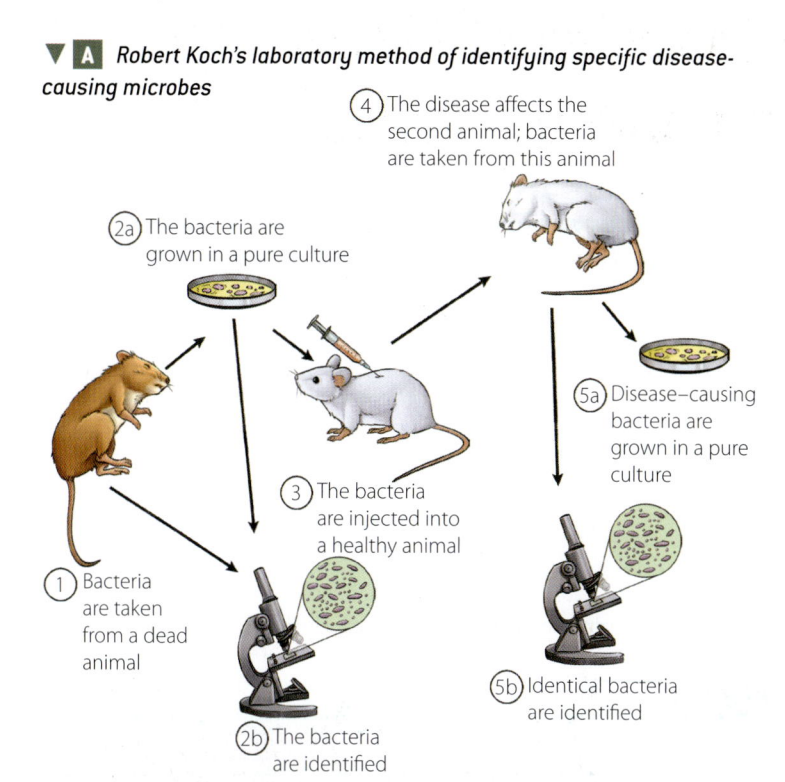

1. Bacteria are taken from a dead animal
2a. The bacteria are grown in a pure culture
2b. The bacteria are identified
3. The bacteria are injected into a healthy animal
4. The disease affects the second animal; bacteria are taken from this animal
5a. Disease-causing bacteria are grown in a pure culture
5b. Identical bacteria are identified

Koch didn't work alone – he had a team working with him, and also trained many young scientists to use his methods. Scientists produced a string of discoveries in the decades to follow, identifying the specific germs responsible for typhoid, pneumonia, meningitis, plague and tetanus.

Reactions to Koch's and Pasteur's work in Britain

Role of Tyndall

As the debate about typhoid rumbled on in mid-1870s Britain (remember that Emanuel Klein thought he had identified the typhoid bacterium in 1874, but was mistaken), Germ Theory was finally starting to win acceptance. Firstly, a number of British germ studies were published between 1873 and 1875: these used microscope evidence and answered many questions about germs. For example, in 1874, William Dallinger and John Drysdale published a paper describing the life cycle of microbes. Secondly, John Tyndall continued to promote Pasteur's Germ Theory widely, and in 1876, he lectured to British doctors on Koch's discoveries about anthrax.

Work

1. Explain some of Koch's principles in your own words.
2. Discuss in groups or in pairs: in your opinion, which was the more important achievement of Robert Koch – his discoveries, or his methods? Why?
3. Add the contributions of William Roberts, William Cheyne and Robert Koch to your timeline from Work question 2, page 49.
4. Who was most responsible for the acceptance of the Germ Theory in Britain? Explain your answer.

Key Word

vaccine

Roberts and Cheyne

In the end, it was the crucial contributions of two British doctors that won over opinion about Germ Theory in Britain. A Manchester doctor, William Roberts, who had supported Tyndall's criticisms of spontaneous generation, developed a doctor's version of the Germ Theory of disease: he linked all the laboratory research work with the practical evidence of surgeons and public health doctors. In particular, he used the work of Koch to draw attention to germs and their role in human infections.

Then, in 1879, Joseph Lister's deputy surgeon, William Cheyne translated Koch's work into English. He also wrote a paper based on Koch's findings. Cheyne explained that some microbes present in healthy tissue and wounds were harmless and did not always produce disease.

By the 1880s, British doctors accepted Germ Theory and its role in explaining infection. Surgery and public health benefited from Germ Theory, but doctors dealing with disease deep inside the body could not use intense heat or powerful antiseptics. Nobody had yet come up with a way to kill or alter microbes in the body without damaging healthy tissue. Despite this, there was great optimism that, as more specific microbes were isolated and identified, appropriate **vaccines** would follow.

Practice Question

Compare the work of Pasteur and Koch. In what ways were they different?

8 marks

Study Tip

Consider how much change each scientist brought about in medical thinking. You could refer to how many lives were affected by their work.

Britain: Health and the people 51

8.2 The search for vaccines and cures in Europe and Britain

As more specific disease-causing germs were identified, many doctors and scientists were eager to produce vaccines for the diseases. The two great giants of bacteriology – Louis Pasteur and Robert Koch – fought to make the next breakthrough.

Objectives

- **Summarise** Pasteur's and Koch's work in the 1880s.
- **Explain** the factors involved in the search for vaccines between 1800 and 1900.

Pasteur and Koch were not the only ones making scientific discoveries in the second half of the nineteenth century, but they were the most famous. There were several main factors that contributed to scientific breakthroughs in the 1880s and 1890s, as seen through the rivalry of Pasteur and Koch.

1 War

1871: The rivalry between Pasteur (a Frenchman) and Koch (a German) increased after France had lost a war against Germany. At this time, nations were interested in medical research because armies could lose more men to illness than to bullets. Defeating diseases could have a big impact on the battlefield.

2 Government and finance

Both Pasteur and Koch were equipped with a laboratory and a team of scientists, paid for by their governments. They both were recognised internationally with many honorary awards and prizes, including the Nobel Prize in 1905 for Koch, and the Copley Medal in 1874 for Pasteur.

3 Individual character

Pasteur: 1860s: He was a determined and hardworking scientist, despite suffering a stroke and losing his daughter to typhoid.

1871–75: He returned to work and continued to investigate agricultural problems, studied the fermentation of beer, and defended his ideas about Germ Theory.

1876–81: Koch's success in identifying the anthrax germ in 1876 spurred Pasteur and his team on to quickly develop vaccines for two animal diseases: cholera and anthrax.

Koch: 1882: Koch was also a strong-minded and rigorous scientist and doctor. After his first discovery, he went on to study tuberculosis (TB). The rivalry was further inflamed when Koch made a great breakthrough in 1882 by identifying the TB germ.

1883: Koch's team of scientists also beat a French team to identify the cholera germ.

Fact

TB was the largest cause of adult deaths in Western Europe. Throughout the 1870s, it killed over 50,000 people a year in Britain.

SOURCE A A cartoon from the 1880s; it shows Koch conquering the bacteria responsible for tuberculosis

KOCH AS THE NEW ST. GEORGE.

4 Luck

1879: Pasteur was investigating chicken cholera, a disease that was crippling the French poultry industry. By accident, Charles Chamberland, one of Pasteur's assistants, used an old and weakened sample of the disease microbes. When the chickens were injected, they survived. More importantly, these chickens also survived when they were then injected with fresh strong germs. Pasteur showed that the weakened microbes built up the chicken's own defences against the stronger ones. This was how vaccines, or the prevention of diseases, worked!

5 Communication

Pasteur developed a vaccine against the deadly animal disease anthrax. He demonstrated his vaccine in front of an audience of politicians, farmers and journalists in France in May 1881. News of this success was quickly sent around Europe by electric telegraph. News of Koch's discoveries was spread by scientific articles and at conferences.

Impact of Pasteur's and Koch's work in Britain

Between them, Pasteur and Koch encouraged a whole new generation of scientists to study deadly diseases and to find ways of preventing them.

Many of these discoveries soon spread to Britain. For example, Joseph Lister introduced the French serum for diphtheria to Britain, and it was widely used after 1895. Within 10 years, the mortality rate in England dropped to less than half.

Work

1. Why did governments pay for scientific research?
2. **Source A** shows admiration for Koch's achievement. How do you know?
3. Explain the contributions of the following people to the development of effective treatment for diseases: Pierre Roux, Emil Behring, Paul Ehrlich.
4. How did Pasteur's discoveries help people understand how vaccinations worked?

6 Teamwork

1880–84: Working with Charles Chamberland and Pierre Roux, Pasteur developed a vaccine for rabies, based on the dried spinal cords of infected rabbits. But he was reluctant to test it on a person.

1885: Pasteur proved that vaccines worked on human, as well as animal, diseases when he gave a boy who had been bitten by a rabid dog the rabies vaccine.

1888–90: The rivalry continued over research on diphtheria, a highly contagious disease that affects the nose and throat. In France, Pierre Roux, one of Pasteur's scientists, showed that the diphtheria germ produced a poison or toxin. In 1890 in Germany, Emil Behring, one of Koch's students, showed that weakened diphtheria germs could be used to produce an antitoxin.

▲ **INTERPRETATION B**
Pasteur and his team collecting the saliva from a rabid dog

Fact

As well as the search for biologically-based vaccines to prevent illnesses, scientists also tried to find chemicals that would attack the specific germs that caused illnesses, and cure them. In 1909, Paul Ehrlich (a German doctor who had been part of Koch's team), developed the first chemical cure for a disease: he found that the chemical Salvarsan 606 cured syphilis. He described it as a 'magic bullet', because it targeted the harmful germ specifically, and destroyed it without harming the rest of the body.

Practice Question

Was luck the main factor in the development of vaccines between 1880 and 1900? **16 marks** **SPaG: 4 marks**

Study Tip

Write about luck and choose two other factors you think were important.

Britain: Health and the people

9.1 How dirty were Britain's towns in the early 1800s?

Public health – the health and well being of ordinary men, women and children – was in a poor state in 1800s Britain. The average age of death for a working man was about 30 years of age. In some places, such as Liverpool, it was 15! In Manchester, one in every five children died before their first birthday and one in three died before they reached the age of five. In fact, despite improved medical knowledge and understanding, people's health in general may even have been worse in the early 1800s than in earlier centuries. What happened to public health at that time? Why was it in crisis?

Objectives

- **Examine** public health problems in industrial Britain.
- **Explore** the causes of public health problems.

The growth of towns and cities

Britain's towns and cities grew very quickly in the first 50 years of the 1800s, and the health of the people living in them grew steadily worse. For example, Sheffield had a population of just 12,000 people in 1750, but by 1850, the number had risen to over 150,000. People had flocked to Sheffield for one simple reason: to get a job in one of the new factories, and the promise of the new life that went with it. Many new factories were built in the north and midlands of England in the early 1800s, and needed thousands of workers to operate the machinery that made cloth, pottery, iron or steel. And as a single factory alone might employ hundreds of people, rows of houses were built quickly, 'back-to-back'.

B A plan of back-to-back housing in Nottingham, 1845

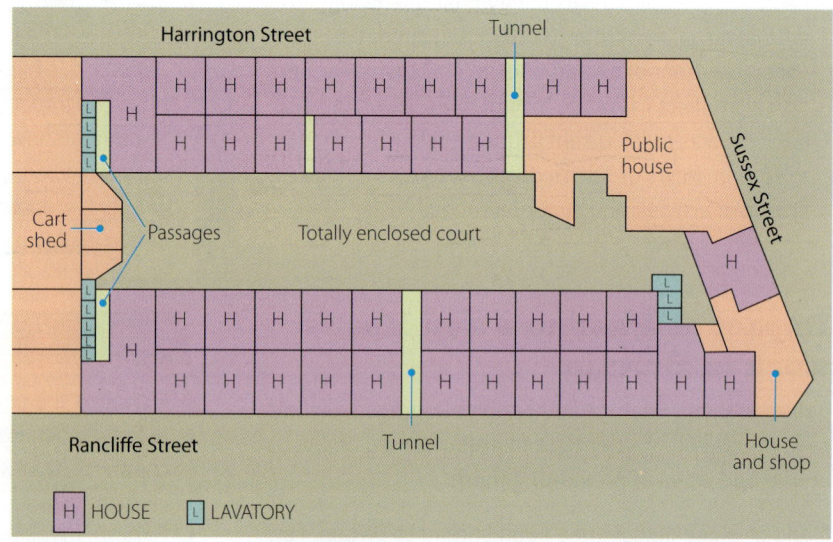

SOURCE C Late nineteenth-century back-to-back housing in Staithes, Yorkshire

A The population of British towns and cities, 1801–51

Town	1801	1851
Bradford	13,000	104,000
Glasgow	77,000	329,000
Liverpool	82,000	376,000
Birmingham	71,000	233,000
Manchester	70,000	303,000
Leeds	53,000	172,000
London	957,000	2,362,000
Bath	33,000	54,000
Norwich	36,000	68,000
York	17,000	34,000

These squeezed as many workers as possible into each street. Almost all the houses were crowded, often with five or more people living in one small room. In 1847, 40 people were found sharing one room in Liverpool.

Disease in the slums

Few of the houses had toilets. The best some families could manage was a bucket in the corner of the room that would be emptied now and again, into the street, or stored outside the door until there was enough to sell to a farmer as manure. Occasionally, there was a street toilet (a deep hole with a wooden shed over it) but this would be shared by lots of families. Sometimes a water pump provided water, but often the water only came from the local river or pond, and this would be as filthy as the water in the streets.

There were no rubbish collections, no street cleaners or sewers, and no fresh running water. Sewage trickled down the streets and into nearby rivers, yet most families washed their clothes, bathed in and drank from the same river. It was little wonder that terrible diseases like typhoid, tuberculosis and cholera were common. No one really knew how people caught diseases, or how to avoid catching them.

A government response?

Governments in all major European nations were concerned about the outbreaks of serious disease in their towns and cities, but were unclear as to how to deal with them. A link had been made between the poor conditions in Britain's towns and cities and the rising death rate, but in the early 1800s people still did not know what really caused disease, so there were no clear strategies to deal with it.

▼ **SOURCE D** *From a report on the 'Prevalence of Certain Physical Causes of Fever' (1838) by the doctors Neil Arnott and James Kay:*

> In Glasgow, which I first visited, it was found that the great mass of the fever cases occurred in the dirty narrow streets and courts, in which, because lodging there was cheapest, the poorest naturally had their homes. Seven hundred and fifty four of about 5000 cases of fever which occurred in the previous year were from one such locality, between Argyle Street and the river.
>
> We entered a dirty low passage like a house door, which led from the street through the first house to a square court immediately behind, which court, with the exception of a narrow path around it leading to another long passage through a second house, was occupied entirely as a place to keep dung.

▼ **E** *Some of the most common diseases of the 1800s*

Disease	Cause	Description
Typhoid	Contaminated water or food	Spread by poor sanitation or unhygienic conditions; sewage would get into the water supply that people drank
Tuberculosis (TB)	Germs passed in the air through sneezing or coughing	Spread rapidly in crowded conditions; another type of TB was caused by infected cows' milk
Cholera	Contaminated water or food	Several cholera epidemics swept the country in the early 1800s

Work

1. Define 'public health'.
2. Give as many reasons as you can why it was so easy for disease to spread in cities in the early 1800s.
3. Look at plan **B**.
   a. Copy the plan of back-to-back houses in your notebook.
   b. What is missing from these houses that we take for granted today?
   c. On your plan, mark which house (or houses) you would least like to live in. Give reasons for your choice.

Extension

Back-to-back housing was built in many towns and cities all over Britain. By the mid-twentieth century, most of it had been knocked down. Identify a town or city near you and try to find out about its back-to-back housing. Where was it? When was it built? Who lived there? When was it knocked down? What is built there now? Note: some back-to-back housing still exists. In Birmingham, for example, it is preserved as a 'living museum' (see www.nationaltrust.org.uk/birmingham-back-to-backs).

Britain: Health and the people

9.2A Fighting one of Britain's deadliest diseases: cholera

In the early nineteenth century, disease spread quickly in filthy, overcrowded cities such as Leeds, Liverpool, Bradford and Manchester. But people at this time didn't understand that germs caused their illnesses. Far away in laboratories, scientists like Louis Pasteur had started to make the connection, but down in the streets and slums of Britain, people continued to live their lives and get their filthy water in the same ways as they had always done. And then, in 1831, a new and frightening disease arrived in Britain: cholera. What was the impact of this deadly disease, and how did the government react?

Objectives

▶ **Examine** the main cholera epidemics of the nineteenth century.

▶ **Explore** the role of public health reformers.

▶ **Assess** the impact of local and national government initiatives to improve public health, including the 1848 Public Health Act.

Cholera: the first outbreak

In 1831 alone, cholera killed around 50,000 people. Victims were violently sick and suffered from painful diarrhoea; the skin and nails turned black just before the victim fell into a coma and died. So many people were dying that cemeteries had to be closed because they were too full: bodies had started to poke through the ground's surface, letting off a disgusting stench. One vicar in Bilston, West Midlands, even wrote that 'the coffins could not be made fast enough for the dead'.

What frustrated many was the complete lack of understanding of this new killer disease – there was no cure. People knew of diseases that killed more people than cholera, but this was something they hadn't experienced before, and it struck with such devastating speed, killing thousands in a few days.

▼ **SOURCE A** *A Dudley Board of Health poster, from the 1840s, announcing the burial procedure for people who had died of cholera*

CHOLERA.
THE DUDLEY BOARD OF HEALTH,
HEREBY GIVE NOTICE, THAT IN CONSEQUENCE OF THE
Church-yards at Dudley
Being so full, no one who has died of the **CHOLERA** will be permitted to be buried after **SUNDAY** next, (To-morrow) in either of the Burial Grounds of *St. Thomas's,* or *St. Edmund's,* in this Town.

All Persons who die from CHOLERA, must for the future be buried in the Church-yard at Nethertor

BOARD of HEALTH, DUDLEY.

What did people think caused cholera?

Many people at this time commonly believed disease was spread by miasma: an 'infectious mist' given off by rotting animals, rubbish and human waste. This led some towns to clean up their streets. But the importance of clean water still wasn't understood. The cholera epidemic passed after a few months and life was getting back to normal. Some thought that cholera would never return.

Action at last

After more outbreaks of cholera in 1837 and 1838, the national government decided to act. In 1839, they set up an inquiry to find out what the living conditions and health of the poor were like all over Britain. The man in charge was a government official named Edwin Chadwick.

Chadwick's report shocked Britain. Over 10,000 free copies were handed out to politicians, journalists, writers and anyone who could change public opinion. Twenty thousand more were sold to the public.

It didn't really matter that Chadwick mistakenly believed in the miasma theory: what was important was that the report highlighted the need for cleaner streets and a clean water supply. And it showed that most people were wrong in thinking that the poor were to blame for bad housing and living conditions. In fact, there was little they could do about it; it was parliament who would have to do something to improve public health.

Chapter 9 Improvements in public health

▼ **SOURCE B** *A drawing from the 1830s showing barrels of tar being burned on the streets of Exeter; the smell from the tar was thought to stop the miasma spreading cholera along the street*

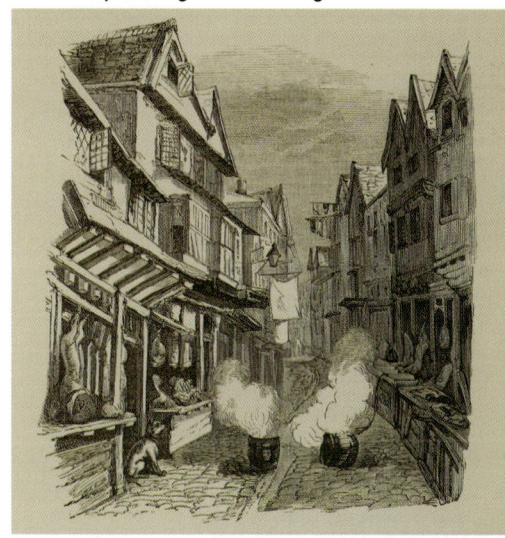

▼ **SOURCE C** *Excerpts of conclusions of Chadwick's 1842 report on the 'Sanitary Conditions of the Labouring Population of Great Britain':*

> Disease is caused by bad air and these diseases are common all over the country.
>
> The bad air is caused by rotting animals and vegetables, by damp and filth, and by overcrowded houses. When these things are improved, the death rate goes down.
>
> A medical officer should be appointed to take charge in each district.
>
> More people are killed by filth and bad ventilation each year than are killed by wars.
>
> People cannot develop clean habits until they have clean water.
>
> The poor cost us too much; the rich pay to feed and clothe orphans. Money would be saved if fewer parents died of disease. A healthier workforce would work harder too.
>
> The poor conditions produce a population that doesn't live long, is always short of money, and is brutal and rough.

Key Biography

Edwin Chadwick (1800–90)

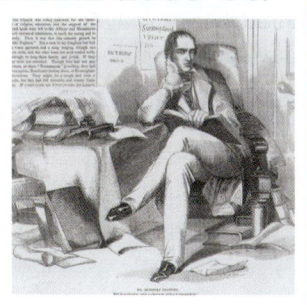

Chadwick was a lawyer who devoted his efforts towards health and social reforms. Over a two-year period, he worked on his famous public health inquiry by sending out doctors to most major towns and cities; they set questionnaires and interviewed hundreds of people. The results of the report were published in 1842.

Work

1. Why do you think cholera was one of the most feared diseases of the 1800s?
2. Look at **Source B**. Why are these people burning tar in the streets?
3. Read **Source C**.
   a. Make a list of changes Chadwick wanted to make.
   b. What evidence is there that Chadwick believed in the miasma theory?
   c. Do you think Chadwick felt sorry for the poor? Explain your answer carefully.

Practice Question

How useful is **Source C** to a historian studying public health problems in industrial Britain? **8 marks**

Study Tip

Write about what the report says and the person writing it. Say why he was well placed to comment on conditions.

Extension

Chadwick's report showed that the length of people's lives was greatly affected by where they lived. The table below shows the average age of death for different classes of people in two different places. Give reasons for the differences between and within classes in different areas.

	Leeds (town)	Rutland (country)
Upper class	44	52
Middle class	27	41
Working class	19	38

Britain: Health and the people

9.2B Fighting one of Britain's deadliest diseases: cholera

Cholera returns

A lot of people paid attention to Chadwick's pleas for improvements, but the government didn't do anything. In the 1800s, many people thought politicians had no right to meddle in the private lives of citizens. This attitude was known as **laissez-faire**, French words meaning 'leave alone': the government should not interfere in the lives of ordinary people and force them to change. These people said it was the government's job to keep law and order, not to keep people clean. And some Members of Parliament were making vast fortunes from rents in the slums; tearing the slums down and rebuilding them would cost them money!

But cholera changed their minds. As news reached Britain of another cholera epidemic sweeping across Europe, the government decided to act at last, and passed a Public Health Act in 1848.

▼ **D** *The main points of the 1848 Public Health Act:*

> A 'Central Board of Health' is to be created in London. This is a group that will work to make any improvements that might improve public health.
>
> They can force some areas to set up their own 'Local Board of Health' where there is a high death rate, or where more than ten per cent of ratepayers ask for one. These boards will have the power to appoint a specialist Medical Officer, provide sewers, inspect lodging houses and check food quality which is offered for sale.

The act gave local town councils the power to spend money on cleaning up their towns, but this was not compulsory. Some towns, such as Liverpool, Sunderland and Birmingham, made huge improvements. However, many others didn't bother to do anything. By 1853, only 103 towns had set up their own Boards of Health, and in 1854 the Central Board of Health was closed down because of strong resentment of government interference.

▼ **SOURCE E** *Adapted from the Liverpool Health Committee, 1849, listing what needed to be done in the city; 'water closets' were simple holes in the ground, covered by a small shed, which collected human waste; 'privies' were much healthier because they contained a seat, with a bucket underneath, which was removed and emptied by the local council on a regular basis:*

> The substitution of water closets for privies, the abolition of cesspools, the banishment of all toxic factories from inhabited areas, the removal of slaughterhouses, an abundant supply of water, and widening of streets.

Dr John Snow's discovery

Meanwhile, the plague of cholera continued. In 1848, 60,000 people died of cholera; 20,000 died of it in 1854. During the 1854 epidemic, a doctor named John Snow made a major breakthrough in proving there was a link between cholera and water supply.

The discovery that cholera was a water-borne disease (a disease carried in water) was a remarkable achievement. The government now had a growing batch of evidence about

Key Biography

John Snow (1813–58)

Snow was a famous surgeon who worked in Broad Street, Soho, London. In 1854, over 700 people living in this street, or in nearby streets, died of cholera within ten days, so Snow began to investigate. Through meticulous research, he found that all the victims in this small area got their water from the Broad Street water pump. Those who didn't die seemed to be getting their water from other places. Snow asked permission to remove the handle of the water pump so people were forced to use another. There were no more deaths in the street! Snow investigated further and found that a street toilet, only one metre from the pump, had a cracked lining that allowed polluted water to trickle into the drinking water. Snow had proved that cholera was not carried through the air like a poisonous gas or miasma. Instead it was caught through contagion: by coming into direct contact with a cholera sufferer; or in this case, drinking some water contaminated by a victim's diarrhoea.

the state of the nation's health within the dirty, overcrowded towns. They even had medical evidence that made a link between cholera and water supply. But the government did not do much about it, until a 'Great Stink' would finally force them into action.

SOURCE F *John Snow's map showing cholera deaths (shown as black blocks) between 19 August and 30 September 1854*

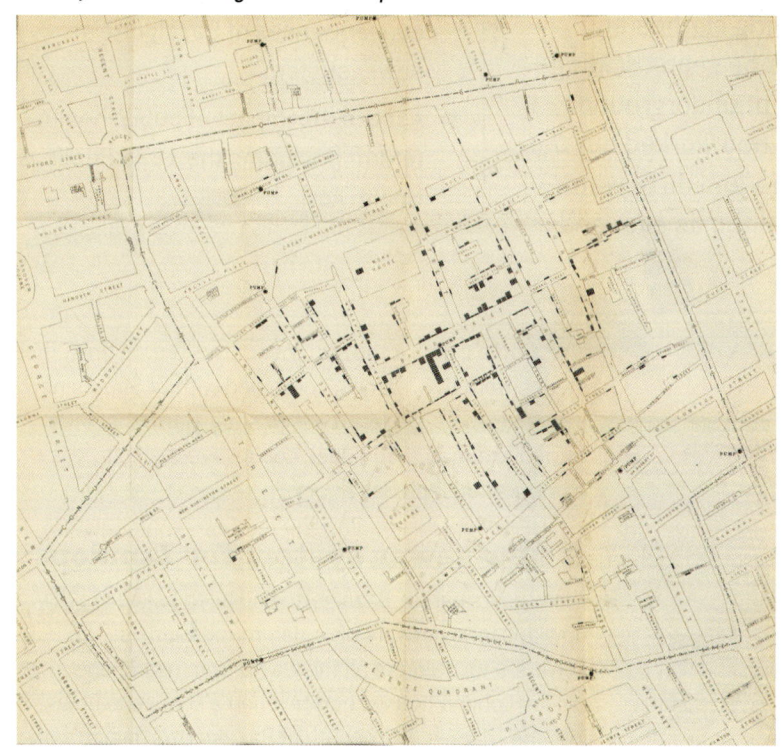

SOURCE G
An English engraving from 1866 called 'The Death Dispensary'; it appeared in Fun *magazine, commenting on London's polluted water supply. This magazine was published weekly and contained amusing poems and parodies, as well as sports and travel information and topical cartoons (often of a political nature).*

Key Word
laissez-faire

Fact
John Snow used scientific observation to show how cholera spread, but he didn't know why it spread. Louis Pasteur didn't publish his Germ Theory until 1861 (see pages 44–45), which would have helped to explain the results Snow had recorded.

Work

1. a What is meant by the term laissez-faire?
   b Why do you think so many politicians believed in laissez-faire?
2. a List some of the things that Local Boards of Health could do.
   b Why do you think public toilets were far more important in the nineteenth century than they are today?
   c What were the limitations of the 1848 Public Health Act?
3. Imagine you are Dr John Snow. Write a letter to the National Board of Health explaining:
   a how you think cholera is spread (you will need to summarise your evidence)
   b what you think should be done about it.
4. Look at **Source E**.
   a In your own words, explain how Liverpool tried to improve public health in the city.
   b How close were their ideas to those suggested by Chadwick?
5. Look at **Source G**. What point is the person who drew this cartoon trying to make?

Britain: Health and the people

9.3 The Great Stink

London in 1858 was a dirty, overcrowded, unsanitary city. Its main river, the Thames, was a dumping ground for human sewage, household rubbish, horse dung, slaughterhouse waste and chemicals from factories. The river water was also used for washing clothes and cooking! Raw sewage could sometimes be seen trickling out of the pumps that pulled water out of underground streams. Despite the fact that Dr Snow had worked out the link between the deadly disease cholera and dirty water supplies, the city streets remained as filthy as ever and were a breeding ground for disease.

Objectives

- **Describe** the 'Great Stink' of 1858.
- **Examine** the reasons for and the consequences of Bazalgette's sewer system.
- **Assess** the impact of public health reform (including the 1875 Public Health Act).

The Great Stink

SOURCE A *A Punch cartoon commenting on the state of the River Thames in 1858; 'Father Thames' introduces his children, Diptheria, Scrofula and Cholera, to London*

In the summer of 1858, a heat wave caused the filthy River Thames to smell worse than ever. The smell was so bad that the politicians in the Houses of Parliament (right next to the river) demanded to meet somewhere else. Some called it the summer of the 'Great Stink'. The stench from the Thames, combined with Dr Snow's new evidence about cholera, caused such alarm that MPs turned to a man they hoped could save their city. His name was Joseph Bazalgette.

A new sewer system for London

Three years earlier, Bazalgette had been asked to draw up plans for a network of underground tunnels – or sewers – to intercept all the waste from nearly one million London houses before it had a chance to flow into the Thames. The beauty of Bazalgette's design was that it used gravity and the slope of the London river basin to get the sewers to flow downstream towards the sea. At Crossness he built a pumping station where pumps, the largest ever made at the time, pumped the sewage up to the level of the Thames; at high tide, it was released into the river and the river did the rest, taking it out to sea. MPs wanted London's streets free of sewage quickly. Bazalgette was given £3 million (about £1 billion today) in 1858 and told to start immediately. Using 318 million bricks, he built 83 miles of sewers, removing 420 million gallons of sewage a day. The

Timeline: Public health reforms

1842	1848	1853	1858	1866	1875
Chadwick Report	First Public Health Act	Compulsory vaccination	Work on London sewer system begins	Sanitary Act: this makes local councils responsible for sewers, water and street cleaning; each town has to have a health inspector	Artisans Dwelling Act (also known as the Housing Act): this makes house owners responsible for keeping their properties in good order; it also gives local councils the power to buy and demolish slum housing if it is not improved

Chapter 9 Improvements in public health

▼ **SOURCE B** *Bazalgette standing, on the right, above a London sewer during construction; many of Bazalgette's sewers are still in use today*

sewers were finished in 1866, and when fully operational, cholera never returned to London. Soon, parliament went into a flurry of action to improve public health.

Of course, other measures improved life expectancy too, including better nursing and surgery techniques, but the nineteenth century saw government take much more responsibility for the state of public health.

The death of laissez-faire?

In 1867, working-class men living in towns were given the vote. It was these same people who had been suffering most from poor living conditions. Soon, political parties realised that if they promised to improve conditions in the towns, the working-class people living there would vote for them. When the Conservative Party won the general election in 1874, it was largely due to working-class votes. Soon after, they introduced many new public health reforms. Many historians today think that working-class people getting the vote is one of the most important reasons why politicians began to improve the nation's health.

1875
Second Public Health Act: local councils forced to appoint Medical Officers to be responsible for public health; councils are also ordered to cover up sewers and keep them in good condition, supply fresh water, collect rubbish and provide street lighting

1875
Sale of Food and Drugs Act: this introduces guidelines for the quality and sale of food and medicines

Fact
The death rate (the number of people dying per 1000 of the population) fell from about 39 in 1800 to 18 in 1900. The average age of death rose from 30 to 50, and the total population of the country rose from about 10 million in 1801 to 38 million in 1901. So the population increased nearly four times – mainly because people were living longer.

Extension
Study **Source A**. How useful is it to a historian studying the development of public health in Britain?

Work

1. Cholera never returned to London after Bazalgette's sewers were fully operational. Should Bazalgette receive all the credit for this? Explain your answer.

2. Look at **Source B**. What does this photograph tell you about:
   a. the scale of the work involved in building the sewers
   b. the building methods of the time?

3. Design a diagram that explains the improvements made in public health in the nineteenth century. Include information on: diseases, death rates, influential people like Chadwick, Snow and Bazalgette, and government action.

Practice Question
Compare a Medieval town with early nineteenth-century London. In what ways were they similar? **8 marks**

Study Tip
Write about the ways in which clean water and sewage were treated as well as the town authorities' attitudes to public health.

10.1A What can a study of penicillin tell us about the development of modern medicine?

A recent exhibition at the British Museum in London estimated that the average number of pills that a person takes in his or her lifetime in the UK is around 14,000! Indeed, the chances are that in recent weeks or months you might have taken a variety of pills for aches and pains. And if you have had an infection, many of you will have been given a drug called penicillin, which was the world's first **antibiotic**. The industry that develops and produces all these drugs for use in medicine and health care is known as the **pharmaceutical industry**. So how did this industry develop? And what can a study of the world's first antibiotic tell us about the development of modern medicine?

Objectives

- **Explore** the development of the pharmaceutical industry.
- **Outline** the factors in Fleming's discovery and the development of penicillin.
- **Assess** the impact of this discovery and development.

Prevention and cure

During the late nineteenth century, knowledge about disease increased greatly. Soon after doctors and scientists started to identify which bacteria caused which diseases, a search began to find ways of preventing people from getting the diseases, and also curing people who already had them. These two lines of research – prevention and cure – led to some dramatic advances in the understanding of health and medicine.

Prevention

When Louis Pasteur published his Germ Theory in 1861, the world began to realise that bacteria were the cause of many diseases; not miasma, or God's punishment, or any of the other causes that people had believed for centuries. And after Pasteur and Robert Koch identified different types of bacteria that caused specific diseases, doctors began to use weakened forms of the bacteria to allow the body to build up immunity to the disease if it struck again. This was something that had been successfully tried – but not understood – by Edward Jenner with smallpox in 1796. Soon vaccines, as they became known, were created to prevent diseases such as diphtheria, TB, rabies and anthrax.

Cure

Koch found that certain chemicals sought out and found specific bacteria in the body. His assistant, Paul Ehrlich, worked at finding a chemical that would not only stain a specific type of bacteria – but kill it too! After Ehrlich's discovery of a chemical cure for syphilis in 1909, other 'magic bullets' were found by scientists over the next 20 years. Most notable was prontosil, a red chemical that worked against the germs that caused blood poisoning. Prontosil's active ingredient was sulphonamide (a chemical from coal tar). More magic bullets or 'sulpha drugs' were soon developed to cure or control meningitis, pneumonia and scarlet fever.

Staphylococcus

By the 1920s, one nasty germ in particular, named staphylococcus, remained undefeated by any magic bullet. It was a highly resistant form of bacteria that had over 30 different strains, and it caused a wide range of illnesses and diseases, especially different types of food and blood poisoning.

However, a way to kill staphylococcus was close at hand. Scientists had known since the 1870s that some **moulds** (yes, the stuff that grows in an unwashed coffee cup or on your wet football boots after a week out in the rain!) could kill germs. One type of mould – penicillin – proved particularly good at killing staphylococcus. Its discovery, and the eventual development of penicillin as the world's first and most famous antibiotic, is a fascinating story. It's a tale of luck, individual brilliance, war, and huge breakthroughs in scientific and technological understanding. As you work through this case study, try to look out for each of the complex factors that contributed to the penicillin story.

Key Words

antibiotic   pharmaceutical industry   mould   bacteriologist   spore

Key Biography

Alexander Fleming (1881–1955)

During the First World War, the **bacteriologist** Alexander Fleming was sent by St Mary's Hospital in London to study the treatment of wounded soldiers. Many were suffering from the ill effects of the staphylococcus germ. Ordinary chemical antiseptics, which were not used as much by this time, were not working on some of the deeper wounds and Fleming saw at first hand the agony suffered by the soldiers. In 1928, he published findings on the effects of the penicillin mould. He won a Nobel Prize in 1945 (along with Howard Florey and Ernst Chain) for the 'discovery of penicillin and its curative effect'.

Fleming's discovery

After the First World War, Fleming became determined to find a better way to treat infected wounds and conducted detailed experiments. By 1928, he was still working on the hard-to-kill staphylococcus germs. When he went on holiday, he left several plates of the germs on a bench. When he came home, he noticed a large blob of mould in one of the dishes. Upon investigation, he noticed that the staphylococcus germs next to the mould had been killed.

Fact

An antiseptic is a chemical that is mostly used outside the body, on the skin and on objects, to kill germs. An antibiotic is a medicine that can be digested or injected into the body, and kills certain germs as it travels around the body. Penicillin is an antibiotic.

An excited Fleming took a sample of the mould, and found it to be the penicillin mould. It appeared that a **spore** from a penicillin mould grown in a room below Fleming's had floated up the stairs and into his laboratory.

Fleming realised the germ-killing capabilities of penicillin and published his findings that year. Even though we know today that penicillin is an antibiotic, Fleming did not realise this and concluded that it was a natural antiseptic. But the one test that was missing from his work was the test of injecting penicillin into an infected animal. This would have shown that penicillin could be used as a medicine, and could kill infections in the body without harming living cells. The results of such a test would likely have sparked great interest in penicillin and could have advanced its development. As a result, few people regarded Fleming's work as a major breakthrough and gradually even Fleming himself lost interest in it. However, the story didn't end there: soon, other key factors played a role in the success of penicillin.

Work

1. Explain what is meant by the term 'magic bullet'.
2. How was Ehrlich's work different from Pasteur's?
3. Discuss in groups or in pairs: why do you think Fleming is usually thought of as the discoverer of penicillin?

Britain: Health and the people

10.1B What can a study of penicillin tell us about the development of modern medicine?

The development of penicillin

In the 1930s, a research team from Oxford University began compiling a list of all the natural substances that could kill germs. They got hold of Fleming's article on penicillin and began to get very excited. Two of the scientists, Howard Florey and Ernst Chain, applied to the British government for some money to begin further research into the germ-killing powers of penicillin. They received only £25; not nearly enough to even start their research properly. In fact, they were probably lucky to get £25: the British government, by 1939, was far more interested in the Second World War that had just started. However, Florey and Chain pressed on and, despite the fact that penicillin is extremely difficult to grow and extract (from the mould), they managed to produce enough to successfully test it on eight mice.

Their next move was to test it on humans, but they needed 3000 times the amount they had used on the mice. So, over a couple of months, the two scientists turned their university department into a penicillin-producing factory. Using old milk bottles, hospital bedpans and a bath in which to grow the bacteria, they slowly collected enough penicillin to use on one human.

A 43-year-old policeman, Albert Alexander, was selected because he had been scratched by a rose bush and a nasty infection had spread all over him. All other drugs had failed on him. When he was injected with penicillin, the infection began to clear up. Tragically though, after five days, the penicillin ran out and the patient died; but the success of penicillin had been noted by all involved. The next step was to try to work out how to produce masses of it.

How was penicillin mass-produced?

▼ **SOURCE A** *Penicillin being mass-produced in the 1940s; a worker at Pfizer is shown carefully preparing vials of penicillin solution*

The Second World War was a vital factor in transforming the supply of penicillin. The growing number of soldiers with infected wounds meant that more penicillin was needed – and quickly. In June 1941, Florey went to America to meet with the US government. Realising the lifesaving properties of this new wonder treatment, they agreed to pay several huge chemical companies to make millions of gallons of it. By 1943, enough had been made to treat just 1000 wounded soldiers, but by 1944 there was enough to treat 40,000. By the end of the war in 1945, Britain and the USA were working closely together and 250,000 soldiers were being treated. Drug companies began using their production methods to make penicillin for public use as soon as the war ended.

The need to produce huge quantities of penicillin was a key factor in the growth of the pharmaceutical industry. In the early 1800s, drugs and medicines were generally produced by small-scale businesses. However, towards the end of the nineteenth century, some of the larger companies we know today, such as GlaxoSmithKline, Hoffmann-La Roche and Pfizer had begun: they started out as chemists and pill-makers, or producers of chemicals used by scientists. The discovery of penicillin as a 'wonder drug' in the early twentieth century led to huge government-sponsored programmes to develop and produce it. This meant that the pharmaceutical industry had both the finance and the technology to research and develop medicines for all sorts of diseases. Today, the pharmaceutical industry is one of the biggest in the world, worth an estimated £200 billion to £300 billion and employing nearly 80,000 people in the UK alone.

> **Fact**
>
> Pharmaceutical drug production became industrialised in the late nineteenth century with the growth of pharmaceutical companies and also with new technological advances: for example, the invention of the gelatine pill capsule (1875), and the first tablet-making machine (1843, in England).

The impact of penicillin

SOURCE B *A British soldier being treated with penicillin in June 1944*

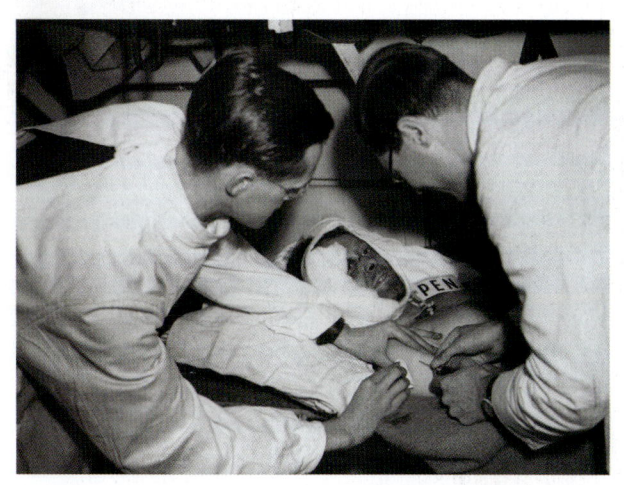

It has been estimated that, during the Second World War, around 15 per cent of wounded British and American soldiers would have died without being given penicillin to fight their infections. Also, thousands of injured soldiers returned to service much quicker than they would have done without penicillin treatment. After the war, penicillin became available for doctors to use as a means of prevention and cure for their patients. It was classified as an antibiotic, and has gone on to save the lives of millions of people. Indeed, unless you have an allergy to penicillin (around ten per cent of people do), almost all of you will probably have been prescribed penicillin by a doctor at some time.

Other antibiotics followed: streptomycin (1944), for example, proved an excellent treatment for tuberculosis, while tetracycline (1953) was great for clearing up skin infections. Mitomycin (1956) has been used as a chemotherapy drug for treating several different types of cancer.

Who gets the credit?

If you were asked on a television game show, 'Who discovered penicillin?' then the answer would almost definitely be 'Alexander Fleming'! This is due to the very well known story of the mould floating into his laboratory and attacking the bacteria on his germ dish. But Fleming certainly didn't develop penicillin, nor was he the first to use it to treat an infection.

So perhaps Florey and Chain should be included in any answer to the question, 'Who developed penicillin?' They were the first to test it directly on a human body, and were the first to develop a way to produce large quantities of the drug. So who does deserve the credit for giving the world penicillin?

> **Work**
>
> 1. Explain the part played in the penicillin story by: Joseph Lister; Alexander Fleming; Florey and Chain; Albert Alexander; the US government.
> 2. How was the discovery of penicillin quickened by luck, and by war?
> 3. a Explain what is meant by the term 'antibiotic'.
>   b List some of the antibiotics mentioned on these pages. State the approximate dates they were introduced and give an example of the types of disease they fought.

Practice Question

Has science been the main factor in the development of penicillin?

16 marks
SPaG: 4 marks

Study Tip

Refer to two other factors such as government and the role of the individual.

Extension

Challenge yourself to do further research on penicillin. Find out about the role of: Norman Heatley; Andrew Moyer; Alfred Richards.

Britain: Health and the people 65

10.2A How have drugs and treatments developed since 1945?

Great changes in understanding disease had taken place in the years up to 1945. The government had started to take more responsibility for public health too, including clearing the worst of the overcrowded slum areas of the dirtiest towns and building proper sewer systems. The widespread use of anaesthetics and antiseptics, and now the discovery of the first antibiotics, meant that life expectancy had increased from the age of 46 (men) and 50 (women) in 1900 to just over 60 (men) and 65 (women) in 1945. What were the medical discoveries and developments that happened in the latter half of the twentieth century?

Objectives

- **Examine** the key developments in new knowledge about the body and disease, surgery and treatments since 1945.
- **Assess** how these developments have been affected by a variety of factors.

The second half of the twentieth century saw an explosion in scientific and medical discoveries and developments that proved significant in achieving a fuller understanding of health and medicine. This resulted in life expectancy levels increasing to around 79 (men) and 83 (women). Indeed, a recent UK government article claimed that one in two babies born today is expected to live until its 100th birthday.

The timeline below charts some of the most significant changes in the fields of knowledge about the body and disease, surgery and treatment.

1948
Free vaccine for TB in the UK

1950
Canadian surgeon William Bigelow performs the first open-heart surgery to repair a 'hole' in a baby's heart

1951
Mexican company Syntex develops norethisterone: a human-made hormone that prevents women ovulating; this leads to the production of the first contraceptive pill

1952
First miniature hearing aid is produced

First kidney transplant is carried out (the first in the UK is in 1960)

1953
American Leroy Stevens discovers stem cells; these are cells in multi-cellular organisms that are able to renew themselves and differentiate into specific cell types

Scientists Francis Crick and James Watson map out the **DNA** structure; the understanding of DNA leads to such developments as gene therapy, genetic **screening** and genetic engineering

1954
Free vaccine for diptheria, whooping cough and tetanus (the 'triple vaccine') in the UK

1955
Free vaccine for polio in the UK

1957
The drug thalidomide is developed in Germany; it is used to treat morning sickness during pregnancy but it causes terrible deformities in babies; today it is used in the treatment of AIDS and some cancers

1958
First pacemaker is fitted (in Sweden); this is a mechanical device that maintains a regular heartbeat (the first in the UK is in 1960)

1962
Surgeons at a hospital in America re-attach the arm of a 12-year-old boy

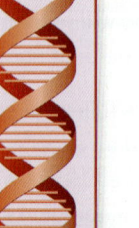

1964
Free vaccine for measles in the UK

66 Chapter 10 Modern treatment of disease

Timeline key:
Purple: relates to body and disease
Orange: relates to surgery
Green: relates to treatment

1973
British scientist Geoff Hounsfield invents the CAT scanner, which uses x-ray images from many angles to build up a 3D image of the inside of the body

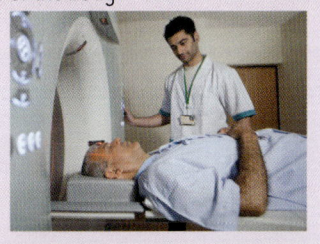

1978
Doctors use IVF fertility treatment to help childless women become pregnant throughout the 1970s, and in 1978, Louise Brown from the UK becomes the first 'test tube baby'

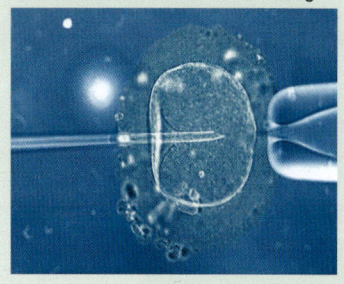

Key Word
DNA (deoxyribonucleic acid) screening

Work
1. Write a sentence or two about the following:
   a. IVF treatment
   b. DNA.

1969
Free vaccine for rubella (German measles) in the UK

1970
British scientist Roy Calne develops the drug cyclosporine, which prevents the body rejecting transplanted organs

1975
Endoscopes are developed; these are fibre-optic cables with a light source that allow doctors to go into small cuts in the skin to 'see' inside the body

1984
At Harvard University in the USA, two burn victims are given skin grafts; the skin had been grown in a laboratory 'skin farm' from tiny pieces – one square centimetre grew to half a square metre

1986
British woman Davina Thompson becomes the first heart, lung and liver transplant patient

1972
British surgeon Sir John Charnley develops hip replacements

1970

1980

1968
First British heart transplant at Papworth Hospital

1980
After a global vaccination campaign, smallpox is officially declared eradicated; so far, the only human disease where this has been possible

1987
MRI scanning is widely used to monitor brain activity, which is especially useful for finding brain tumours or stroke damage

1967
Christian Barnard, a South African heart surgeon, performs the first heart transplant; the patient lives for 18 days (the first in the UK is in 1968)

Fact
DNA (*deoxyribo nucleic acid*) is the material that makes up genes. It is like a long list of instructions, or a code, that operates every one of the cells in your body: there are 3000 million letters in the code. The instructions are grouped together in genes, and each gene has a different function. Some genes determine your eye or hair colour, for example. Others determine whether you will develop a disease or a disability. All genes can be passed from parent to child. An expert in X-rays called Rosalind Franklin photographed DNA in 1951 and identified the DNA structure. However, it was Crick and Watson at Cambridge University who publicised the mapping of the DNA structure and the fact that genes could pass information from one generation to the next.

10.2B How have drugs and treatments developed since 1945?

1996
Researchers in Scotland breed the first cloned animal: a sheep called Dolly, cloned from a cell taken from a six-year-old ewe. Cloning is the process of creating an identical copy of an original organism. Dolly died in February 2003 from a lung disease. The idea of using cloning technology on humans is one of the medical world's most controversial issues

2002
American surgeons implant electrodes connected to a miniature computer into the visual cortex of a blind man; using a video camera mounted onto his glasses, the man is able to 'see' well enough to drive a car

2008
First full face transplant

2006
First HPV (anti-cancer) vaccine approved

2013
First human liver is grown from stem cells

1990 — **2000** — **2010**

1990
The **Human Genome Project** formally launches: it is the world's largest collaborative biological research project that aims to decode all the genes in the human body and identify their roles; the money for this international scientific project comes from the governments of the USA, Britain, Japan, China, France and Canada, as well as drug companies that hope to profit from developing drugs based on understanding DNA

2003
The Human Genome Project is declared complete with the final sequencing of the entire human genome, which is a huge breakthrough in understanding how genes help determine who a person is; ongoing research into links between genetics and treating diseases come from the information produced by this project

2006
First partial face transplant is carried out

2007
Huge breakthrough in visual prosthetics (bionic eyes) with the release of the Argus II prosthetic eye

Technology

New technologies such as **keyhole surgery** and MRI scanning have helped doctors and surgeons to develop new techniques for identifying illnesses and operating on them. Discoveries, such as understanding more about DNA, have helped gene researchers work out family relationships, trace ancestry, use DNA analysis to solve crimes, and find specific genes involved in diseases. With the ongoing research on the human genetic code (made possible by the Human Genome Project), scientists are optimistic that soon doctors can better understand cancer and lots of other illnesses.

War

Two world wars meant that the government spent a fortune on research and testing so that the latest drugs and surgical techniques were available for wounded soldiers. Doctors had to find better ways to treat casualties too, thus advancing medical knowledge. Sadly, wars and conflict continue to take place and the research, testing and development continue.

Government and finance

Governments spend far more money on research and care than ever before. For example, the British government has a huge breast and cervical cancer screening programme which aims to identify illness before it develops. Drug companies too, spend huge amounts on research and development, hoping to make money from cures.

Key Words

Human Genome Project   keyhole surgery

Communication

New ideas spread rapidly due to the increased use of television, news media and the Internet. Television and radio advertisements have made more people than ever before aware of health risks associated with smoking and alcohol, for example.

No wonder smokers cough.
The tar and discharge that collects in the lungs of an average smoker.

Change in attitudes

Modern politicians have realised that one of their main priorities is to help and protect the people they serve. In recent years the British government has introduced 'Healthy Eating Standards'. This means that food served in schools must include high-quality meat and fresh fruit and vegetables. Schools cannot serve drinks with added sugar, crisps, chocolate or sweets in school meals and vending machines.

Reasons why drugs and treatments have developed greatly in the late twentieth century

Individual character

As across all periods of history, the late twentieth century saw some geniuses in action: Crick and Watson, and Geoff Hounsfield in Britain, for example.

Extension

Which do you think is the main factor affecting medical progress? Write a paragraph (no more than 250 words) explaining your reasons why. Make sure you mention at least two other factors and why you think they are not the main factors.

Practice Question

Explain the significance of the individual sciences – physics, chemistry and biology – for medical progress in the twentieth century.   **8 marks**

Study Tip

Show how each branch of science has contributed to progress in medical treatments.

Work

1 What is the Human Genome Project?
2 Imagine you have to choose three medical developments from the twentieth century to include on a web page entitled 'The greatest advances in medical history'. Which three developments would you choose? Give reasons for your choices.
3 **a** In your own words, explain how medical progress has been affected by:
   - government and finance
   - technology
   - war
   - individual character
   - communication.
   b Can you find examples on the timeline on pages 66–68 that match these factors?

Britain: Health and the people

10.3 Beyond mainstream medicine

Researchers predicted in 2002 that by 2070, people would live to the average age of 100 (it stood at 80 for women and 75 for men at the time the prediction was made). They put this down to the advances made in medicine in the twentieth century. So what happens if people develop immunity to prescribed drugs? How do things like '**positive health**' and '**alternative medicines**' fit into all this?

Objectives
- **Define** antibiotic resistance.
- **Describe** alternative treatments.
- **Explore** advances in healthcare in the latter half of the twentieth century.

Antibiotic resistance

The battle against disease, and other causes of death, continues in the same way as it always has. The range of new drugs being produced every year is huge. Drug companies spend billions of pounds on research, knowing that enormous profits can be made. Since the development of penicillin, there have been many more discoveries of different types of antibiotics that kill all sorts of bacteria, including tuberculosis; and lots of different vaccines that prevent and control diseases such as polio, measles, mumps and whooping cough.

However, despite the development of new drugs, not all drugs work: even proven antibiotics can fail. In fact, the effectiveness of antibiotics can lead to their overuse, prompting bacteria to evolve and become increasingly resistant to common antibiotics. An example of an antibiotics-resistant bacteria is called MRSA (methicillin-resistant Staphylococcus aureus), first reported in a British study in 1961.

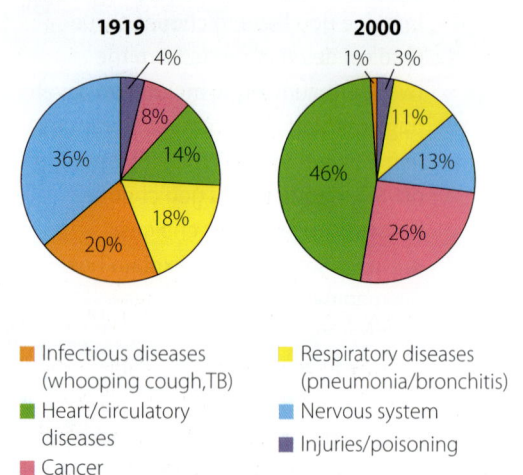

A *Causes of death in the UK, 1919 and 2000*

- Infectious diseases (whooping cough, TB)
- Heart/circulatory diseases
- Cancer
- Respiratory diseases (pneumonia/bronchitis)
- Nervous system
- Injuries/poisoning

Alternative treatments

Doctors are still not able to cure some diseases, such as viruses like AIDS and the common cold. Cancer – although treatable depending on the type – is still a major killer disease. As a result some people turn to alternative therapies to find ways of improving their health and treating their illnesses.

Alternative medicine is the term used to describe any other way of treating an illness or health condition that doesn't rely on mainstream, doctor-dispensed scientific medicine, or on proven evidence gathered using the scientific method. It includes a wide range of practices and therapies.

B *An extract from a survey on the popularity of alternative therapies, in which 2000 British people took part*

Alternative therapy	Tried by (%)	Satisfied (%)	Not satisfied (%)
Herbal medicine	12	73	18
Homeopathy	4	66	16
Acupuncture	3	50	47
Chiropractic	2	68	19
Hypnotherapy	2	43	50

Those in favour of alternative medicine argue that these treatments consider the patient as a whole, instead of beating a disease down by finding the cause and then hitting it with drugs. However, some have put the increase in popularity of alternative healthcare down to a lack of confidence in conventional doctors and hospital care. In Britain in the 2000s, a number of scandals (such as that concerning Dr Harold Shipman, who murdered his patients and stole their money) reduced public confidence. However, generally speaking, satisfaction levels with the treatment people get from their hospitals and GPs remains quite high. A 2014 survey of nearly 2000 people found that 71 per cent were satisfied with the service they received from their doctor.

Since the 1980s, alternative medicine has become more and more popular in Britain, and some of it (such as acupuncture) is now available on the NHS.

Chapter 10 Modern treatment of disease

Aromatherapy

What is it? Aromatherapy is the use of essential oils from flowers, fruits, roots and leaves. The oils are inhaled or massaged into the skin.

Effect? The inhaled scents are said to stimulate particular parts of the brain, which promote healing, while massaged oils pass into the bloodstream and can influence nervous system function, mental function and emotions.

Hypnotherapy

What is it? A therapist hypnotises the patient. When totally relaxed, the patient can be relieved of stress, allergies or even physical addictions such as smoking.

Effect? It is based on positive thinking – that the power of a patient's own mind can bring about their healing.

Homeopathy

What is it? Patients take a medicine (a plant, animal or mineral material soaked in alcohol) which causes similar symptoms to the illness they are suffering from.

Effect? The idea is that tiny doses of the medicine that causes similar symptoms will cure the patient by stimulating his or her natural defences. Studies have shown homeopathy to be effective in treating hay fever, insomnia, depression and eczema.

Examples of alternative or complementary medicine

Key Words

positive health   alternative medicine

Acupuncture

What is it? Fine needles are placed at key points around the body. The places chosen are thought to be linked with particular needs or illnesses. Acupuncture has been a key part of traditional Chinese medicine for thousands of years.

Effect? The needles are said to release blocked energy and balance it properly. Acupuncture allows the energy to flow again; and it stimulates healing and relieves pain. It has been used as an anaesthetic during major surgery.

▼ **SOURCE C** *Acupuncture charts in an alternative therapy clinic*

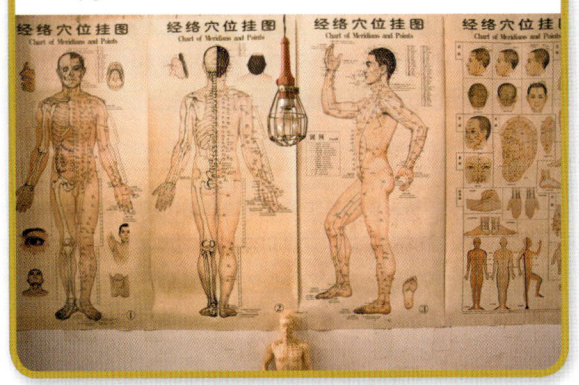

In fact, a recent survey indicated that one in five people in Britain have consulted alternative healers and used alternative medicines. Today one in ten doctors is actively involved in the promotion of alternative medicine, and they sometimes offer 'complementary' medicine, which is when an alternative practice is used together with conventional medicine.

In recent years, there has been a greater emphasis placed on prevention rather than cure – this is sometimes known as 'positive health'. People are learning that regular exercise is very important for health; and that a good diet which avoids sugary, fatty foods can help prevent some of the twenty-first century's biggest killers, such as obesity and heart disease. There is also a lot of emphasis on making 'lifestyle changes' and publicising the dangers of tobacco and the misuse of alcohol and drugs.

There has also been an increase in screening, which focuses on checking people who seem to be healthy, aiming to find those who have the early signs of a serious illness like lung or breast cancer.

Work

1. Why do you think doctors and scientists are particularly worried about bacteria such as MRSA?
2. a What is meant by the term 'alternative medicine'?
   b Why has there been a rise in the popularity of alternative medicine in recent years?

Fact

One of the criticisms of alternative medicine is the lack of regulation. While mainstream medicine can only be practised by a doctor who has studied in medical school and been certified, alternative medicine can be prescribed by almost anyone. However, this is slowly changing as some alternative treatments such as osteopathy and chiropractic have professional regulations and licensing in the UK.

11.1A The impact of war and technology on surgery and health

Throughout history, one of the key times when the latest medical techniques and the most up-to-date medical technology are needed is during wartime. If medical services are good, then more soldiers have a chance of survival; and the more soldiers there are available, the greater the country's chances of victory. Medicine usually develops at a greater rate during wartime than in peacetime. Governments pour a lot of money into developing ways of getting their injured soldiers back 'fighting fit' as soon as possible. Doctors and surgeons work very hard in wartime, often in battlefield situations, to develop their ideas in order to treat the injured. The huge numbers of wounded soldiers give doctors and surgeons more opportunities than are available in peacetime to test their ideas out.

Objectives

- **Examine** the links between the two world wars and medical progress.
- **Assess** the impact war and technology has had on surgery and health.
- **Explore** the latest technological breakthroughs since the Second World War, including radiation therapy and keyhole surgery.

The two world wars that took place during the twentieth century were huge conflicts that killed and wounded millions more people than in any wars before them. New and deadly weapons – high explosive shells, gas bombs, hand grenades and machine guns – were used on a massive scale for the first time, and inflicted terrible – often fatal – injuries. Over 10 million people were killed in the First World War (1914–18) and over 20 million in the Second World War (1939–45). These figures overlook the huge amount of people who were injured. Despite the great suffering caused by these two horrific wars, a number of improvements in surgery were made as a direct result.

Impact of the First World War on surgery

The diagram on these pages outlines the impact of the First World War on surgery and health. Advances made during and as a result of the Second World War are shown on pages 74 and 75.

Positives and negatives

As you can see from some of the examples on these pages, war can often bring about a great many medical developments and advances. But some historians argue that war can have a negative effect on medical progress too. For example, it could be argued that the First World War actually hindered the development of medicine because thousands of doctors were taken away from their normal work to treat casualties. Furthermore, lots of medical research was stopped during wartime so countries could concentrate everything on the war effort. Also, throughout history, warfare has disrupted towns and cities, sometimes destroying libraries and places of learning. Medical advances may have been delayed because these places were destroyed and manuscripts and research lost.

Work

1. In what ways can war have both a positive and a negative effect on the development of medicine?
2. Imagine you are an army surgeon in the First World War. Write a short letter home to your friends and family explaining how the latest scientific and technological developments have helped you in your work.

Shell shock

The mental strain of war could cause psychological damage known as shell shock. Some shell shocked soldiers had panic attacks; others shook all the time or were unable to speak or move. To begin with, the British army refused to believe that shell shock existed and many of the men were treated as cowards. However, by the end of the war, there were so many cases that shell shock was officially recognised. Today the condition is known as PTSD, or post-traumatic stress disorder.

Blood transfusions

Although blood transfusions had been tried for centuries, it wasn't until 1900 that scientists worked out how to do them successfully. Karl Landsteiner discovered blood groups, which helped doctors to work out that a transfusion only worked if the donor's blood type matched the receiver's. Even then it wasn't possible to store blood for long because it clotted so quickly. As a result, many people still died from loss of blood, so a solution to the problem of storing blood was needed. In 1914, Albert Hustin discovered that glucose and sodium citrate stopped blood from clotting on contact with air. Other advances meant that blood could be bottled, packed in ice, and taken to where it was needed by surgeons operating on soldiers.

X-rays

X-rays were discovered in 1895, and soon hospitals were using them to look for broken bones and disease. However, it was during the First World War that X-rays became really important. Mobile X-ray machines were used near battlefields to find out exactly where in the wounded soldier's body the bullets or pieces of shrapnel had lodged – without having to cut him wide open!

Plastic surgery

During the First World War, the hard work and dedication of Harold Gillies, a London-based army doctor, led to the development of what we now call plastic surgery. He set up a special unit to graft (transplant) skin and treat men suffering from severe facial wounds. He is commonly recognised as one of the first surgeons to consider a patient's appearance when treating wounds. Queen's Hospital in Kent opened in 1917 and by 1921 provided over 1000 beds for soldiers with severe facial wounds. Gillies and his colleagues treated over 5000 servicemen by 1921.

Infection

Battlefields are very dirty places and lethal wound infections such as gangrene were common. Through trial and error, surgeons worked out that the best way to prevent this was to cut away any infected flesh and soak the wound in salty (saline) solution. This wasn't ideal, but as a short-term answer in a battle situation, it saved many lives.

Broken bones

New techniques were developed during the First World War to repair broken bones. For example, the Army Leg Splint (or Keller-Blake Splint) was developed, which elevated and extended the broken leg 'in traction'. This helped the bones to knit together more securely. The splint is still in use today.

Britain: Health and the people

11.1B The impact of war and technology on surgery and health

The First World War sped up developments in surgery, health and medicine that probably would have happened anyway. For example, scientists had been working on blood transfusions for many years, but the amount of blood needed by soldiers in the war meant that scientists worked even harder to make blood transfusions a success. X-rays had been discovered in 1895, but it was during the First World War that X-ray technology became really important.

Impact of the Second World War on surgery and health

It was a similar situation in the Second World War. The millions of wounded soldiers meant that doctors, surgeons and scientists worked hard to develop new medicines and techniques – but they also tried to improve on some of the advances made in earlier years.

Blood transfusions

Advances in storing blood in the years after the First World War meant it could be kept fresh and useable for longer. This led to the British National Blood Transfusion Service opening in 1938. Large blood banks were developed in both the USA and Britain during the Second World War.

Heart surgery

Heart surgery progressed during the Second World War. American army surgeon Dwight Harken, stationed in London, cut into beating hearts and used his bare hands to remove bullets and bits of shrapnel. His findings helped heart surgery develop greatly after the war.

The National Health Service

When the Second World War broke out, the British government increased its involvement in medical care. After the war people started to think about how best to organise health care on a national basis. In 1942, a civil servant named William Beveridge proposed a free National Health Service for all – and just after the war finished, the NHS was born.

Impact of the Second World War on surgery and health in Britain

Plastic surgery

A doctor from New Zealand who trained and worked in Britain, Archibald McIndoe (a cousin of Harold Gillies), used new drugs such as penicillin to prevent infection when treating pilots with horrific facial injuries. His work on reconstructing damaged faces and hands was respected all over the world.

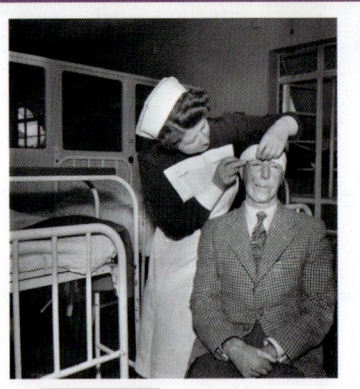

▲ **SOURCE A** A soldier, wounded in the Second World War, after treatment by Archibald McIndoe

Diet

Shortages of some foods during the war meant that the government encouraged people to grow their own food. This improved people's diets because the food they encouraged civilians to grow – fresh vegetables for example – was very healthy.

▲ **SOURCE B** A government poster issued during the Second World War

74 Chapter 11 The impact of war and technology on surgery

Hygiene and disease

In order to keep Britain 'fighting fit', posters were produced to encourage people to keep healthy. They warned against the dangers of poor hygiene, for example. A national immunisation programme against diphtheria (a bacterial infection which killed many children) was launched too.

Drug development

Penicillin, the first antibiotic, was developed in the years leading up to the war. The British and American governments realised how important this new 'wonder drug' could be in curing infections in deep wounds. By 1944, enough penicillin was produced to treat all the Allied forces in Europe.

Poverty

During the war, over one million children were evacuated from Britain's towns and cities into the countryside. Many of the children were very poor and the cleaner, healthier, lifestyle they enjoyed in the countryside improved their health. The whole experience highlighted the levels of poverty endured by some children in Britain, and increased the government's commitment to improve things after the war.

Impact of technology on surgery

Major technological breakthroughs continued in the field of surgery after the world wars. Improved anaesthetics allowed patients to be unconscious for longer, so more complicated operations could be attempted; while better antiseptics increased the success rate of difficult operations because they cut down the chances of deadly infection. When transplant surgery became more common, new drugs helped to prevent a patient's body from 'rejecting' their new organs. Keyhole surgery, using small fibre-optic cameras linked to computers, meant surgeons could perform operations through very small cuts. Microsurgery allowed them to magnify the areas they were working on so they could re-join nerves and blood vessels — allowing feeling to be returned to damaged limbs.

Radiation therapy (also known as radiotherapy) has been used for the treatment of cancer and other diseases for over 100 years. However, the methods of treatment are developing all the time and it is estimated that about half of all cancer patients will receive some type of radiation therapy during the course of their treatment. Broadly speaking, radiation therapy involves the use of high-energy radiation to shrink tumors and kill cancer cells. The radiation may be delivered by a machine outside the body — or it may come from radioactive material placed inside the body near cancer cells. Sometimes a radioactive substance such as radioactive iodine is used, which travels in the blood to kill cancer cells.

Surgery using lasers (rather than a scalpel) has become increasingly popular since a laser was first used in an eye operation in 1987. Lasers are still commonly used in eye surgery, but are increasingly used to treat a variety of skin conditions, help clear blocked arteries, remove tumors and ulcers and control bleeding.

Extension

The Second World War had a major impact on healthcare — and not just in Britain. For example, the World Health Organisation (WHO) was set up in 1946 to help people worldwide attain the highest possible level of health. Research WHO to see the work it has done over the years. What is their current opinion of the state of public health in Britain?

Practice Question

Has war been the main factor leading to improvements in surgery?

16 marks
SPaG: 4 marks

Study Tip

You can refer to periods outside the twentieth century in your answer, for example, the Medieval period or the nineteenth century.

Work

1. **a** Study the diagram of the impact of the Second World War. Explain how each of the advances, ideas and developments improved surgery and health.
   b Which of these developments would not have happened if it wasn't for the Second World War?
2. In your own words, explain how technological developments since the Second World War have made an impact on surgery and health.

Britain: Health and the people

12.1A Why did the government try to improve the nation's health after 1900?

Before the two world wars, the British fought a war in southern Africa called the Boer War (1899–1902). However, at the time around 40 per cent of the men who volunteered to fight were too unhealthy to be soldiers. In some big cities, 90 per cent of men weren't fit enough! This worried not only army leaders but also the British government too. But within five years of the end of the Boer War, the government had begun to introduce reforms aimed at getting Britain fitter and healthier — including free school meals for Britain's poorest children, school medical inspections, and a National Insurance Act which gave people the right to free medical treatment. So how exactly did the Boer War lead to free school meals? And what impact did the changes have on Britain's citizens?

Objectives

- **Explore** how and why public health was improved after 1900.
- **Outline** the Liberal social reforms of 1906 onwards in relation to poverty and housing in Britain.
- **Assess** the importance of Booth, Rowntree and the Boer War.

The Boer War

In 1899, a large-scale army recruitment campaign took place to find men to fight in the Boer War. But army chiefs were alarmed by the fact that 40 out of every 100 young men who volunteered were unfit to be soldiers — and the army didn't have particularly high entry standards either! The government was also shocked, so it set up a special committee to enquire into the 'Physical Deterioration of the People'. In 1904, the committee released its report. Among the many conclusions was the acknowledgement that many men were failing to get into the army because they led such unhealthy lives.

> **Fact**
>
> In the Boer War, the British and the Boers (descendants of Dutch settlers in Africa) competed for control of land in southern Africa.

The reports of Booth and Rowntree

Around the same time, several special investigations into the lives of the poor started to make headlines. For example, reports by Charles Booth, called *Life and Labour of the People in London*, found that around 30 per cent of Londoners were so poor that they didn't have enough money to eat properly, despite having full-time jobs. He demonstrated that there was a link between poverty and a high death rate.

In York, Seebohm Rowntree's *Poverty: A Study of Town Life* (1901) found that 28 per cent of the population did not have the minimum amount of money to live on at some time of their life. This fuelled fears that the unhealthy state of Britain's workers could lead to the decline of the country as a great industrial power. Germany, for example, which had a good system of state welfare for workers, was beginning to produce as much coal, iron and steel as Britain.

These reports, and the Boer War itself, highlighted the fact that poverty and poor health had become one

▼ **SOURCE A** An extract from Rowntree's *Poverty: A Study of Town Life* (1901):

> These children presented a pathetic sight; all bore some mark of the hard conditions against which they were struggling. Puny and feeble bodies, dirty and often sadly insufficient clothing, sore eyes, in many cases acutely inflamed through continued want of attention, filthy heads, cases of hip disease, swollen glands — all these and other signs told a tale of neglect.

of the big issues of the time. They came at a time when more people were beginning to feel that one of the key responsibilities of any government was to look after people who can't look after themselves. Some politicians, including many from the Liberal Party (including Winston Churchill and David Lloyd George), believed that direct action from the government was the way to improve the public health, welfare and productivity of the nation. They were also worried about the popularity of the Labour Party, which had been founded in 1900, so they wanted measures that would appeal to working people and stop them voting for Labour. In 1906, the Liberal Party won the general election, and set to work.

The Liberal social reforms

School meals

In 1906, the School Meals Act allowed local councils to provide school meals, with poor children getting a free meal. By 1914, over 158,000 children were having a free school meal every day. However, lack of food was only part of the problem.

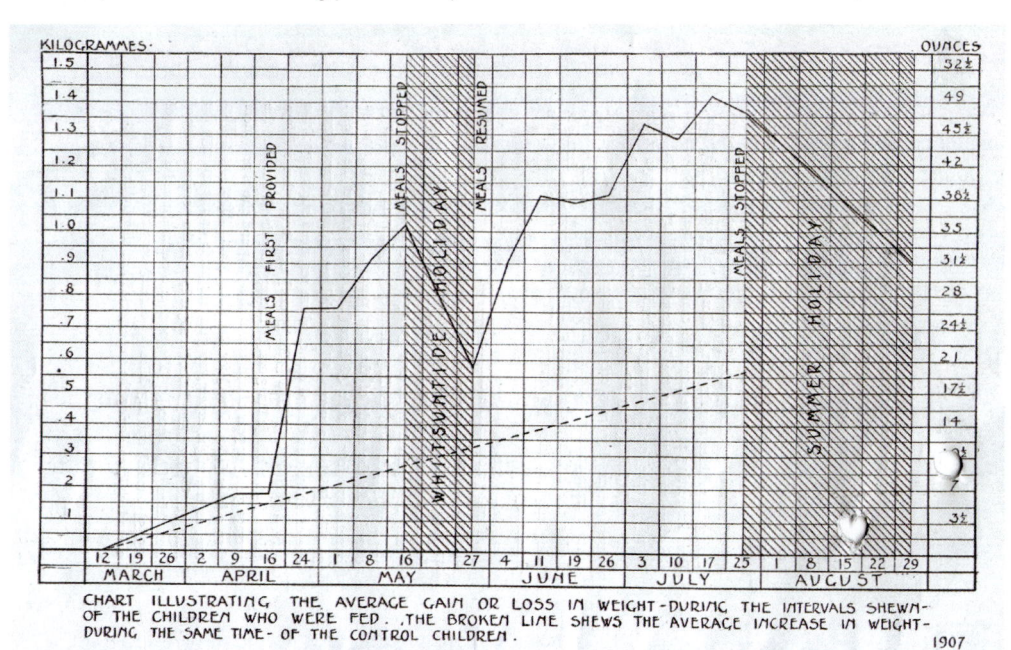

THIS WEEK'S MENU

Monday: Tomato soup – Currant roly-poly pudding

Tuesday: Meat pudding – Rice pudding

Wednesday: Yorkshire pudding, gravy, peas – Rice pudding and sultanas

Thursday: Vegetable soup – Currant pastry or fruit tart

Friday: Stewed fish, parsley sauce, peas, mashed potato – Blancmange

▲ **B** *Bradford was the first city to offer free school meals. They were introduced at a time when research showed that a poor child was, on average, nine centimetres shorter than a rich one.*

◀ **SOURCE C** *This graph from 1907 shows the impact of the free school meals; it charts the weight children gained (and lost) during part of the school year*

Work

1. In what ways did the following affect the way the government felt about the health and welfare of British citizens: the Boer War; Charles Booth's report; Seebohm Rowntree's report; Germany.

2. Look at the menu in **B**.
   a. Why were menus like this introduced in schools in the early 1900s?
   b. Write down at least two reasons why many viewed this as a healthy menu.
   c. In what ways have modern governments today tried to improve the eating habits of young people at school?

3. Look at **Source C**.
   a. What effect did providing meals have on the weight of the children?
   b. What happened to the weight of the children during the holidays?
   c. What is the dotted line – and why does the dotted line go up?

Britain: Health and the people

12.1B Why did the government try to improve the nation's health after 1900?

Children's health

In 1907, the government told all councils that they should have a school medical service. At first, doctors examined the children and then parents paid for treatment. When lots of parents failed to follow through with treatment – because they couldn't afford it – the government paid for school clinics to be set up with free treatment.

Other measures continued to help children. The Children and Young Person's Act of 1908, for example, made children into 'protected persons', which meant that parents were breaking the law if they neglected their children.

SOURCE D *A school doctor consulting a mother during a medical examination of her young son, London 1911*

The school system was also seen as a way of improving children's health and well being. From 1907, special schools were set up to teach young women about the benefits of breastfeeding, hygiene and childcare.

Poverty and housing

After helping children, the government moved onto other sections of society. A National Insurance Act introduced unemployment benefit ('the dole'), free medical treatment and sickness pay. Old Age Pensions were introduced and Britain's first job centres were built.

SOURCE E *Adapted excerpt from the Children and Young Person's Act, 1908. This was nicknamed 'The Children's Charter', and laid down in law many of the things that still protect children today:*

> Children are 'protected persons': parents can be prosecuted if they neglect or are cruel to them.
>
> Inspectors are to regularly visit any children who have been neglected in the past.
>
> All children's homes are to be regularly inspected.
>
> Youth courts and young offenders' homes are to be set up to keep young criminals away from older ones.
>
> Children under 14 are not allowed into pubs.
>
> Shopkeepers cannot sell cigarettes to anyone under 16.

Over the next 30 years, successive governments continued to take measures to improve the welfare of Britain's citizens. The building of overcrowded back-to-back housing was banned, for example, so fewer people would have to live in the crowded, filthy, disease-ridden slums. In 1918, local councils had to provide **health visitors**, clinics for pregnant women, and day nurseries. A year later, councils began to build new houses for poorer families and, by 1930, a huge slum clearance programme began, finally clearing away the breeding grounds of so much disease.

Impact of social reforms on public health

Gradually, during the twentieth century, infant mortality began to drop. A further boost to children's welfare was given in the 1940s with the introduction of the National Health Service (NHS). So, in today's world, health care begins before a baby is born: a pregnant woman will get free treatment and advice at antenatal clinics, and all hospital care and nursing are free. When the baby is born, it receives cheap milk, food and vitamins if required; then a free education, cheap (or free) school meals, dental treatment and eye care. And if a child has any need that requires a special school, for example if they are blind or deaf, this costs the parents nothing. In 2015, the infant mortality rate in the UK was 4.2 per 1000: meaning that for every one thousand babies born, fewer than five die before they are one year old.

Key Word

health visitor

SOURCE G *A line graph showing the effect of a 1940 government campaign to get all children immunised against diphtheria; this disease causes a fever that makes sufferers short of breath, and it killed many children in the nineteenth century*

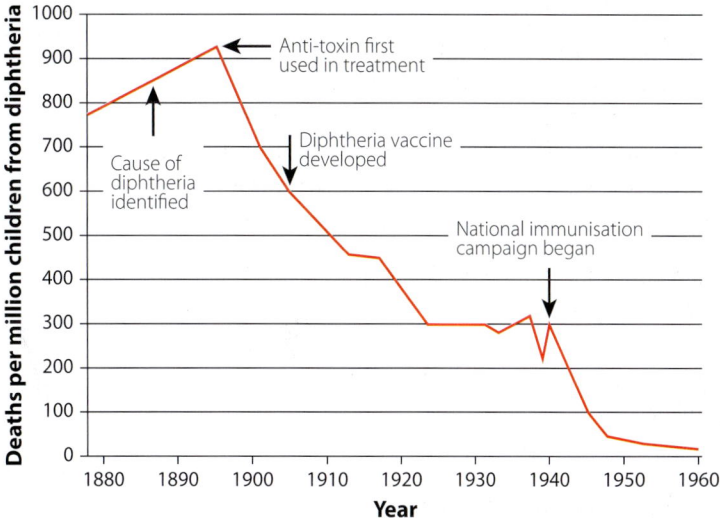

Deaths per million children from diphtheria (1880–1960):
- Cause of diphtheria identified
- Anti-toxin first used in treatment
- Diphtheria vaccine developed
- National immunisation campaign began

Extension

Health issues are major news items. What topics related to health have been in this week's newspapers or TV news broadcasts?

SOURCE F *A bar graph showing infant mortality in Britain, 1840–2010*

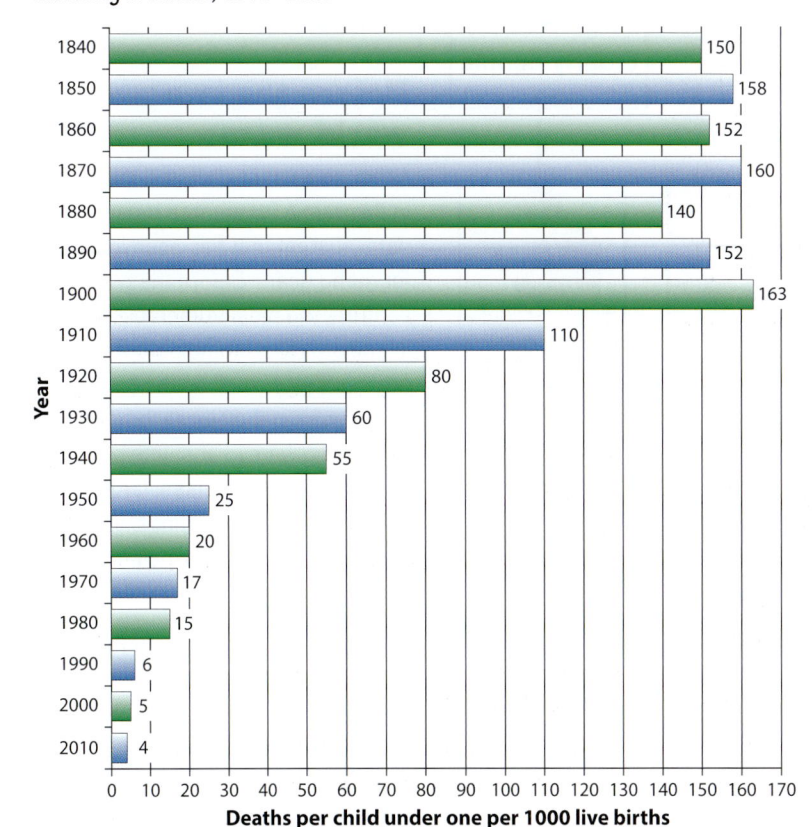

Deaths per child under one per 1000 live births:
- 1840: 150
- 1850: 158
- 1860: 152
- 1870: 160
- 1880: 140
- 1890: 152
- 1900: 163
- 1910: 110
- 1920: 80
- 1930: 60
- 1940: 55
- 1950: 25
- 1960: 20
- 1970: 17
- 1980: 15
- 1990: 6
- 2000: 5
- 2010: 4

Work

1. Apart from the introduction of school meals, how else were children helped in the early 1900s?
2. Study **Source F**. In pairs or in groups, discuss why the infant mortality rate dropped between 1900 and 1945. You may want to review what you learned about the impact of the two world wars (pages 72–75) to help you with the discussion.
3. Look at **Source G**. Why do you think a national immunisation campaign for diphtheria was started in 1940?

Practice Question

Explain the significance of the Liberal social reforms for the prevention of disease. **8 marks**

Study Tip

Refer to different groups of people at the time and how the reforms relate to the NHS.

Britain: Health and the people

12.2A Into the twenty-first century

There is almost no-one in Britain who isn't helped at some time or another by the **welfare state**. This is the name of the system by which the government aims to help those in need, mainly the old, the sick, the unemployed and children. You and your family will almost certainly have been helped out by this system at one time or another. Sometimes also known as 'social security', the welfare state aims to ensure that nobody goes without food, shelter, clothing, medical care, education or any other basic need simply because they can't afford it. How did Britain develop into a welfare state in the twentieth century? What are the issues for public health in the twenty-first century?

Objectives

- **Examine** the impact of the two world wars on public health.
- **Explore** the concept of the welfare state and the development of the NHS.
- **Evaluate** the impact of the NHS.
- **Explore** the costs, choices and issues relating to healthcare in the twenty-first century.

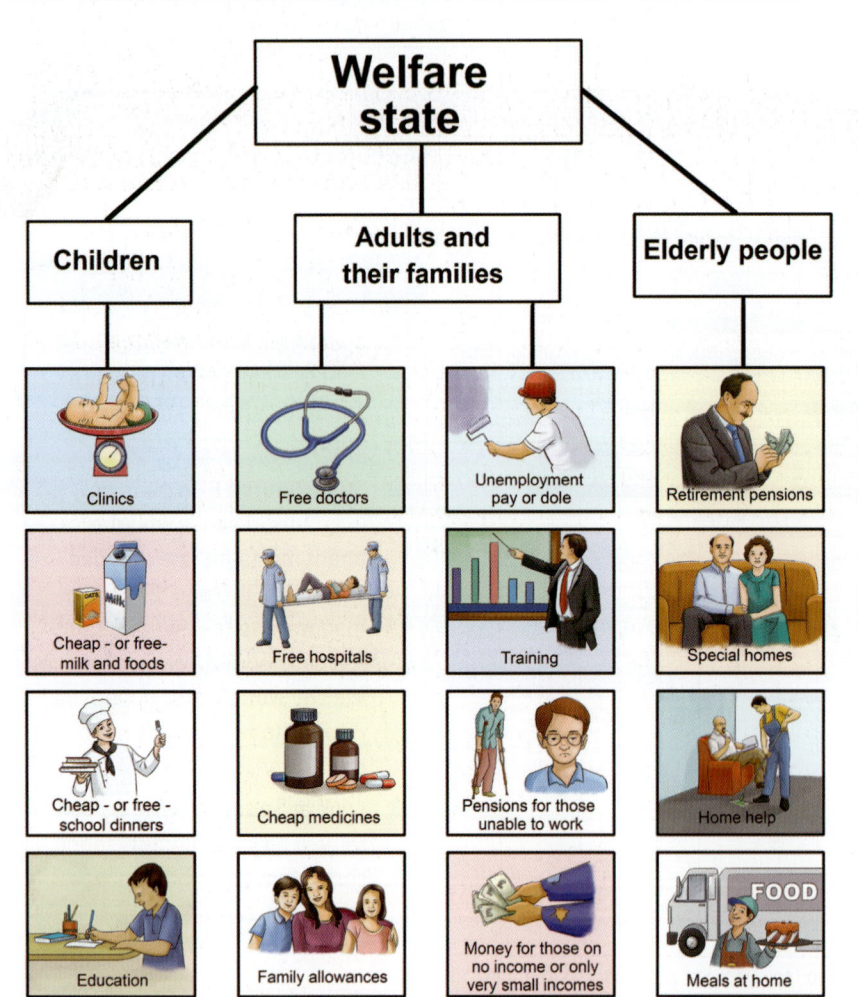

A *The twentieth century saw the government accept the need to care for its citizens 'from the cradle to the grave'; this diagram gives a basic outline of how the welfare state in Britain works*

Before the two world wars

Although we take things illustrated in diagram A for granted today, it is not a system that has been in place for many years. Before the twentieth century, the most vulnerable people in society relied on help from charity organisations, such as the Salvation Army, or from their local church. Those who were in absolute poverty ended up in **workhouses**: large, cold, intimidating buildings where people had to work for their food and accommodation.

From 1906, a few years after the Boer War ended, the government introduced some help for the most vulnerable sections of society: free school meals for poorer children, free school medical check-ups and treatment, small old-age pensions for the over 70s, and basic sick and 'dole' pay. But this was not on the same scale as what was introduced after the two world wars.

80 Chapter 12 Modern public health

SOURCE B Speaking in 2006, Ivy Green from Nottingham remembers medical care in the 1930s:

> You paid National Insurance as soon as you got a job. We called it 'the stamp' and it worked like any insurance policy does today. You paid a set amount each week into a central fund and this entitled you to some basic sick pay and care from a 'panel doctor' if you were ill … but because you only paid your stamp if you had a job, it meant you missed out on doctor's care when you lost your job. So when there was high unemployment in the 1930s, loads of people were unable to get any medical treatment because they hadn't been paying their stamp. You could pay for a doctor to visit you – six pence I think. It wasn't a lot of money but it still made you think twice about calling him. I'm sure lots of people mustn't have bothered to call a doctor because of the money.

Impact of the two world wars on public health

The death and destruction of the two world wars didn't just have an impact on people's lives – it had a major impact on attitudes too. It wasn't just the men fighting at the front that were dying: many people back in Britain suffered too, from shortages and bombing attacks. People felt that the sacrifices made at home and abroad should mean that the future should be a lot better for them. They felt that a better, fairer healthcare system should be part of this. And many middle-class people in the countryside had been genuinely shocked by the state of some of the dirty, under-nourished children who had been evacuated out of the cities during the Second World War. They felt that winning the wars should mean a better future for them too.

Beveridge Report

Towards the end of the Second World War, Sir William Beveridge wrote a report about the state of Britain. The Beveridge Report (1942) said that people all over the country had a right to be free of the 'five giants' that could ruin their lives:

- disease
- want (need)
- ignorance
- idleness
- squalor (very poor living conditions).

The report suggested ways to improve quality of life, and said that the government should 'take charge of social security from the cradle to the grave'. In a nation where people hoped that life would be better once the war was over, the report became a surprise bestseller, selling over 100,000 copies in its first month of publication.

Key Words

welfare state   workhouse

SOURCE C Sir William Beveridge (1879–1963)

The Labour government

As the Second World War ended, an election was held to decide who would run the country after the war. The Labour Party promised to follow Beveridge's advice, while the Conservative Party, led by Winston Churchill, refused to make such a promise. The Labour Party won the election easily – and Winston Churchill, the man who had led Britain during the war, was out of power.

Work

1. In your own words, describe how the most vulnerable people in society were looked after before the Second World War.
2. a. Explain what is meant by the term 'welfare state'.
   b. What was the Beveridge Report?
   c. In your own words, explain what you think was meant when the report said that the government should 'take charge of social security from the cradle to the grave'.

12.2B Into the twenty-first century

The welfare state

The new labour government, led by Clement Atlee, kept its promise: within the next few years, they put many of Beveridge's reforms into practice:

- The National Health Service (NHS) was set up in 1948 to provide health care for everyone. This made all medical treatment – doctors, hospitals, ambulances, dentists and opticians – free to all who wanted it.
- A weekly family allowance payment was introduced to help with childcare costs.
- The very poor received financial help or 'benefits'.
- The school leaving age was raised to 15 to give a greater chance of a decent education, and more free university places were created.
- The government's programme of 'slum clearance' continued as large areas of poor-quality housing were pulled down and new homes were built. Twelve new towns were created and by 1948, 280,000 council homes were being built each year.

Fact

The NHS scheme was originally opposed by doctors who didn't want to come under government control. Many felt that they would see a decline in their income because they could no longer charge what they wanted for their services. In a survey of around 45,500 doctors, nearly 41,000 didn't want a National Health Service! However, Aneurin Bevan, the Minister of Health, won them over by promising them a salary and allowing them to treat private patients as well.

Development of the NHS

Aneurin Bevan was the Minister of Health appointed by the government to introduce the NHS. And almost immediately, the NHS made an enormous impact. Up until 1948, around eight million people had never seen a doctor because they couldn't afford to. Now everyone could get free medical treatment and medicines.

It seems that Bevan's words hit home with health care providers – women's needs became a priority and they are now four times more likely to consult a doctor than men. Life expectancy for women has risen from 66 to 83 since 1948, and for men the figure has risen from 64 to 79. However, even in these modern times, your life expectancy can be affected by your wealth and living conditions. For example, in 2014, life expectancy for newborn baby boys was highest in the wealthy London areas of Kensington and Chelsea (83.3 years) and lowest in Blackpool (74.7 years), where there is far less wealth.

SOURCE D *From a speech by Aneurin Bevan in 1946:*

> A person ought not to be stopped from seeking medical assistance by the anxiety of doctors' bills … medical treatment should be made available to treat rich and poor alike in accordance with medical need and no other criteria. Worry about money in a time of sickness is a serious hindrance to recovery apart from its unnecessary cruelty. Records show that it is the mother in the average family who suffers most from the absence of a full health service. In trying to balance her budget she puts her own needs last.

SOURCE E *From an interview with Frederick Rebman, speaking in 2004, remembering the introduction of the NHS:*

> We were sorry to see Churchill voted out – he was our war leader, but he never promised to give the new ideas a go. The Labour Party did you see, and they publicised this in all the papers … servicemen like me expected so much after the war, perhaps Utopia, and the welfare state seemed to be a good start. I didn't mind paying a bit more of my salary to know that a doctor or a dentist was there if I needed them. I felt it was worth it, that the government cared about us a bit more I suppose. I think there was a bit of a rush when the NHS first started. There were stories of people going and getting whole new sets of teeth, new glasses, even wigs. Perhaps they'd have struggled on before with their short-sightedness or their painful teeth, but now they didn't have to.

▼ **SOURCE F** *The cost of the NHS, 1950–2010*

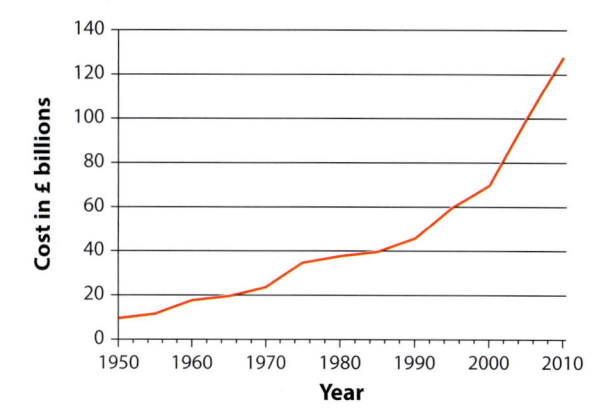

Costs of the welfare state

Of course, this all cost money. All workers had to pay for the NHS service through taxation, and over the years, the cost of welfare state services like the NHS rocketed. In fact, the NHS did not stay totally free for long. Working people today have to pay for doctors' prescriptions and dental treatment, for example, but the NHS ensures that no one is deprived of services such as family planning, physiotherapy, child care, cancer screening, asthma clinics and minor surgery simply because they can't afford it.

Healthcare in the twenty-first century

The NHS is rarely out of the news, mainly due to the fact that it has problems: waiting lists seem to be getting longer and doctors and nurses are overworked. There is rarely a month that goes by without some big media scandal about 'dirty wards', 'crumbling hospitals' or 'nurses doing long hours', or a news headline such as 'Doctors strike in UK-wide protest over pensions'. The main problem, of course, is money. Modern drugs are very expensive and modern medicine means that people are living longer – so there are more elderly people than ever before, and older people tend to use the services of the NHS more than younger people. The NHS has always been, and should continue to be, a really hot topic in British society.

The quest to improve medical treatments and public health continues today. Healthy eating campaigns and new laws try to protect Britain's citizens and prevent them from needing expensive medical care in the future. Tobacco advertising, for example, was banned in 2005 and in 2007 a smoking ban made it illegal to smoke in all enclosed public places. In 2015, drivers in England were banned from smoking in cars while carrying children as passengers.

Initiatives such as checking for the early signs of cancer, understanding how to spot (and deal with) a potential stroke victim, and trying to encourage people to eat five portions of fruit and vegetables a day are all aimed at making Britain healthier. In 2016, the British government unveiled plans to introduce a 'sugar tax', adding an additional cost to the price of high-sugar drinks, particularly fizzy drinks.

Technological breakthroughs and developments will also continue to improve the health and wellbeing of people. 'Digital therapy', for example, is designed for patients who need at-home care or who can't travel to a doctor's surgery or hospital. It is hoped that, in the future, mobile technology, combined with artificial intelligence (AI), will provide patients with a daily to-do list and a tracker for diet and exercise, based on results provided from patient scans.

Work

1. How did Beveridge and the Labour government win doctors over to accept the NHS?

2. Read **Source D**.
   a. Who was Aneurin Bevan?
   b. What point does he make about women in his speech?

3. Read **Source E**.
   a. According to the source, why did the Labour Party win the election in 1945?
   b. Why do you think people rushed out to get 'whole new sets of teeth, new glasses, even wigs' when the NHS first started?

4. Why do you think the NHS is still such a controversial topic today?

Practice Question

Have governments been the main factor in the development of public health?

16 marks
SPaG: 4 marks

Study Tip

Write about two more factors, for example, the role of individuals and religion. Refer to earlier periods in your answer.

Britain: Health and the people

How to... analyse significance

In your exam, you will have to deal with a question about analysing the significance of something, such as an event, an issue or a person.

Practice Question

Explain the significance of the work of William Harvey.

8 marks

Study Tip

Judging the *significance* of a person (such as Harvey) is about looking at the impact that he or she had *at the time*, how his or her work affected people *in the long term*, and whether his or her work is still relevant *today*.

Over to you

When we say an event, idea or person is *significant*, we mean more than just that it is important. Judging the significance of an event, idea or person is about looking at the impact that it had *at the time* and how it affected people, and whether it had long-lasting effects or caused important change. You should also consider whether the event, idea or person is still *relevant* to the present day. Now, work through the following questions.

1. Start by planning out your response: what do you know about the work of William Harvey? Try to make notes about what Harvey did at the time.

2. Consider Harvey's impact at the time of his discovery. Write about how people thought or did things before Harvey completed his work, and why Harvey's work was a change compared with what went before.

3. After you have written about Harvey's impact at the time, move on to consider how his work might have an impact in the long term.

4. Lastly, does Harvey's work directly affect our world today? Remember that the significance of an event, idea or person can *change* over time, so sometimes a lot of time will need to pass before they are recognised as being significant. Something might not be seen as significant *at the time*, but years later, when more is known, they can be identified as having had a key impact. Equally, something that was significant at the time may lose its significance as a result of later developments, and no longer influence our thinking or world *today*. So, considering all these points, what do *you* think is Harvey's significance?

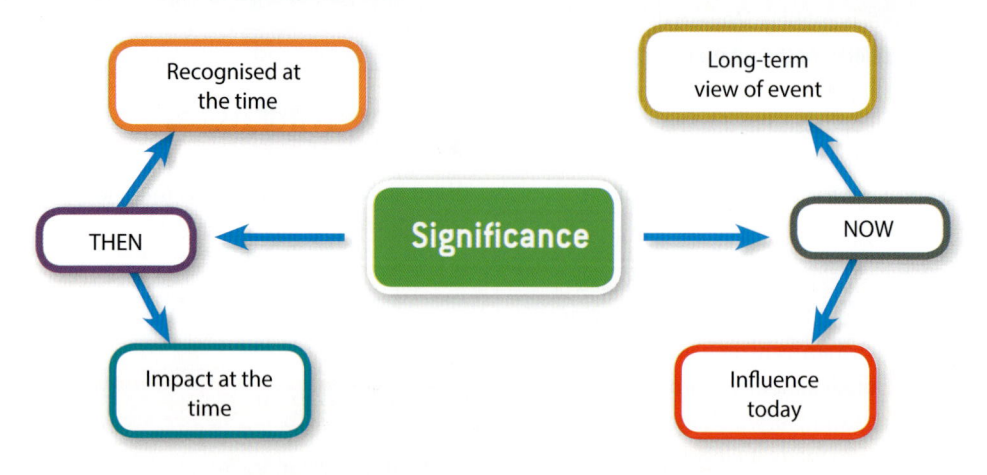

Significance diagram:
- THEN → Recognised at the time / Impact at the time
- NOW → Long-term view of event / Influence today

5 Read the following response. Can you identify where the answer explains about recognition of Harvey's work at the time, his immediate impact as well as his long-term impact, and his relevance today?

> Harvey's discovery was recognised at the time as a great challenge to the view of Galen. It sparked a fierce debate between those who supported Galen and those who favoured Harvey's new theory. Harvey's discovery was not immediately useful for treatments, and further scientific discovery was needed. Eventually, however, in his lifetime the theory was accepted as correct.
>
> At the time Harvey's discovery was not seen as useful. Although it did not help to cure any patients at the time, within a few years knowledge of the circulation of the blood prompted other scientists to carry out experiments.
>
> Harvey's approach was an experimental and scientific one. In the Middle Ages doctors studied the words of Galen without questioning his ideas. In the Renaissance, Vesalius advocated visual demonstration and learning from observing dissection. In the seventeenth century, Harvey was increasing medical knowledge and learning through scientific experimentation. However, doctors would not be able to replace or transfuse blood until 1901 when they knew more about blood groups. Still, understanding the circulation of the blood was a vital stage in the development of surgery and the diagnosis of illness. There are a vast number of modern medical techniques that could not work unless we understood about the circulation of the blood, such as blood tests and heart transplants.

6 Now try to answer the Practice Question yourself!

How to... analyse sources

In your exam, you will have to deal with a question about analysing the usefulness of a source to a historian studying a particular area of history. You will be asked a question that directly relates to a source.

▼ **SOURCE A** *Drawn in 1802 by a British cartoonist, this picture is generally thought to show Edward Jenner giving his patients 'the new inoculation' at St Pancras Hospital in London. However, historians have suggested that the doctor is actually William Woodville, who ran the hospital. He was in dispute with Jenner after some of his patients died from smallpox when he used Jenner's technique.*

Study Tip

The provenance (for example, the place and date of publication, the type of source, and the title) can help you assess the usefulness of a source. What do you know about the topic that you can link with the information from the provenance?

Study Tip

The content of the source is the image itself. Begin by describing what you can see. What do you know about the history of vaccination that you can connect with what you see in the image?

Practice Question

Study **Source A**. How useful is **Source A** to a historian studying vaccination?

8 marks

[Taken from AQA 2016 Paper 2 specimen material]

Over to you

The usefulness of a source is what it could tell you about the history of the time. A source might be useful because it reveals something new, why events turned out the way they did or why people acted or thought in a particular way at that time. This question suggests that the source has a use for historians studying vaccination: remember this as you work through the following questions.

1. Start by analysing the content of **Source A**. Describe what you see. What is the cartoonist trying to say about vaccination? And what does it tell us about the topic that makes it useful or not? The content of the source should be checked against your own knowledge of the topic.

2. You should also consider the provenance of **Source A**:

    a. What does it tell you about how useful, or not, the source might be? Provenance could mean who produced the source, why it was produced, who it was produced for, where and when it was produced. Remember that to asses the usefulness of a source, the provenance of a source is just as important as the content.

    b. What was the context of the time in which the source was created? This source dates from 1802, which was only a few years after Jenner's discovery about cowpox. The provenance suggests that this is not Jenner but another doctor using Jenner's method. Perhaps you could argue that this source is useful because it gives historians the evidence that Jenner's method is popular because someone else is using it.

3. Recall the actual question: it asks about a historian studying vaccination. In **Source A**, the patients are growing small cows from different parts of their body, which suggests that the cartoonist does not approve of vaccination. Why might this be? It is helpful if you try to use the provenance and the content together. The provenance said that some patients had died from smallpox when using Jenner's technique. It might seem that vaccination did not work. Do you remember that people used inoculation before vaccination? Perhaps the cartoonist thinks that inoculation is safer.

4. What are the strengths and weaknesses of the following answer?

> The source is useful because it comes from near the time when Jenner made his discovery in 1798 about vaccination. So the source will show what people were thinking at the time about vaccination. The picture shows people with cows growing out of them and this suggests that the cartoonist did not approve of vaccination or did not understand it. He is poking fun at vaccination and suggesting that there are side effects. The provenance suggests that people had come across severe side effects like death! The source is useful because it shows the historian that people did not accept vaccination immediately. I know from my own knowledge that people were inoculated with weak smallpox to give immunity. Doctors made a lot of money from this. Perhaps the cartoonist prefers those doctors and their methods. At the time, Jenner could not explain why his method worked so people were reluctant to accept it. If doctors used Jenner's method incorrectly or with dirty instruments they could infect people with smallpox.

5. Now try to answer the Practice Question yourself!

How to... compare similarities

In your exam, you will have to deal with a question about comparing the similarities of two things, such as two events or developments.

Practice Question

Compare the Black Death in the Middle Ages with the cholera epidemics in the nineteenth century. In what ways were they similar?

Explain your answer with reference to both epidemics. **8 marks**

[Taken from AQA 2016 Paper 2 specimen material]

Study Tip

Write something about both events, and compare them for their causes, development and consequences.

Over to you

This style of question asks you to compare what you know about two topics or aspects of the history you have studied. You are looking for similarities between the two events: remember this as you work through the following questions.

1. Start by planning out your response: what are the similarities between the Black Death and cholera epidemics? Make a list or mind-map to help you analyse the similarities. For example, when comparing events, consider:

   a. causes: why did the event happen?

   b. development: how did the event develop?

   c. consequences: events will have results.

2. Try to organise your response in three sections, covering causes, development and consequences. Remember that you will need to show how well you have understood both events by explaining the similarities that you can find.

3. Read the following response. Can you identify where the answer explains about similarities in terms of causes, development and consequences?

> Cholera came to England in 1831. It was not surprising that it killed more of the poor who lived in low-quality housing and often had a water supply that was contaminated with sewage. A shared water supply was a very simple and effective way for the disease to spread. Both diseases had effective ways to spread. The Black Death was really two sorts of plague, one pneumonic, the other bubonic, so it could be spread by a flea's

bite but also by droplets in the breath of someone who was infected. Because of the effectiveness of the method of spreading, many thousands of people died from both diseases. Both the Black Death and cholera led to changes in the lives of those people who survived it. Cholera did not respect the rich and powerful. If their water became contaminated it was likely that they would die. Cholera drew attention to the conditions in which many lived.

The effects of cholera influenced the work of people like Chadwick and Farr who believed that cleanliness would reduce disease. Cholera epidemics seem to underline the importance of Public Health Acts such as in 1848 and 1875. So cholera contributed to better sanitation through legislation. The Black Death killed so many people in Medieval times that those who survived received better wages in the decades after the Black Death. This was because England was agricultural and the landowners needed the hard work of the ordinary people to bring in harvests and tend the land. The Statute of Labourers in 1351, which tried to set wages at the rate they were at before the Black Death, was not successful. So the epidemics are similar because they had a big impact on those who survived them.

4. As you can read, this answer compares both events for the way they developed and their consequences. Can you write a paragraph that compares both events for a similar aspect connected with what caused each epidemic?

5. Now try to answer the Practice Question yourself!

Timeline

Britain: Power and the people

This thematic study covers over 800 years in the history of the relationship between the citizen and the state in Britain. Beginning in the twelfth century, you will explore how the power and authority of different kings and parliament have been challenged. By examining the journey from feudalism to democracy and equality, you will discover how, in different periods, the state has responded to challenges to its authority and the impact of this.

You will explore how the balance of power changed, why change happened when it did, whether change brought progress, and the significance of the changes. You will also consider how factors — such as war, chance, religion and the economy — sometimes worked together to bring about particular changes at a particular time.

And although the focus of this study is the development of the relationship between power and the people in Britain, it will show how ideas, events or developments in the wider world affected the course of Britain's political development.

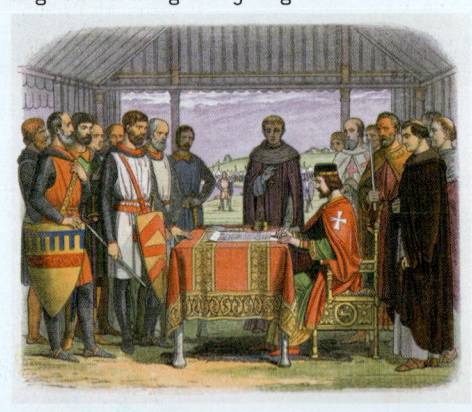

1215
Magna Carta is signed by King John

1381
Local uprisings lead to the Peasants' Revolt; the leader, Wat Tyler, is killed

1200

1300

1500

1600

1700

1265
Simon de Montfort calls a parliament that has 'commoners' in it

1536–37
People from the north of England start a pilgrimage to protest about King Henry VIII's changes to the Church

1642–51
English Civil War occurs between those who support King Charles I and those who support parliament

1819
The Peterloo Massacre: protestors demanding the vote are attacked by the authorities

1981
Brixton Riots take place and lead to the Scarman Report into institutional racism in the police

1775–82
Britain's defeat in the War of Independence results in the loss of the American colonies

1838–48
Chartism movement tries to secure more representation for the working class

1833
Factory Reform Act reduces the amount of hours women and children can work

1918
Women over 28 get the vote

1800

1900

2000

1804
Toussaint L'Ouverture leads a rebellion against slavery; the new independent island of Haiti is created

1834
Tolpuddle Martyrs are arrested for holding a union meeting

1948
Empire Windrush arrives in Britain, beginning a new wave of West Indian migration to the country

1897
The National Union of Women's Suffrage Societies is set up; the campaign for women's suffrage becomes organised

1926
General Strike takes place in support of British miners

Britain: Power and the people 91

1.1 What did people want from the Medieval King John?

This topic focuses on the topic of power and its impact on Britain and Britain's people from 1170 to the present day. To understand the topic, you will need to explore how power has been challenged and enforced over the centuries. To begin you will need to understand what Medieval kings were like in Britain, starting with King John.

When John became king in 1199 he had a lot to live up to. His father, Henry II, was viewed as a successful king, and his brother was Richard the Lionheart. Richard was a fantastic soldier who had captured and controlled land in France and fought in a **crusade**. A Medieval king was expected to defend his people by leading his army well and maintaining the support of important people in the kingdom, such as the **barons**. He should also keep the country peaceful, successfully deal with rebellions, and try to maintain good relations with the Church. So, did King John have what it took to be a good king?

Objectives

- **Outline** the qualities of a good Medieval king.
- **Explain** why King John was unpopular.
- **Analyse** interpretations of King John and come to a judgement.

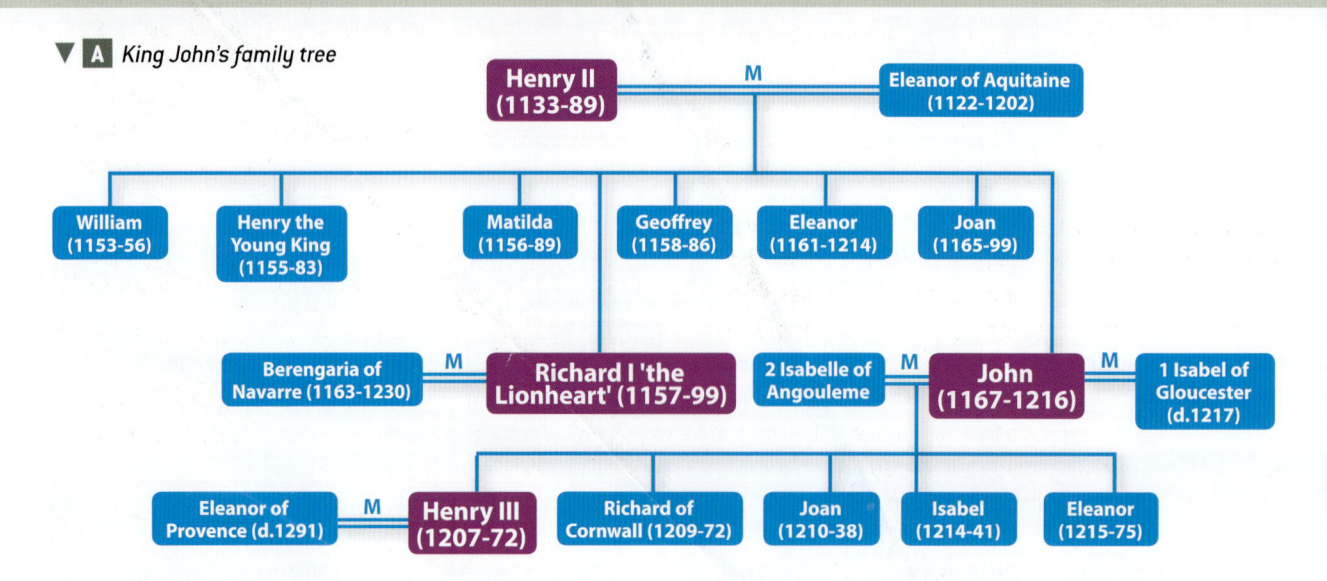

A King John's family tree

- Henry II (1133–89) M Eleanor of Aquitaine (1122–1202)
  - William (1153–56)
  - Henry the Young King (1155–83)
  - Matilda (1156–89)
  - Geoffrey (1158–86)
  - Eleanor (1161–1214)
  - Joan (1165–99)
  - Richard I 'the Lionheart' (1157–99) M Berengaria of Navarre (1163–1230)
  - John (1167–1216) M 2 Isabelle of Angouleme; M 1 Isabel of Gloucester (d.1217)
    - Henry III (1207–72) M Eleanor of Provence (d.1291)
    - Richard of Cornwall (1209–72)
    - Joan (1210–38)
    - Isabel (1214–41)
    - Eleanor (1215–75)

Medieval society

Medieval society was built on the **feudal system**. The king was at the top of this system and gave the barons land, in return for money and men to fight in wars. The barons would then give some of their land to the **knights** if they promised to fight when needed. There was a Great Council where the barons could meet and have their views and concerns heard. However, Medieval kings did not always listen to the Great Council.

'Bad' King John

The Christian religion was an important part of Medieval life. Medieval kings believed they were appointed by God, but the Pope was also the head of the Church and had great power over many European countries. John had a disagreement with the Pope when he refused to support the appointment of Stephen Langton as Archbishop of Canterbury. The Archbishop of Canterbury often found himself as a key adviser to the king; thus, it was a very powerful role. John was against Langton's appointment because he did not want someone who would obey the Pope and go against the king's wishes. In retaliation, the Pope banned church services in England; even marriages and funerals. This frightened the people as they thought that without regular attendance at **mass** they would go to hell. The barons were nervous, as this breakdown in relations between king and Church could lead to an invasion from a foreign king.

SOURCE B A painting of King John, painted between 1250 and 1259 by Matthew Paris, a monk who did not think highly of John; most images from the time show the king holding a church, trying to show that the king and the Church worked well together

Key Words

crusade   baron   feudal system   knight
mass   scutage   occupy

his father's and brother's great reputations: he would always look inferior. Richard had left John in debt because of his wars with France, so John struggled to raise enough money to govern and defend the country. John himself did win some wars against the Scottish and the Welsh, and strengthened the English navy.

John also ensured that the people of England could have a fair trial with a judge and jury: he sometimes even delayed proceedings so he could be there himself to ensure a trial was fair. This helped everyone in England, not just the rich barons.

John and the barons

Fed up with John, the barons put an army together under the leadership of Robert Fitzwalter, and sent it to **occupy** London: the barons were ready to fight the king. If John wanted to gather an army of his own, he would need the barons' support. He therefore had no choice but to negotiate with them. On 19 June 1215, King John met the barons at Runnymede, near Windsor. They would negotiate the way in which the country should be governed.

Another cause of poor relations was high taxes – known as **scutage** – which John charged barons to help him fight wars in France. The barons became angry because John was not living up to their expectations: he was given the nicknames 'lackland' and 'softsword' due to his poor record in battles. This affected the barons as it meant they lost their lands in France, so they lost money. Despite this loss, John continued to charge them even higher feudal payments. To make matters worse John managed to lose the crown jewels in an area of marshland called the Wash! Although this didn't affect the barons as much as raising taxes, it did make people question his competence.

According to the barons and to church officials, John was not doing well as a king, and the barons started to become restless. Few people could read or write in the Middle Ages, so it was down to the educated monks and barons to record the events of the day. As a result, there are many negative historical accounts of John and what kind of king he was, mainly because he came into conflict with the very people who could write down their opinions!

'Good' King John

There was much evidence that John was a terrible king. However, some historians have argued that to be fair, John would never have been able to live up to

Work

1. a Draw a mind-map of the ideal qualities a Medieval king should have.
   b Annotate your mind-map with comments to explain the ways John did or did not live up to these expectations.
2. Explain why the barons were angry with John.
3. Study **Source B**.
   a How did Matthew Paris portray King John and his relationship with the Church? Think how he has drawn the church and John's crown.
   b Why would he present John in this way?
   c Is this a good source for explaining what kind of king John was? Why or why not?

Fact

To determine whether a source is 'good' or not you should think about the information it gives you and if this is accurate. Then think about what information is missing from the source. Does that make it a 'bad' source? Why has the information been left out?

Britain: Power and the people

1.2 What was Magna Carta?

In 1214, the English barons lost patience with their king and raised an army. England was now effectively in a state of **civil war**. It was not uncommon for Medieval kings to face attacks from the barons but this time it was different. The barons would force the king to agree to conditions about how the country was run. John had no option but to agree. Magna Carta was signed on 15 June 1215. What did it mean for John? Would all kings have to agree to it?

Objectives

- **Identify** key features of Magna Carta.
- **Explain** why Magna Carta was significant.
- **Analyse** the significance of Magna Carta.

How did the barons deal with John?

One of the main reasons the barons were angry with John was because of his taxation policy. The most hated tax was scutage. Barons had to pay this if they did not fight for John when he asked. The problem was that the more the barons disliked John, the less likely they were to fight — so the higher the scutage they would have to pay. But there were other reasons why the barons were unhappy; for example, John lost important land in France and fell out with the Pope many times.

On several occasions, the barons drew up a list of complaints about the way John ruled, but he refused to change. Now he had no choice: the barons were prepared to fight him. They had the upper hand and John needed their support to keep power. At Runnymede, the barons got John to sign Magna Carta; Latin for Great Charter. But could the barons trust John?

▼ **INTERPRETATION A** A print of an engraving by Edmund Evans in 1864, showing King John signing Magna Carta

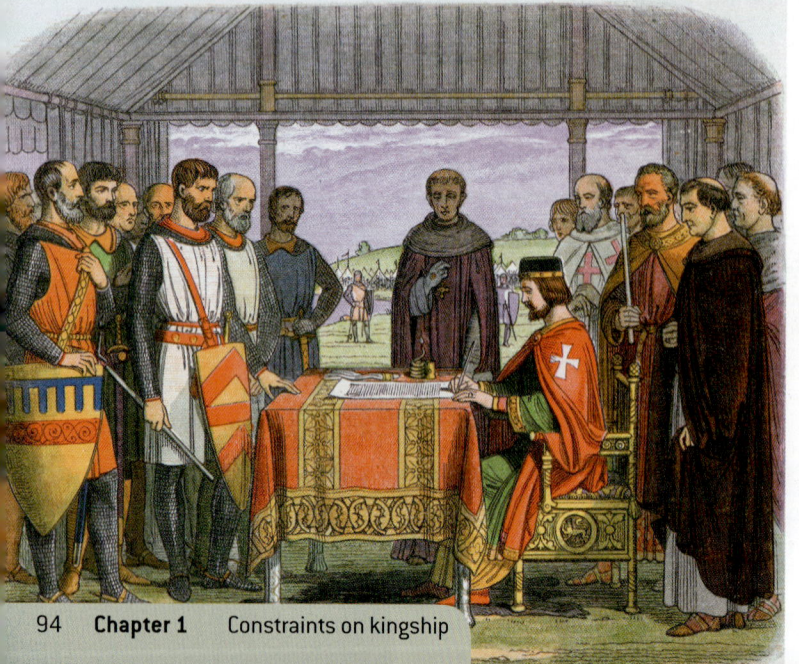

Clauses of Magna Carta

Magna Carta contained 63 promises that the barons wanted John to keep. These would change the power of the king and give the barons more control.

▼ **B** The six main clauses of Magna Carta

We grant to all **freemen** all the liberties written below:

- a baron's heir shall **inherit** his lands on payment of £100 to the king
- no scutage shall be imposed on the barons except with the common counsel of the realm
- no freemen shall be arrested or imprisoned without a proper trial and according to the law of the land
- the English Church shall be free to make make its own appointments
- all **merchants** shall have safety, in staying and travelling in England, for buying and selling goods, free from evil tolls
- a group of 25 barons will be created to monitor the king and ensure he commits to Magna Carta (Clause 61).

John had no intention of sticking to the promises he made that day at Runnymede. He only agreed so the civil war would end, and so he could get the barons back on side. Many people consider it a failure in the short term, because John quickly backed out of the agreement, saying he had been forced to sign it.

▼ **SOURCE C** *Part of the original Magna Carta*

Why is Magna Carta significant?

It is widely accepted by historians that Magna Carta was not important to all the people of England at the time it was signed. It only referred to freemen, such as barons; **peasants** and **villeins** were not free. The barons were looking out for their own interests when they drew up Magna Carta, and only included the Church and merchants because they needed to get more support against John. Magna Carta changed nothing for the ordinary people of Medieval England, only the politically powerful.

However, as the years passed, Magna Carta developed a greater significance. It applied to more people as they gained their freedom. It introduced the idea that there are some laws and rules that even kings have to follow: kings cannot just do whatever they want. After King John died, other kings signed similar versions of Magna Carta and today it is viewed as one of the first major steps in Britain's journey to becoming one of the world's best-known democracies.

▼ **SOURCE D** *The American Bar Association (of lawyers) erected this monument at the site where Magna Carta was signed. Although the charter did not change anything for ordinary people at the time, it would become known as a symbol of 'freedom under law'. It was used by the Americans to draw up their constitution when they became independent from Britain in 1776.*

Key Words

civil war   freeman   inherit
merchant   peasant   villein

Extension

The Republic of India also has a plaque at Runnymede that reads: 'As a tribute to the historic Magna Carta, a source of inspiration throughout the world, and as an affirmation of the values of Freedom, Democracy and the Rule of Law which the People of India cherish and have enshrined in their Constitution.'

Research why Magna Carta would be important to the people of India. Does it have the same relevance it has in America?

Work

1. Discuss in your group which clauses of Magna Carta you think are the most important. Decide on your top three clauses.
2. Write a paragraph explaining which clause you think would be most likely to make the barons happy.
3. Make a table in your book showing the impact of Magna Carta. One column should be headed 'short-term impacts' and the other should be headed 'long-term impacts'.

Practice Question

Explain the significance of Magna Carta.

8 marks

Study Tip

Remember that something is significant if was important at the time *and* is also important today. Research the extension task to further develop your response.

Britain: Power and the people

1.3 The impact of Magna Carta

King John quickly went back on his word. He had used the signing of Magna Carta as a stalling tactic to allow him to gather troops and rally support. In August 1215, the Pope came out in support of John stating that, as he had been forced to sign Magna Carta, it was invalid. John had the support of the Pope but the barons had the support of the French, whose king was ready to fight John. By May 1216, it looked like a war was about to begin. Would John keep the throne? Would he finally accept Magna Carta?

Objectives

- **Describe** the ways in which King John restored royal control.
- **Explain** the causes and consequences of the Barons' War.
- **Assess** the impact of Magna Carta.

The Siege of Rochester – softsword no more

War had been declared. The barons had taken control of London and had requested support from France, so the French king sent some knights to help secure London. John was in Dover organising his army. Rochester Castle, which lies between the two cities, became vitally important for both King John and the barons.

In a bid to gain an advantage, the barons occupied Rochester Castle. In October 1215, John's men arrived with five **siege** engines, consisting of **catapults** and **trebuchets**. They bombarded the castle with stone balls but they were not strong enough to break through the 3.6-metre-wide stone walls of the castle.

John then waited. He tried to starve the barons out. On 25 November he sent an order to Canterbury to have pickaxes made: he was going to dig beneath the castle. He sent out another order for forty fat pigs to be brought to him. By the end of November, the king's men had dug a tunnel under the castle's stone foundations. The tunnel's ceiling was supported by wooden props.

▼ **SOURCE A**
Rochester Castle today; after the 1215 siege it was rebuilt during the reigns of Henry III and Edward I

▼ **B** *A map of the south of England and northern France, showing London, Dover and Rochester*

When the pigs eventually arrived, they were slaughtered and their fat was used to cover sticks that were packed under the wooden props. These were set on fire. The fat burned at such a high heat that the wooden props holding up the castle's wall burned away — and the wall collapsed. John and his men stormed the castle. The siege was over by 30 November. John now held the power, but for how long?

The Barons' War and the re-signing of Magna Carta

Everything seemed to be going John's way. Small rebellions in Scotland and Wales had been settled after his cunning victory at Rochester. John now had control of most of England, as far north as Berwick-upon-Tweed.

However, John felt his fortune change in May 1216. While in Kent, he saw the French Prince Louis arrive with troops. The barons had called for him and promised him the English throne. John fled to southwest England. Louis, with the support of the barons, managed to take control of most of England. He did this by capturing strategic towns and castles. John took land from the rebel barons and gave it to his supporters in a bid to regain control. The barons would not be put off. With the support of a foreign power they could still defeat John: his royal authority had been diminished.

Prince Louis was announced (but not crowned) king at St Paul's Cathedral on 2 June 1216. Even the Scottish King Alexander II swore allegiance to Louis. It seemed like John had lost power and the barons had won.

We cannot be sure that John failed in his last attempt for control as, in October 1216, King John died. The barons decided that they did not need a French king and they crowned John's young son, Henry, instead. This worked in the interest of the barons as Henry, being a child, was easy to deal with. His **regent**, the Earl of Pembroke, called for Englishmen to defend the country against Louis. So, on 28 October 1216, Henry III became king. The barons reissued Magna Carta and the young king agreed to the conditions. Power had been restored and the king had to follow the rules set out. The events of the Barons' War had made it clear what would happen if he didn't.

▼ **INTERPRETATION C** *From the official Magna Carta 800th anniversary website, 2015. There were many events to mark the anniversary, with a ceremony held at Runnymede attended by the Archbishop of Canterbury, Queen Elizabeth and Prime Minister David Cameron:*

> It has transcended barriers of language and the divisions of cultures and ideologies. 800 years on, the rule of law, individual freedom and human rights are foundational principles of modern societies.

Key Words

siege   catapult   trebuchet
regent   parliament

Was Magna Carta a failure?

It is safe to say that the power of the monarch was limited after the signing of Magna Carta. However, the king could simply go against it if he wished. This was a feature of the reign of John's son, Henry III. It was not until 1295, during the reign of Edward I, that there was a **parliament** that represented people other than the barons.

Some historians argue that Magna Carta was a base for the freedom and justice mentioned in Interpretation C to grow. Others argue it was merely a negotiation between John and the barons, not the basis for human rights as we know them today. It is fair to say that although Magna Carta was important to the barons at the time it was only in the long term, when its full impact could be evaluated, that its significance was clear.

Work

1. Draw a timeline of the events from the signing of Magna Carta to the end of the Siege of Rochester.
2. a. Create a table showing the ways Magna Carta was a success and the ways it was a failure.
   b. Use two different colours and mark which points are short-term and which are long-term successes and failures.
   c. Do you think Magna Carta was a success or a failure at the time? Discuss this with your partner.
3. How did the barons try to protest against King John? Explain your answer.
4. In groups, research Magna Carta and its legacy. Create a presentation evaluating the impact of Magna Carta and whether it has been a success. You should look at the commemorations, human rights law and the impact at the time.

2.1 Simon de Montfort and King Henry III

Magna Carta was a series of written promises between the king and his subjects stating that the king would govern the country with respect for the law. The barons were given the responsibility of making sure the king carried out these promises, and the document clearly stated that they could use force if they felt it was necessary. So Magna Carta put the barons in a much more powerful position: surely there was now nothing that could upset the barons and cause more unrest. Wrong! In 1216, King John died and his son became King Henry III, at only nine years old. Over the next few years, the country was run by a series of advisers, including the king's mother. Henry personally took over in 1234, and before long, his relationship with the barons was at breaking point. There was one baron in particular who came to the fore at this time – Simon de Montfort. Who was de Montfort and what was his relationship with Henry like?

Objectives

- **Summarise** the role of Simon de Montfort in Henry III's court.
- **Explore** the problems between Henry III and the barons.
- **Evaluate** the actions of Henry III in dealing with de Montfort and the barons.

Who was Simon de Montfort?

After the Norman invasion of 1066, the de Montfort family was one of the first **aristocratic** families to come to England from Normandy. However, over the next 200 years they had lost more and more of their land to the king. In 1229 Simon, the leading member of the de Montfort family, tried to reclaim some of the family land, so he approached Henry.

Henry agreed to give the family some land back. Even better, Henry made de Montfort one of his favourites, and gave him the job of **steward**. De Montfort enjoyed this role as it put him in a position to meet rich widows: marrying one might be a way to sort out the family finances. He eventually married Henry's sister, Eleanor. She had been married before, at the age of nine, and was a widow by the time she was 16. De Montfort was then given special favour and sent to represent the king abroad. This position helped him in what was arguably now his main aim — reclaiming land that he felt his wife was owed by her first husband's family. For de Montfort, marrying the king's sister opened up the door to wealth and opportunity.

De Montfort eventually became an opponent of the king and a controversial figure. Some people view him as a hero and the creator of modern **democracy**. Others view him as an opportunistic baron, who got lucky marrying the king's sister.

Key Biography

Simon de Montfort (1208–65)

- The Earl of Leicester from 1239 until his death, de Montfort worked for the king but eventually led a rebellion against him, which resulted in the Second Barons' War.
- He became ruler of England for a short time when the king was imprisoned. He became famous for calling two parliaments. Some people believe these parliaments were the model for our parliaments today; others disagree.
- He died in the Battle of Evesham, August 1265, fighting against the king.

Henry and the Pope

Henry was as a **pious** king. Although this was normally seen as a good thing, his links with Rome created financial problems for England. Henry had increased payments to Pope Innocent IV to help the Pope fight wars in Europe. The Pope had convinced Henry to help him remove the royal family of Sicily and put his young son, Edmund, on the throne instead. Four years later, when Henry failed to pay the promised money, another Pope (Alexander IV) threatened to excommunicate Henry — remember how the people of England reacted when this happened to John. Furthermore, the Pope suggested that

Henry's brother, Richard, become Holy Roman Emperor: an important job that would bring part of Europe under the control of the Pope. This was a clever move by the Pope as it meant Henry and England would foot the bill for the Sicilian war. This would also mean an increase in taxes for the barons.

Henry then gave away top jobs in English churches to Italian clergy. This stopped English men being promoted in the Church. This led to the barons becoming increasingly frustrated by Henry's subservience to the Pope.

Henry and France

Henry had close ties with the French, especially the House of Lusignan, due to his marriage. This relationship alarmed the barons, as the English severely disliked the French. Their alarm increased when Henry started to allow French men into parliament. This was also down to his tutor and adviser, Peter de Roches: a French man. The barons started to feel that England was coming under foreign rule.

▼ **SOURCE A** *A painting of Henry III at his coronation, showing him holding a church and having the crown placed on his head*

The Gascon campaigns

Henry raised taxes to fund his campaigns to win back the land his father had lost in France. In 1230, he took his army to Brittany and Gascony. He lost the campaign and returned to England. In 1248, Simon de Montfort was sent over to France to try again. He had been training to go on crusade so was ready to fight. He crushed the rebellions and established order with a combination of military skill and ruthlessness. The previously lost land was now under the control of Henry and de Montfort.

The king was happy until reports reached him about de Montfort's use of force against the French in the occupied towns. The king was sympathetic to the French, so he called de Montfort back to England for an inquiry. Despite being found innocent, de Montfort was furious with the king. This anger intensified when Henry insisted his son, Edward, should take charge of the campaign when de Montfort returned to France. De Montfort felt so let down by the king he considered fighting with the French, against the king! He returned to England at the request of the barons, feeling betrayed by the king and bitter at his perceived fall from grace.

Key Words

aristocratic steward democracy pious

Henry needs the barons

By 1254, the relationship between the king and the barons had deteriorated. Henry's various schemes, involving land lost in France or more money to the Pope in Rome for wars against Sicily, angered the barons. De Montfort was fast becoming their spokesperson. They refused to fund Henry's schemes. Henry now faced a crisis on two fronts. He needed the support of the barons but they did not support increased taxes. This meant that Henry could not provide the funds the Pope desired. Without the money from increased taxes it was likely he would be excommunicated. Would the barons help him?

Extension

Research a biography of Henry III's son, Edward I. Did he learn from observing his father's struggle with de Montfort?

Work

1. Using the biography of Simon de Montfort and the information given, create a CV for him to present to Henry. It should have information about: his personality; his strengths; the reasons why he would a good person to work for the king; his bad points; whether his bad points might make him a bed person to work for the king.
2. Working in groups, write the main problems between the king and the barons on cards. Order these in a 'diamond nine' to show which problems could be the most important.
3. Write a letter to King Henry advising him on his actions towards the barons. What should he have done differently? What did he do well? Can you predict future issues he should try to deal with?
4. Study **Source A**. What impression does this give you of Henry? Think back to the similar portrait of King John.

Britain: Power and the people

2.2 The Provisions of Oxford and the Second Barons' War

By 1254, the relationship between the king and his barons was bad. The barons refused to fund Henry's schemes, so he faced a crisis on two fronts. He would either be excommunicated by the Pope for not paying the money he owed, or he would have to get the support of the barons. So he asked the barons for help: they refused. There was a meeting of the Great Council in 1258 and it was here that the barons set out to change the shape of royal control in England. What would this mean for the balance of power?

Objectives

- **List** the changes to power made by Simon de Montfort.
- **Explain** the significance of the Battle of Lewes.
- **Compare** the First and Second Barons' Wars.

The Provisions of Oxford, 1258

Simon de Montfort led the barons who called the Great Council against Henry in 1258. Having previously secured his position of wealth, he became obsessed by the reform of royal control and influence. During the Great Council meeting, the king agreed to the Provisions of Oxford. This stated that from now on a council of 15 barons would be in charge of the Great Council. They would be elected by 24 men: 12 appointed by the king and 12 by the barons. By agreeing to the provisions the king agreed, among other things, that:

- foreign members of the royal household would be banished
- castles would be held by Englishmen
- each county would have a sheriff and taxes would be decided locally.

This settled some of the grievances the barons had about foreign control of England. The barons also refused to fund the planned payment to the Pope over the wars in Sicily.

The Provisions of Oxford gave the barons the majority of power, as they stated that the barons could make decisions without the king's presence or approval. Moreover, the king could not make decisions without approval of the council. The Provisions of Oxford had a real impact on royal authority.

SOURCE A *From a section of the Provisions of Oxford, 1258, outlining the powers of the* **chancellor** *– the person responsible for the creation of official documents and laws:*

> The chancellor of England will not seal any writ without the order of the king and of the councillors who are present.

Opposition to the Provisions of Oxford

However, some barons were angered by the Provisions of Oxford, especially Richard de Clare, the Earl of Gloucester. He and many other older barons felt that the reforms were interfering with their local interests. The younger barons also disliked the Provisions of Oxford because they had not been elected to the council, and had therefore lost their influence. Furthermore, those lower in society were given a greater say. The barons longed for the feudal system when knights and **burgesses** had much less influence!

The Provisions of Oxford were extended in October 1259, with the creation of the Provisions of Westminster. These provisions reformed local government and were popular among the less powerful and wealthy members of society. Many barons resented the provisions, as they forced them to accept reforms demanded by their **tenants**.

SOURCE B *Henry III being forced by his barons to implement the Provisions of Oxford*

Therefore the barons had another reason not to be happy with the settlement de Montfort had agreed to. The barons were clearly divided.

▼ **INTERPRETATION C** *From the website of the British parliament, which provides information about the work of parliament and Members of Parliament. It ran a campaign in 2015 to celebrate the 750th anniversary of Simon de Montfort's challenge to Henry:*

> These reforms show the growing power of social groups beyond the major barons, who though still leading the reform, evidently felt they could not ignore popular discontent. In this regard they introduced reforms that were even harmful to their own local interests.

Henry's return to power

The bickering barons led the way for Henry to return to power and reject the Provisions of Oxford and Westminster. Henry wrote to the Pope and asked for his permission to cancel the provisions. In 1261, Henry received confirmation from the Pope that he would be released from the provisions. He appointed his own men to the council. Henry was back in power and de Montfort left for France in disgust.

Why is the Battle of Lewes significant?

After three years of Henry's revived rule, the barons sent for de Montfort: they had had enough. De Montfort returned and started the Second Barons' War. England was now in the midst of another civil war. The barons were fed up with negotiating and were now using military strength instead. As a result, de Montfort and his men were victorious at the Battle of Lewes in 1264. De Montfort captured the king and imprisoned his son, the young Prince Edward. England was now without its king, and in charge was the opportunistic baron, de Montfort. England was on its way to being a **republic**.

Extension

The Simon de Montfort Society run tours along key sites that involved de Montfort. They are considering starting a tour on the site of the Battle of Lewes. They want you to write the script for the tour guide. People need to know why it is significant but they also need to be entertained. You should think about the language you use: try to build a narrative. This means you can give your opinion and you can add in interesting facts about the battle.

Key Words

chancellor   burgess   tenant   republic

▼ **SOURCE D** *A stained glass window at Chartres Cathedral in France showing Simon de Montfort on horseback*

Work

1. a. Make a timeline of the key events between 1259 and 1264.
   b. Above each event note its cause, and below each event note its consequence.
   c. Colour code the causes and consequences into long-term ones and short-term ones.
2. What can we learn from **Source A** about the power of the king under the Provisions of Oxford?

Practice Question

Compare the First Barons' War with the Second Barons' War. In what ways were they similar?

8 marks

Study Tip

When dealing with comparison questions you should try to think of different aspects. For example; causes, key features and consequences/outcomes. These will show similarities or differences and you can then explain in more detail using specific evidence.

Britain: Power and the people

2.3 The king and a new parliament

King Henry was captured and young Prince Edward was being held in prison. Simon de Montfort had become the most powerful man in England. England was set to become a republic, ruled by a parliament and not a monarch. However, Edward made sure his father regained full control and de Montfort's life ended with him being cut into pieces. Would kings now continue to overrule the demands of the barons? Would the next council come from war or from more peaceful methods?

Objectives

- ▶ **Describe** the key features of the barons' challenge to power.
- ▶ **Categorise** the consequences of the changes to royal authority.
- ▶ **Analyse** the significance of Simon de Montfort.

The Commons: the road to parliament

When Simon de Montfort ruled over England, some barons began to get worried that he was too powerful. Not all the barons supported the new system of the Great Council, as de Montfort had appointed a council of nine which consisted of his own friends and allies; he reconfirmed Magna Carta and the Provisions of Oxford. The barons who had supported Henry wanted their old lives of influence and money back.

In 1265 de Montfort started to worry that he was losing his grip on the country and so he called a meeting of the Great Council. Unlike previous meetings, he invited burgesses and knights from every county. This increased support for de Montfort, which he was lacking from the powerful barons. The burgesses represented the growing merchant class who were making money in the growing towns all over England. So ordinary people – sometimes known as commoners – had been invited to the Great Council to have their voices heard for the first time, in what became known as the Commons. This was indeed a historic event.

The Battle of Evesham, 1265

The barons were concerned with their own interests and were also beginning to think that de Montfort was ruling as an **autocrat**. They began to put all their support behind Henry. His son, Prince Edward, had been released and had raised an army: they were out to get de Montfort.

Later, on 4 August 1265 at the Battle of Evesham, de Montfort fell from his horse, crying 'God's grace!' before he landed. His body was then cut into pieces – even his genitals were cut off – and the pieces were sent around the country as a warning.

▼ **SOURCE A** An undated painting of de Montfort's death at the Battle of Evesham

Fact

When de Montfort was killed, his head was cut off and his testicles were hung over his nose. This was sent to Roger Mortimer's wife, who was a big critic of de Montfort. She apparently had a party on receipt of the 'present' and put it pride of place on a lance in the great hall of Wigmore Castle.

Edward and future parliaments

Henry ruled until 1272 and never called another meeting of the Great Council. However, when Prince Edward became King Edward I, he knew he would have to tread carefully with the barons. He had learned from his father's and grandfather's mistakes.

When Edward needed money to fight the Scots and the Welsh to secure his territory and authority, he knew what would happen if he simply demanded the money from the barons, instead of negotiating with them. Therefore, he called many parliaments to raise the funds required. In 1295, he called what would be known as the **Model Parliament**. This is the parliament that most

Key Words

autocrat   Model Parliament

▼ **SOURCE B** *A painting of Edward I and his Model Parliament, from the 1300s; notice that some people are smaller than others – a reminder that this is not a completely equal parliament*

▼ **INTERPRETATION C** *Adapted from* A History of England, *written in 1830 by Sir James Macintosh; he was a supporter of the French Revolution that saw the removal of the French king and royal family:*

> De Montfort summoned a parliament of which the lower house was composed, as it has ever since been, formed of knights of the shires and members for cities and boroughs. He thus unknowingly determined that England was to be a free country.

▼ **INTERPRETATION D** *Adapted from* Simon de Montfort, *written by J. R. Maddicott in 1994; this gives a more balanced account of de Montfort and his parliament:*

> It was the most fundamental attempt to redistribute power within the English state before the seventeenth century. The 1265 parliament was a partisan [biased] assembly in which ecclesiastics [priests] were much over-represented and earls and magnates under-represented.

resembles ours today. The lords were invited to attend but the commoners (by far the largest group) were elected. This was still not a perfect system as only the elite of society, such as the barons, could vote, and voting was not done in secret.

Does de Montfort deserve to be remembered 750 years on?

De Montfort's parliament was not perfect, and parliament and its powers would continue to change throughout the Middle Ages. The king's power was not totally challenged until the English Revolution, when parliament gained more control than the monarch in 1688. Regardless, what most people agree is that de Montfort was influential in the common man's growth of power; however, women had to wait a few hundred years more for their voices to be heard.

Work

1. Why did the barons turn against de Montfort?
2. How was the 1295 parliament different from the 1265 one?
3. There are many different consequences to events. Can you explain the political, economic and social effects of the changes between 1265 and 1295?
4. Complete a table with one column for reasons de Montfort should be remembered and another column for reasons he shouldn't.

Practice Question

Explain the significance of Simon de Montfort for the development of democratic government.

8 marks

Study Tip

Something doesn't have to be good to be significant. Split your points into long- and short-term significance. Is there a difference between why de Montfort is significant in 1295 compared to today?

Britain: Power and the people

3.1 Were rats to blame for the Peasants' Revolt?

Life for the peasants of England was hard. They were at the bottom of the feudal system, working for a lord and serving the king. In the fourteenth century the peasants decided they had had enough. Not only were they having to pay high taxes to fund the king's lifestyle, but they were also being killed off by a terrible plague that seemed to affect them more than the barons. The peasants fought back against a king and a system that treated them unfairly. What were the main causes of this revolt?

Objectives

- **Outline** the impact of the Black Death.
- **Categorise** the causes of the Peasants' Revolt.
- **Analyse** causes to make a judgement on the most important.

The Black Death arrives

▼ **A** *A map showing the spread of the plague through Europe in the 1300s*

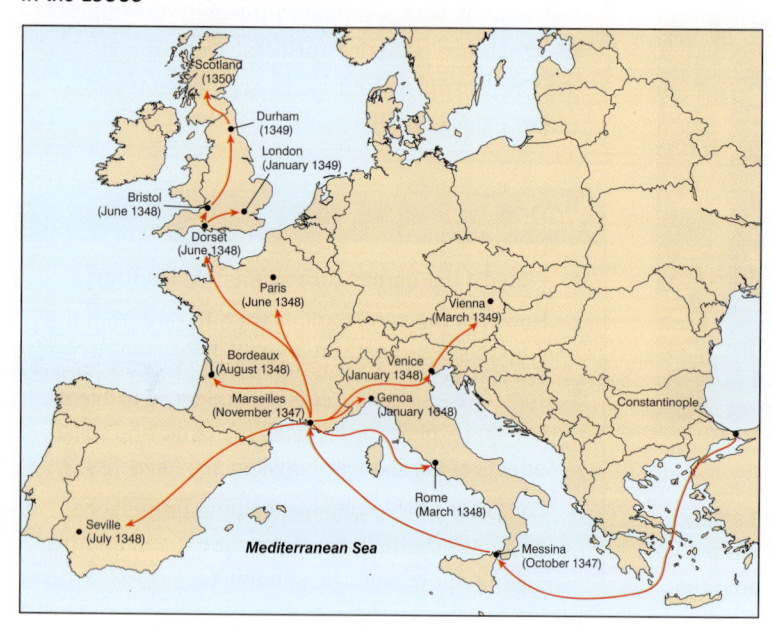

▼ **B** *Bar graphs showing the decrease in the number of days worked after the Black Death, and the increase in wages paid after the Black Death*

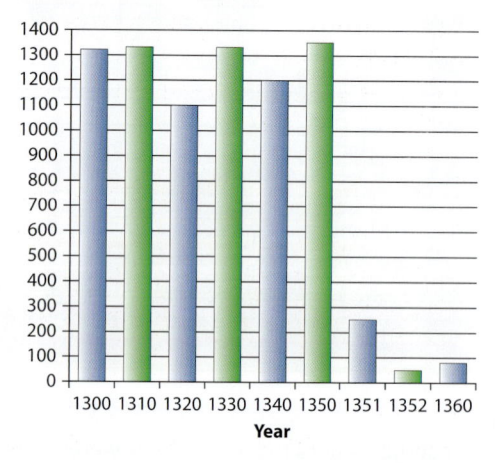

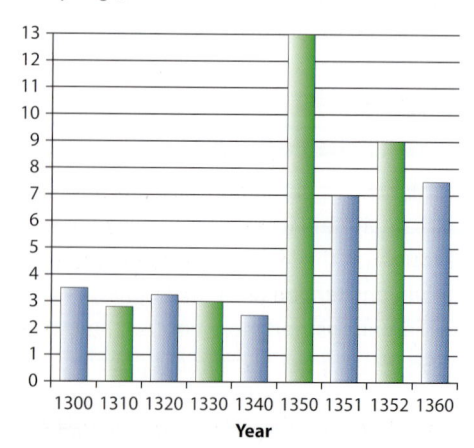

In 1348, a ship arrived at Melcombe Regis in Dorset, bringing goods from Europe. However, also on board the ship was something that quickly swept across England, getting as far as Scotland by 1350, and would eventually go on to kill a third of the population: the plague. The poor were more likely to be affected by the plague. This had a big impact on Medieval society, and became known as the Black Death.

The Statute of Labourers, 1351

The Black Death had the greatest impact on peasants, who made up the majority of the workforce. It led to fields of crops being left to rot, since there weren't enough people to bring in the harvests, and some villages being abandoned. However, for the surviving peasants, there were big advantages.

As there were far fewer workers after the Black Death, the peasants started to demand higher wages. Good, strong and hardworking peasants were now in demand. And so to look for better pay, or a fairer lord, many peasants moved to neighbouring villages.

Local lords and even the king started to become worried that the peasants were gaining too much power, and that the feudal system was starting to break down. So, in 1351, Edward III passed the Statute of Labourers.

▼ **SOURCE C** *Adapted from the Statute of Labourers, 1351:*

> Every man and woman in the realm must work for those who want them, and shall only receive the same wages as before the plague.

This angered the peasants. Some who had left their manor (the area their lord owned) were now captured and forced to work for their lord again. However, the peasants didn't just passively accept this new situation. Between 1377 and 1379, 70 per cent of the people brought before the **Justice of the Peace** were accused of breaking the Statute of Labourers. It was clear that the peasants who survived the Black Death were not afraid to stand up for themselves.

Causes of the Peasants' Revolt

The Statute of Labourers tried to control the peasants and their rising wages — but some peasants were in quite a powerful position. After all, the Black Death had killed so many workers, and landowners needed workers to bring in the harvests. The peasants started to question the way the government was running the country. Furthermore, the new king, Richard II, was young and inexperienced. He had taken over from his very able father and his much preferred brother had just died. Richard's reputation was not helped by his association with John of Gaunt, his main adviser and one of England's most hated landowners. Gaunt advised Richard to raise taxes.

Richard was also fighting unsuccessful campaigns against the French in the **Hundred Years War**. To help fund these campaigns he introduced a **poll tax**. In fact, he introduced three in as many years! By 1380, every person over the age of 15 had to pay four **groats** per year to the king. This was a massive increase from the one groat they had previously paid.

Furthermore, many priests started to preach about how the Church had been exploiting the peasants. The key people doing this were John Wyclif and John Ball. They

Key Words

Justice of the Peace   Hundred Years War
poll tax   groat   pardon

argued that the Church should not be charging **pardons** for sins and that the Church should not have so much property when others were starving.

In 1381, the peasants had had enough. They started a revolt against the system that they felt suppressed them. The Peasants' Revolt had begun.

▼ **D** *Adapted from one of John Ball's speeches, quoted in* The Chronicles of Froissart, *written c1400:*

> My good friends, things cannot go well in England until everyone is equal. They are dressed in velvet while we are forced to wear rags.

Fact

Historians sometimes add a 'c' before dates. This stands for 'circa', which means 'around' or 'approximately'.

Work

1. How did the Black Death arrive in England?
2. Why did the Black Death mean peasants could demand higher wages?
3. Why did King Edward III pass the Statute of Labourers?
4. a Make a list of as many causes of the Peasants' Revolt as you can think of.
   b In groups make colour coded cards of the causes to sort them into factors (political, social, economic and religious).
   c Use the cards to create a mind-map showing the causes of the revolt.
5. Were rats the most important cause of the Peasants' Revolt? Use your own knowledge and the sources to help you. Hint: when thinking about which cause was the most important, try to divide your answer into long- and short-term causes. You could even try to show how these causes link together.

3.2 The Peasants' Revolt of 1381

Life under the Statute of Labourers and an ever-increasing poll tax was hard for ordinary people. To make matters worse, there was a new king in June 1377, Richard II. He was young and inexperienced. Landowners, the Church and the king were taking lots of money from people by raising taxes. Many peasants were returning home from fighting in the Hundred Years War and were being forced back to their old lives — but were now paying far higher taxes. Disgruntled, many peasants refused to pay the poll tax. They threatened violence and decided to march to London, to take their grievances straight to the king. Would be listen?

Objectives

- **Identify** the aims of the Peasants' Revolt.
- **Compare** the actions of both the peasants and the king.
- **Evaluate** the tactics of the peasants.

'When Adam delved and Eve span'

The peasants were inspired by the preaching of John Ball who said, 'When Adam delved and Eve span, who was then a gentleman?' This reference to the creation of man and woman outlined in the Bible shows that there was no rich and poor, thus everyone was equal. The king had Ball arrested so his preaching couldn't influence any more people against the feudal system and the unfair distribution of wealth. The king was clearly worried.

Ball's arrest came too late however, as the peasants had had enough. Uprisings started in Essex and Kent; the men involved in these uprisings eventually joining forces. They were not necessarily angry with the king, but more with the oppressive system they lived under. They were more interested in removing bad priests and evil landowners, as these were the very people who directly exploited them.

The actions of the rebel peasants and the government

A The key areas and events in 1831, as the peasants made their way to London to see the king

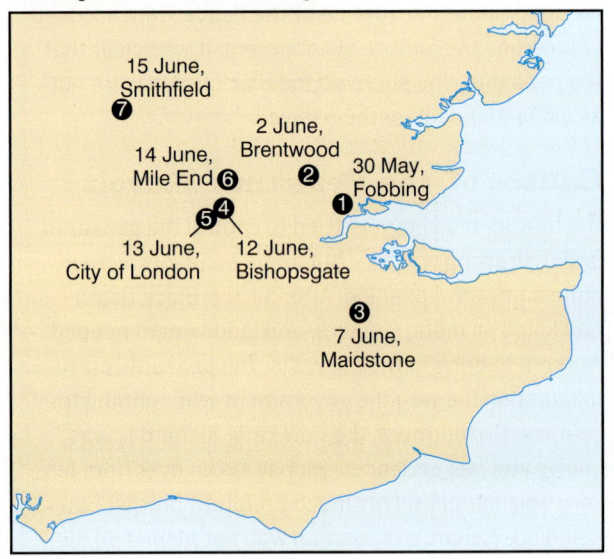

- 1. 30 May, Fobbing
- 2. 2 June, Brentwood
- 3. 7 June, Maidstone
- 4. 12 June, Bishopsgate
- 5. 13 June, City of London
- 6. 14 June, Mile End
- 7. 15 June, Smithfield

1. 30 May, Fobbing

Soldiers turn up to support the tax collector John Bampton who has come to collect the poll tax. The peasants refuse to pay and threaten Bampton with his life. Scared, he rides straight back to London. The villagers hide in the woods as they are worried they will be punished for their actions.

2. 2 June, Brentwood

Rebels from other villages join forces. When the Chief Justice is sent to the village to get what Bampton had failed to, the men return and threaten him with death. When the Chief Justice leaves, the men find Bampton's clerks and behead them. They start setting fire to the houses of Bampton's supporters.

3. 7 June, Maidstone

Peasants in Kent march to Maidstone. When they get there they hear a man called Wat Tyler speak; the rebels make him their leader. They also free John Ball from Maidstone prison, and storm Rochester Castle. They destroy tax records by burning down government buildings.

106 Chapter 3 Medieval revolt and royal authority

4 12 June, Bishopsgate

The men make it to the outskirts of London's city walls and set up camp. Leaving the Tower of London, the king sails to meet the peasants. When they see his barge there is so much shouting and booing that the king's men will not let him get off the boat. Convinced they will not breach the city walls, Richard II says he will meet the rebels on 17 June.

5 13 June, City of London

The rebels enter the through the city gates, opened by supporters. They storm the Savoy Palace of John of Gaunt and burn it to the ground. They kill foreign merchants and supporters of the king. However, not all the peasants are violent, as Wat Tyler has given explicit orders for the peasants to be peaceful. The king offers to meet the rebels and their leader at Mile End the next day.

6 14 June, Mile End

Wat Tyler meets the king and outlines the peasants' demands. The king is to give a royal pardon to all involved and all villeins are to be made freemen. The king agrees and asks the peasants to go home in peace. Some of the peasants go on another killing spree. These men also kill the Archbishop of Canterbury.

7 15 June, Smithfield

Richard II meets the rebels again. Tyler is bold and refuses to leave until the king agrees to his demands. He wants a full change to the system of law. He wants Church lands to be given to the people and to get rid of all bishops bar one. The king agrees. However, one of his men steps forward and kills Wat Tyler. The peasants are confused and some are ready to fight. The king rides forward shouting, 'Will you shoot your king? I am your leader, follow me!' The peasants follow the king out of London. The revolt is over.

▼ **SOURCE B** *An illustration from* The Chronicles of Froissart, *written c1400; Froissart was a monk who recorded the events of the revolt. This illustration shows the Archbishop of Canterbury being killed by the rebels.*

Practice Question

How useful is **Source B** to a historian studying the tactics used by the peasants during the revolt?

8 marks

Study Tip

What tactics does the source show you? Does it tell the whole story? You should focus on the content of the source and mine it for all the information you can. Then think about who produced it – can we trust that person?

Work

1. List the aims of the peasants during the revolt.
2. Create and complete a table with one column headed 'Peasants' actions' and the other headed 'King's actions'.
3. a Discuss with your partner whether you think the peasants used the correct tactics. Explain your answer.
   b Write a speech for Wat Tyler to deliver to the peasants on 13 June. Use your points from your discussion to help. Will you encourage violence or peaceful tactics?

Britain: Power and the people

3.3 The impact of the Peasants' Revolt

It was common for Medieval kings to go back on their word. King John and King Henry both went against the wishes of the people. It seemed to be happening again after the Peasants' Revolt. King Richard had made promises, and the peasants went back to their respective towns and villages. Their leader's head was put on a spike and supporters were hanged from the gallows. Some uprisings took place in other towns but they were easily squashed by local officials. There are many interpretations of the final minutes of the revolt at Smithfield and about the impact of the revolt on society. Did the revolt change anything? How do people view it now?

Objectives

- **Describe** the different interpretations of Wat Tyler's death.
- **Explain** the impact of the Peasants' Revolt.
- **Evaluate** interpretations of the revolt.

The murder of Wat Tyler

When the revolt was over Richard did not keep his promises. He stated, as kings had done before him, that he was forced to make these promises. The rebel leaders were rounded up and hanged. John Ball was hanged and then his body was cut into pieces. His head was stuck on a spike of London Bridge. Next to it was the head of Wat Tyler. There are many different interpretations of the killing of Tyler.

INTERPRETATION A A painting from 1460 showing the death of Wat Tyler; the king is painted twice, once watching the murder of Tyler and again talking to the rebels

SOURCE B Interpretation from *The Chronicles of Froissart*, written c1400; Froissart recorded the events of the revolt, but wasn't actually there to witness any of it:

> Tyler still kept up the conversation with the mayor. The mayor replied, 'I will not live a day unless you pay for your insolence.' Upon saying which he drew his sword and struck Tyler such a blow on the head as felled him. As soon as the rebel was down, he was surrounded on all sides so his own men might not see him.

SOURCE C Interpretation written by a monk in York, 1399; again this monk would not have been there, and is creating the account from word of mouth:

> Tyler dismounted his horse in front of the king, carrying his dagger. He called for some water and then spat it out in front of the king. Tyler then went to strike the king's valet with his dagger. The mayor of London tried to arrest Tyler and because of this Tyler stabbed the mayor with his dagger in the stomach.

INTERPRETATION D An engraving from around 1840 showing the death of Wat Tyler; this is a dramatic interpretation of his death, portraying Tyler as the victim

Short- and long-term impact of the revolt

The revolt was not a total failure. The poll tax was never repeated, although there were similar charges, and taxes were never as high again. Workers' wages began to rise, as the situation from before the revolt was still the same: there was still a lack of workers, so the peasants could demand higher wages. The landowners paid up, as they needed the workers. Also, parliament eventually gave in and stopped trying to control the peasants' wages.

The demands of the rebel peasants were further realised when some were able to buy their own land, because there was so much unused after the Black Death. This freed them from having to work the lord's land. Gradually peasants became independent and within 100 years the peasants were freemen. They had got what they wanted.

What does history say about the revolt?

The Peasants' Revolt is generally considered a significant event in history. It led to change for the peasants and was the first time ordinary people had started a revolt: this had previously been done only by barons and nobles. However, history is written by people with different opinions, which means some people think the revolt is more significant than others. This means we have different interpretations of it.

Some historians believe the revolt was unnecessary. Their interpretations suggest that society was already changing and that serfdom was coming to an end. **Socialist** historians believe the revolt was significant because it was the first working-class rebellion. Some take this further and present the peasants as politicised and organised. This, they believe, marked the beginning of English ideas of freedom.

Key Word

socialist

Extension

Research the connection between the Peasants' Revolt, the poll tax, and the Community Charge of 1989/1990–1993.

Work

1. a What are the different interpretations of Wat Tyler's death? Include brief quotations to support your answers.
   b Why might there be different interpretations of his death?
   c How does **Interpretation A** show the different views of Wat Tyler's death?
2. Explain the impact of the Peasants' Revolt.
3. Which interpretation of the Peasants' Revolt do you think is the most convincing?

Practice Question

Explain the significance of the Peasants' Revolt for the development of democracy and equality. **8 marks**

Study Tip

Refer to the results of the revolt at the time and how people have thought about it long after the event.

4.1 How did Henry change the Church?

Henry VIII became king in 1509. He is best known for having six wives and being desperate for a son to rule after him. His first wife, Catherine of Aragon, was unable to provide him with a son, so he planned to divorce her and marry Anne Boleyn. But Henry was unable to do so because, as a devout Catholic, he was not allowed to divorce without permission from the Pope. And the Pope would not allow it. However, Henry eventually got his divorce – and managed to change England forever in the process. How did he do it? What exactly did he change, and who did these changes affect?

Objectives

- **Outline** the problems Henry VIII had during his reign.
- **Explain** why the monasteries were useful to Henry.
- **Compare** different reactions to Henry's actions.

England before the Reformation

The Reformation was a religious movement in the 1500s that began as an attempt to reform the Roman Catholic Church. Many people believed that there was a problem with the Church's wealth and its influence in society. Even the king started to question the Church.

The Church had always been an important part of Medieval life. Monasteries were at the centre of many communities, acting as hotels, hospitals and refuges for the poor. Most people were happy with the role of the Church but others started to feel that the monasteries and nunneries were becoming too powerful. It was said that many people inside had forgotten their vows of poverty and were living a life of luxury, while people outside starved. These changing attitudes to the monasteries and the Catholic Church in general were further fuelled by the writings of Martin Luther in 1517.

Henry and the Reformation

Henry VIII was a devout Catholic but he was unhappy with the wealth and the power of the Church. Henry saw the Pope as a competing power. People would take direction from the Pope as the head of the Church, but Henry wanted the people of England to listen to him only. He was not a supporter of Luther and the new Protestant religion, but he used these new ideas to go against the Pope and, most importantly, to get a divorce from Catherine of Aragon. The Pope refused to give Henry a divorce, so Henry made himself the head of the Church of England through the Act of Supremacy, 1534. This gave him full control and he no longer had to pay taxes to the Pope in Rome.

Many people refused to recognise Henry as the head of the Church; most famously his Lord Chancellor, Thomas More. Henry had created a law, with the help of Thomas Cromwell, to make it treason to not accept Henry as the head of the Church. Before he was beheaded, More said that he died 'as the king's good servant, but God's first.'

Key Biography

Martin Luther (1483–1546)

- He became increasingly angry about the clergy selling indulgences for sin: this was when people would give the priests money to get forgiveness for their sins. He believed that Christians were saved through their own faith.
- He translated the Bible into German. His ideas spread throughout Europe and started the Protestant Reformation.

Key Biography

Thomas Cromwell (1485–1540)

- He was a blacksmith's son, and was well travelled.
- He became part of Henry VIII's court, soon becoming his most faithful servant. He helped secure Henry's divorce and make Henry wealthy again.
- Historians have differing views about him.

SOURCE A *Adapted from the Act of Supremacy, 1534:*

> The king, our sovereign lord, and his heirs and successors shall be taken, accepted and reputed the only supreme head on earth of the Church of England.

Dissolution of the monasteries

Henry's divorce was not the only problem he had. Although he had made himself head of the Church of England and had stopped sending taxes to the Pope, he was still spending far too much money. His conflict with the Pope had angered Catholics in other European countries, and he began to worry about invasion by these foreign Catholics. He therefore made sure every change he wanted was made through parliament. This way, he could blame his government for the changes.

Cromwell promised Henry that he would make him the richest king in Europe. One way to do this would be to take the money from the monasteries: these actions became known as the dissolution of the monasteries. The monasteries controlled a quarter of all the land in England and had a combined annual income of £200,000. This was nearly double that of the king. In 1536, parliament passed an act closing all small monasteries that had an annual income of less than £200. Cromwell then set up *Valor Ecclesiasticus*, which was an evaluation of monastery finances. He sent inspectors to the monasteries to see what they were spending their money on. If they were seen to not be run properly they would be closed down and the Crown would take the finances. Reports were sent to Cromwell, and if they were positive they were sent back to be rewritten in a way that showed them in a less positive light.

Responses to the changes

Not everyone was happy with the changes Henry made. The people of England were used to their king increasing taxes. They were used to quarrels with the Pope. They did not, however, support a complete break with Rome, leaving the king in full control.

Why were people unhappy about Henry's changes?

Rising prices
Prices normally stayed the same every year, but they continued to rise under Henry. People blamed his advisers.

Changes to religion
Many people disliked the changes made to the Church. They wanted the monasteries back and the Pope as head of the Church.

Landowners lost influence
Many landowners who had been advisers to the king fell out of favour after the divorce. They had been supporters of Catherine and felt pushed out. They blamed Cromwell.

Cromwell's power
Cromwell was seen as the creator of the new religious policies and he had helped Henry get a divorce from Catherine. Many of the landowners disliked him, as he was the son of a blacksmith and therefore seen as not good enough to advise the king.

Work

1. Why did Henry VIII want to be head of the Church?
2. Why did Henry let Thomas Cromwell make so many decisions?
3. Explain how the monasteries could solve Henry's problems.
4. Create a conversation between a peasant and a landowner. You should explain why the peasant is angry with Henry, and the same for the landowner. Do they agree with each other's points? Are there some points they disagree on?

Practice Question

Was religion the main factor that made Henry VIII want to take control of the English Church?

16 marks
SPaG: 4 marks

Study Tip

You will need to explain your answer with reference to religion and other factors. Consider the economic, political and personal factors. Can you create links between these factors? Does one have more importance than the others?

4.2 The Pilgrimage of Grace

By 1536, King Henry VIII had divorced Catherine of Aragon, married Anne Boleyn (who had a baby on the way), and had taken a firm grip of the Church. He had got what he wanted; he controlled the Church, and had a new wife and possibly a son. He had another surprise waiting for him though — an uprising. Peasants from Yorkshire started to march towards London. They wanted Henry to listen to their demands and return the Pope as the head of the Church. They also wanted the return of the monasteries. Did Henry return the monasteries to his people? How did the protestors present their demands?

Objectives
- **List** the demands of the pilgrims in 1536.
- **Explain** the causes of the Pilgrimage of Grace.
- **Compare** and contrast the rebellion with the Peasants' Revolt.

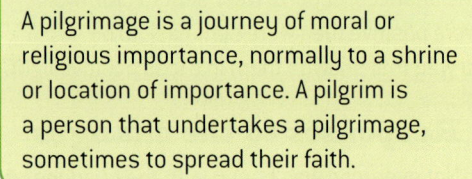

Fact
A pilgrimage is a journey of moral or religious importance, normally to a shrine or location of importance. A pilgrim is a person that undertakes a pilgrimage, sometimes to spread their faith.

SOURCE A *The banner under which the pilgrims marched, showing the five wounds of Christ*

Demands of the pilgrims

In 1536, a rebellion broke out in Yorkshire. It was an uprising by devout Christians who were worried and angered by the changes that Henry had made to the Church. They had to be careful because the change in law meant that criticism of religious changes was a criticism of the king. They could be charged for treason. They found a leader in a lawyer called Robert Aske. He was able to put the case together for the group to show that they were not against the king. In fact, Aske and his fellow protestors all believed in the social hierarchy and royal authority. They had no intention of challenging Henry. They just wanted him to:

- restore the monasteries (in the north of England the monasteries did important social work and were not as corrupt as some in the south)
- recognise the Pope as the head of the Church
- dismiss Cromwell and other ministers who were giving the king poor advice.

The king and others would be in no doubt of the purpose of this pilgrimage, known as the Pilgrimage of Grace, since the marchers carried a banner showing the five wounds of Christ. This uprising was about religion and was against those who were seen to be corrupting it.

SOURCE B *Adapted from a speech by Robert Aske, 1536:*

> The closing of the monasteries means that religious services will not be carried out, and the poor will not be looked after. The monasteries are much loved by the people.

Norfolk marches north

Throughout October 1536, the pilgrims captured key locations. The rebellion began in Lincoln with Lord Hussey, who had been a staunch supporter of Catherine. He, and others, wanted a removal of taxes in peacetime. Then York and Pontefract Castle, which had been held by Lord Darcy, a supporter of Henry, were captured. Darcy surrendered to the pilgrims and joined their campaign. By the end of October they had control of most of England, north of Cheshire and Lincolnshire.

Chapter 4 Popular uprisings against the Crown

▼ **INTERPRETATION C** *An engraving from 1870 showing marchers taking part in the Pilgrimage of Grace in 1536*

Henry was worried. However, he chose just the right man to represent him and negotiate with the pilgrims: the Duke of Norfolk. Norfolk was a Catholic and a critic of Cromwell. The king was sure he would be the man to deal with the pilgrims. On 27 October he met the pilgrims at Doncaster Bridge; he had an army of 8000 men, and Aske had one of 30,000. Norfolk reassured Aske that he would present a list of demands straight to Henry. The rebels took a month to draw up their demands. They were the same as before except this time they added that a parliament must meet in York. They now wanted better representation for the north.

Norfolk reassured Aske and the rebels that royal pardons would be given. Aske took off his pilgrim's badge and the rebels went home.

Aske and Henry

In December 1536, after the list of demands had been given to the king, Robert Aske spent the Christmas holiday with Henry at his palace in Greenwich.

▼ **SOURCE D** *From a quote by Henry VIII to Robert Aske, December 1536:*

> Be you welcome, my good Aske; it is my wish that here, before my council, you ask what you desire and I will grant it.

▼ **SOURCE E** *From Robert Aske's reply to Henry VIII, December 1536:*

> Sir, your majesty allows yourself to be governed by a tyrant named Cromwell. Everyone knows that if it had not been for him the 7000 poor priests I have in my company would not be ruined wanderers as they are now.

Henry did not disagree with Aske regarding Cromwell. He reassured Aske that he, and the other rebels, had his support. Meanwhile, news was reaching the rebels that the king was strengthening his garrison in the north: he had no intention of sticking to his word. The rebels decided to strike first.

The revolt breaks out again

In January 1537, castles in Hull, Beverley and Scarborough were attacked by the rebels. This gave Henry the excuse he needed to cancel the pardons. Norfolk travelled north again and a further rebellion took him to Carlisle. The rebels surrendered and 74 of them were hanged in their own gardens. Norfolk did not hang more because he felt they had been humiliated enough. The second wave of the rebellion had been squashed.

Work

1. a List the aims of the Pilgrimage of Grace
   b Pick the one you think is the most important. Explain why you picked this one.
2. Why was the Duke of Norfolk the right man to negotiate with the pilgrims?
3. Create a story board showing the causes of the Pilgrimage of Grace. You should think about the different types of causes and explain them with captions.
4. Which factor do you think was the most important for causing the Pilgrimage of Grace?
5. Draw a Venn diagram. One circle is for the Peasants' Revolt and the other is for the Pilgrimage of Grace. The overlap of the circles should show similarities between the rebellions.

Practice Question

Compare the Peasants' Revolt with the Pilgrimage of Grace. In what way were they similar?

8 marks

Study Tip

You should focus on causes, the methods of the rebels, and the king's responses. Plan out your answer so you can structure this carefully.

4.3 Impact of the rebellion

King Henry VIII had been challenged by the Catholic landowners who had lost their influence after his divorce from Catherine. He was challenged by peasants who were worried about the changes he was making to the Church. They wanted their monasteries back. The one uniting factor for these different social groups was their distrust and distain for one of Henry's advisers – a man named Thomas Cromwell. How did Cromwell deal with the rebels?

Objectives

- **Describe** the end of the Pilgrimage of Grace.
- **Explain** the impact of the rebellion.
- **Analyse** the role Cromwell played in key events.

Thomas Cromwell takes charge

In the aftermath of the Pilgrimage of Grace, Henry called for Aske, Darcy and Hussey. When they arrived in London they were immediately arrested. Cromwell took a harder line than Norfolk: he was adamant that all those who had gone against the king should be killed. Cromwell was keen to remain as Henry's most faithful servant, and he was also annoyed at people getting in the way of his reforms. Aske was killed in York on 12 July 1537. All local landowners were required to come and watch his execution. Darcy and Hussey had been beheaded the previous year in London. Lord Darcy, at his beheading, told Cromwell that the rebellion was his fault and warned him that there may be one noble left in the country that may take his head, like he had taken Darcy's and Hussey's.

The end of the monasteries

Henry's reaction to Pilgrimage of Grace sealed the fate on the monasteries. The campaign against smaller monasteries in 1536 now gave way to the dissolution of larger monasteries in 1539. Some abbots tried to resist the closures, for example, the Abbot of Glastonbury. He was dragged through the town, hanged, and had his head placed on a spike on the abbey gates. The monasteries were coming to an end.

Monastery land was bought by some landowners. Many monasteries were left empty, having been stripped of the gold and jewels by the monks. The doors, beams, lead and stained glass windows were taken by locals. It is thought that many Tudor houses still standing today have monastic beams in them.

▼ **SOURCE A** Many abbeys, such as Byland Abbey, were left in ruins after Henry's actions

▼ **SOURCE B** The Mary Rose, one of the first ships to be able to fire a full broadside of cannons; the ship was built in Portsmouth, 1509–10, and is thought to be named after King Henry VIII's sister Mary and the rose, the Tudor emblem

Henry gets what he wants

Court finances improved greatly after the pilgrimage, with the money from the monasteries. Henry spent this money developing the Royal Navy, building more ships like the *Mary Rose*, and reinforcing fortifications; he was still worried about foreign attack.

In the long term Henry consolidated his control in the north with the Council of the North. He increased the power of loyal families and secured the border with Scotland. In the short term Henry was convinced about the need for the end of the monasteries and was adamant that he should have control over all people and institutions.

No more rebellions took place during Henry's reign. He had dealt with the Pilgrimage of Grace with deceit and ruthlessness. The 200 executions that took place at the end of the uprising were a warning to those that dared to challenge Henry's authority. Even Thomas Cromwell was executed. He had fallen out of favour with the king and was charged with treason and corruption. One of the things Henry blamed Cromwell for was encouraging him to marry Anne of Cleves, his fourth wife, who was not to his liking. Cromwell was beheaded in July 1540: Darcy's prediction had come true. King Henry VIII now had full control of the Church and his country.

▼ **SOURCE C** *A woodcut showing Henry sitting on his throne with the Pope under his feet, as a foot stool*

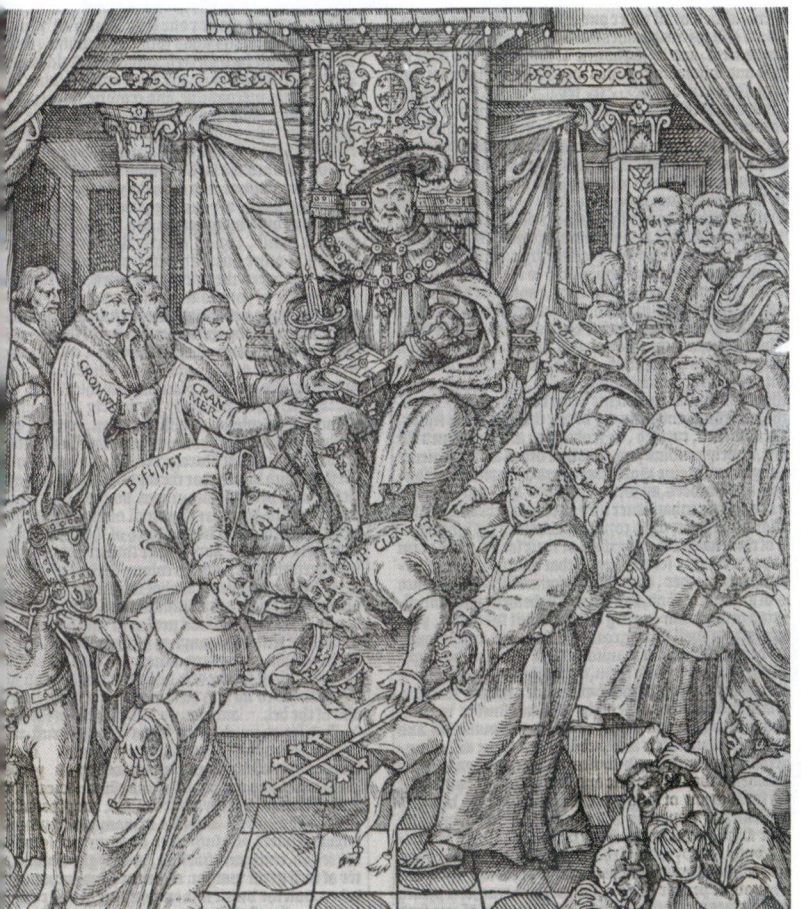

Extension

Wolf Hall and *Bring up the Bodies* are novels written by Hilary Mantel that explore the life of Thomas Cromwell. Many historians have criticised Mantel for distorting the truth, and accuse her of trying to rescue Cromwell from his bad reputation. Research this on the Internet to see what historians have said about the novels. Do you think her account stands up to what you know about Cromwell? You should read them and see what you think!

Work

1. **a** Describe the end of the Pilgrimage of Grace.
   b Would you say the pilgrimage was a defeat or a victory for the rebels?
2. **a** Explain the impact of the rebellion.
   b With two different colours, underline the short- and long-term impacts in your answer.
   c Go back and look at your comparison to the Peasants' Revolt. Do you think they are more similar, now you know the impact the pilgrimage had?
3. **a** Study **Source B** and **Source C**. Make notes about what each one shows you about the impact of the Pilgrimage of Grace.
   b Why were these sources created? Do they have a clear purpose?
   c Which source do you think is the most useful for a historian studying the impact of the Pilgrimage of Grace? Explain your answer.
4. Henry VIII called Cromwell his 'most faithful servant'. Do you think this was the case when you consider Cromwell's role in controlling the rebellion? Show both sides of the argument.

Britain: Power and the people

5.1A The causes of the English Revolution

In the seventeenth century England faced a civil war, with parliament fighting against the king. It involved Scotland and Ireland, and ended with parliament executing the king. This was a British revolution, and there were many reasons why it took place. What were the key causes of the revolution? Was the king ultimately to blame?

Objectives

- **Consider** the differences between King James I and King Charles I.
- **Categorise** the long- and short-term causes of the English Revolution.
- **Analyse** the different causes of the civil war to make a judgement.

James I & VI

When Elizabeth died in 1603, James VI of Scotland became James I of England and, for the first time, Scotland and England shared the same monarch. James was an extravagant king who spent money unwisely, and this led to tension with parliament when they refused to give him any more money or raise it through taxes. They knew James would give the funds to his favourites at court. However, one area that James succeeded at was religion. He managed to keep the majority of Catholics and Protestants content throughout his reign.

Charles I

When Charles I became king in 1625 he was keen to keep order in his court. He believed in the **divine right** of kings and felt that the royal court should be removed from everyday life. He believed he had been appointed by God and did not want many people involved in the decisions about the country. Where his father had been open and had many in his court, Charles closed the doors to allow only a privileged few. He wanted to make decisions that suited him without being challenged. He made the Duke of Buckingham a favourite (he had also been a favourite of James), which alarmed parliament because of the influence Buckingham had over the king. Charles responded by simply dissolving parliament in 1629, and did not call it for another 11 years. Some people refer to this as the period of personal rule but others call it the 'Eleven Years' **Tyranny**'.

▼ **SOURCE A** Anthony van Dyck's painting of Charles I, painted 1637–38

▼ **INTERPRETATION B** Adapted from A History of England, written in 1920 by the historian James Oliphant; he writes about Charles's personality:

> Charles I was a handsome man with cultivated tastes, but he was unfit for the position of king. He was too stupid and cold-hearted to understand or sympathise with the feelings of the people, and events were to prove that he was hopelessly obstinate, self-centred, and untrustworthy.

Foreign policy and the economy

King Charles, like King James before him, had a persistent problem: money. They both needed lots of it from parliament to fight wars, specifically with Spain. James was refused this money as he spent much of it on gifts for his favourites. Charles was refused it because parliament felt they couldn't trust

116 Chapter 5 Divine right and parliamentary authority

him. There were concerns about the sincerity of his religious tendencies; not helped by his marriage to a Catholic. There was also a fear that he would use the money to become independent from parliament. Charles, who believed it was his divine right to have the money, introduced a tax known as 'Ship Money' in 1637. This was a tax that was normally paid by those in coastal towns as a means of raising money to build the navy. Charles made everyone pay the tax. Parliament was concerned about Ship Money because it could make Charles financially independent and therefore able to make decisions without consulting parliament.

People refused to pay Ship Money. One Member of Parliament, John Hampden, refused and was taken to court. He was narrowly convicted, and the case publicised the opposition towards Charles and his personal rule.

Tensions over religion

After Henry VIII's changes to the Church, England had gradually become more Protestant. However, there were still many Catholics in England – many of them worshipping in secret – and some Protestants regarded them as a threat. After all, there were Catholic plots against Queen Elizabeth, and the famous Gunpowder Plot of 1605 was a Catholic attempt to kill Charles' father, James. Religion was a contentious issue in the seventeenth century.

Charles was not Catholic but he did marry a Catholic princess from France, Henrietta Maria. When Buckingham was killed in 1628, she became Charles' closest adviser. The people of England were scared of her influence and what this could mean for their Church.

The person who went on to have the most influence over religion in England was William Laud. He was made Archbishop of Canterbury in 1633 and felt the same as Charles about bringing conformity back to the Church. Laud was not Catholic, but he was Arminian, which meant he thought people should worship in a similar way to Catholics. For example, he wanted the church clergy to be more separate from the congregation and to be dressed in robes that showed their importance; he also wanted churches to be more decorated, with candles, crosses, statues and paintings.

Laud's changes met so much opposition because many **Puritans** – who were Protestants who wanted the king to reverse the **Laudian** reforms – had become prominent in parliament. They were vocal in their opposition. One famous case of opposition was from three men: Prynne, Bastwick and Burton, who wrote a **pamphlet** criticising the Church. The men were tried in the **Star Chamber**, which had become a substitute for parliament during Charles' personal rule. It was used against anyone who spoke out against the king and Laud, and was known for being corrupt because it always came down on the side of the king. Prynne, Bastwick and Burton were punished as thieves would be: **pilloried**, their faces branded, and their ears cut off.

What Laud and Charles had not expected was the widespread support for the men. When they were released from prison they were met by a large cheering crowd, and when their ears were cut off people crammed to dip their handkerchiefs in the blood. These men were seen as heroes.

Key Words

divine right   tyranny   Purtian   Laudian
pamphlet   Star Chamber   pilloried

▼ **SOURCE C** *A cartoon from c1635, showing the Archbishop of Canterbury, William Laud, choosing a meal made from the ears of Puritans rather than food fit for a prince*

Work

1. a Write three things that you know about James I & VI.
   b Write three things you know about Charles I.
   c Are there any ways that the kings are different?
2. Explain the grievances that parliament had with King Charles. Try to categorise these into economic, religious and political grievances.
3. a What information does **Source C** give us about the problems people had with Charles?
   b Why was this cartoon created? What was its purpose?

Britain: Power and the people   117

5.1B The causes of the English Revolution

The Scottish rebellion and the Covenanters

Charles' changes in religion also caused unrest in Scotland. The Scots had always had their own Church which by this time was **Presbyterian**, which is a type of Protestantism. However, in 1637, the king insisted that everyone in Scotland should use the new Laudian prayer book. This relied on the **catechism** – religious instruction from the priest – and moved away from the Protestant method of personal worship. There were riots in St Giles' Cathedral in Edinburgh: the Scots would not be told how to worship. In 1638, they signed an agreement called a covenant, saying they would not accept the changes. The people who signed it and its supporters became known as the Covenanters. When Charles sent an army to Scotland in 1639, the Covenanters defeated it. They then invaded England.

SOURCE A *Rioting at a church service in Scotland, as worshippers reacted angrily to the king's proposed changes to worship in Scotland*

The Short Parliament and continued opposition

Charles needed more money if he was going to defeat the Scots. Eleven years after he had dissolved parliament, he needed to ask it to meet again, in April 1640. Parliament agreed to provide Charles with funds to fight the Scots, but only with conditions. He had to promise not to pass laws without parliament's agreement, not to raise unpopular taxes, and to stop Laud's religious changes. This parliament was called the Short Parliament as it lasted only a month. Charles would not give in to parliament's demands.

The Earl of Strafford

One of Charles' favourites was Thomas Wentworth, the Earl of Strafford. He had been sent to Ireland to keep control. There was tension in Ireland between Catholics and Protestants in social and political life. Many of the Protestants were from Scotland and England, and had been originally sent to Ireland by James and Charles to keep order and prevent any rebellions; these postings were known as plantations.

Parliament was not happy about Strafford's control in Ireland. He had a strong and loyal army and parliament was concerned that Charles would try to bring this army to England and use it against the English. When parliament refused to give Charles the funds to fight the Scots, Strafford encouraged Charles to rule England on his own, without parliament.

The Long Parliament

Another parliament was called by Charles in November 1640. Charles was running out of options and was keen to defeat the Scots and restore order. He knew he needed parliament.

B *The demands of parliament, November 1640, and what the king had agreed to by the summer of 1641*

Parliament's demands:	The king agreed that:
• Wentworth and Laud must be removed. • Ministers should be appointed from parliament to advise Charles. • The king must get rid of the Star Chamber. • Parliament must meet regularly. • No taxes without parliament's approval. • Reversal of Laudian reforms.	• Strafford was executed and Laud was imprisoned. • Some of Charles' critics were appointed as his advisers. • Courts of the Star Chamber were abolished. • Parliament would meet every three years. • The Long Parliament could be dissolved by Charles without its permission. • Ship Money was made illegal.

Many people were convinced that the agreements would mark an end to the unrest. However, in August 1642 the English Civil War began. What led to this?

Rebellion in Ireland

When Strafford returned to England in 1640, riots broke out in Ireland. Thousands of Protestants were killed by Catholics. Many people in England thought that Charles supported the rebellion: they saw it as a Catholic plot. Parliament was willing to give money to suppress the Irish rebellion but they did not want Charles in charge of the army. Despite Charles' response to parliament of, 'By God! Not for an hour!', parliament took control of the army. The king was furious.

1642 and the Five Members

By 1642, relations had deteriorated again between the king and parliament. John Pym, a leading opponent of the king, presented the Grand Remonstrance This was a list of grievances towards Charles, and was the straw that broke the camel's back. Charles would not be made of a fool of by parliament. He raised an army and marched to parliament to arrest the five men – the Five Members – who led the opposition. They had already escaped but now everyone knew how far Charles would go to protect himself. This was even more proof that he was a tyrant who would not listen to the people.

▼ **INTERPRETATION C** *An engraving, from 1803, showing Charles I attempting to arrest the Five Members*

Key Words

Presbyterian   catechism

Work

1 a Put the events from 1637 to August 1642 on a timeline.
   b Above the timeline, describe the event; below it, explain why it would cause unrest.
   c Pick the event that you think was the spark for the English Civil War.

2 It has been said that Charles' problem was not England but how he dealt with Scotland. How far do you agree?

Extension

Research the lives of each of the Five Members. Who were they and what happened to them – Hampden, Haselrig, Holles, Pym and Strode?

Practice Question

Was religion the main factor in causing the English Civil War?

16 marks
SPaG: 4 marks

Study Tip

You need to explain your answer with reference to religion and other factors. Plan out your answer with all the different events and people you will talk about – see how many link to religion and how many link to other factors. Is there a difference between the short- and long-term factors?

Britain: Power and the people

5.2 The English Civil War and the role of the New Model Army

In August 1642, Charles was in Nottingham. He called on his loyal supporters, and declared war on parliament. England was now at war, with itself! The English Civil War had begun. For the next six years parliament and the king fought each other using their loyal forces. Mothers, sons, fathers and daughters fought in a quest to win the war, even if it meant fighting against each other. What were they fighting for? How did they fight the war?

Objectives

- **Define** the different sides of the English Civil War.
- **Explain** the key events of the civil war.
- **Evaluate** the role of the New Model Army in the civil war.

Who fought whom?

The war was fought on two sides: the Roundheads (parliament) against the Cavaliers (royalists). It is generally agreed that people's social class affected who they supported. The wealthy landowners supported the king, as a way to show personal loyalty and to keep in place the social structure they benefited from. The middle classes and peasant workers supported parliament, as there was a less rigid social hierarchy in parliament.

There were also clear geographical allegiances. The king's support was mostly from the north, and parliament had support in the south and in London. This was partially due to a merchant class (traders and business men, for example) who were not happy about the taxes Charles had been imposing.

Religious and political reforms brought in by Charles gave many people good reason to go against him and support parliament. Furthermore, many people simply felt that Charles' personality did not make him a good king.

There were reports that some families divided their loyalties so that no matter who won, they would be on a winning side. Many poorer people were forced to support whoever their lord supported.

Propaganda as a tactic

The war started with a draw at the Battle of Edgehill, 1642. The king tried to take London but failed, and withdrew to Oxford. Both sides fought using **cavalry** and **infantry**, and used tactics that had been seen in many battles before.

The king's nephew, Prince Rupert, was one of the most prominent royalist commanders. He led successful campaigns against parliamentary forces and this earned him a bad reputation among the Roundheads.

To combat his successes, parliamentary forces created **propaganda** against Rupert and his trusty dog, Boy, who would accompany him into battle. Propaganda is still used today; it is designed to wear the opponent down and make people turn against them. This worked in the case of Rupert, as it made people think he was weak; it created the idea that the king was weak. Look at the following examples of propaganda and consider why they would have been created.

▼ **A** The land held by Charles I and key battles of the English Civil War

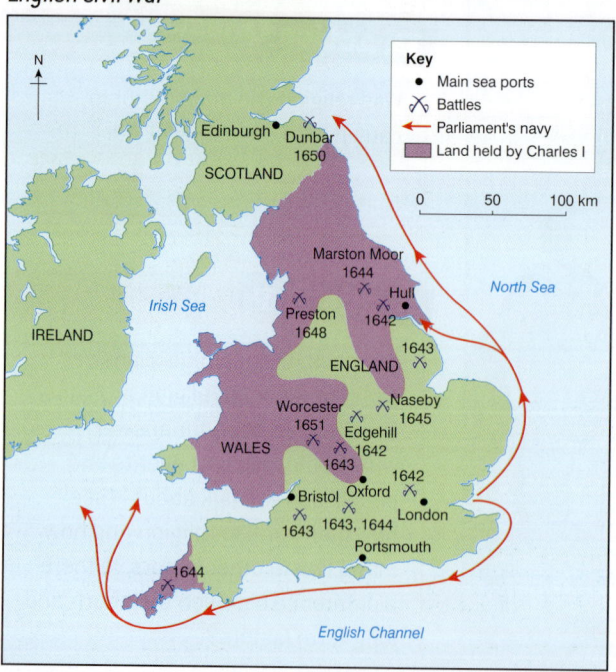

▼ **SOURCE B** *A Puritan propaganda drawing from 1644 showing royalist forces murdering women and children*

▼ **SOURCE C** *A woodcut showing Prince Rupert hiding in a bean field at the Battle of Marston Moor, 1644, with the dog Boy lying dead in the battlefield*

▼ **SOURCE D** *A drawing showing parliamentary forces smashing up a church*

Key Words

cavalry   infantry   propaganda

The New Model Army and Naseby, 1645

It is important to remember that not all parliamentarians wanted the full removal of the monarchy. They just wanted the removal of royal reforms. This attitude angered Oliver Cromwell. He was the Member of Parliament for Cornwall and had been leading the Roundheads against the Cavaliers, with Thomas Fairfax. Fairfax was a lord who had once worked with Charles to fight the Scots; he joined the parliamentary forces in 1642.

Cromwell was committed to removing the king. He knew that the Battle of Marston Moor could have been a defeat for his side and he did not want that to be the case again. He trained a new army which would be known as the New Model Army. He recruited men based on their ability, rather than their privilege. The army was disciplined and lived by a strict religious and moral code. The men were not allowed to drink or swear.

This army was used for the first time at the Battle of Naseby in 1645. The New Model Army, with 14,000 men, outnumbered the king, with 9000 men. They defeated the royalist cavalry by slowly approaching, rather than charging. They overcame the royalist infantry by manoeuvring behind them and attacking from the rear. Naseby was the end of the king's last great army. The New Model Army, under Cromwell, went on to capture Bristol and then Oxford in 1646. There was now little doubt about who would win the war.

> **Fact**
>
> Women played a big part in fighting the civil war. They mostly worked as nurses but they did defend castles from enemy forces. There are accounts that at Marston Moor, Jane Ingleby of Ripley Castle charged with the royalist forces.

Work

1. Create a profile for each side during the war. You should include details of location, religion and social class.

2. Copy and complete the table below for **Sources B, C** and **D**. Which source is the best for finding out about the civil war?

Source	What does it tell us?	Who is winning?	Why was it produced?

3. Could parliament have won the war without the New Model Army? Try to show both sides of the argument.

Britain: Power and the people

5.3 Were the English right to kill their king?

The king had tried to restore his control over England and Scotland but Cromwell's New Model Army proved too strong. Charles was captured in 1647 by the Scots in Nottinghamshire, and imprisoned. He would go on trial accused of treason. The king was killed on a cold January day in 1649. Why did parliament feel the only option was **regicide**? Did everyone agree? Who ruled now the king was dead?

Objectives
- **Describe** Charles I's execution.
- **Explore** the reasons why the king was executed.
- **Assess** the evidence to make a judgement about the execution.

Second Civil War
While Charles was imprisoned he was keen to negotiate with parliament to secure a peaceful end to their disagreements. However, at the same time, he was writing to the Scottish parliament to convince them to raise arms against the English parliament and the New Model Army. He promised them a Presbyterian Church in England. The Scots did raise an army against Cromwell and so the Second Civil War began. The two sides met at the Battle of Preston, 1648. The Scots were defeated and Charles had proved he could not be trusted.

The Rump Parliament
In December 1648, the regiment of Colonel Thomas Pride surrounded the Houses of Parliament and refused entry to Members of Parliament who were known to support negotiations with the king. Thomas Pride was a soldier in the civil war and had fought with Cromwell against the Scots. His actions became known as 'Pride's **Purge**', and meant the king would stand trial with no supporters. The remaining members formed a parliament that was known as the Rump Parliament.

The trial of Charles I
Charles was called before parliament where a special commission had been put in place to try him for treason. However, out of the 135 commissioners due to attend, only 68 turned up. They were scared, as they had openly fought against him; this was not the way society worked. Even Thomas Fairfax did not attend. His wife did, and is reported to have supported the king. For many people things had gone too far. However this was not the case for Oliver Cromwell. When Charles walked into court Cromwell said, 'I tell you we will cut his head off with the crown upon it.'

Another problem parliament encountered was that Charles refused to give a plea – he would not say whether he was guilty or not guilty. He said parliament had no right to act as judge and jury. They could not try the king for treason.

On the second day, the court president, John Bradshaw, allowed the king to speak. They exchanged angry words and Bradshaw ordered the king removed. Bradshaw must have known that there was a chance that proceedings would get heated as he wore a specially made bulletproof hat!

SOURCE A King Charles responded to the charges against him:

> I would know by what power I am called here. I want to know by what authority, I mean lawful. Remember I am your king, your lawful king.

With no progress yet made, on 24–27 January witness statements were heard – none in support of Charles. The court heard that Charles:

- was guilty of starting the war by trying to raise an army in Nottingham
- approved of the ill-treatment of parliamentary forces during the war – calling his own subjects enemies
- was plotting with his son to start another war while negotiating with parliament.

On 27 January 1649, parliament found King Charles I guilty of treason and sentenced him to death. Bradshaw justified this by saying that Charles had not done his duty by calling regular parliaments, attacking the basic liberties of the country. Charles would be beheaded.

SOURCE B An engraving showing the trial of Charles I

Execution

At 10:00am on 30 January 1649, the king was taken to Whitehall to be executed. Parliament made Charles wait hours. This was partly down to the executioners not turning up – they were too scared to be the one to kill the king – and partly down to **legislation**. Parliament had to secure a law that said no new monarch could be installed on the king's death. The axe fell and the English Revolution was over.

SOURCE C A painting of the execution of Charles I

Was Charles a danger to democracy?

People were motivated by many factors to support the execution of the king. There were religious, political and moral objections to the way Charles had been ruling. As far as the soldiers were concerned, Charles' defeat in battle was a sign that God was against him. Other people wanted an end to the taxes they had endured under his reign. Many enjoyed the new sense of freedom – ordinary men could now have influence too. Cromwell described the king's execution as a cruel necessity.

Key Words

regicide   purge   legislation

SOURCE D Adapted from The History of the Rebellion, written by the Earl of Clarendon and published in 1702; this was the first full history of the civil war; Clarendon sat in parliament and was a supporter of the king:

> It is most certain that, in that very hour when he was thus wickedly murdered in the sight of the sun, he was the worthiest gentleman, the best master and Christian.

SOURCE E Adapted from a contemporary pamphlet about Charles' death:

> Even the crucifying of our blessed saviour did not equal this, and Christ was yet judged at a lawful court.

Work

1. **a** Write an account of the king's execution from either a royalist or a parliamentarian viewpoint. Think about key dates, times and people.
   b Swap books with someone who wrote from the other point of view. How are the accounts different?
2. Put the king on trial. In groups allocate roles and play out the trial of Charles I. Remember to focus on why he is being tried. Does everyone have the same reasons?
3. Parliament was right to sentence the king to death. How far do you agree?

Practice Question

Explain the significance of the execution of Charles I.   **8 marks**

Study Tip

Try to explain that people at the time realised that the king's execution was a historic event.

Britain: Power and the people   123

5.4 How should Cromwell be remembered?

The Commonwealth was the name for the republic under the leadership of parliament after Charles' death. With Charles dead, the parliamentary army was the strongest force in the Commonwealth and its leader, Oliver Cromwell, the most powerful man. Cromwell is one of the most disputed characters in history. The opinions of him tend to change with shifting political events. When, in the nineteenth century, Britain moved towards a democracy and parliament became more important, historians became more sympathetic towards Cromwell. However, during the time of the restoration of the monarchy under Charles II, Cromwell was regularly depicted in royalist propaganda as the devil. Many people in Ireland have their own interpretations of Cromwell too. So how should he be remembered?

Objectives

- **Identify** the different views of Cromwell.
- **Analyse** the interpretations of Cromwell.
- **Compare** and contrast the Protectorate to earlier parliaments.

Fact

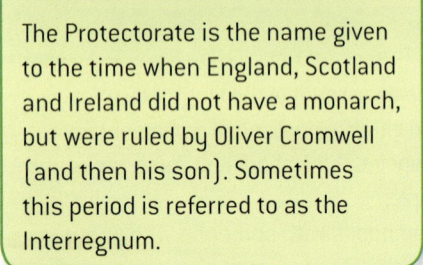

The Protectorate is the name given to the time when England, Scotland and Ireland did not have a monarch, but were ruled by Oliver Cromwell (and then his son). Sometimes this period is referred to as the Interregnum.

Cromwell and the Commonwealth

Positive views of Cromwell's rule?

There were many reasons people supported Cromwell. For example, he won wars against the Dutch and the Spanish and restored England's reputation abroad, and he introduced the Navigation Act in 1651, which stated that any ship coming into or leaving England had to be English. People were free to worship in any way they liked, and many ordinary people felt that Cromwell was on their side.

SOURCE A Samuel Cooper's painting of Cromwell, 1656. Cromwell is said to have told Cooper to paint him exactly as he saw him, 'warts and all'.

SOURCE B Written by a bishop, 50 years after the Protectorate:

> Cromwell would rather have taken a shepherd's staff than the Protectorship. Nothing went more against his feelings than a show of greatness. But he saw it was necessary at that time to keep the nation from falling into extreme disorder.

SOURCE C Although Cromwell had always declined the Crown he was given a state burial on his death in 1658. This painting was produced in 1659. It shows Cromwell wearing the crown and holding the royal sceptre and orb.

Negative views of Cromwell's rule?

Cromwell didn't please everyone. He appointed Major Generals to the 11 districts he created. People resented their presence because they kept such strict control on many aspects of life: they even tried to stop Christmas celebrations. The Levellers, a religious group who believed in equality, were imprisoned by Cromwell, and their leaders were killed. In Ireland, Cromwell laid siege to the town of Drogheda, and even when the townspeople surrendered he killed them – women and children included. Land was taken from Catholics in Ireland and given to Protestants, so England would always have allies in Ireland.

▼ **SOURCE D** *A Dutch drawing of Cromwell dressed as a king, with Charles I being executed in the background. The drawing was made at the time the Dutch were fighting a war against England.*

Positive or negative views of Cromwell's rule?

Some aspects of Cromwell's rule can be viewed as positive or negative! For example, Cromwell ended up with more power than Charles, and he secured his son as his successor. He felt that his victories since Naseby meant it was God's **providence** that he should be in charge, and sinful activities were banned to ensure that the Commonwealth was Godly.

Challenges to the Commonwealth

There were many challenges to Cromwell's Protectorate and from this emerged a political and religious **radicalism** that had never existed before. The civil war saw the development of many Protestant groups, which would challenge Cromwell's authority. The biggest challenge came, however, from a political group. This group was the Levellers. They wanted a reform to political representation for the men who had fought in the New Model Army. Cromwell met with them and their leader, John Lilburne, during the Putney Debates in 1647 where their demands were heard. Support for them soon decreased and Lilburne was imprisoned. Cromwell was able to rule for 10 years.

The end of Cromwell and the Commonwealth

When Cromwell died in 1658 his son, Richard, took over the role. However, Richard was not interested in politics and resigned in 1659. In 1660, Charles II rode into London and was crowned king of England, Scotland and Ireland.

Cromwell's body was dug up from its grave and hung in Tyburn. His head was placed on a spike where it stayed for decades. Most people were happy to have a king back on the throne.

Key Words

providence   radicalism

Work

1   a   Pick the top three things you think show Cromwell in a good light, and the top three things that show him in a bad light.
    b   Share your lists with your partner. Discuss your choices.
2   Study **Sources C** and **D**. Explain the impression that each one gives of Cromwell.

Practice Question

Compare the achievements of the Protectorate to the rule of Simon de Montfort. In what ways were they similar?   **8 marks**

Study Tip

Separate your points into political and religious outcomes and put all the key information into these factors. Think about how long they lasted and what kind of opposition they had.

6.1A What was the impact of the American Revolution?

Britain had become one of the most powerful countries during the seventeenth century and used this power to take over other parts of the world, including large parts of North America. However, by the mid-1700s the people of America no longer want to be part of the British **Empire**. They considered themselves American, and in the late 1700s fought a war against the British; and they won an unlikely victory. Why did these people want to be free of British rule?

Objectives

- **Explain** why the colonists in America were unhappy with British rule.
- **Analyse** the defeat of the British to show the consequences of this.
- **Compare** and contrast the revolution with past events.

Long-term causes of the American Revolution

The control of large areas of land in North America had been fought over by Britain and France for many years. Britain eventually defeated the French and used the **colonies** there to make money, growing crops like cotton, tobacco and sugar to sell all over the world. By the early 1700s, there were 13 separate English colonies in North America, and by 1775 there were around 2.5 million settlers living in them. Many people also made huge amounts of money buying and selling the slaves that were used in the colonies to farm the land.

Countries such as Britain wanted empires because they could tax the people who lived in the colonies, and ensure that they bought British goods. However, many of the **colonists** in America, despite being of British descent, now considered themselves American.

The American colonists started to resent the economic support they had to give to Britain. One tax they resented was to pay for the British army. The British felt it was acceptable to tax the Americans as the army had, after all, been 'protecting' the colonists from other foreign powers. Throughout the 1760s, the American colonists were also forced to comply with Navigation Acts, which ensured that only British goods were imported into America. There could be no trading with other countries. If Britain produced something, the colonists could not buy it from another country.

In addition, the colonists felt bossed about by the British because they were given boundaries on the land that they could not cross. The British had made these agreements with the **Native Americans** without consulting the colonists. These boundaries stopped them accessing good farmland: the colonists wanted to have more of a say.

No taxation without representation: short-term causes of the revolution

The citizens of America were ruled directly from Britain yet they had no representatives in parliament in London. So they felt there was no-one to speak up for them. Throughout this thematic study, from the barons to the working class, this is a common thread – the desire for representation. People wanted a voice in what was done to them and for them, especially if they were expected to pay for it through taxes! So the colonists, who had started to identify as American rather than as British, stated: No taxation without representation!

One key event considered the spark of the fight against the British was the Boston Massacre of 1770. When some anti-British colonists jeered, and threw snowballs and sticks at the British army on 5 March, the army opened fire and killed some of them. Unrest in Boston continued to grow when some of the colonists, unhappy with the heavily taxed British tea they were forced to buy, boarded a ship and poured the tea out into the harbour. This became known as the Boston Tea Party. This act of defiance scared the British and in retaliation they closed the port of Boston.

By 1775, anti-British feeling was so strong that when the British army tried to seize a supply of gunpowder in Concord they were fired on by 20,000 'minutemen'. These men were local farmers, clerks and ploughboys who had had enough of British rule. This became known as the Lexington incident and marked the start of the revolution against the British.

SOURCE A A 1789 painting of the Boston Tea Party, showing Americans throwing the teaship cargoes into the river

Key Words

empire   colony   colonist
Native American   Congress

Declaration of Independence

The Americans were quick to organise themselves. They met in **Congress** to decide what to do, and by 1775 they had made George Washington the leader of their army.

In 1776 Congress had a meeting in Philadelphia where a Declaration of Independence was issued. This stated that the 13 colonies were free and that all control from Britain had ended. This was the easy step; the hard part would come in making the declaration a reality. There would be seven years of fighting before the colonists were victorious and an independent America was a reality.

SOURCE B Adapted from the American Declaration of Independence, written by Thomas Jefferson in 1776:

> We hold these truths to be self-evident, that all men are created equal, that they are endowed by their Creator with certain unalienable rights, that amongst these are Life, Liberty and the Pursuit of Happiness. That whenever any Government becomes destructive of these ends, it is the right of the people to alter or abolish it.

Extension

Look back to Chapter 1. In what ways is the American Declaration of Independence similar to Magna Carta? Do you think the Americans are right to compare the two? Think about the quote on the monument at Runnymede.

Work

1. a Make a list of the reasons the colonists were dissatisfied with British rule. Use **Source B** to help you.
   b Colour code your reasons – the factors for unrest – into economic, social and political factors.
2. a What taxes were the colonists forced to pay?
   b In what ways did the colonists lack representation?
   c Do you think the British government understood how serious the colonists were?
3. a In your groups make a list of the rules you would have in the Declaration of Independence.
   b How similar is your declaration to the section in **Source B**?

Britain: Power and the people   127

6.1B What was the impact of the American Revolution?

It would be astonishing if one of the biggest and best-trained armies in the world were to be defeated by a group of American farmers and clerks. How could this happen, and if it did, what would it mean for Britain's imperial power?

Yorktown and the defeat of the British

The British had won most of the battles during the American War of Independence. They had a world-class army that was well trained and well supplied. However, many of the battles took place in forest and mountain areas, in land the British did not know well.

▼ **C** *A map showing some of the War of Independence battles and the movements of the British, Americans and French that resulted in the British being trapped at Yorktown*

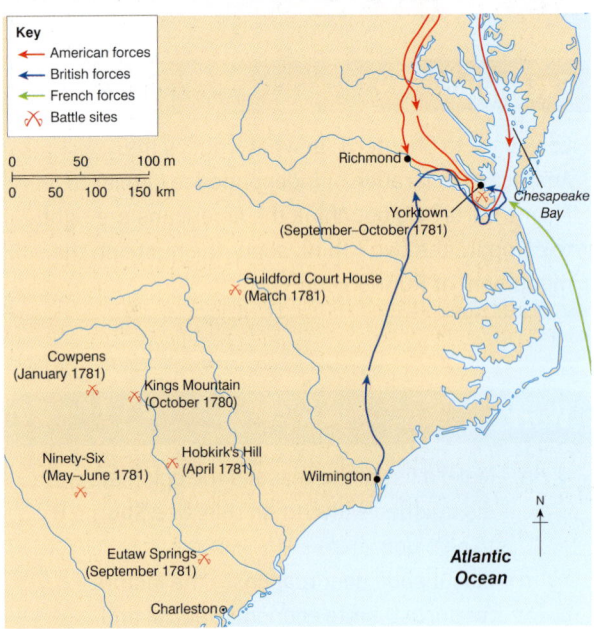

The decisive battle of the war was at Yorktown in 1781. The American troops, who were perceived to be weak, had reinforced themselves with 3000 extra men. Added to this they had the support of the French, who had secured control of the waters around Yorktown. This was important as the British needed to get their supplies in from the sea.

The British commander, Charles Cornwallis, unwittingly helped the Americans by moving his troops onto a **peninsula** as they awaited supplies. They were now cut off and in a weak position. George Washington, sensing the advantage he could have, attacked the British. With few weapons and no supplies the British were forced to surrender.

The battle at Yorktown saw the immediate defeat of the British and the end of the War of Independence. America was now an independent country, and proclaimed itself the 'land of the free'. This was an unprecedented victory. It showed what could be achieved with a clear cause against an opponent that underestimated your ability.

▼ **SOURCE D** *An engraving from 1781 showing British General Charles Cornwallis surrendering to General George Washington, ending America's War of Independence*

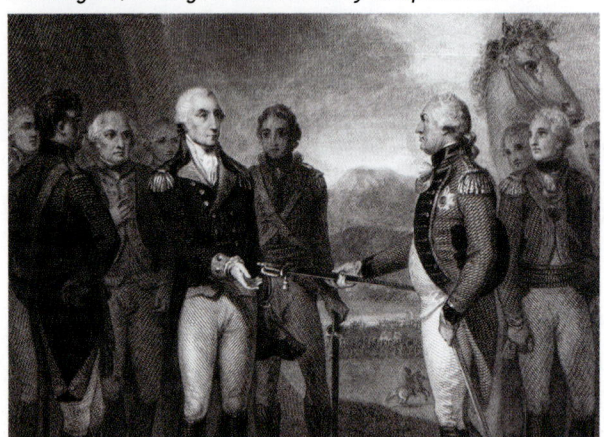

Consequences for America

The Americans were delighted with their victory. Using their determination they had defeated the most powerful country in the world. However not all of the people in America were happy with the outcome, and many moved north to Canada which was still under the control of Britain.

The Americans set up their own system of government with a written set of rules (called a constitution), a parliament (Congress) and a President. This system still exists today. Americans now had the representation they desired.

However, not everything was perfect. Many poor farmers, who could not afford to buy their land, could not vote. The rich were represented but not the poor. Furthermore, slavery still existed and Native Americans were widely discriminated against: this was not equality. However by the early twentieth century, America had developed into the most powerful independent country in the world.

Consequences for Britain

Britain had spent a lot of money on the war and had lost a lot of men. The involvement of France on the side of the revolution had worsened relations between the two powers. Britain was able to use the strength of its navy to make up for the loss of America by colonising other parts of the world. America had been used as a **penal colony**, where criminals were sent to work on the **plantations** alongside **indentured servants** who worked to pay off the cost of their passage across the Atlantic. Britain now turned its focus to Australia and New Zealand as a place to send convicts.

Relations with America improved as the years went by and the two countries started to trade with each other. The loss of America was not an issue by the late nineteenth century because by then Britain had a colony in every time zone of the world. The sun never set on the British Empire. And although America had once been considered the most important of the colonies it was soon replaced by India: the 'jewel in the crown'. The main problem for Britain's leaders was that the idea of overthrowing authority was one that might spread to Britain itself. With a growing working population this was possible.

▼ **E** *The extent of the British Empire by 1921*

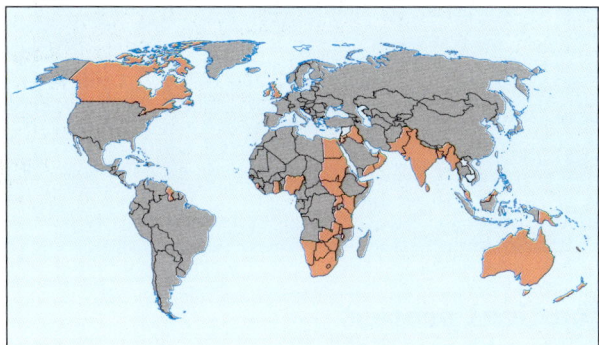

Consequences for the world

The success of America and its fight against British authority inspired one of the most important events in European history. The French were fed up with their king, Louis XVI. People were starving while he and his wife ate lavish breakfasts and lived in luxurious palaces. The French people decided to take action, and the French Revolution began. There were many long-term factors that caused this revolution but the success of the American Revolution acted as a spark for the people of France to remove the **autocratic** rule of their king, Louis. This would go on to inspire the working class in Britain when it came to their voting rights and representation in parliament.

Key Words

peninsula   penal colony   plantation   indentured servant   autocratic

Work

1. Write a news report to explain how the British lost at Yorktown. Use the sources to help you add detail.
2. a. What were the consequences of American Independence? Create a diagram showing this. You could have three circles, which show the economic, social and political consequences, or you can have a go at creating your own style of diagram.
   b. Colour code your consequences to show long- and short-term ones.
   c. Can you think of any other consequences for Britain?
3. Write a letter from George Washington to the British government, explaining how Britain should treat its new colonies across the world if it doesn't want another revolution. You should think about what had made the Americans so unhappy.
4. Create a grid for every revolt you have studied thus far. Have one column for similarities and one for differences. Which revolt do you think is most closely linked to the American Revolution?

Practice Question

Was the economy the main factor that caused the American Revolution?   **16 marks**   **SPaG: 4 marks**

Study Tip

You will need to explain your answer with reference to the economy and other factors. Think about using specific examples that strengthen your points. Can your examples support another judgement? Explain why they support your points more. The Boston Tea Party could support both economic and political factors so you have to use your evidence to say which it supports the most.

Britain: Power and the people

7.1A Give us the vote!

Since the thirteenth century, power had shifted between the monarch, the landowners and parliament. On a few occasions, when ordinary people had challenged the authority of those at the top (such as during the Peasants' Revolt), the challenge had never lasted and control of the country had ultimately remained in the hands of a very small minority. But in the nineteenth century, the Industrial Revolution created a large working class. They wanted, and demanded, representation. Did they use violent methods to try to achieve this? How did the government respond?

Objectives

- **Describe** the problems with voting rights before the early nineteenth century.
- **Explain** the forms of protest for voting reform.
- **Analyse** the impact of the Great Reform Act.

The problem with who could vote

In the early nineteenth century, the king and those who owned land and titles were the people who controlled the country. They made decisions about how the country should be run and what should happen to everyone else in society. This became a problem when the population increased during the Industrial Revolution. Many factory owners became very wealthy — but they, and their workers, had no political power.

One of the main complaints was about the so-called rotten boroughs. These were areas that sent two Members of Parliament (MPs) to parliament even though no one lived there. In one case there was a mound of grass, called Old Sarum, where a village used to be: still, two MPs went to parliament to represent it! Birmingham, on the other hand, was one of the largest and fastest growing towns, yet it had no MPs to represent its people in parliament. Pocket boroughs were also an issue. These were boroughs that were controlled by rich individuals who did not represent the needs of everyone.

When people did go to vote there was no secret **ballot**. This meant that people had to say in public who they were voting for. Therefore, they could be easily bribed, and in some cases people were sacked if they did not vote for the 'right' candidate. This was not true representation, as the same corrupt people continued to hold the power.

Unfairly, some people were allowed to vote purely because they had a fireplace and a locked door! These were called potwalloper boroughs because in order to prove their assets, the men would rattle their keys in a large cooking pot. On top of all of this, women did not have the vote. Despite how much money, how many fireplaces, and how many locked doors they had!

SOURCE A *A painting by William Hogarth, from 1755, called* The Polling; *it shows disabled men being helped up the stairs to vote for a particular candidate*

Radical protest

In Britain, both rich and poor alike noted the effect of the French Revolution, an event in which the ordinary people of France rebelled violently against the ruling class. This coincided with the end of the Battle of Waterloo, when many soldiers were returning home and needed work. The introduction of Corn Laws and a poor harvest meant people were starving. People were now no longer in a position to wait for change — they needed representation in parliament, and radical speakers started to demand it.

Case Study: Peterloo

In 1819, there was a gathering in St Peter's Field in Manchester, of people who were demanding the vote. This was a peaceful protest where the 60,000 protestors listened to speeches by radicals such as

Henry Hunt. Hunt inspired the crowds with his speech that called for the reform of parliament.

The local magistrate panicked when he heard how many people had gathered, and called the local militia in. It is reported that they were drunk, and so events escalated quickly. Within ten minutes, 600 people had been wounded and 15 had been killed. These figures included women and children. Working-class people making clear demands had scared the authorities into responding with violence.

After the event, which became known as the Peterloo Massacre, the government introduced the Six Acts. These stated that any meeting of more than 50 people for radical reform was an act of treason. Anyone doing this was now breaking the law.

▼ **SOURCE B** *This is the official plaque that was put up in Manchester to commemorate the events at Peterloo. Many people felt it did not reflect the true events, and it made no mention of the people killed.*

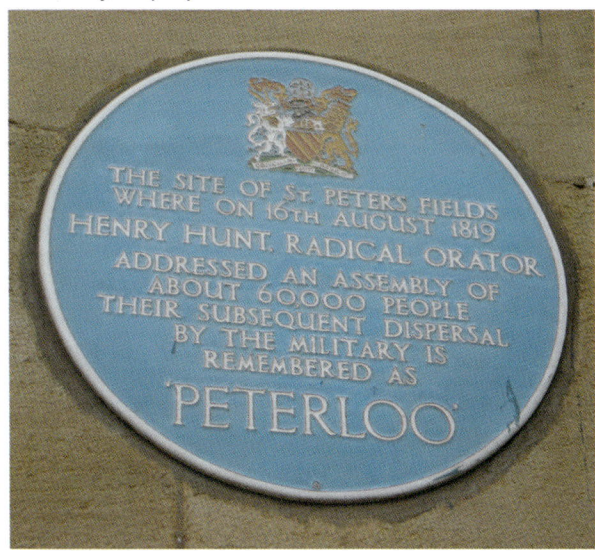

▼ **SOURCE C** *This alternative plaque replaced the blue plaque in 2007. It gives a more accurate account of the events at Peterloo.*

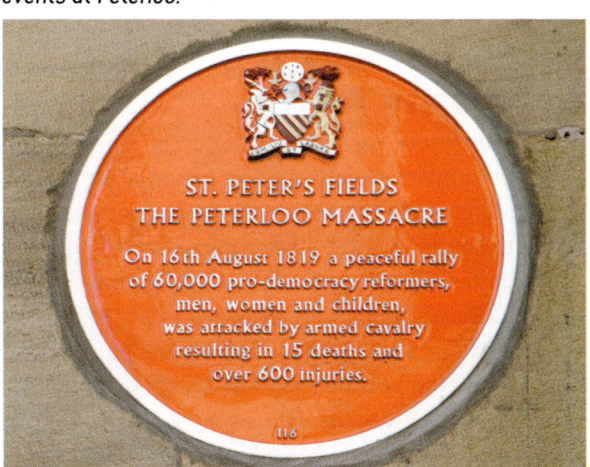

Key Word

ballot

▼ **SOURCE D** *A 1819 painting called* The Massacre of Peterloo, *showing Henry Hunt and his supporters waving the revolutionary flag of France. You can see women and children being attacked by the soldiers on their horses.*

Work

1. a. Who could vote in the early nineteenth century?
   b. How does **Source A** support your list of who could vote? Can you spot the woman in the distance? Why might she be painted far away?
   c. Can you see any other problems with the voting system, from the details given in the painting?
2. Write a letter to the Prime Minister in 1819 describing the reasons why there should be voting reform.
3. List the key differences between **Source B** and **Source C**.
4. a. Explain the key features of radical protest for voting reform. Use the sources to help you.
   b. Which of **Source B**, **Source C** and **Source D** is the most accurate as a piece of evidence about the events at Peterloo? Explain your answer.

Extension

A public survey voted the events at Peterloo as more significant than the Putney Debates (see page 125). In groups, carry out more research on both and create a presentation that states whether you agree or disagree.

7.1B Give us the vote!

So far, nothing had changed for working-class people, or for the middle classes. They still needed change, but instead of protesting they now tried to convince the government to change things and extend the franchise (give more people the vote) through legislation.

Who was in charge?

The political party that had been in charge at the beginning of the nineteenth century was the **Tory** party, who were against reform. They were voted out of government in 1830 and replaced by the **Whig** party, led by Earl Grey.

This coincided with the death of King George IV. He had been considered insane and had not been running the country well: he was extravagant and was not interested in making life better for ordinary people. George was replaced by King William IV in 1830, who was more open to reform and improving society.

How did people try to convince the king?

The government had cracked down on public gatherings and protests for change. However, a Birmingham man called Thomas Attwood formed the Birmingham Political Union of the Lower and Middle Classes of People in 1829. Attwood, along with 8000 others, sent a **petition** to parliament for reform. They wanted shorter parliaments, the end of property qualifications and a vote for all men who contributed to local or national taxes. However, the petition was rejected.

▼ **SOURCE E** The Meeting of the Birmingham Political Union, painted in 1832–33 by Benjamin Robert Haydon

By the end of 1829, the union was renamed the Birmingham Political Union (BPU). The group vowed to cooperate with the law – this would make it harder for the BPU to be banned – and it was agreed that the lower and middle classes would unite for the cause.

The BPU model was copied around the country, so when Attwood called for people not to pay their taxes, the king and the government started to worry.

The Great Reform Act, 1832

Earl Grey's Whig government tried to pass laws for a reform act. In fact they tried three times to get a reform act through! This is how the system works: when the government wants to pass a law, they have to send it through the House of Lords. The House of Lords is the part of parliament that is not elected. In the first parliament – the Great Council – they were the barons and nobles. So, can you see the problem? The House of Lords did not want to pass an act that would give more power to the ordinary people by having them represented in parliament.

On the third attempt, Earl Grey went to the king and requested that lords be appointed who were Whigs, or at least sympathetic to reform. The existing lords were horrified at the idea, because it would mean that Tory lords would lose their some of their power to the Whigs, so they passed the Reform Act in 1832. It had been such a fight to get the act passed that it was called the Great Reform Act.

How great was the Great Reform Act?

The middle class did well out of the Great Reform Act. Merchants and industrialists gained more representation and were happier that their interests were being considered. Rotten boroughs were removed and new towns, such as Birmingham, were allowed to elect MPs. The working class, however, were unhappy about the Reform Act being called 'Great'. They had not been given the vote, as most only earned around £50 a year. There was no secret ballot

SOURCE F This painting, by Sir George Hayte in 1833, hangs in the National Portrait Gallery. It shows key individuals involved in the Great Reform Act of 1832.

Key Words
Tory Whig petition

G The main points of the Great Reform Act

- 56 very small locations lose the right to elect their own MPs
- 30 other smaller towns lose one MP
- London and other large towns and cities are given more MPs
- People who earn £150 a year can vote
- Voters increase from 435,000 to 652,000

Work

1. Create and complete a table with two headings: People who opposed reform; People who supported reform.
2. How did the BPU try to convince the government to extend the franchise?
3. a The National Portrait Gallery paid a lot of money for **Source F**. Was it worth the money? Should the Great Reform Act be remembered?
   b Write a letter to the National Portrait Gallery explaining your judgement.

until 1872, so the lucky few working-class people who could actually vote were effectively forced to vote for their factory or landowner, rather than their chosen candidate. The act meant that only one in seven men could vote; this didn't represent the people of Britain.

The Reform Act did not change things for working-class people in the short term. However, it had been proven that change was possible, and over the next decades the call for further parliamentary reform continued. Furthermore, the Reform Act reduced the power of the king and landowners. The middle class had joined the electorate: they now had influence and this could only mean more change.

Practice Question

Compare Peterloo and the Newport rising (see page 135). In what ways were they similar?

8 marks

Study Tip

Remember in your answer to compare the reasons for, the development of and the consequences of each event.

Britain: Power and the people

7.2A What was the impact of Chartism?

Working-class men had fought hard and supported the campaign for reform in 1832. However, they were left feeling bitter after the Great Reform Act: they were still unable to vote because they did not qualify under new rules that said voters must own property worth at least £10. Lots of other factors came together to fuel further unrest. Through the anger, the **Chartist movement** was born. The Chartists were a group of like-minded people with clear aims that focused around equal representation for the working class. What specifically did the Chartists want, and how did they go about getting it? Did the Whig government support the movement?

Objectives

- Describe the aims of the Chartists.
- Examine the tactics of the Chartists.
- Evaluate the impact the Chartists had.

Poor harvests and the Poor Law

Working-class people were becoming more and more disgruntled due to their poor living and working conditions. They found it hard to find work because of the new machines being invented: one machine could do the work of ten men, and faster. This meant that most jobs no longer required skill; even children could do them. The Industrial Revolution had created problems that the government needed to solve, and so it reformed the Poor Law in 1834. This was done through a desire to help people in the new industrial society, by offering help to those who struggled financially. People who needed Poor Law assistance would be sent to the workhouse: this was seen as help at the time. However this did not solve the problems faced by most people. Bad harvests in the 1830s added to the troubles of the poor. When were the working class going to get the help and representation they deserved?

William Lovett and the birth of the Chartist movement

In 1836, the Chartist movement was born when William Lovett, from the London Working Men's Association, started a campaign that was quickly adopted around the country. Thomas Attwood and the Birmingham Political Union joined the campaign. This led to a national Chartist convention being held in Birmingham in 1839.

The movement was a peaceful one, due to Lovett's Christian faith, and organised the mass signing of petitions to be sent to parliament. The Chartists had six main aims, set out in a document called the People's Charter.

A The demands of the People's Charter

- Votes for all men!
- Equal-sized constituencies!
- Voting in secret!
- Wages for MPs!
- No property qualifications to be able to vote!
- An election every year!

The demands would make voting, and therefore society, fairer. If MPs were paid then working-class people could become MPs. They could then promote the interests of the working class in parliament. This was truly a charter for equality. In 1839 the first petition was sent to parliament. However it was rejected.

134 Chapter 7 The extension of the franchise

SOURCE B Adapted from a speech by William Lovett, before 1839:

> Let us, friends, seek to join together the honest, moral, hardworking and intelligent member of society. Let us find out our rights from books. Let us collect information about our lives, our wages and our conditions. Then let us publish our views. Then MPs will agree there must be change, without having to use violence and arrest.

Moral force or physical force?

The rejection of the petition was a real blow to the Chartist movement and some supporters decided that peaceful methods of protest were not enough. Chartists in South Wales, for example, were particularly angered by the rejection. Here, unemployment was higher than average and many people were starving. They decided to march on Newport in November 1839. One of their leaders had been imprisoned and many planned to attack the prison and free him. However, when they reached Newport the authorities were ready for them, and had soldiers guarding the prison. The soldiers opened fire and 22 men were killed. The attack was over.

By 1842, another petition was being sent to parliament. This also coincided with the emergence of Feargus O'Connor. He became the undisputed leader of the movement when the 1842 petition was rejected, and called for violent actions to pressurise parliament into agreeing to the demands. Many workers in factories in the north of England started to vandalise machinery. These actions became known as the 'plug plot'. They demonstrated that people would stop at nothing to get the charter passed through parliament.

O'Connor called for a **general strike** of all workers and even went as far as calling for a British republic. He was determined to remove the people who kept working men down. The government became so concerned it moved Queen Victoria to the Isle of Wight, for her own safety.

By 1847, the economic and agricultural **depression** had returned to Britain. There was a surge in support for the Chartists. A third petition was signed and taken to parliament. Did it succeed?

Key Words

Chartist movement   general strike   depression

Work

1.
   a. Write a list of the six aims of the Chartists.
   b. Beside each aim, write what it would change.
   c. Which aim do you think would have the most impact?
2. Create a conversation between Lovett and O'Connor. They should be trying to convince each other of their tactics. Use examples of successes and failures that could support their points.
3. Group discussion: Who do you think had the right idea? Which tactics worked better?

▶ **SOURCE C** *A sketch by John Leech that appeared in* Punch *magazine in 1849, called 'The beginning and the end'; it shows a Chartist at the beginning of the protests who is shouting about freedom and liberty, but then shows the same man next to a policeman who has put down the aspirations ('liberty') of the people, who have been forced to accept the norm and carry on because of the show of force*

THE GREAT CHARTIST DEMONSTRATION.

NO. IX.—THE BEGINNING AND THE END.

Britain: Power and the people

7.2B What was the impact of Chartism?

The Chartists were divided between those who believed in moral force and those who believed that physical force was the solution. Also, there were many other areas of life, in addition to politics, that the Chartists want to reform. But did they achieve their six main aims, as set out in the People's Charter?

Other areas of reform

Lovett was committed to education and reform through the cooperative movement. This movement was inspired by Robert Owen and helped bring a better standard of living to working-class communities. Many Chartists became heavily involved in the **trade union** movements that would become important in the latter half of the century.

Lovett and other leaders also promoted **temperance**. This is zero tolerance of alcohol and was a popular movement in the early nineteenth century. It was believed that parliament would have to take the Chartists seriously if they were sober. This would show that working-class people were disciplined and worthy of the vote.

O'Connor was interested in land reform. He felt that everyone was entitled to land, and that if they had land, they could leave the factory towns and the problems they faced there. There were several sites where this kind of land reform took place, and one of the most significant was named 'O'Connorville'. The scheme worked for a while but the land was poorly farmed by the settlers and eventually the scheme failed. Despite their differences, it is clear both that Lovett and O'Connor wanted to improve life for the working class.

Government responses

The government feared the Chartists, who were able to mobilise large groups of people from all classes. In addition, they had respectable leaders, and even a newspaper they could use to promote their agenda. The government took decisive action against them, in addition to rejecting their petitions. Local government officials put up posters in towns asking people to not attend Chartists meetings. They would freely arrest Chartists, with Lovett and O'Connor being arrested on more than one occasion.

One tool the government used to deter people from pushing for reform was transportation. It had been decided that the death penalty was too harsh for many crimes. Therefore, people were transported to other countries, such as Australia, as punishment. This threat from the government was enough to dissuade people from joining the Chartist movement.

> **Fact**
>
> William Cutty was a black man who was the son of a former slave. He supported the physical force Chartists. He was transported to Australia for his activities, where he quickly set up Chartist groups to support the freedom of indigenous people. The Chartist movement travelled elsewhere around the empire, where others, like Cutty, were transported. Chartism continued to challenge the British government even on different continents!

One of the most significant actions by the government was when the third Chartist petition was taken to parliament in 1848.

The end of Chartism?

O'Connor and fewer than 50,000 supporters met on Kennington Common in London on 10 April 1848. Expecting more, the Duke of Wellington had prepared troops and police. Some 85,000 special constables were

▼ **SOURCE D** *The Great Chartist Meeting at Kennington Common, 10 April 1848, just before the presentation of the third Chartist petition. This image is an early photograph called a daguerreotype, which usually reversed the image. The technology was replaced by easier methods after 1860.*

enrolled for the day: they were not going to let O'Connor and his followers disturb London.

Wellington stopped the crowd from entering the city, and O'Connor was forced to take the petition into London himself. The petition was said to have over five million signatures: in fact it had fewer than two million.

The petition was read out in parliament and it transpired that thousands of the signatures were forged. Many were seemingly from Queen Victoria herself! O'Connor argued that this was because workers had to keep their identity a secret from their employers. Parliament saw the whole thing as a farce.

The Chartist movement was not a complete disaster, as in the end all but one of the six aims in the People's Charter were achieved by 1928.

Why did the Chartist movement fail in the short term?

There are many reasons why the Chartist movement failed to have an immediate impact. There was strong parliamentary opposition, with clear strategies being used; mainly government suppression of local meetings and gatherings. The standard of living started to increase during the 1850s and there were many alternative working-class movements such as trade unionism and cooperatives. The divided leadership of Lovett and O'Connor was certainly a cause of failure. Without one clear message, and with too many fringe groups, the movement was doomed to failure.

SOURCE E *A cartoon published in* Punch *magazine, May 1859, mocking the petition*

Key Words

trade union   temperance

F *The Chartist aims and the dates they were met*

Votes for all men!
1918

Equal-sized constituencies!
1884

Voting in secret!
1872

Wages for MPs!
1911

No property qualifications to be able to vote!
1918 (men)

An election every year!
Never

Work

1 a Which tactics did the government use to defeat the Chartists?
   b Which tactic had the biggest impact?
2 a What is the message of the cartoon in **Source E**?
   b Why was this cartoon created?
3 Do you think **Source E** is useful as evidence of why Chartism failed?
4 Create your own cartoon showing another reason for Chartism's failure.

Practice Question

How useful is **Source D** to a historian studying support for the Chartists?   **8 marks**

Study Tip

Refer in your answer to the type of source it is and what it shows.

8.1 The Anti-Corn Law League

The early nineteenth century had seen a number of reform movements. There were campaigns to change voting rules, to end slavery and to improve living and working conditions, for example. At the same time another movement developed, called the Anti-Corn Law League. This group campaigned over the price of wheat, which was a very contentious issue in the nineteenth century. So why were there laws about wheat at this time? What methods did the Anti-Corn Law League use? Did it change the lives of poor people?

Objectives

- **Identify** the reasons the Corn Laws were passed.
- **Analyse** the factors that led to the repeal of the Corn Laws.
- **Evaluate** the impact of the Anti-Corn Law league.

Fact

The price of wheat affected everyone because it was used to make bread – a staple food for many people.

What were the Corn Laws?

Britain had been at war with France (1803–15) and thus had stopped trading with the French. During the war, British farmers had the monopoly on wheat sales and the prices soared. When the war ended there were calls to start trading with France, which had cheaper wheat. However, the politicians in government were wealthy landowners. They had made money from the high wheat prices and were reluctant to see their profits fall. So, the government passed the Corn Laws in 1815. These laws were designed to keep the price of wheat high. If the price fell too low, imports of wheat would be stopped. This kept the wealthy landowners and farmers happy, but were the manufacturers and workers happy?

Why and how did the 'Leaguers' protest?

Many people were unhappy with the Corn Laws and their impact on the price of bread. There were riots up and down the country, from Westminster to Dundee, as the Corn Laws made their way through parliament.

The Anti-Corn Law League was mostly made up of middle-class men who felt that the restrictions were unfair to the poor and the manufacturing middle class. Two prominent 'Leaguers' were Richard Cobden and John Bright. Both men were excellent **orators** and toured the country, giving speeches and spreading support for the league. They created pamphlets and published newspaper articles in sympathetic newspapers. They were quick to take advantage of new technology by using the railway to travel faster, and spreading their pamphlets through the penny post: this was a cheap post that most people could afford. They used it to send a pamphlet to every eligible voter in the country, and easily obtained nationwide support. Their main arguments were:

- The laws were unfair to the poor because they increased the price of a basic food – bread!
- Cheap wheat could help to lower living costs.
- People could spend more money on other foods, such as meat, which would help farmers.
- People could also spend more money on industrial goods, thus benefiting the manufacturers.
- Countries who could export their wheat to Britain would have the money to invest in industry.
- The relationship built up through trade with these countries could ensure peace in Europe in the coming years.

The league had a lot of support, which increased when both Cobden and Bright were elected as MPs, in 1841 and 1843 respectively. In parliament they found the support of the new Prime Minister, Robert Peel.

Peel was a supporter of **free trade** and saw the benefits of **repealing** the Corn Laws. However, he was also the leader of the Conservative Party, whose members were mostly wealthy landowners: they would not support changes to a law which protected their wealth.

▼ **SOURCE A** *Adapted from a quote by an MP in Scotland, Joseph Hume, in the 1830s:*

> Every man who earns his bread by his labour, should raise his voice against the Corn Laws, as they produce stagnation in trade, a want of work, and starvation.

138 Chapter 8 Protest and change

Famine and crop failure: other factors for reform

There had been attempts at reforming the Corn Laws in the 1820s but none had done enough for the poor and starving of Britain. It would be the plight of the poor that would eventually push Peel's dithering hand.

In the early 1840s, there was a potato failure in Ireland. This was caused by the crop disease, blight, which had spread across Europe. This was a problem for the poor in Ireland as they relied heavily on potatoes and bread for their diet. By 1846, Ireland was experiencing a terrible famine and millions of people were starving. The Corn Laws meant that there was no spare wheat to send to Ireland. Something had to be done.

Simultaneously, there were crop failures in England and Scotland and reports of suffering started to reach London. The bad harvest, the lack of work for **tenant farmers** and the high price of bread was about to cause a similar crisis to the one in Ireland.

Corn Laws repealed

In 1846, Robert Peel repealed the Corn Laws. In his final speech in parliament, he stated that he hoped people would remember him as someone who did the right thing. It is fair to say that he understood the problems faced by the Chartists and the workers; he did change conditions for the workers. But in doing so, he faced so much backlash from his own political party that he had to resign. He would never hold office again.

Impact of repeal

The repealing of the Corn Laws did not have the devastating effect on wheat prices as anticipated. What British farmers hadn't realised was that the low price of wheat after the end of the war with France was not because of foreign imports but because of wheat over-production in Britain during the war years.

The increase in population and the return to normal prices of wheat meant that farmers and landowners did not suffer. The poor were able to afford wheat and the price of barley, oats and meat actually increased, which helped those farmers who had been affected.

Many historians argue that the influence of the landowning class was challenged by the repeal of the Corn Laws and led to more protection for the working class in future years.

Key Words

orator   free trade   repeal   tenant farmer

▼ **SOURCE B** *A drawing seen in the* Illustrated London News, *December 1849, showing an Irish woman, Bridget O'Donnel, with her children; they are starving because of the famine*

Work

1. **a** Who would benefit from the Corn Laws? Why?
   b What did the Corn Laws mean for the working class?
2. Write a speech for a public meeting about the Corn Laws. You want to persuade people to vote against them. Pick the three best arguments and focus on them in your speech.
3. Explain the importance of the famine in Ireland in influencing the repeal of the Corn Laws.

Practice Question

Compare the Anti-Corn Law League with the Chartists. In what way were they similar?   **8 marks**

Study Tip

Explain your answer with reference to both the Anti-Corn Law League and the Chartists.

8.2A What was the impact of the anti-slavery movement?

For hundreds of years, from the 1500s onwards, Britain had made money from slavery. However, in the nineteenth century, Britain's involvement in the slave trade stopped. There were a number of reasons for this. For example, people campaigned to abolish slavery, and the slaves themselves rebelled, until any involvement in slavery was made illegal in Britain in 1833. So why was Britain involved the slave trade? What was life like as a slave? And who led the movement to end slavery?

Objectives

- **Identify** the motivations for Britain's involvement in slavery.
- **Explain** the factors that led to the end of slavery.
- **Make** a judgement on why slavery ended and the consequences of this.

What was the slave trade?

Britain had been involved in slavery since the fifteenth century. For hundreds of years, British traders had made money by selling people to work in the West Indies and then America. Some slaves were bought to Britain to work too. The British, along with other European nations, had set up plantations growing mainly cotton and sugar; they needed people to pick the crops. They got their slaves from the west coast of Africa. There, many tribal leaders were happy to sell people to the slave traders. In return they were given goods such as cloth, guns, glass and iron.

Britain made lots of money from slavery. Evidence of this can be seen in cities such as Bristol, Liverpool and Glasgow, where houses and iconic buildings were built using money made through the slave trade.

Life as a slave

Conditions were dreadful on the ships that took the slaves across the Atlantic. The men, women and children were crammed in on top of each other. On average, one third of the passengers died on each crossing.

▼ **SOURCE A** William Cunninghame, who made his fortune from tobacco plantations, built this grand mansion in 1870. Today the building is Glasgow's Gallery of Modern Art.

When the slave ships arrived at their destinations, the new slaves were treated like animals during the auctions, where people bid for them. Life on the plantations was extremely difficult. Slaves were expected to work all their lives; if they didn't work hard enough or tried to escape they would be severely punished. They had no legal rights. The average life expectancy for a slave was only 27.

▼ **SOURCE B** A drawing from 1787, which appeared in newspapers, pamphlets, books and posters, showing the cramped conditions endured by slaves on slave ships. The ship in this drawing, the Brookes, had 454 slaves crammed into its hold.

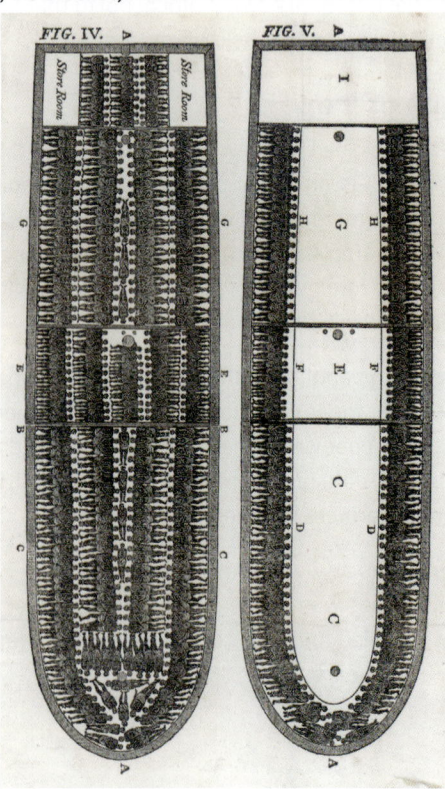

140 Chapter 8 Protest and change

Abolition movement: William Wilberforce and friends

After hundreds of years of slavery, many people started to accept that it was wrong. One of the main motivations for this new view was the comparison to the working conditions in the factories; the workers had been referred to as 'white slaves'. It became clear that if they opposed the horrible conditions of the British factories, they should also oppose slavery. Others were led by their religious convictions that slavery was not Christian. One group that believed this was led by William Wilberforce. He, and likeminded others, created the Anti-Slavery Society.

The society held public meetings to educate people, they produced pamphlets and posters, and society members wore a badge to display their membership. These actions were designed to raise awareness and show support for the abolition of the slave trade. Different Anti-Slavery Society members made different contributions to the cause.

Many working-class people supported the movement, with workers in Manchester signing a petition to parliament. By 1792, a quarter of the population of Manchester had signed the petition.

SOURCE C *The badge of the Society for the Abolition of Slavery, designed by the famous pottery owner, Josiah Wedgewood, in 1787*

William Wilberforce:
- MP for Hull
- motivated by his Christian faith
- spoke in parliament and pushed several **bills** through to abolish slavery
- held meetings to convince other prominent members of society to end slavery and in 1797, presented a petition to parliament – it had more signatures than the Chartist petition
- secured the Abolition of the Slave Trade Act in 1807, which would make it illegal to buy and sell slaves in the British Empire (but people were allowed to keep the slaves they already owned).

Thomas Clarkson:
- collected information about slavery and the conditions on board slave ships
- considered slavery evil and saw it as his job to do something about it
- produced drawings of the conditions on slave ships and pamphlets to show everyone how horrible the conditions were for slaves.

Granville Sharp:
- in the late 1700s, supported cases of black slaves in Britain who wanted to be free
- motivated by his studies and his interest in politics and law
- in the famous case of Jonathan Strong, who was recaptured by his former slavemaster and sent back to the West Indies, Sharp won his case for freedom
- his work showed how unclear the law was in Britain about owning slaves
- brought to public attention the case of the slave ship *Zong*, where 133 slaves were reportedly thrown overboard.

Olaudah Equiano:
- had been a ship-master's slave and had travelled the world
- lived in England where he was educated and converted to Christianity
- finally gained freedom and wrote a book, *The Interesting Narrative of the Life of Olaudah Equiano or Gustavus Vassa, the African*, giving an account of his time as a slave
- his autobiography was used by the abolition movement to win the support of people; it made people aware of the horrors of slavery.

Key Word

bill

Work
1. List three reasons why Britain was involved in slavery. What do you think was the most important reason?
2. a Can you think of two categories that the motivations of the abolitionists fit into?
   b Use your categories as headings and write all the methods they used to end slavery below these.

8.2B What was the impact of the anti-slavery movement?

Wilberforce and his supporters campaigned for a long time for the abolition of slavery. After 20 years of campaigning, in 1807 the British parliament abolished the slave trade, making it illegal to buy and sell slaves. However, people were allowed to keep the slaves they already owned. This changed in 1833 when parliament banned slave ownership too – not only in Britain but throughout the British Empire. So who deserves credit for their role in ending British involvement in slavery altogether?

Anti-abolitionists

The abolition movement was not fully supported within government. This was because many of the MPs and lords had made their money from slavery, or a link to it. If slavery ended, plantation owners would have to pay their workers and this would mean they could lose money.

Those who were supporters of the slave trade created their own propaganda supporting the view that black people were inferior, and that Britain had a responsibility to keep black slaves locked up. This was called the 'white man's burden'.

SOURCE D *A 1789 cartoon by William Dent opposing the abolition of slavery; the heads at the bottom are 'Abolition' (labelled 'Folly') and 'Regulation' (labelled 'Wisdom'). The cartoon argues that regulation of the slave trade would be better than abolition.*

Women and the abolition movement

Despite women not yet having the vote, and playing little role in politics, many women got involved in the abolition movement. One of these was Hannah More, who wrote poems for the movement. More met Wilberforce in 1787 and they formed a firm friendship, based around their faith and commitment to social reform.

There were many anti-slavery societies run by women; in fact, by time slavery was abolished in 1833, there were 73 such organisations. They were located across the whole of Britain, demonstrating that women nationwide were concerned about the issue of slavery and were willing to take action.

SOURCE E *Adapted from Hannah More's poem, Slavery, written in 1788:*

> Was it decreed, fair Freedom! At thy birth,
> That thou should never irradiate all the earth?
> While Britain basks in thy full blaze of light,
> Why lies sad Africa quenched in total night?

Slave resistance

It would be wrong to assume that the abolition of slavery was achieved only by middle-class white people in Britain. There were many instances of slave rebellions that changed the way people thought about slavery.

The Maroon slaves in Jamaica had escaped from their plantations when the British took control of Jamaica in 1655. They lived in the mountains and celebrated their native African culture. The British knew that if word spread of this group, they would face slave rebellions everywhere. Thus, they negotiated with the Maroons, and managed to control rebellions for a time.

It was harder to supress rebellions after the French Revolution spread new ideas of freedom and equality. Two years after the revolution, the slaves of St Dominique, a French-controlled island, rebelled. They killed the white plantation owners and set fire to the sugar crops. The French and British tried to control and stop this rebellion, but failed. This was partly because of the brilliant leadership of Toussaint L'Ouverture. He led fellow slaves to victory and slavery was abolished on the island in 1804. The island was declared independent and given the new name: Haiti.

The rebellions sent a clear message that the slaves were not willing to accept slavery, and expected more from life. They also proved they would use any means to gain freedom.

The economic factors of abolition

Some historians now argue that the abolition of slavery was less to do with a surge of social consciousness, and more to do with a decline in the economic benefits of slavery. In other words, slavery was making less money than it used to! Sugar could be imported more cheaply from Brazil and Cuba; there was no need for the British to grow it themselves.

Was the abolition movement a complete success?

The Abolition of Slavery Act 1833 only instantly freed those slaves under the age of six. The rest were put into age categories and were promised freedom after four years. William Wilberforce has been widely criticised for supporting this staged abolition. He argued that slaves had not been educated and they would have to be trained to live outside the shackles of slavery. Many others, however, disagreed with this strategy and campaigned for the immediate release of all slaves.

The road to freedom was not a smooth one. Many slaves were sacked if they refused to live in their old slave quarters. Smuggling of slaves became a problem: as it was carried out in secret, it made conditions even worse as there was no one to **regulate** it. The smuggling was carried out by former slave traders who did not want to give up the money they could make from slavery. For many slaves, freedom resulted in a decline in living standards as they tried to compete for work and wages.

In the long term the success of the abolition movement was undoubtedly a positive change for black people globally, as Britain increased the pressure on other nations to abolish slavery.

▼ **SOURCE F** Adapted from a book, *The Black Jacobins*, written in 1938 by a West Indian historian, C. L. R. James:

> Those who see in the abolition of slavery the awakening conscience of mankind should spend a few minutes asking themselves why it is that man's conscience, which has slept peacefully for so many centuries, should awaken just at the time that men began to see the unprofitableness of slavery.

Practice Question

How useful is **Source D** to a historian studying the anti-slavery campaign? **8 marks**

Key Word

regulate

Extension

In 2001, the World Conference against Racism met in South Africa. One member addressed the conference to say that he wanted Britain and the other nations involved in the slave trade to admit that slavery was a crime against humanity. He also called for compensation for the descendants of slaves and nations that had been impacted on by slavery. Britain refused to do either. The debate for compensation found support again in 2015. Research the various groups campaigning for this and create a presentation saying whether you agree or disagree.

Work

1. Complete the diagram below to explain how each factor led to abolition. In the parts that overlap put events that could be linked to more than one factor.
2. Which factor do you think had the most impact? Explain your decision.
3. Imagine it is the 200-year anniversary of the abolition of slavery. Write a post for your school's website explaining the impact the acts of 1807 and 1833 had.

Economic factors — Slave resistance — Anti-abolition movement

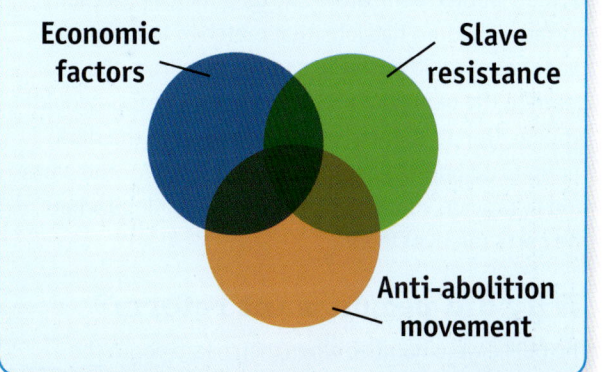

Study Tip

Write about what the cartoonist wants you to think about the opposition to the anti-slavery campaign. Why is the date of the cartoon important? Explain your answer.

8.3A Factory and social reform

The Industrial Revolution started around 1750. Before this, most people had worked at home, in the 'Domestic System'; this normally involved the whole family. They had managed their own time and took breaks when they wanted. With the building of factories and the demand these created for coal, working conditions changed. The new factories were often dangerous, noisy, dirty buildings, controlled by factory owners and managers who were more concerned with making money that with the health and wellbeing of their workforce. Several people campaigned to try to improve working conditions in factories. How did people react to reform, and did it make life better for everyone? How successful were the reformers?

Objectives

- **Describe** attitudes to reform in the nineteenth century.
- **Explore** the results of factory and social reform.
- **Analyse** the impact of reform on society.

Factory conditions

Textiles such as woollen and cotton cloth were the main products being made in factories in Britain during the Industrial Revolution. The factories were built because the new machines that made production more efficient, cheaper and quicker were too big for people's homes. With the new factories came new, longer working hours and new dangers. Children as young as six worked in some factories. Accidents were common, in which young people might lose limbs and, in extreme cases, their lives.

Mine conditions – a family affair

Coal mines provided jobs for the whole family. Men manually cut the coal away from the **coal seam**, and women worked as bearers carrying the coal to the surface. Children had jobs that matched their age. Older boys would push the coal in carts from the coal seam to the bearers. Children as young as four would work as trappers. They would have to sit in the dark for up to 12 hours a day, opening the door for the carts and to provide ventilation. Many lost their legs when the carts ran over them.

Why did people want reform?

The public were horrified when they heard about the conditions people worked in. Men's work was hard but people were shocked when they heard about women and children. Reports started to come from inspectors and from those who supported the reform of working conditions. One supported was an MP called Michael Sadler. His report showed that factory children were being caught under machines and injured, and were being mistreated by factory owners. Because of this,

Sadler suggested that those under 18 years old should not be allowed to work more than 10 hours a day; this became known as the 10-hour movement. Other reports highlighted that girls were carrying baskets of coal weighing up to 150 kilogrammes, and that women were dragging carts of coal on their hands and knees. Most people were appalled.

Lord Shaftsbury was another keen reformer. He made it his personal mission to improve the lives of children both at work and socially. He wanted reforms to apply to

▼ **SOURCE A** *A drawing from 1881 that appeared in the* Illustrated London News, *showing a government inspector visiting a factory where children are employed*

144 Chapter 8 Protest and change

all factories, not just textile factories. He was led by his Christian beliefs and what he felt was the humane way to treat people, regardless of their social status. Shaftsbury, like Sadler, gave support to the 10-hour movement; he was also an important supporter of the Mines Act of 1842 and a campaigner for more education for children who worked in factories.

It is important to remember that the campaign for the abolition of slavery was happening at the same time: people started to refer to the factory workers as 'white slaves'.

Why were people against reform?

Many people were against reform because of **laissez-faire** politics. This was the belief that politics should not be involved in people's personal lives. In terms of factory reform, it was believed that working conditions were a private arrangement between a person and his or her employer. In terms of social reform – making people's lives better outside the workplace – there was a belief that people were poor because of their own bad choices. Why should the rich have to pay for the poor when they were feckless and undeserving?

▼ **SOURCE B** *A portrait of Lord Shaftesbury, Anthony Ashley-Cooper*

Key Words

coal seam   laissez-faire

▼ **C** *Some points of the acts for reform*

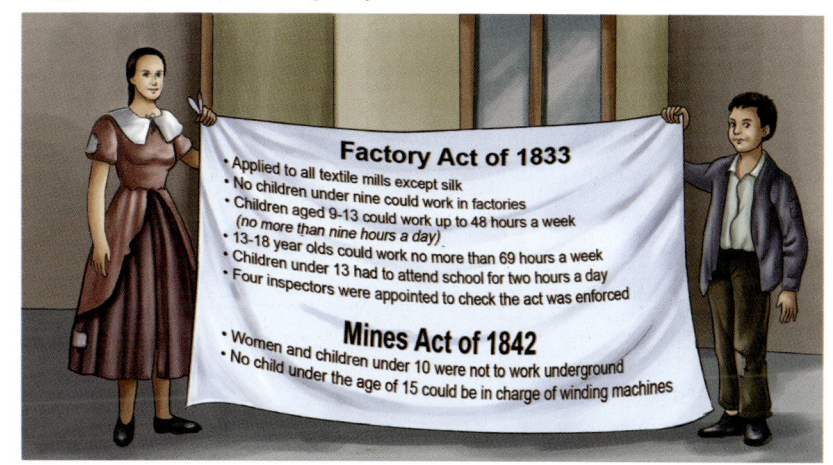

Factory Act of 1833
- Applied to all textile mills except silk
- No children under nine could work in factories
- Children aged 9-13 could work up to 48 hours a week (no more than nine hours a day)
- 13-18 year olds could work no more than 69 hours a week
- Children under 13 had to attend school for two hours a day
- Four inspectors were appointed to check the act was enforced

Mines Act of 1842
- Women and children under 10 were not to work underground
- No child under the age of 15 could be in charge of winding machines

Problems with the acts?

Many workers did not support the factory reform acts as they limited the amount of money coming into a household. The acts did not cater for all workers and all factories. Furthermore, the reforms put poor people at a disadvantage and the existing poor relief did not support everyone. This led to the Poor Law Amendment Act of 1834. However, this law increased the pressure on workers: if they could not make enough money they were put into the dreaded workhouses. Families would be separated and lives ruined. Would life ever improve for the poor of Britain?

Work

1. What would each of the following think about factory reform:
   - a factory owner
   - a child worker who wants to go to school
   - a mother who has nine children to feed and little money
   - an upper-class lady who had read Lord Shaftsbury's report
   - a politician who believes in laissez-faire politics?

2. a Write two diary entries for a child in a factory. One should be from before 1833 and the other from after the factory reform act. You should try to show the good and bad consequences of the act.
   b Include a third entry about your little brother who was a trapper in the mines. Has his life changed after 1842?

Britain: Power and the people

8.3B Factory and social reform

The reform acts brought some improvements in working conditions. Mostly, they paved the way for further reform later in the nineteenth century, which reduced working hours, increased hours of education and made factories and mines safer. Who were the individuals – called **philanthropists** – behind reform, and why were they motivated by it?

> **Fact**
>
> Quakers are Protestants who believe in peaceful principles. They are **pacifists** and are committed to an equal society. This is why they were so heavily involved in social reform.

Name: Robert Owen and New Lanark

Biography: Owen had run a successful mill in Manchester where he had treated his workers well. In 1800, he became manager and part-owner of his father-in-law's mill in Scotland. This was south of Glasgow and was called New Lanark.

Famous quote: 'Eight hours labour, eight hours recreation, eight hours rest.'

Politics: He was a socialist: this meant he was not led so much by profits, but more about the wellbeing of his workers. He believed in a more equal society. Owen was also aware that happy workers would work better, and then he would have a better business.

Religion: He was not driven by religious motivations but did receive funding from a Quaker. They were renowned for their desire to help the most vulnerable people in society.

What he changed: By 1810, he had introduced an 8-hour day (this was decades before the success of the 10-hour day campaign, which he was part of). He also opened a school in 1816 and all children had to have a certain number of hours of education, depending on their age. New Lanark had a social club and meeting areas for workers to visit in their time off. Drinking alcohol and swearing were banned in these places. New Lanark was visited by members of the royal family and MPs, and everyone agreed that it was a successful town.

Name: Edwin Chadwick

Famous quote: 'The formation of all habits of cleanliness is obstructed by defective supplies of water.'

Biography: Chadwick was from a **progressive** family and studied law at university. His father was a progressive.

Politics: He made friends with people who were political philosophers; they were interested in social reform.

What he changed: He was responsible for the reform of the Poor Law that resulted in record numbers of people entering the workhouse in the 1830s; this made him very unpopular. However, he did write a report called 'The Sanitary Conditions of the Labouring Population'. This report showed that there was a link between the poor housing and sanitation of the factory workers and the outbreaks of killer diseases such as cholera. Most middle- and upper-class people had blamed the workers themselves.

Name: Elizabeth Fry

Biography: Fry was born to a Quaker family. Her mother helped various charities and her father was a well-respected Quaker who owned a factory.

Politics: She was a social reformer who believed in the poor being helped; she also believed in prison reform.

Religion: She was a strict Quaker.

Famous quote: 'Punishment is not for revenge but to lessen crime and reform the criminal.'

What she changed: She was shocked by the conditions she had heard of in Newgate Prison. In the prison she saw hundreds of women and children huddled on the floor in two cells. They had to sleep, cook and clean themselves in the cell. Children, there with their arrested mothers, sometimes had to share cells with murderers. Fry visited the prison regularly and soon established a school and a chapel. Her brother-in-law was an MP; he raised the issue of prison reform in parliament. As a result, prisons were reformed, as were the conditions for women on transportation ships.

Extension

Research individuals such as George Cadbury, Titus Salt and Robert Peel Snr. What kind of reform did they engage in? What factors pushed them to become reformers? How much did they change things?

Practice Question

How far was religion the main factor that brought about improvements in the lives of working people in the nineteenth century?

16 marks
SPaG: 4 marks

Study Tip

Refer to individuals, governments and pressure groups. Use Chapters 7, 8 and 9 to help you with your answer.

Key Words

philanthropist   pacifist   progressive

Name: Josephine Butler

Biography: Butler was from a family of social reformers: her father was involved in the abolition of slavery.

Politics: She was a social reformer; her second cousin was Earl Grey.

Religion: She was an evangelical Christian.

Famous quote: 'It is unjust to punish the sex who are the victims of a vice, and leave unpunished the sex who are the main cause both of the vice and its dreaded consequences.'

What she changed: She was concerned with the issue of child prostitution, and campaigned for the age of consent to rise from 13 to 16. She was appalled by the way women were treated when they were arrested for being prostitutes. Society regarded these women as ungodly and unworthy of help. Butler saw their problems as poor wages, and men! In 1869, the Contagious Disease Act was introduced as a way of keeping sexually transmitted infections away from the armed forces. Women could be examined by a police officer if she was thought to be a prostitute. Butler's campaigning saw the repeal of the act in 1883.

Work

1. a. What are the differences between factory reform and social reform?
   b. Which one do you think made the biggest changes to people's lives?
2. a. Elizabeth Fry's face is on a British £5 note. Explain why.
   b. Do you think she deserves to be on the note more than the other reformers you have read about? Create a proposal in your groups to either keep Fry on the note or put another reformer on it.

Britain: Power and the people

9.1 The development of trade unionism: a new workers' paradise?

During the Industrial Revolution the working class grew in numbers. However, the relationship between factory owners and their workers was not always a good one. The workers often felt exploited by the factory owners, and sometimes grouped together to form trade unions. They felt that their working conditions were not good enough and the factory owners didn't look after the welfare of their workforce. Did the factory owners support the unions? Did trade unions make things better for the workers?

Objectives

- **Consider** the reasons people wanted trade unions.
- **Summarise** the key acts and movements in trade union history.
- **Analyse** the success of trade unions.

Workers' guilds

Since Medieval times there had been workers' **guilds** that controlled prices and wages. Before the Industrial Revolution businesses were small and the terms and conditions of service were negotiated person-to-person. Most business owners worked with their employees in small workshops so work was fair and conditions were good.

Once the Industrial Revolution took hold things changed. Work that had previously been done at home or in workshops was moved into factories. Wage competition was a massive problem, with immense increases in the working population. If someone had a grievance about their wages or working conditions they would simply be invited to leave, and someone else would be ready to take their job, often for a lower wage.

Opposition to new technology

There were many groups who fought against the changes in industry. The Luddites would deliberately break machinery in the hope that factory owners would turn away from technology. This did not have the desired effect.

▼ **SOURCE A** *A letter from 'Captain Swing', the fictional leader of the movement; no one knows who actually wrote the letter, but it was probably an angry agricultural worker:*

> This is to inform you that if you don't pull down your machines and raise the wages of married men to two and six pence a day and single men to two shillings, we will burn down your barns and you in them. This is the last notice.

Another group, the Swing Rioters, were angered by the depression in agriculture after the Napoleonic wars, and by the new threshing machines that took their jobs. They set fire to farms and damaged the machines.

The Combination Act of 1825

There had been various combination acts since 1799. They put restrictions on groups of workers combining to form trade unions. After a wave of strikes in 1824, the Combination Act of 1825 was passed. This defined the rights of trade unions as meetings to discuss wages and conditions. Anything outside of this was illegal. The act was brought about to stop the perceived threat of intimidation by groups of workers. It also stopped them **picketing**. The problem with the act was that it was not clear about exactly what intimidation meant. However, the trade unions had been weakened.

Grand National Consolidated Trade Unions

Robert Owen, a mill owner in Scotland, was a keen supporter of workers' rights. He set up the Grand National Consolidated Trade Union (GNCTU) in 1834. This was to bring all workers together under one umbrella organisation.

Owen's cooperative movement saw the workers buying goods in bulk to sell on in their cooperative member shops. The profit from these shops was then shared among the working members.

Within a week of being set up the GNCTU had half a million members. The government was worried. However, the success of the GNCTU was short lived. The reality was that factory workers had different grievances from mine workers, and conflict between the two groups weakened the union. Its fate was sealed in 1834 when six farm labourers were arrested for swearing an oath to protect their income. Although union activity was not illegal, the swearing of an oath was.

In 1837 the Scottish Friendly Association of Cotton Spinners took **strike action**: when they were unhappy with something to do with their job, for example, pay, they would refuse to work until their demands were met. They used violent methods, such as harassing people who were willing to work for less, and in extreme cases shooting them. Eventually, the spinners ran out of funds and their leaders were arrested. The strike ended in disaster.

New Model Unions

In 1851, a new type of union was set up: the Amalgamated Society of Engineers (ASE). This was a union of highly skilled men who could afford to pay weekly subscriptions: this would ensure they received sick pay and other benefits. Furthermore, if they threatened to strike their employer would suffer, as they could not replace them. This then sparked a wave of New Model Unions, with carpenters in 1860 and then tailors in 1866.

These New Model Unions were very successful, with the ASE boasting 33,000 members by 1868. The reason they were seen as 'new model' was because they were moderate in their outlook: they accepted the structure that they worked in, and did not want to destroy it. Rather, they wanted to negotiate improvement from within. This helped trade unionism gain support from the government. By the 1870s, trade unions had legal status and members could picket for their rights.

▼ **SOURCE B** *A trade union scroll from 1851 for the Amalgamated Society of Engineers, Machinists, Millwrights, Smiths and Pattern-Makers; this was presented to members when they joined*

Key Words

guild   picket   strike action

▼ **SOURCE C** *From a speech by William Allen, the General Secretary of the ASE, given in the 1850s:*

> The union does all it can to prevent any strike. We believe strikes to be a waste of money, not only in relation to the workers, but also to the employers.

New Unionism

The success of the New Model Unions had only benefited the more affluent skilled workers. There was a whole class of unskilled workers who were still unhappy. During the 1880s, this group organised themselves into action, and they had some success. The two most high-profile cases were the match girls' strike of 1888 and the dockers' strike of 1889. These strikes were successful: the trade union movement was strong.

This strength and order paved the way for a move into politics, with the creation of the Independent Labour Party; at the turn of the twentieth century this became the Labour Party we still have today. Trade unionism realised that it could best support and improve the lives of members by creating a political voice that could be heard.

Work

1. Write a definition for the following: New Model Union; workers' guilds; Luddites; GNCTU.
2. Write a list of all the reasons why someone would want to be a member of a trade union.
3. Draw a timeline of all the important events in trade union history.
4. Only the New Model Unions were a success. How far do you agree?

Practice Question

Explain the significance of New Model Unions for the development of workers' rights. **8 marks**

Study Tip

Refer to the influence of New Model Unions both at the time and during later trade union history.

9.2 The Tolpuddle Martyrs

The Industrial Revolution had brought new machines, new factories, new towns and new workers to the UK. Alongside this, workers had started to organise themselves into trade unions, to try to negotiate better pay and conditions. By 1834, unions were legal and growing in numbers. However, for six men in Dorset, union activity would result in them being put on a boat to Australia – and not for a holiday! Why, and how, were these people punished for being in a union? What were the consequences of this?

Objectives

- **Outline** the reasons why the Tolpuddle Martyrs were arrested.
- **Describe** why people were unhappy with their punishment.
- **Explain** the consequences of the Tolpuddle arrests.

Fact

This was a period when society moved from a focus on farming in the countryside and manufacturing on a small scale to a focus on machines, factories, and industry in towns and cities. Large factories and large machines were built to do things people used to do by hand.

Who were the Tolpuddle Martyrs?

In a small village in Dorset called Tolpuddle, farm labourers had formed a union to try to negotiate better pay and conditions. The new farm machinery that had been invented meant fewer labourers were needed. Furthermore, anyone could operate the machines and no special training was needed, so wages dropped.

Being part of a trade union had been made legal so the men were not breaking any laws. They met under a sycamore tree in the village, or in a room in one of the members' cottages. Their leader was George Loveless. In February 1834, Loveless left for work and would not see his family again for years. He had been arrested.

The 'crime'

The men had not broken the law by being part of a trade union. However, part of the act to legalise unionism had stated that no secret oaths were to be taken. The men had all taken an oath to keep their union a secret, and so they had, in fact, broken this law.

The local landowner heard about this and was worried that the men had formed a union in the first place. Because of the French Revolution (a time when ordinary French citizens rebelled violently against their rulers), landowners and the government were scared that the ideas of equality and freedom would spread through Britain's working-class population. The Luddites and the Swing Riots had not helped to ease their worries.

Luckily for the Tolpuddle landowner, and those in power who were also against trade unions, the six men could be arrested. The exact crime was, in a way, irrelevant. The message to the working class was clear – no unions!

SOURCE A *A poster warning that people found guilty of uttering illegal oaths and joining unions would be transported; this was put up in Dorset in February 1834*

The punishment

The men were found guilty of making an unlawful oath, and were sentenced to seven years' transportation to Australia. There they would endure hard labour.

Public reaction and consequences

Word spread quickly about the sentences the men had received. Soon there were various organisations and groups who were committed to overturning the decision made about the group, now named the Tolpuddle Martyrs. Robert Owen called a meeting of the GNCTU; 10,000 people arrived to attend.

The march at Copenhagen Fields was attended by thousands of working class supporters, and many prominent individuals such as William Cobbett and Robert Owen. The supporters gathered petitions and demanded that the Tolpuddle Martyrs be returned to England.

The government was originally reluctant to reverse the decision made, but eventually the persistent campaigning paid off. On 14 March 1836, all six of the men were given a full and free pardon. The trade unions had won.

Many of the people involved in the movement to free the Tolpuddle Martyrs also got involved in Chartism, and cooperative societies, as a way to make the lives of all working ordinary people better.

SOURCE C *A drawing of the demonstration in support of the Tolpuddle Martyrs, held at Copenhagen Fields in London on 21 April 1834*

SOURCE B *Maps showing where the six Tolpuddle Martys went to in Australia*

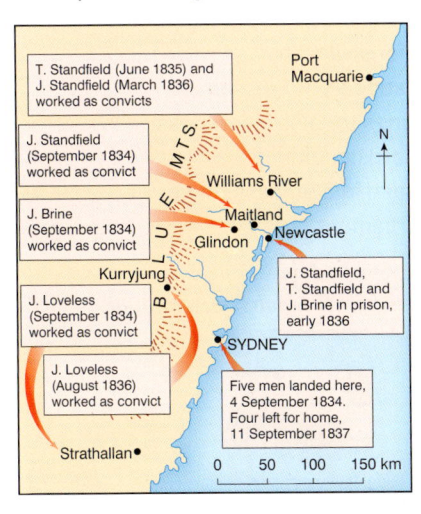

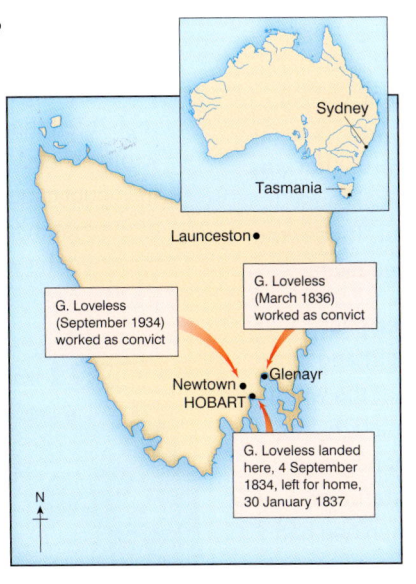

Work

1.
   a. Write as many reasons as you can for why the Tolpuddle Martyrs were arrested.
   b. Next to each reason provide a statement about why this would upset the government.
   c. Now write another statement saying why it was important for the workers.

2. Why would people be upset that the Tolpuddle Martyrs had been transported? Use the map showing the work they did, and think about the workers who were left in Britain.

3. Why did many people who campaigned for the Tolpuddle Martyrs go on to join Chartism? How similar were the movements?

4. Create the table below in your book. Complete it for the Topuddle Martyrs, then go back to look at the trade unions on the previous pages, and add to the table. Leave room so you can add to it when you look at other working-class unions.

	Date	Successful?	Not successful?	Sources to support?
Tolpuddle Martyrs				

Extension

Find out what happened to all the Topuddle Martyrs after they were pardoned.

Britain: Power and the people 151

9.3 New Unionism: how successful were working class unions?

In the 1850s, the New Model Unions made life better for specialised, highly skilled workers, such as engineers and carpenters. However, unskilled workers still had difficulty organising themselves to improve their conditions. The growth of New Unionism, as it was called, was spurred on by two strikes in the 1880s. This New Unionism would ensure the voices of the unskilled working class were heard; things were about to change. What tactics did New Unionism use? How successful were they?

Objectives

- **Compare** the causes of the strikes in the 1880s.
- **Explain** why the strikes were successful.
- **Assess** evidence to analyse how successful working-class unions were.

Why did matchbox factory workers go on strike?

One of the most prominent factories making matches was the Bryant & May factory in London. It employed women to make the matches, many of them young girls. The conditions in the factory were poor and many of the girls and women working there became very ill; some even died. The most common illness was 'phossy jaw'. This was caused by the white phosphorus that was used to make the matches light. The chemical caused their jaws to rot, meaning their teeth fell out. Those who survived the illness were left with disfigured faces.

If that wasn't enough, the workers were paid poor wages: around twenty pence a week for a girl and forty pence for a woman. They were often fined at the whim of the factory owner, for not working fast enough or for being late to work, for example. In 1882, money was deducted from their wages to fund a new statue of Prime Minister William Gladstone. The women had had enough, and in July 1888 they decided to go on strike.

Strike action and support

A journalist, Annie Besant, had become aware of the conditions the women worked in. She helped to organise the strike action, and supported the workers. The strike quickly caught the imagination and sympathy of the general public. Here were young women, being paid little for hard and dangerous work.

Besant organised the grievances of the women in a publication: 'White Slaves of London'. With it she called for a boycott of the matches made at Bryant & May. The factory owners put pressure on the women who were not striking to deny the claims made by Besant. When one refused she was dismissed from her job. As a result, a further 1400 workers came out in support of the strike, during which Besant:

- asked for higher wages for the women and registered them for strike pay
- wrote articles in support of the women
- held public meetings to raise awareness of the match factory conditions
- marched the women in a procession to the Houses of Parliament.

▼ **SOURCE A** *Workers from the match factory, 1888*

Lucky strike!

All of the strike action paid off. The employers agreed to the demands and removed the system of deductions and fines. The matchbox workers were also given a pay rise. This was the first successful strike by unskilled manual workers.

The dockers' strike

A year after the match girls' strike, the London dockers went on strike, demanding better pay and working conditions. They were also inspired by the successful gas workers' strike. The dockers were striking for a wage rise, from five pence an hour to six pence (the 'docker's tanner'). They also wanted eight pence an hour for any overtime work. The dockers had the added problem of having to compete for work. They would regularly go days without work – just turning up in the morning to see if they were needed. They needed to change this and wanted to secure at least four hours a day.

Tactics of the dockers

The New Unionism strikes were more **militant** than the actions of the New Model Unions, mostly because the New Unionism leaders were socialists. The dockers' leader was Ben Tillet; he was adamant the men should get better working conditions. He encouraged them to march through London to raise the profile of the strike and get support. The men carried rotten vegetables and fish heads to show the public what they and their families were living on.

The men also picketed the gates of London docks. This way they could continue to put pressure on the managers and stop any 'blackleg' labourers entering the docks to do the work. This was certainly a move away from the negotiations of the Amalgamated Society of Engineers.

Did the dockers get their tanner?

The strike action closed London docks and gained the support of some influential people, including the Lord Mayor of London and Cardinal Manning, who mediated between the dock owners and the workers. The public, as with the match girls, were sympathetic to the dockers' plight and supported their demands. A generous donations of £30,000 from unions in Australia helped support the strike action. This forced the hand of the dock owners and the men received their pay rise and a guaranteed four-hour day.

The success of the match girls' strike and the dockers' strike was an important milestone in union history. Union membership increased and unskilled workers now had a voice. Did this pave the way for other groups in society to find their voices?

Key Word

militant

SOURCE B *A poster appealing for donors to the striking dockers' relief fund*

DOCK LABOURERS' STRIKE! RELIEF FUND.

Fellow-workmen—An earnest appeal is made to you to help your fellow-workmen, the half-starved, under-paid Dockers, in their great struggle. The men MUST win, or so much the worse for all of us. It will be our fault if they do not. Their cause is the most righteous and reasonable in modern times.

GIVE LIBERALLY & SECURE THE VICTORY!

Work

1. List the similarities and the differences of the two strikes.
2. What lessons do you think workers in other industries learned from the match girls' strike?
3. Complete the table you started on the Tolpuddle Martyrs. Pick out the successes and find a source that supports your point.
4. Use the table to answer the question: How successful were working-class unions? Try to show both sides of the argument.

Practice Question

Compare Chartism with New Unionism. In what ways were they similar? **8 marks**

Study Tip

It would be easy to confuse New Model Unions and New Unionism, so make sure you know exactly what you are comparing! Think about the kind of people who were involved, and the outcomes of the movements.

10.1 Where was a woman's place?

By 1913, the suffragette movement was in full swing. The Prime Minister had been attacked, buildings had been burned down, some women were starving themselves to death and others had been arrested. One suffragette even died after being hit by a horse during the world famous Derby horse race. Why did such a violent movement emerge, just for the vote? How did the government react? Did the violent methods work?

Objectives

- **Identify** attitudes to women in the nineteenth century.
- **Describe** why women wanted the vote.
- **Predict** which group would have the most success.

A woman's place?

During the Industrial Revolution, women had started to work in factories and to earn more money than they ever had working from home. There were many reforms that improved the working conditions for women in factories and mines. For middle-class women, however, their world still revolved around the home. In addition, many people believe that the reforms for the working class were actually an attempt to put women back in the home, where they could look after their husbands and children.

There were some acts during the nineteenth century that made life better for women, such as the Married Women's Property Act, 1870. This allowed women to control their own income and property after marriage. Previously, their income and property had been under the control of their husbands. This had meant women were dependent on men, but the new act started to change this.

Despite the changes, women had certainly not achieved equality by the start of the twentieth century. Most professions expected women to leave when they got married: their job was now to be a wife and a mother. Even if women did the same jobs as men they were paid less. As was the case for many groups before, the one way to bring about change would be for women to have representation in government. Women needed the vote!

Millicent Fawcett and the National Union of Women's Suffrage Societies

The need to persuade men that women deserved the vote became organised in 1897. By this time women had been able to vote in local elections and school board elections. However, for real change, women would need to be able to vote at a national level.

Millicent Fawcett, the wife of the **Liberal** MP Henry Fawcett, brought all the groups campaigning for women's suffrage together to form the National Union of Women's Suffrage Societies (NUWSS). They became known as the Suffragists. This was a collection of middle-class women who believed in peaceful methods. They felt that to persuade men to give women the vote, women would have to show that they were kind and gentle. This was what men expected women to be.

The Pankhursts and the Women's Social and Political Union

Some Suffragists became frustrated with how long it was taking for change to occur. In 1903, a member of the Manchester branch of the NUWSS — Emmeline Pankhurst — decided that it was time to take more direct action. Mrs Pankhurst and her

▼ **SOURCE A** *An NUWSS poster showing the root of the campaign and the different branches that made up the NUWSS*

▼ **SOURCE B** *Millicent Fawcett, pictured around 1890*

two daughters, Sylvia and Christabel, formed the Women's Social and Political Union (WSPU). They believed in 'deeds not words' and were not scared to live up to their motto.

The Pankhursts were middle class and had a long history of supporting women's causes. Emmeline's husband had been Richard Pankhurst. He was a lawyer who had written the Married Women's Property Act.

The Women's Freedom League

By 1907, the WSPU had many members who engaged in the militant tactics promoted by the Pankhursts and other leaders. However, there were many who wanted change but did not believe in violent methods. They were mostly pacifists. These women broke away and created the Women's Freedom League (WFL). As well as campaigning for the vote, they also campaigned for equal pay for women. There were now three different groups, all campaigning for the same cause. They all wanted the vote; they just had different ways of campaigning for it.

▼ **SOURCE C** Emmeline Pankhurst; born in 1858, she founded the Women's Franchise League in 1889. This fought to allow married women to vote in local elections.

Key Words

liberal

▶ **SOURCE D** An original WSPU rosette; the colours used were for specific reasons – purple signified dignity, green showed hope and white symbolised purity

▼ **SOURCE E** A Women's Freedom League demonstration, June 1908

Work

1. Copy out the following statements about women in the nineteenth century. Next to them write TRUE or FALSE:
   - Women could vote in national elections.
   - A woman was expected to leave her job when she got married.
   - A woman's husband would legally own all her money and property on marriage.
   - A woman was paid less than a man for doing the same job.
2. Explain what Millicent Fawcett, Emmeline Pankhurst and a member of the Women's Freedom League would agree and disagree about, concerning women's suffrage.
3. Which group do you think would have had the most success? Write a letter to the leader explaining why you would like to join them.

Extension

The idea of equality for women was not a new concept by the twentieth century. Research the work of Mary Wollstonecraft. Why do you think nothing changed for women when she was writing in the eighteenth century? What else was happening in the world that might have led Wollstonecraft to believe change was possible?

Britain: Power and the people 155

10.2A What was the impact of the campaign for women's suffrage?

By 1914, the campaign for women's suffrage had gathered pace; it now had many supporters. The women were developing their tactics and gaining support. However, the First World War caused a change in the role of women. Did it help with their campaign? Which branch of the movement gained most support and which had the most success? Did women get the vote?

Objectives

- **Describe** the different tactics used in the campaign for the vote for women.
- **Explain** the government response to the suffragettes' actions.
- **Evaluate** the success of the violent tactics used in the campaign.

Give peace a chance

The NUWSS used their political contacts to lobby MPs. They pledged to support MPs who believed in universal suffrage. Their members were trained to speak publicly, in a persuasive but non-violent way. They created petitions and pamphlets to persuade the nation and those in government that women deserved the vote. Many people were persuaded by the campaign, but some members felt that the Suffragists' actions were too easy to ignore.

Despite their placid tactics, the NUWSS did have many supporters throughout the early twentieth century. When the government did not pass an act in 1912 to extend the vote to women, the NUWSS started a pilgrimage from Carlisle to London. Thousands of people joined the march in support.

We need change now!

Led by Emmeline Pankhurst, some WSPU members decided to use more militant tactics. They were prepared to use more extreme, often violent methods. They were referred to as suffragettes, to distinguish them from the Suffragists. To begin with, they had the support of the Liberal Prime Minister, Henry Campbell-Bannerman, who told the women to pester the government and not to show patience.

Their tactics included heckling members of parliament during speeches. They stood outside the House of Commons and held demonstrations. In 1912, they started a stone-throwing campaign. Hundreds of windows were smashed and over 200 suffragettes were arrested. This was all part of their plan: the court cases got them extra publicity.

The suffragettes took their actions further, making arson attacks and blowing up buildings. MPs were put on high alert. They were warned to be suspicious of parcels in case they contained explosives. In 1913, parliament made another attempt to give women the vote. This failed.

Derby Day, 1913

At the Derby horse race at Epsom in 1913, the king's horse was running round the racecourse when it was brought to the ground by a woman who had deliberately walked onto the racecourse as the horses approached. This woman was Emily Wilding Davison, and she died of her wounds in hospital, soon after the incident. She was a suffragette, and became the first **martyr** of the suffrage movement. Historians are divided about whether Davison had planned to kill herself that day. It seems she might have been trying to stick a suffragette rosette on the horse, but she was trampled as the horse was going too fast. There is uncertainty about her intentions and whether she meant to kill herself because she had bought herself a return ticket home.

▼ **SOURCE A** *A portrait of Sir Thomas Carlyle that was slashed by a suffragette; the way she slashed the face made people worry that suffragettes may do this in real life*

> **Key Word**
>
> martyr

Regardless, the movement now had evidence of how committed their members were. They were so serious about getting the vote that they were willing to die for it. Emily Davison was given a headstone that said: Deeds not words.

SOURCE B The cover of *The Suffragette* magazine, 13 June 1913

Due to the dangers of force-feeding, the government passed the Prisoners (Temporary Discharge for Ill Health) Act in 1913. This would allow them to release the women when they became too weak from starvation. Once they had been rehabilitated and were healthy enough to return to prison, they would be re-arrested. The act thus became known as the 'Cat and Mouse Act'.

SOURCE C Adapted from an account of a suffragette on hunger strike; the WSPU were able to publish her account in a pamphlet while she was still in prison before the Cat and Mouse Act:

> I was then surrounded and forced back onto the chair, which was tilted backwards. There were about ten persons around me. The doctor then forced my mouth so as to form a pouch, and held me while one of the wardresses poured some liquid from a spoon; it was milk and brandy. While I was held down a nasal tube was inserted. It is two yards long, with a funnel at the end; there is a glass junction in the middle to see if the liquid is passing. Great pain is experienced during the process, both mental and physical.

SOURCE D A suffragette poster about the 'Cat and Mouse Act', showing a cat (representing the police, the prison authorities and the government) holding a mouse (representing a suffragette) in its mouth. Many people were against this act, which seemed to prolong the suffering of women by repeatedly re-arresting them, and public sympathy for the suffragette movement grew as a result.

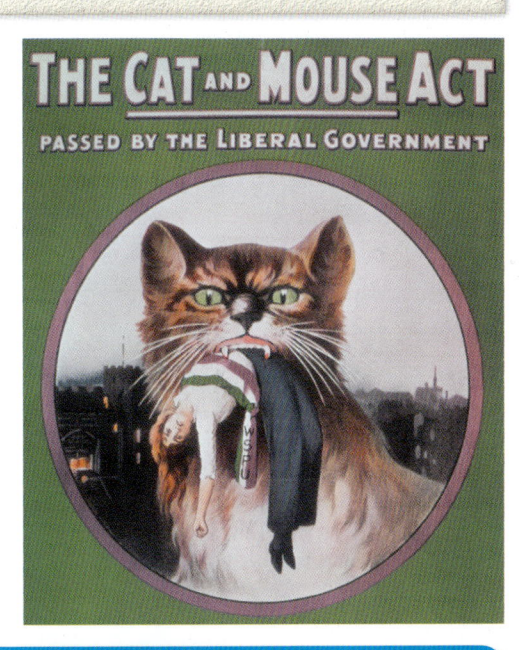

Why does the cat chase the mouse?

The suffragette tactics extended to their time in prison. They were often arrested for their violent attacks, or for disturbing the peace by chaining themselves to railings. When they were in prison, many went on hunger strike. This is a tactic used by prisoners as a way to continue their campaign by gaining publicity. The government knew they could not have women dying in prison: these women were middle-class, and many had husbands or fathers who held influential jobs. Prison officers initially tried force-feeding the suffragettes. However, this was dangerous and could lead to disabilities and death.

> **Work**
>
> 1. Write out as many tactics as you can that the different groups used. Colour code them to show which would have a long-term impact and which would have a short-term impact.
> 2. a What tactics do **Sources A**, **B** and **C** tell you about?
>   b Why is Davison portrayed as an angel in **Source B**?
>   c Do you think this would convince people to support the suffragettes?
>   d Which one of the sources gives details of the most effective tactic, in your opinion?
> 3. Why did the government introduce the 'Cat and Mouse Act'?
> 4. Look at **Source D**. Create your own propaganda poster that shows a tactic and the response it got. You can create the poster from government's or the WSPU's perspective.
> 5. How useful is **Source B** to a historian researching suffragette tactics?

10.2B What was the impact of the campaign for women's suffrage?

Responses to militancy

The suffragettes were starting to gain criticism for their actions, with many people at the time feeling that they were actually preventing women getting the vote, rather than helping. Their violent actions made them look, in some people's eyes, irrational and unbalanced. These were exactly the reasons that many people had used to not give women the vote.

Even many women objected to the campaign for universal suffrage. These women believed a woman's place was at home, supporting her husband and caring for her children. They did not think politics was a world women belonged in. This was a view held by the Liberal Prime Minister, Herbert Asquith. Asquith did not support votes for women; he believed the decision should only be made if it improved government and the political process. He could see no argument for why it would and therefore opposed extending the franchise to women.

▼ **INTERPRETATION E** Adapted from *The Place of Women: 1700 to the Present Day* (1971), written by John Ray:

> The opposition was great. Some men objected to women having the vote because they believed them to be inferior. It was suggested that women could not think out matters coolly and calmly. Others would not agree to women's suffrage because they did not want change. Women had never voted before. Why should they start now? A further objection involved property. In 1900, few women were householders or lodgers. If the vote were given to them, then it would have to be given also to men who were not householders or lodgers. At that time political parties were not prepared to do this.

▼ **SOURCE F** A poster, produced by the National League for Opposing Woman Suffrage, called 'A Suffragette's Home'; the note stuck on the poster says, 'Back in an hour or so'

The angel of the factory

When war broke out in 1914, the NUWSS and WPSU united to support the war effort. The suffragettes stopped their militant and violent campaign, and as a result of the work they did they earned themselves the nickname of 'angel of the factory'. The Women's Freedom League, however, refused to support the war effort. As pacifists, they did not want to support the men fighting in Europe.

It is widely accepted by historians that women's war work helped them get the vote. They worked in factories, on farms and even at the front line, as nurses. This showed that women could do the same jobs as men. It also proved that women could make clear-headed decisions, not only in factories but in running family businesses and driving ambulances in dangerous circumstances at the front line. Lastly, the argument that women were not as intelligent was contradicted by the fact they managed to successfully look after the family, run the home and do the jobs their husbands had done. Women proved they could do it all.

The post-war situation

After the war, the men who returned from the trenches moved back into their jobs. Many women moved back into the home. Before the outbreak of war, the government had accepted that some women should have the vote. The government also had to consider that a lot of the men who had gone to fight did not have the vote: this was recognised as unfair. Thus, in 1918 the Representation of the Peoples Act was passed. This gave all men over the age of 21 the vote, and some women over the age 21, if they owned property, otherwise they had to be over 30. This was a success for the wealthy middle-class women but did nothing for working-class women. Some women continued to campaign until, in 1928, women were given the vote on equal terms with men.

Women throughout the twentieth century

The campaign for women's rights did not stop in 1928. In the 1960s, a new movement developed in Britain and the USA. This was the Women's Movement. Women were no longer campaigning for the vote but for a different kind of equality. They wanted equal pay with men, increased numbers of women in higher education, 24-hour child care, free contraception and abortion on demand. They wanted women to have the same rights and freedoms as men. The movement was successful, with the government passing the Divorce Reform Act in 1969, arguably an extension of the Married Woman's Property Act. The 1969 act allowed women to divorce their husbands easily, and they were entitled to claim any property owned in the divorce settlement. In 1970 the Equal Pay Act and in 1975 the Sex Discrimination Act gave women more rights and protection in the workplace. This was all happening during a time of social change: the government of Harold Wilson was creating a more liberal society. Not only were women's lives changed: Wilson also changed the law so that homosexuality was no longer illegal; he tried to end discrimination against ethnic minorities; and he abolished capital punishment.

There is still a disproportionately low percentage of women in higher education compared to men, and there remains today a wage gap in Britain. Women are still not completely equal with men, but the suffragettes ensured that women could do something to change it. They could vote and be part of the political process.

Extension

Research the impact of the following: the New English Law of Property (1926), the Law Reform Act (1935), the Education Act (1944), the Abortion Act (1967), the Equal Pay Act (1970), the Employment Protection Act (1975), and the publication of *The Female Eunuch* (1969) and *Spare Rib* (July 1972).

SOURCE G *Women marching in New York to commemorate the fiftieth anniversary of women's suffrage in the USA, August 1970*

Work

1. Give three reasons against universal suffrage that were used before 1914.
2. Why do you think women did not get the vote before 1914?
3. a Create a timeline showing all the key acts/events in the journey for women's suffrage. Which events were indirect reasons why women got the vote? Which was the spark?
   b Make your timeline a 'concept timeline' by showing periods of tension and good relations between the government and the suffragettes.
4. 'Women's war work got them the vote.' How far do you agree? You need to compare their war work with their militant tactics. Which one had the biggest impact?
5. How do you think Emmeline Pankhurst would feel if she could see **Source G**?

Practice Question

Compare the Chartist campaign with the campaign for women's suffrage. In what ways were they similar? **8 marks**

Study Tip

Explore the split in both groups – they both had peaceful and militant branches. Both had clear leaders as well: did their leadership help or hinder the success of each movement?

11.1A The General Strike, 1926

In May 1926, Britain was almost at a standstill. Coal miners across the country were angered by falling wages and increased working hours: they decide to go on strike. Britain faced the prospect of no transport, coal or electricity. In order to prevent disaster the Conservative government had to act quickly. In the end, the General Strike lasted for nine days, with workers from heavy industries such as the steel industry, shipbuilding and the railway industry supporting the striking miners. Did the strike result in better working conditions for the miners? Did the government and unions work together to resolve the issues?

Objectives

- **Explain** the causes of the General Strike of 1926.
- **Analyse** the causes and consequences of the strike.
- **Evaluate** evidence using your own knowledge.

Britain after the First World War

During the First World War, because of the demand for armaments, Britain's heavy industries enjoyed high output and a dramatic increase in people working for them. All coal mines had been **nationalised** during the war, and the miners had hoped that they would be continued to be owned by the country when war ended. This would mean the government would be obliged to invest money, thus their jobs would be safe. However, after the war the government was quick to return control of the mines to their private owners.

After 1918, the future was not looking good for Britain's mining industry, as there was a fall in the demand for coal. So, the mine owners needed to dramatically reduce costs: their mines had to become more efficient in order to make money. One option the owners had was to close down mines that were inefficient: this meant they could concentrate production on the mines that were making the most money. Another option was to start introducing new automatic machinery: this meant fewer men were needed as the machines could do a lot of the work, a situation similar to the one at the start of the Industrial Revolution.

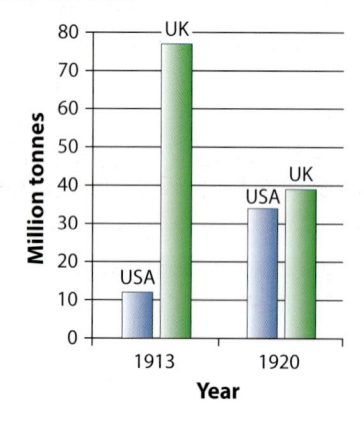

British mines were the pits

Foreign competition and a lack of modern technology pushed British coal mine owners further into crisis. Mines in countries such as Germany had more modern equipment, as they were owned by big companies that could invest lots of money in new technology. Increasingly, British mines could not compete with their output. The unions wanted the government to **re-nationalise** the mines; the mines needed investment.

▼ **INTERPRETATION B** *Adapted from* British Economic and Social History, *1987, written by modern historian Philip Sauvain:*

> [By the early 1920s] Poland and Germany, as well as the United States, were challenging Britain's supremacy in the export of coal. Their coal was easier to mine. They had lower labour costs and often lower transport costs as well.

Black Friday

On Friday 15 April 1921, mine owners announced an extension of the working day, along with a drop in wages. The miners were outraged and decided to strike. Worried that other employers would do the same as the mine owners, the Trades Union Congress (TUC) called other industries out on strike in **solidarity**. However, at the last minute the railway and dockers unions pulled out. They did not feel the immediate concerns as the miners did; they were not as worried for their jobs. And so, left alone without any support from other industries, the miners felt that they had no other option but to return to work with longer days and for lower wages.

▼ **A** *Bar graphs showing the output of coal in the UK and the USA in 1913 and 1920*

Chapter 11 Workers' rights

Red Friday

In 1925, the price of coal fell again and the mine owners declared further changes to hours and pay. Prime Minister Stanley Baldwin knew that the other unions would support the miners this time. He was worried about a workers' revolution and knew he had to do something to stop the unrest. On Friday 31 July 1925, Baldwin agreed to subsidise the coal industry. He also set up the Samuels Commission, the job of which was to reach an agreement between the miners and the mine owners. Many people believed that Baldwin was just buying time with the commission, so he could prepare Britain for the inevitable General Strike. But the miners were happy, for now.

Workers, unite!

In April 1926, Baldwin's subsidy money ran out: the TUC met to discuss action. On 1 May – May Day: a day when workers' rights are celebrated – they agreed to strike. On 3 May, Britain's first General Strike began: ships sat unloaded in docks, trains didn't move and coal wasn't mined. The strike divided the country.

Fact

Friday 15 April is known as Black Friday because many workers felt betrayed by their union leaders. Friday 31 July is known as Red Friday because the workers achieved a victory with the government subsidies.

SOURCE C *A cartoon shown in a trade union magazine in 1925; it is called 'The Subsidised Mineowner – Poor Beggar!'*

THE SUBSIDISED MINEOWNER—POOR BEGGAR!

Key Words

nationalise   foreign competition
re-nationalise   solidarity

SOURCE D *Arthur James Cook, a trade union leader, addressing miners in October 1929*

Work

1. Why had Britain's heavy industries enjoyed a boom period before 1921?
2. a. Create a mind-map showing the causes of the General Strike in 1926. You should annotate it with detail from the text and the sources. Try to categorise the causes.
   b. Can you justify why one cause was more important than the other?
3. a. What information about the General Strike can you infer from **Source C**?
   b. Which side is being represented in **Source C**? Explain your answer using the source and your own knowledge.
   c. Is **Source C** a good source for researching the causes of the General Strike?

Extension

Research the issues that lead to large numbers of workers going on strike in Britain today.

Britain: Power and the people 161

11.1B The General Strike, 1926

The nine days

The General Strike lasted for nine days in May 1926. The table below shows the actions taken by each side to either make the strike effective or try to limit its impact.

E *Government and TUC actions*

Government actions:	TUC actions:
Used the Emergency Powers Act from the First World War to arrange for the army to take over the jobs of the striking workers.	Created their own newspaper, *The British Worker*, and used it to explain the motivations for the strike.
Encouraged middle-class students to take a break from university and work in heavy industries; more than 226,000 student volunteers did this.	Also used the paper to remind strikers to remain peaceful and not use violent tactics.
Started a propaganda campaign with their own newspaper, *The British Gazette*, which tried to turn the public against the strikers; the newspaper was edited by Winston Churchill.	Some strikers did become violent and there were clashes with the police.
Stanley Baldwin made speeches referring to the strike as a revolution; this fuelled the public's fear of **communism**.	Strikers travelled the country to picket with other industries in solidarity.
Armoured cars, driven by the army and police, were sent to key cities to stop the violent clashes between the strikers and government supporters. They were armed with machine guns.	Funds were set up to help feed the strikers and their families. This would ensure the strike could keep going.

SOURCE F *A volunteer worker helping a railway passenger during the strike in 1926*

SOURCE G *The front page of* The British Gazette, *5 May 1926; this was the government newspaper*

SOURCE H *The front page of* The British Worker, *13 May 1926; this was the official strike news bulletin*

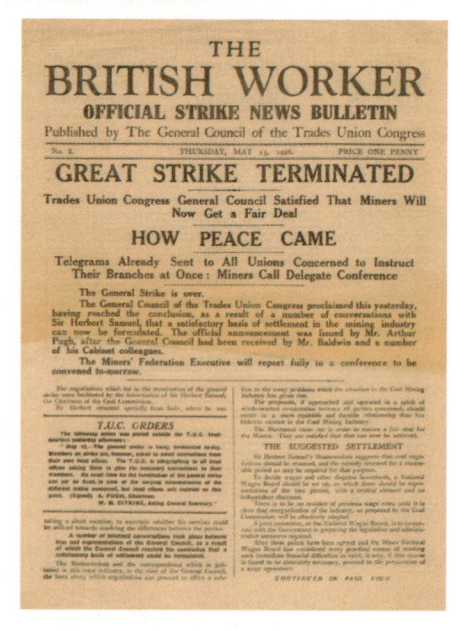

Back to work

After nine days, on 12 May, the strike ended with the TUC deciding to negotiate with the government and finally accepting the findings of the Samuel Commission.

The miners' federation had refused to take part in these negotiations. Some slight changes made to Samuel's report were enough for the TUC leaders, and they encouraged the miners to return to work. By this time, the TUC had run out of money and could not possibly continue with the strike action. They had been defeated by the government who had been preparing for the strike for nine months; it had been paying the subsidy to the mine owners. Furthermore, the violent actions of some meant that public opinion had gone against the strikers. Moreover, the party that was meant to represent the workers, the Labour Party, was not in full support of the strike action. Workers in all industries, apart from the miners, returned to work. The miners did not fully return to work until November, when they were forced back by hunger and disillusionment. They worked longer hours for lower wages: many felt that the strike had been for nothing.

Consequences of the strike for the unions

After the failure of the General Strike, union membership fell dramatically. This coincided with a rise in unemployment. The government passed the Trade Disputes and Trade Unions Act in 1927, which made it illegal for unions to join together to strike. Unions could no longer use money from union memberships to fund political parties: all members had to agree for this to happen. This had an impact on the unions' relationship with the Labour Party and weakened the power of the unions. Union membership would not reach peak levels again until the Second World War.

▼ **SOURCE I** *A Punch cartoon from 1926 showing the constitutional government and the TUC lever breaking under it; this showed the weakness of the TUC*

THE LEVER BREAKS.

Key Word

communism

Work

1. **a** Describe three tactics used by each side during the General Strike.
   b Explain why the tactics were used. Can you say which was the most effective?
2. What can you learn from **Source I** about why the strike failed?
3. **a** Work with a partner. One of you should write an article for *The British Gazette*, outlining the causes and events of the General Strike. The other person should write an article for *The British Worker*. Your articles should be no longer than 200 words.
   b In what ways are your articles similar?
   c In what ways are they different?
   d Can you suggest reasons why they are different?

Practice Question

How useful is **Source I** to a historian studying the General Strike and the reasons for its failure?

8 marks

Study Tip

Remember that sources can have clear opinions about the General Strike. You have to be able to explain why it has this view and if this makes it more or less useful. You should try to refer to the source being one-sided; this way you will always consider the other side.

Extension

The left-wing historian A. J. P. Taylor has written lots about the twentieth century, with a focus on the Second World War. His politics mean that he supported workers' revolutions; but he was also a pacifist. He stated, 'The strikers asked nothing for themselves. They did not seek to challenge the government but still less to overthrow the constitution. They merely wanted the miners to have a living wage. They were loyal to their unions, as they had been loyal during the war to their country and their generals. They once more went into the trenches, without enthusiasm and with little hope.' How has Taylor presented the strikers? Why does he have this interpretation?

11.2 Trade union reform

In 1900, only 12 per cent of Britain's labour force had been in a trade union. By 1984, the proportion had grown to around 50 per cent. One of the key tactics available to workers in a trade union is to go on strike if they are unhappy about something relating to their job. By the 1980s, British workers were going on so many strikes that striking became known as the 'British disease'. Why, after the General Strike of 1926, did workers continue to strike on such a large scale? Did the government use the same tactics to deal with striking workers as they had done during the General Strike?

Objectives

- **Examine** the British economy after the Second World War.
- **Describe** the changing relationship between the government and the unions.
- **Explain** the reasons for union failure in the 1980s.

Post-war nationalisation and reform

After the Second World War, there were many changes in British society. There was a strong belief that life should be better for the majority of people; this after all was what people had been fighting for during the war.

The creation of the welfare state, the National Health Service and the nationalisation of key industries were all features of post-war Britain. Nationalisation started with the Bank of England, civil aviation, coal, and cables and wireless. Then came railways, canals, road haulage and trucking, electricity, and gas. The nationalisation of industries played a key role in creating a good relationship between the government, employers and union members. The appointment of Ernest Bevin as a moderate union leader helped to gain union support after the General Strike.

In 1946, the new Labour government passed the Trades Disputes and Trade Unions Act; this amended the same act of 1927. Union membership flourished. This was great news until the 1960s, which brought an increase in prices and a drop in wages.

Industrial disputes: the road to unrest

A *Government successes and the fate of the unions*

1960s Country suffers from periods of inflation; unions demand wage increases to match rising prices

1969 MP Barbara Castle produces a plan calling for a secret ballot and a 28-day cooling-off period before a strike is approved

1969–71 Smaller unions join together; membership continues to increase

1971 Industrial Relations Act introduced: makes ballots compulsory

1972 and 1974 National Union of Miners vote for coal strikes; leads to shortage of coal; government rations electricity and brings in 3-day working week

1974 New Labour government abolishes Industrial Relations Act and introduces social contract instead, securing regular wage increases for workers

1976 Social contract challenged by Grunwick dispute, a strike by Asian women working in Grunwick Film Processing Laboratories in London; they strike for two years in protest of poor working conditions; their leader goes on hunger strike

SOURCE B *Jayaben Desai, picketing during the Grunwick dispute*

Winter 1978–79
Strikes in many industries, leads to 'Winter of Discontent'; reports of rubbish piling up in streets and bodies piling up in morgues as workers strike

1984
Thatcher's government introduces Trade Union Act; this states 80 per cent of members must agree for strikes to be called; closed shops are illegal unless 85 per cent of workers are happy with situation; secondary picketing (of companies that do business with employer) is outlawed

1985
Miners' strike ends in government victory. Inflation falls, unemployment rises above three million

1979
Conservatives win election, Margaret Thatcher becomes Prime Minister; government begins to challenge strength of unions

Government success

Extension

In 2014, the film *Pride!* told the story of the LGBT (lesbian, gay, bisexual and transgender) community and their organisation, Lesbian and Gays Support the Miners. Research the impact this group's support had on the miners' strike in 1984.

1980 and 1982
Employment Acts introduced, changing rules on picketing and making it unlawful for someone to be dismissed because of a closed shop

Fate of unions

Industry continues to decline

1984
Miners' strikes, led by Arthur Scargill, sweep country; Women Against Pit Closures set up to rally support in communities and help feed families

▼ **INTERPRETATION C** *Adapted from an account by a striking miner, John Moulson, in 2015; he remembers what it was like being on the picket line:*

> I lived in a mining town and it was expected that every man would join the picket lines to cause as much disruption to coal movements as possible. It started to get really scary, as not only could we have been seriously injured, we could also have ended up with a criminal record. Throughout the strike the camaraderie between the communities was unbelievable, and the support given by local people enabled many of the miners and their families to survive.

Huge stockpiles of unsold coal, split in miners' union, well organised policing of pits that continue to work, lack of support from other unions, and negative press attention means miners' strike ends

Laws introduced by Conservatives in early 1980s do not end confrontations between employers and workers; disputes by print industry workers, teachers and miners. None is particularly successful

Work

1. List all the reasons people went on strike in the late twentieth century.
2. Create a graph showing the power struggle between the government and the unions. Put dates along a line, and above put the key events that made the government more powerful in relation to trade unions. Below put the events that made it less powerful.
3. Was the failing economy the main factor, among others, for the failure of the trade unions?

Practice Question

Compare the reasons for strikes in the nineteenth century with the reasons for strikes after the Second World War. In what ways were they different?

8 marks

Study Tip

Try to explain the reasons for each by considering society at the time. Why might one have different reasons from the other? Is it because they had different motivations, or was society different?

Britain: Power and the people

12.1 Was the 'mother country' a good mum?

On 22 June 1948, the ship *Empire Windrush* docked at Tilbury, near London. On board were 492 people from the Caribbean. During the 1950s, more people arrived from the Caribbean and from Asia. It is this **migration** that helped make Britain the multiracial nation it is today. Why did this migration take place and how did Britain respond to the new arrivals?

Objectives

- **Identify** reasons for immigration to Britain after the Second World War.
- **Describe** the experience of the immigrants.
- **Evaluate** the usefulness of a source about the immigrant experience.

Britain, the mother country

At the beginning of the twentieth century, Britain had a large empire. After the First and Second World Wars Britain started to lose this empire, with many countries becoming independent. Some of these countries kept ties with Britain by becoming part of the Commonwealth. These countries had fought for Britain in both wars, and in 1948, the British Nationality Act gave all 800 million Commonwealth citizens the chance to come to the 'mother country' and gain full British citizenship. Many decided to take this opportunity.

Why were immigrants encouraged to come to Britain?

There were many reasons why people from Commonwealth countries were encouraged to come to Britain. Citizenship in Britain was initially awarded to those that had fought alongside Britain in the Second World War. Many other people were keen to take advantage of the British Nationality Act. They had heard so much about Britain and were keen to see the country that had ruled over them for so long. There were also many other reasons why immigrants were encouraged to come.

Loans for transport

It was easy for people to emigrate to Britain: their governments gave out interest-free loans so they could afford the ship fare.

Shortage of labour

There was a shortage of labour for low paid and unskilled jobs in Britain. The British government was trying to rebuild the country after the war, and needed people to fill these jobs. One example is London Transport, who recruited people from Barbados and Jamaica to drive buses and trains. The job opportunities were not always there in their home countries. Furthermore, Britain wanted to secure the loyalty of these countries in case they were needed again.

▼ **SOURCE A** *Men being interviewed during a recruitment fare for London Transport, 1956*

Opportunity

British companies held recruitment fares like the one in Source A. This meant that, before even leaving home, many immigrants had secured a job. The opportunities seemed endless.

▼ **SOURCE B** *Adapted from a personal account by Arthur Curling, originally from Jamaica, who joined the RAF aged 16:*

> I came to England first in 1944, in the air force. I returned back to Jamaica in 1946. After spending two years there, it was too small for me. But England has something that you want to get back to; you can't put your finger on it.

Chapter 12 Minority rights

The immigrant experience

Not everyone shared Arthur Curling's feelings about wanting to be in Britain. The new immigrants were mostly placed in areas where they were needed for work. Early immigrants from the Caribbean were mostly young men, who had planned to make money to send home to their families. This surge of young black men into communities caused some resentment. Most white people moved out to other areas, a reaction called 'white-flight'. In many areas where the white residents remained there was **segregation**. Resentment boiled between young white and black men. Groups of young white men, such as the Teddy Boys, felt that the young immigrants were stealing 'their women'. This tension exploded in 1958 with the Notting Hill Riots in London.

Many immigrants were highly educated but were forced to take low paid, unskilled work, as their qualifications were not recognised in Britain. However, this was not the case for all immigrants. There were many doctors who arrived from the **Indian subcontinent** who were employed in the new National Health Service. The experience of the Asian immigrants was different from those from the Caribbean. Language barriers and religious differences often meant many Asian immigrants formed their own communities and started their own businesses.

Overcrowding was a big problem for all immigrant communities, as many landlords refused to let them rent their accommodation. Local authorities also tried to stop black and Asian people renting houses in particular areas. A high profile case of this was in Smethwick, Birmingham. The black and Asian residents got the support of Malcolm X, who visited the area in 1965 as a protest against the housing policy towards immigrants.

The British had boasted about their fight against the Nazis in the Second World War. They were proud that they had defeated fascism and racism. However, many groups then experienced discrimination in Britain in the decades that followed. Did Britain, the mother country, really protect all her children?

▼ **SOURCE C** *Malcolm X at Marshall Street in Smethwick, West Midlands, 12 February 1965*

▼ **SOURCE D** *Signs like these encouraged discrimination and hostility towards immigrants*

Key Words

migration   segregation   Indian subcontinent

Work

1. Write out a conversation between a British MP who wants to 'pull' an immigrant to the UK, and an immigrant who explains about the 'push' factors in their home country.
2. a. Study **Source B**. What can we learn from it about immigrant experiences?
   b. Does **Source B** tell us everything about the immigrant experience?

Practice Question

How useful is **Source B** to a historian investigating the immigrant experience in Britain? **8 marks**

Study Tip

Think: the source might not tell us everything, but does it tell us about typical views at the time?

Extension

Find out more about the 1958 Notting Hill Riots. Look at newspaper reports from the time and create a presentation on how the media fuelled discontent in multiracial Britain. Did any media help?

12.2 Did the government make life worse for immigrants?

By 1958, blood had been spilled over immigration. Race riots in Notting Hill and Nottingham resulted in dozens of arrests, many injuries and thousands of pounds worth of damage. Race relations in some parts of Britain were at a low point. There were clear tensions in society and things were getting worse. The government responded by introducing acts that were meant to improve race relations. What were the aims of these acts? Did they work?

Objectives

- **Outline** the events that led to government controls on immigration.
- **Explain** the key features of the controls.
- **Justify** your opinion about the impact of the immigration controls.

Why was government intervention needed?

After the Notting Hill Riots in 1958, relations between immigrant groups and white residents were not good. Factory owners were increasingly reluctant to employ black workers, and segregation became an even bigger problem in housing, employment and even the social lives of this new community. The general feeling was that too many immigrants were settling in major cities, and that this needed to be stopped.

▼ **A** Table showing immigration numbers from the Caribbean and from India, Pakistan and Bangladesh

Year	Caribbean	India, Pakistan and Bangladesh	Total
1956	26,000	8000	34,000
1957	23,000	7000	30,000
1958	17,000	11,000	28,000
1959	20,000	4000	24,000
1960	53,000	10,000	63,000
1961	62,000	50,000	112,000
1962	35,000	47,000	82,000

Government responses

The government had two main aims in responding to the problems. One was to curb the number of immigrants coming into the country; the second was to tackle the racial discrimination that had developed.

The first response was the Commonwealth Immigrants Act, 1962. This controlled the immigration of all Commonwealth passport holders, except the British. It controlled the movement of people by stating that immigrants now needed to apply for a work voucher before they came to Britain. They could only get a voucher if the skills they had were in demand in Britain. This had an effect on many Commonwealth doctors and nurses: they could not find employment in their chosen professions as their qualifications were not recognised.

MPs were divided over Commonwealth immigration controls, but in the 1964 general election those who had been against immigration reform were not re-elected. The people had spoken. They wanted change.

In 1968, another Commonwealth Immigrants Act was passed. This put even tighter controls on immigration, by extending restrictions to those who were part of the Commonwealth but held British passports. If these people did not have a parent or grandparent who was born in, or was a citizen of, the UK, they could not move there. This act confirmed to many immigrants that non-white migration was the problem the government was really trying to stop. The government reforms were perceived as being racist and unfair.

The 1968 act was a reaction to the new politics in Kenya after its independence from Britain in 1963. It had gained independence under Jomo Kenyatta, who had started a policy of Africanisation. Many Asians living in Kenya felt this policy would discriminate against them. Some historians have argued that it was the potential arrival of 200,000 Asians from Kenya that prompted the passing of the Commonwealth Immigrants Act of 1968. It seemed clear that the motivations behind the act were racism and discrimination.

By 1971, the Conservative government was ready to push for even tighter controls, so they passed the Immigration Act. This act replaced employment vouchers with work permits; these permits allowed only temporary residence in Britain. There was also an aspect of the act that encouraged **voluntary repatriation**; this meant the government would assist people in moving back to their country of origin and in changing their citizenship from British to that country. The act still allowed for **chain migration**; this meant families could join those who already had citizenship.

▼ SOURCE B *A march in London, 1962, protesting against the Commonwealth Immigrants Act*

Enoch Powell and political opposition

The feeling that these acts were fuelled by racism was further supported in people's minds by politicians such as Enoch Powell. Powell was a Conservative MP in 1968 when Labour was in power. He made a speech which became known as his 'Rivers of Blood' speech, for the way it highlighted the race issue. He said that immigration posed a threat to British identity and that the future would be violent for a multiracial Britain if immigration was not stopped.

▼ SOURCE C *Adapted extract from Enoch Powell's 'Rivers of Blood' speech, April 1968:*

> We must be mad, literally mad, as a nation to be permitting the annual inflow of some 50,000 dependants, who are for the most part the material of the future growth of the immigrant-descended population. It is like watching a nation busily engaged in heaping up its own funeral pyre. So insane are we that we actually permit unmarried persons to immigrate for the purpose of founding a family with spouses and fiancés whom they have never seen.

Although his views were shocking, Powell represented a large section of society with similar views. He was not the first politician to try to harness support with these views.

Key Words

voluntary repatriation   chain migration
second generation

▼ SOURCE D *Pro-Powell graffiti, London, May 1968*

With its reactions to immigration, the government had made its views clear. How would the immigrant community respond? What about **second generation** immigrants – people who were actually born in the UK?

Work

1. **a** Write on cards as many reasons as you can find for the government's controls on immigration.
   b Which reasons show long-term causes of unrest, and which show short-term causes of unrest?
   c Create a table with three columns. These should have the headings: Act; Improving race relations; Supporting the concerns of those against immigration. Provide information about each act, and in the relevant column explain how it either improved relations or supported the concerns.

2. Which act do you consider to be a turning point in immigration control? Use the sources to help you explain your answer. Can you challenge your judgement?

Extension

Research the politics of Idi Amin and his treatment of Asian people in Uganda. Study the government acts again: can you see where the law was changed to help the Asian people trying to escape Amin's rule?

Britain: Power and the people   169

12.3 Protest, riots and reform: how did the people react?

By the early 1970s, the government had done little to reassure the black and Asian communities of Britain that they were equal and welcome. The black community became even more disillusioned when police policies seemed to discriminate against them. By 1981, there had been riots in London, Birmingham and Liverpool. Why did the riots start? How did the government respond? Did relations with black and Asian communities improve?

Objectives

- **Define** Powellism.
- **Explain** the causes of the riots in the UK in the 1970s and 1980s.
- **Evaluate** the significance of immigration to the UK since the Second World War.

Powellism and the National Front

The politics of Enoch Powell received a lot of support, especially from the working class. This support for Powell (known as Powellism) was based on a type of extreme nationalism that viewed white British people as superior to people who were non-white – even if they had been born in Britain.

Some people felt that Powellism fuelled the rise in popularity of a group called the National Front. This group wanted all non-white immigrants to Britain to return to their country of origin – or the country of origin of their parents or grandparents. Many members identified strongly with Hitler's policies in Nazi Germany.

SOURCE A *A demonstration against immigration and in support of Enoch Powell, September 1972*

Race Relations Acts

The government introduced some laws that were intended to improve relations between different communities. They would have to reform both society and politics if they were to succeed. The existence of Powellism and the National Front meant the black community would need reassurance that the government represented them as well.

Fact

1965 Race Relations Act: prevented racial discrimination in housing and employment. Seen as a failure due to Race Relations Board bringing no criminal convictions.

1968 Commonwealth Immigrants Act: aimed to help the integration of immigrant communities.

1976 Race Relations Act: extended the definition of discrimination to any practice that disadvantaged another group. Race Relations Board was replaced with the Commission for Racial Equality, which had much greater powers.

SOURCE B *Adapted extract from Bernie Grant's archives; Grant was elected MP for Tottenham in 1987, one of only three black MPs at the time:*

> When I arrived here there were still signs on the windows – no black, no Irish, no dogs, no children. Then, there was no Race Relations Act, which outlawed all of that. But what I found was that the problem lay in institutional racism; hidden policies which you found in housing, in education and so on.

Riots: Brixton and the UK

The dream of integration and improved relations was short lived. A year after the 1976 Race Relations Act there was the infamous Battle of Lewisham. This was sparked by a National Front march through the borough. The black community felt let down by the police, as they had allowed the march to happen. Relations between the black community and the police were disintegrating further, as the black community were being blamed for crime in the area. This fuelled the National Front's hatred of the black community further. They claimed, 'a multiracial society is wrong, is evil and we will destroy it.'

▼ **SOURCE C** *The police clashing with protestors in the Battle of Lewisham, 13 August 1977*

Tensions continued to build, and in 1981 there were riots in Brixton and in other major cities. These riots can be seen as a continuation of the situation in Lewisham, as the role of the police and their poor relations with black communities provided the sparks for the riots. Adding to the tension, the late 1970s was a time of **recession** in the UK. The resulting economic hardships hit black communities the hardest with high unemployment, poor housing and higher crime rates.

Many young black men in Brixton and other immigrant communities felt that they were being discriminated against, despite the 1976 act. This discrimination was due to the law that allowed police to stop and search people they suspected were about to commit a crime – know as the 'sus law'. This law led to what many described as **racial profiling**: they believed black people were being stopped simply because of the colour of their skin. Furthermore, Operation Swamp 81 meant Brixton was filled with plain-clothes police officers from other districts, using 'sus law' as a way to prevent street crime. More than 1000 people were stopped in six days, further increasing tensions as young black men felt attacked in their own community.

Key Words

recession   racial profiling   racially prejudiced

This simmering tension boiled over when rumours of police brutality to a black man led to an angry crowd confronting police officers. The arrest of a young black man on 10 April 1981 saw the start of the riot, where for three days young black people fought the police, and set fire to vehicles and buildings.

The Scarman Report

Lord Scarman was asked to write a report on the events in Brixton. Before his report was published, similar riots had taken place in Handsworth in Birmingham, in Toxteth in Liverpool and in Manchester. The Scarman Report found that institutional racism did not exist within the Metropolitan Police Service. However, the report did suggest making **racially prejudiced** behaviour an offence. The report also led to the end of 'sus law' and the creation of the Police Complaints Authority. These measures improved relations between the police and the black community.

However, in 1993 Stephen Lawrence, a young black man, was murdered in London. It was a racially motivated attack. An investigation showed that the Metropolitan Police Service had not responded appropriately due to institutional racism.

Work

1. a. Create a graph with a vertical axis showing tension and a horizontal axis showing the years from 1948 to 1981. Plot the events covered on pages 166–171 that caused racial tension in this period.
   b. From your graph, which cause seems to be the most common cause of tension?
2. How did the government try to improve race relations?
3. Why was it difficult to improve race relations?

Practice Question

Explain the significance of Caribbean migration to Britain after the Second World War.   **8 marks**

Study Tip

You should separate this into short- and long-term significance, and into factors – immigration both influenced politics and changed society.

Britain: Power and the people   171

How to... analyse significance

In your exam, you will have to deal with a question about the significance of something, such as an event, an issue or a person.

Practice Question

Explain the significance of the Peasants' Revolt for the government of Britain. **8 marks**

Study Tip

Judging the significance of a person or events is about looking at their impact on different groups and at different times. Something is significant if it was important at the time *and* is also important today. Even if it only impacted on one group, it can still be significant.

Over to you

When we say an event, idea or person is significant, we mean more than just that it is important. Judging the significance of an event, idea or person is about looking at the impact that it had at the time and how it affected people, and whether it had long-lasting effects or caused important change. You should also consider whether the event, idea or person is still relevant to the present day. Now, work through the following questions.

1. Start by planning out your response: what do you know about the Peasants' Revolt? Try to make notes about what happened in the revolt at the time.

2. Consider the impact of the revolt at the time. Write about how peasants lived and worked before the revolt, and how the revolt was a change compared with what went on before.

3. After you have written about the revolt's impact at the time, move on to consider how it might have an impact in the long term.

4. Lastly, does the Peasants' Revolt directly affect our world today? Remember that the significance of an event, idea or person can change over time, so sometimes a lot of time will need to pass before it is recognised as being significant. Something might not be seen as significant at the time, but years later when more is known, it can be identified as having had a key impact. Equally, something that was significant at the time may lose its significance as a result of later developments, and no longer influences our thinking or world today. So, considering all these points, what do you think is the significance of the Peasants' Revolt?

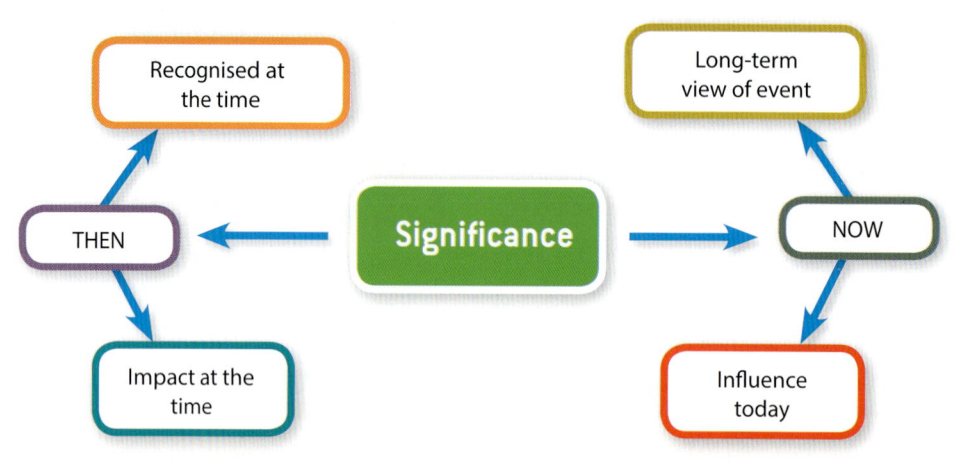

Diagram: Significance branches into THEN (Recognised at the time, Impact at the time) and NOW (Long-term view of event, Influence today).

5 Read the following response. Can you identify where the answer explains about the recognition of the Peasants' Revolt, its immediate impact as well as long-term impact, and its relevance today?

> The Peasants' Revolt was recognised at the time as a great challenge to the king's authority. Medieval kings were used to being challenged by their barons and nobles but not by the peasants. The leader of the revolt, Wat Tyler, was killed by the king and this made him a martyr to many, making him and the revolt significant at the time.
>
> At the time, the Peasants' Revolt was significant for the government as it showed that the peasants could come together and challenge the king. After the revolt, taxes were never increased, which shows it had an immediate impact. Workers' wages began to rise after the revolt but it could be argued that this was due to a lack of workers because of the Black Death. Thus, reducing the significance of the revolt itself. Parliament did, eventually, stop controlling peasants' wages, which shows the demands of the peasants and the revolt itself were successful. However, historians since have suggested that the peasants were already becoming politically organised because of the Black Death. The government did continue with community charges, so the revolt was not that significant for the government at the time. Another impact of the revolt was that some peasants were able to buy land that was unused after the Black Death. They could no longer be controlled by their landlords and were able to work for themselves. However, this did not apply to all peasants.
>
> A hundred years after the revolt, peasants were declared freemen — this is directly linked to the demands of the peasants and shows a long-term impact on society. This would also have had implications for barons and nobles who would no longer have been able to rely on free labour.
>
> Some historians argue that the Peasants' Revolt marks the beginning of British ideas of freedom. If this is accurate then the impact of the Peasants' Revolt can be felt during other peasant and working-class uprisings through history. The chartists and other movements in the nineteenth century used the Peasants' Revolt as inspiration for their movements, as the revolt challenged the ruling class with some successful outcomes. There are many streets and schools in the south-east of England named after Tyler which suggests he was significant.

6 Now try to answer the Practice Question yourself!

Britain: Power and the people 173

How to... analyse sources

In your exam, you will have to deal with a question about the usefulness of a source to a historian studying that particular part of history. You will be asked a question that directly relates to a source.

▼ **SOURCE A** *Drawn in 1649 by Clement Walker, a disgruntled parliamentarian, this is a piece of propaganda called* The Royal Oak of Britain. *Walker was arrested for this drawing and charged with high treason. The drawing shows Cromwell destroying the regime of Charles I.*

Study Tip

Ask yourself, 'what is this source?' The provenance (such as the date of publication, the type of source, and the title) will help you to assess the usefulness of the source. What do you know about the topic that you can link with the information from the provenance?

Study Tip

The content of the source is the image itself. Begin by describing what you can see. What do you know about Cromwell that you can connect with what you see in the image? Look at what is hanging from the tree.

Practice Question

Study **Source A**. How useful is **Source A** to a historian studying Cromwell?

8 marks

[Taken from AQA 2016 Paper 2 specimen material]

Over to you

The usefulness of a source is what it tells you about the history of the time. A source might be useful because it reveals something new, why events turned out the way they did, or why people acted or thought in a particular way at that time. This question suggests that the source has a use for historians studying Oliver Cromwell: remember this as you work through the following questions.

1. Start by analysing the content of **Source A**. What is the author trying to say about Cromwell? What does the source tell us about Cromwell that makes it useful or not? The content of the source should be checked against your own knowledge of the topic.

2. You should also consider the provenance of **Source A**:

   a. What does it tell you about how useful, or not, the source might be? Provenance could mean who produced the source, why it was produced, who it was produced for, and where and when it was produced. Remember that to answer the usefulness of a source, the provenance of a source is just as important as the content.

   b. What was the context of the time in which the source was created? The source dates from 1649, which is the year King Charles was executed. The provenance suggests that it is someone who is unhappy with Cromwell's actions. Perhaps you could argue that this source is useful as it gives evidence that some parliamentarians did not approve of Cromwell as Lord Protector and did not approve of the king's execution.

3. Recall the actual question: it asks about a historian studying Oliver Cromwell. In **Source A** Cromwell is seen to be destroying the 'British Oak' that contains the crown, sceptre and coat of arms; it shows that Cromwell was responsible for destroying the king's rule in Britain. Why might this be? It is helpful if you try to use the provenance and the content together. The provenance says that that the person who created this source was a disgruntled parliamentarian. It might seem that he was unhappy with Cromwell. Did all parliamentarians support Cromwell? Was Cromwell responsible for the king's execution?

4. What are the strengths and weaknesses of the following answer?

> The source is useful because it comes from the time when the king was executed in 1649 and gives the opinion of someone who fought against the king. It shows that not everyone supported the king's execution and Cromwell as Lord Protector. The source shows Cromwell ordering his men to destroy the British Oak that contains the royal crown. From the branches of the tree hang Magna Carta and the Bible. This shows that the Cromwell was viewed as someone who would destroy the rights of the people who had fought in the civil war and that he was against God. I know that at the time there were many people who were unhappy at Cromwell's influence. They were also worried about the changes he would bring to England. Some people, however, did support Cromwell as he was, despite the drawing, seen as someone who would bring religious toleration after Charles' forced reforms under Laud.

5. Now try to answer the Practice Question yourself!

Britain: Power and the people

How to... compare similarities

In your exam, you will have to deal with a question about comparing the similarities of two things, such as two events or developments.

Practice Question

Compare the Magna Carta and the Great Reform Act. In what ways were they similar?

Explain your answer with reference to both.

8 marks

Study Tip

You can compare any aspect of the two events in the question. They may have the same causes but completely different outcomes. It could be that they both have political consequences but one is more significant than the other.

Over to you

This style of question asks you to compare what you know about two topics or aspects of the history you have studied. You are looking for similarities between the two events: remember this as you work through the following questions.

1. Start by planning out your response: what are the similarities between Magna Carta and the Great Reform Act? Make a list or a mind-map to help you analyse the similarities. For example, when comparing the two events, consider:

    a. causes: why did the event happen?

    b. development: how did the event develop?

    c. consequences: events will have results.

2. Try to organise your response in three sections, covering causes, development and consequences. Remember that you will need to show how well you have understood both events by explaining the similarities that you can find.

3. Read the following response. Can you identify where the answer explains about similarities in terms of causes, development and consequences?

> Both events are similar because they were concerned with greater representation. With Magna Carta the barons wanted greater representation in the Great Council, and those campaigning for the Great Reform Act wanted representation in government. The barons were frustrated with King John charging them tax for war and giving jobs to his foreign family; they needed more of a say. Likewise, the emerging middle class in nineteenth-century Britain felt their interests were not represented as they could not vote for a suitable candidate. Another way the events are similar is that they resulted in change for the barons and the middle class. The peasants and working class did not benefit from the changes. Nowhere in Magna Carta did it mention peasants and villeins, and the Great Reform Act could be seen as not that 'great' because it only catered for the middle and merchant class, not the working class.

4. Now try to answer the Practice Question yourself!

How to... evaluate main factors

In your exam, you will have to deal with a question that asks you to evaluate factors.

Practice Question

Have living standards been the main factor in causing unrest in Britain in the nineteenth and twentieth centuries?

Explain your answer with reference to living standards and other factors.

16 marks
SPaG: 4 marks

Study Tip

Write down all the factors you can think of that caused unrest. Next to each one write the event it links to. Then try to show if some factors influence each other. Once you have completed this you should have a clear idea about which is the main factor.

Over to you

Different factors have affected this power and the people thematic study over a long period of time. Those factors are war, religion, chance, government, communication, the economy, ideas such as equality, democracy and representation, and the role of the individual in encouraging or inhibiting change. Frequently, factors worked together to bring about particular developments at particular times. This question is asking about one particular factor and its influence compared with other factors: remember this as you work through the following questions.

1. Start by writing about the factor that has been named in the question: in this case, it is about living standards. You will have come across examples where living standards have appeared in your study of power and the people. Using these examples, write about how the factor had an influence. The factor you are addressing might sometimes have helped and sometimes have hindered the development of power for the people. Try to give two or three examples from different times or places during your study.

2. Next, consider other factors that have influenced the development of power, for example political representation and race relations. Choose two or three other factors from your study and explain, with examples, how those factors changed the development of power. Again, it is useful if you can find examples from across the wide range of your study that both helped and hindered the development.

3. Lastly, you will have to deal with the judgement in the question. The question picked out that the living standards factor was the main factor. You have to say whether or not you agree with this. Try to weigh up or assess the living standards factor against all the other ones, and say which was more important. To back up your conclusion, you should also explain *why*, with supporting evidence.

4. Read the following essay conclusion to the question. Can you identify: the given factor (living standards) and two others factors? The supporting points about each factor? An assessment or judgement about which is the main factor?

> Living standards were an important factor for causing unrest, but they were not the main factor. Although it is true in the last 200 years different groups such as the Tolpuddle Martyrs, the Chartists, the General Strike and the unions of the 1970s all wanted more wages and better working and living conditions, the main factor in causing unrest has been the desire for more representation in government — to have a voice. This is true of the Chartists, the Suffragettes and minority groups in the late twentieth century such as the black and Asian communities. All these groups realised that if they wanted to improve their standards of living, they had to have more of a say and therefore more representation in government.

5. Now try to answer the Practice Question yourself!

Timeline

Britain: Migration, empires and the people

This thematic study covers over 1000 years of the history that shaped much of what Britain is like today. You will get the chance to explore how the identity of the people of Britain has been created by their interactions with the wider world. You will have the opportunity to consider invasions and conquests and study the country's relationship with Europe and the wider world. You will examine the ebb and flow of people into and out of Britain, and will evaluate their motives and achievements. You will also consider the causes, impact and legacy of the British Empire upon the ruled and the ruling in the context of Britain's acquisition and retreat from its empire.

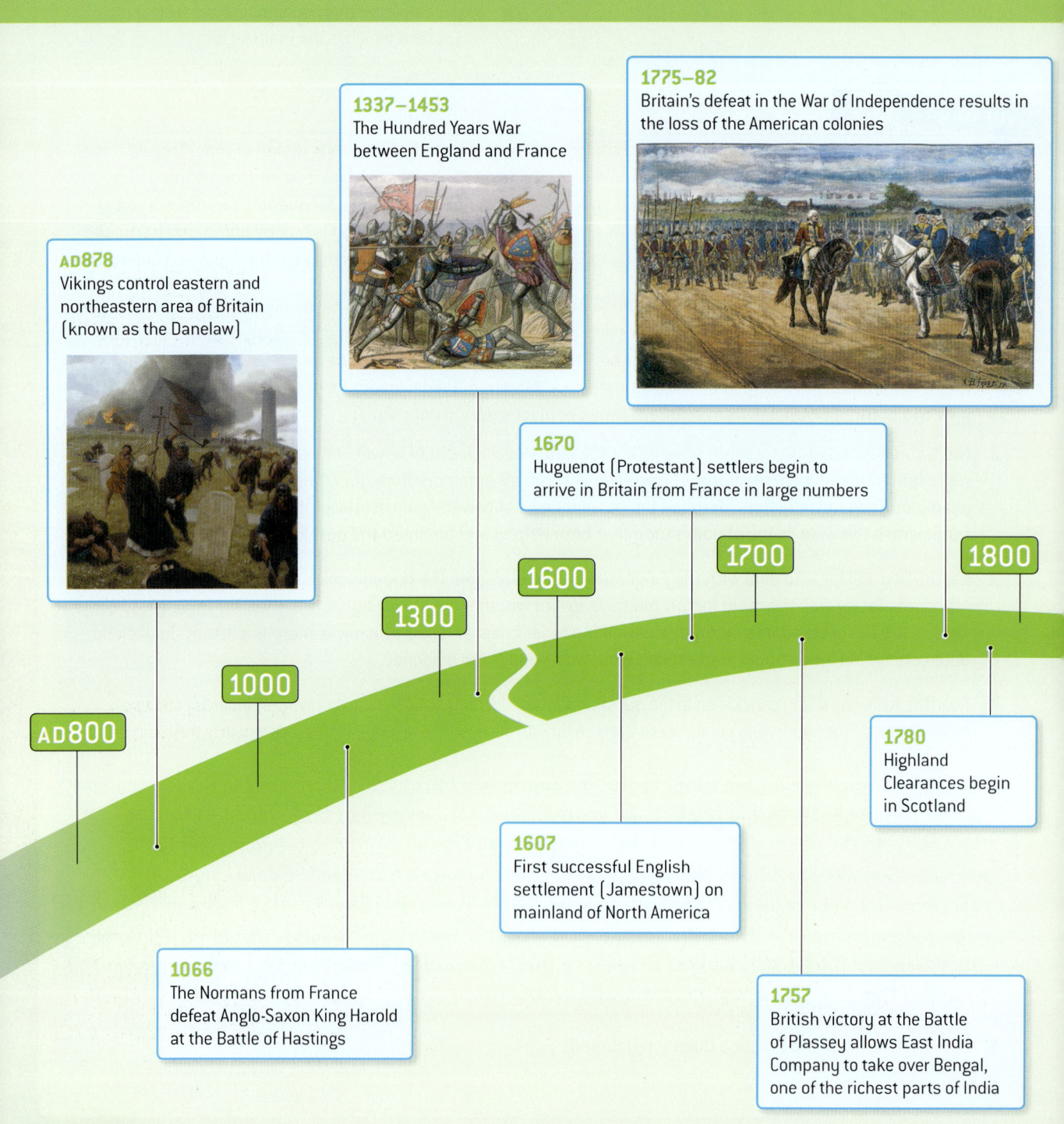

AD 878
Vikings control eastern and northeastern area of Britain (known as the Danelaw)

1337–1453
The Hundred Years War between England and France

1775–82
Britain's defeat in the War of Independence results in the loss of the American colonies

1670
Huguenot (Protestant) settlers begin to arrive in Britain from France in large numbers

1780
Highland Clearances begin in Scotland

1066
The Normans from France defeat Anglo-Saxon King Harold at the Battle of Hastings

1607
First successful English settlement (Jamestown) on mainland of North America

1757
British victory at the Battle of Plassey allows East India Company to take over Bengal, one of the richest parts of India

1948
Empire Windrush arrives in Britain, beginning a new wave of West Indian migration

1881–1914
Scramble for Africa sees the invasion and colonisation of most of Africa by Britain and other European powers

1845–49
Irish potato famine sees mass starvation in Ireland and the emigration of around one million people

1899–1902
The Second Boer War is fought between Dutch settlers (the Boers) and the British army

1973
Britain joins the European Union

1999
Twelve members of the EU adopt the Euro as their currency, but Britain refuses and continues to use the Pound

1900

1950

2000

1857–58
Indian Rebellion results in India coming under the formal control of the British government

1947
India gains independence from Britain

1982
The Falklands War between Britain and Argentina over the disputed Falkland Islands near South America takes place

Britain: Migration, empires and the people 179

1.1 Why did the Vikings invade Britain?

This topic focuses on the people who came to and left Britain, and the different **empires** Britain belonged to and built, from c790 to the present day. Different groups of people have been moving to Britain and settling for various reasons, and have made lasting contributions to British culture. Britain had also taken over land in other parts of the world: at one point in time, the British ruled over more land than any other country before or since. However, there have been times in Britain's history when it has been controlled by another, more powerful nation, and has been part of their empire. What was Britain like before the AD790s?

Objectives

- **Explore** the history of invaders and settlers in Britain.
- **Examine** how Britain came to be under Anglo-Saxon rule.
- **Explain** the reasons why the Vikings invaded Britain in the AD790s.

The first Britons

The timeline below charts the history of settlement in Britain up to the time this thematic study begins.

Fact

Historians sometimes add a 'c' before dates. This stands for 'circa', which means 'around' or 'approximately'.

Timeline

Before c4000BC:
The first people who live in Britain are **immigrants**. They arrive from Europe around half a million years ago and are **hunter-gatherers**. They move around in small groups and learn skills such as lighting fires and making tools

c4000BC:
Around 6000 years ago, farmers arrive from Europe, bringing seeds to grow crops and animals. They begin to clear some of Britain's thick woodland to create farms and build stone houses

c500–43BC:
About 2500 years ago, a new wave of settlers begins arriving from central Europe. They are called the Beaker People after their beaker-shaped pottery cups; they also know how to make things out of metal. The next tribes to arrive and settle in Britain are Celts: they too farm the land and fight fiercely between themselves and with the people already settled here. Over many centuries, they merge with the original population

Fact

The Romans were the first people to use the name 'Britannia' for Britain. The name was based on the word 'Pretannia', which is what the Ancient Greeks called Britain: they thought a Celtic tribe called the 'Pretani' lived there. In fact, the Pretani tribe lived mainly in Ireland, but the name stuck, and later became 'Britannia', and then simply 'Britain'.

From around AD400 onwards, Anglo-Saxons settled in villages next to their farmland. They set up a number of different kingdoms, led by lords and chieftains. The most powerful lords acted like local kings and fought one another to gain more land.

The strongest Anglo-Saxon tribal chiefs were known as Bretwalda or 'Ruler of Britain'. By AD800, most Anglo-Saxons had converted to Christianity, and merchants traded goods all over the country and into Europe, making some Anglo-Saxon kingdoms very wealthy.

◀ **A** Anglo-Saxon treasures like this war helmet were uncovered at the Sutton Hoo Saxon burial site in East Anglia, England

▶ **B** The Anglo-Saxon kingdoms, around AD700. The white areas in the south-west (Wales and Cornwall) were occupied by the original Celtic Britons. Over time, the area of Britain where the Anglo-Saxons settled became known as 'Angle-land', and later 'England'.

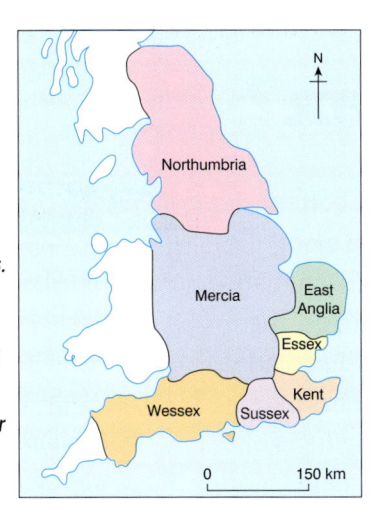

Key Words

empire   immigrant   hunter-gatherer   Viking

The Vikings attacked Britain because they had traded goods with the Anglo-Saxons for many years, and knew of their wealth. The first recorded attack was on the monastery at Lindisfarne in Northumbria in AD793, and two years later they attacked the Isle of Iona in Scotland. To begin with, they attacked in the summer when the seas were calmer for their small ships. They raided villages and monasteries near the coast, and then sailed back with stolen gold and silver, cattle and even slaves. Later, they sailed up rivers and attacked further inland, and they sometimes stayed for long periods of time and built camps.

▼ **INTERPRETATION D**
A twentieth-century interpretation showing Vikings attacking the English; Vikings are often portrayed as wild, unsophisticated and bloodthirsty

Who were the Vikings and why did they attack?

In the mid-700s, the people of Scandinavia (Norway, Denmark and Sweden) began to explore, raid and eventually invade the countries around them. They sailed to Britain, Ireland, France, Spain and Italy. Others travelled by land, going as far as Israel, Greenland and probably America. They were known as **Vikings**, or Northmen, and began their raids on Britain around the AD790s.

AD43–401:

The Romans arrive from Italy and conquer most of the British tribes. The Romans stay and rule for over 400 years, and the country becomes part of the huge Roman Empire

AD401 onwards:

By AD401, the Romans in Britain are called back to Italy to defend their homeland from invasion. The British who have lived under Roman rule are left to fend for themselves, and soon new tribes invade. They come by boat from Denmark and northern Germany looking for a better climate and good farmland. These tribes are called Angles, Saxons and Jutes. They soon become known as Anglo-Saxons and, after fighting with the British tribes, capture most of Britain (except Cornwall, Wales and the far north)

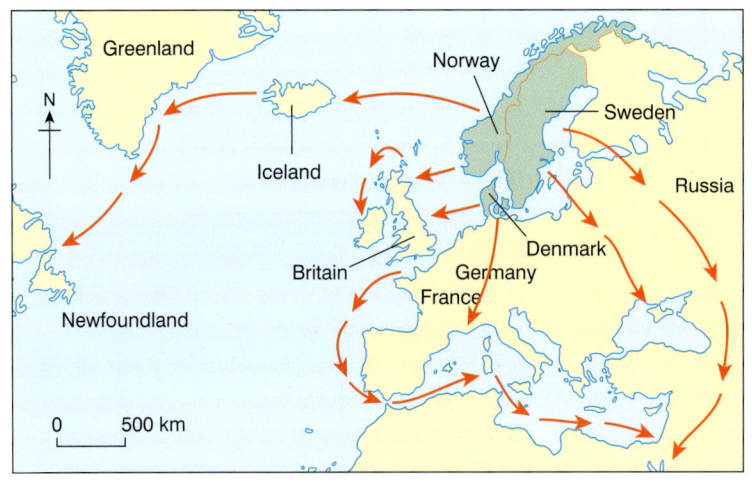

▲ **C** A map of the main Viking voyages

Work

1. Write a sentence or two to explain the following words: immigrant; empire.
2. Put the following groups of invaders and settlers into the correct chronological order: Romans; Anglo-Saxons; Celts; Vikings.
3. a Who were the Anglo-Saxons?
   b Why did Vikings begin to invade Britain in the eighth century?

Britain: Migration, empires and the people   181

1.2 What was 'Great' about King Alfred of Wessex?

Around the year 850, just like the Angle and Saxon tribes before them, the Vikings decided to settle in Britain. They landed along the eastern coast and built large, well-protected camps. Soon they started to venture out and capture British towns and villages. The city of York, for example, was captured in November 866 by an army of Danish Vikings. The Vikings slowly pushed their way across the country, and by 870, had conquered the Anglo-Saxon kingdoms of Northumbria, East Anglia and much of Mercia. What was their impact on the areas under Viking control? To what extent did the Anglo-Saxons, especially Alfred of Wessex, resist the Vikings?

Objectives

- **Describe** who Alfred the Great was, and his successes as King of Wessex.
- **Explain** how the Danelaw was created.
- **Assess** the impact of Viking rule on Britain.

Why did the Vikings choose to settle in Britain?

Although the Vikings and Anglo-Saxons were now fighting each other, they had much in common. Both groups were farming people who had a history of conquering new land to improve their lives, for example. The Vikings realised that Britain offered more opportunities than their homelands: Norway was very hilly and it was a struggle to grow crops there, and Denmark's sandy soil limited the amount of animals that could be reared. Scandinavia was also becoming overcrowded, so many left looking for a new life abroad. Recruiting young men into the Viking armies was relatively easy, since only eldest sons inherited farmland, so younger brothers needed to join the army and make their own wealth by moving to other lands.

What happened to Wessex?

After conquering Northumbria, East Anglia and most of Mercia, the Vikings now turned their attention to Wessex. In 871, Alfred, the 22-year-old son of Aethelred of Wessex, had become king after his father's death. He would go on to be known as Alfred the Great. In 876, the Vikings began a series of ferocious attacks against Alfred's Wessex. After some early successes, King Alfred and his army was driven back and forced to hide on the Isle of Athelney in the Somerset marshes.

After several desperate months, Alfred managed to gather enough support and train an army to attack the Vikings once more. In May 878, King Alfred beat the Vikings at the Battle of Edington in Wiltshire, and the two sides sat down to agree peace terms. Alfred insisted that the Viking leader, Guthrum, had to become a Christian, like Alfred himself, and had to agree never to attack Wessex again. Alfred accepted that the Vikings were here to stay, and the two leaders settled on a boundary between their territories. The Vikings were to live in the north and east of the country (which was called the **Danelaw**).

A The division of Britain at the end of the ninth century. The orange areas show the Danelaw, where the Vikings conquered and settled. Alfred's kingdom of Wessex is yellow.

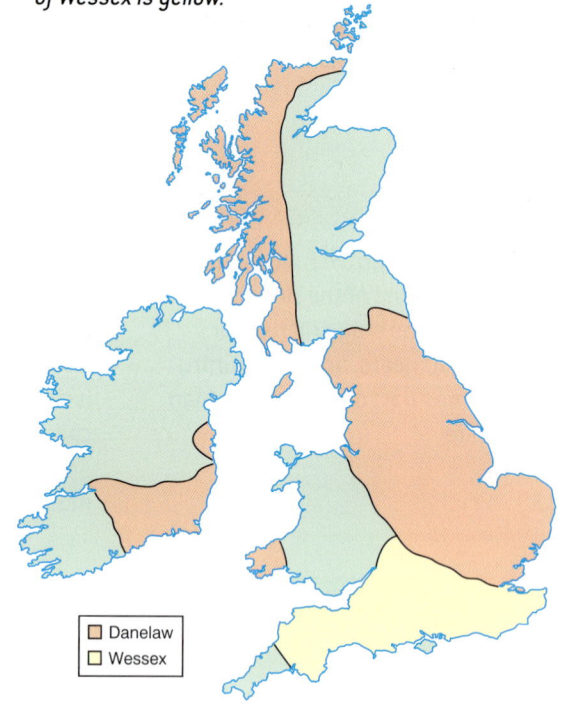

The Danelaw

The part of England under Viking control changed considerably at this time. The Vikings brought their own distinct laws, place names, customs, measurements, skilled crafts and farming techniques to the Danelaw. Many of these Viking influences still survive today. For example, some days of our week have Viking names: Thursday is named after Thor, the Norse god of thunder;

182   Chapter 1   Invasion

Key Biography

King Alfred (reigned 871–99)

- Became the sixth King of Wessex in 871.
- Cultured and academic by ninth century standards, he encouraged learning and said that all young noble men should learn to read English. He translated many books from Latin into English.
- Re-wrote many laws. He took the most just laws from other kingdoms and used them for his.
- To ensure there would be no further Viking attacks in his lifetime, Alfred built burhs (fortresses or castles) across the country from the 880s to strengthen England's defences. The soldiers in these burhs could not only defend Alfred's land in Wessex, they could launch attacks if required. He also fortified existing Roman-era towns such as Oxford. As a result, Alfred had a grid of defensive sites across his territory that made his land more secure. Most importantly, his new defences showed confidence: they gave a sign to the Vikings that invasions were no longer as easy as before.
- Other kingdoms in England acknowledged Alfred to be the 'overlord', or the dominant ruler over them. Under his rule, the Anglo-Saxons began to call themselves Angelcynn – the English.

B *Alfred is remembered as an Anglo-Saxon king who was a 'Great' general in war, a wise and kindly ruler in peace, and a clever scholar. This statue of him was put up in Winchester, his capital, one thousand years after his death.*

Friday after Freya, the goddess of love. Viking settlements can easily be detected through the use of the suffix 'by' (meaning 'homestead' or 'village'), for example Grimsby ('Grim's homestead'), or 'thorpe' (meaning 'new village'), or 'thwaite' (meaning 'meadow' or 'piece of land'). Some British surnames have Viking origins too (such as Adamson, Holt and Thorn), as do many words, such as egg, bread, sister, happy, ill and muck.

After Alfred

During Alfred's reign, there were still Viking raids on Anglo-Saxon territory. For the most part, however, the Vikings in the Danelaw settled down as farmers and lived fairly peacefully side-by-side with the Anglo-Saxons. People travelled and traded between Wessex and the Danelaw, and there was intermarriage between Vikings and Anglo-Saxons.

After Alfred's death, his descendants managed to re-capture parts of the Danelaw and win control over it. Alfred's grandson (Athelstan) conquered Northumbria in 927, and some historians argue that Athelstan could be called the first real 'King of England'. However, the Viking presence and influence still remained: York had Viking rulers until 954, for example. But by the time Alfred's great-grandson (Edgar the Peaceful) became king in 959, the country was as settled as it had been for generations.

Practice Question

Explain the significance of Alfred the Great for the development of English identity. **8 marks**

Key Word

Danelaw

Work

1. Why did the Vikings choose to settle in Britain?
2. a Who was Alfred?
   b How did Alfred gain the upper hand over the Vikings?
   c Why do you think Alfred is known by many as 'Alfred the Great'?
3. What was the Danelaw?
4. Describe the impact of the Vikings on Britain.

Extension

Find out more about what happened at the Battle of Eddington in 878 – who were the leaders, the tactics, and what happened in the battle?

Study Tip

Remember to refer to several aspects of Alfred's achievements and the impact they had for a long time after he had died.

1.3A King Cnut and the North Sea Empire

In the ninth century, Alfred the Great had prevented the Vikings taking over all of England. After winning the Battle of Edington in 878, he made a peace treaty that restricted the Vikings to living only in the north and east of the country, an area known as the Danelaw. In the tenth century the English re-conquered much of the land held by the Vikings. Under King Edgar the Peaceful, the country became both calm and stable; but when he died in 975, things began to unravel. Within 50 years, England had a Viking king once more, and the country became part of the Danish Empire.

Objectives

▶ **Examine** the new Viking raiders of the late tenth century.

▶ **Explore** who King Cnut was and assess the way he controlled England.

▶ **Consider** the importance of Britain to Cnut's North Sea Empire, including the role of Emma of Normandy.

Edward then Aethelred

When King Edgar the Peaceful died, he left two sons by different mothers: Edward (aged 12) and Aethelred (aged 9). As the oldest son, Edward became King of England, but his reign only lasted three years. In 978, he was murdered by supporters of his younger brother Aethelred, who then took over as king. Aethelred's reign was a difficult one. He was only a young boy when he became king, and was not a good judge of character. The advisers that helped him were often corrupt and looked to make as much money and acquire as much land as they could from the king. Many people were also outraged by the murder of his elder brother, Edward. There is little evidence that the young Aethelred had anything at all to do with his brother's death, but one story claims that his mother, Aelthfryth, stabbed Edward (her stepson) so that her own son could become king!

INTERPRETATION A A drawing, published in 1865, showing the victorious Vikings, after the Battle of Maldon, being paid Danegeld

The Vikings return

During Aethelred's reign, new waves of Vikings searching for fame and fortune begin to invade England. In 991, a huge Viking army, led by the Dane, Sven Forkbeard and the Norwegian, Olaf Tryggvason, arrived at Folkestone in a fleet of over 90 ships. Their army defeated the English at the Battle of Maldon in

August. Aethelred paid the Vikings to leave. This payment was called **Danegeld** (money for the Danish). Not all of the Vikings left; some remained as mercenaries to protect the English and others continued to terrorise the English on the south coast for the next three years. After 997, fresh raiding parties of Vikings attacked parts of southern England. They demanded (and received) Danegeld.

Aethelred and Emma of Normandy

The Danegeld that Aethelred was paying the Vikings to stay away from England was costing a fortune. After the Battle of Maldon, the king had given the Vikings around 3300 kilogrammes of silver (about £900,000 in today's money), and the English hated the taxes that were needed to pay it. As a result, Aethelred looked for another way to keep the Vikings away.

The Vikings had been sheltering in Normandy, France, after raiding England. The Normans were descendants of Vikings who had settled in France around 100 years before. So, Aethelred made a deal with the Duke of Normandy that said that they agreed to support each other against their enemies. Aethelred hoped that this would reduce the number of raids because the Vikings would not be able to use Normandy as a base. Aethelred sealed the agreement by marrying the Duke's sister, Emma. However, in November 1002 Aethelred used the popular fear and hatred of the Vikings to carry out a mass killing of all Viking men, women and children that he could find south of the Danelaw. This became known as the St Brice's Day Massacre and caused the anger of King Sven Forkbeard, whose sister Gunhilda was murdered.

Fact

King Aethelred is often called 'Aethelred the Unready' and it is commonly thought that this is because he failed to act quickly enough to stop Viking raids. However, the word 'unready' is not interpreted correctly in this definition. It is based on the Old English word 'unraed', which means 'ill advised', and refers to the poor advice Aethelred received, and his lack of judgement as a young king.

Key Word

Danegeld

Forkbeard attacks

The King of Denmark, Sven Forkbeard, invaded England with a powerful Viking army. He wanted revenge – and some of the great wealth of England for himself. If he achieved this it would strengthen his position against rival Viking leaders. In 1000 at the Battle of Svold, Sven killed Olaf Tryggvason, his former raiding partner who had become King of Norway. Sven also wanted to teach Thorkell the Tall a lesson. Thorkell was a Viking warrior who switched sides to work for Aethelred in 1012. In 1013, Sven summoned a large army and swiftly conquered England.

Fact

Some of the Vikings who sailed to France in the AD900s settled near Paris. They were called the Northmen – or Normans. They soon became rulers of this part of France and the area was named Normandy. William the Conqueror came from this part of France (he was Duke of Normandy) and he was descended from these Viking invaders.

Work

1. Describe the circumstances in which Aethelred became King of England.
2. a What was Danegeld?
   b In what ways did the payment of Danegeld: help Aethelred; hinder Aethelred.
3. Who was Emma of Normandy?
4. Why do you think Aethelred married Emma?
5. Why did Forkbeard attack England?

1.3B King Cnut and the North Sea Empire

Aethelred and Cnut

With Aethelred out of the country and Forkbeard on the throne, it looked as if the fighting between Anglo-Saxons and Vikings was over for a while. But the peace didn't last. Just over a year after becoming king, Forkbeard died. His young son, Cnut (pronounced Canute) became England's new Viking king, but Anglo-Saxon nobles wanted the Anglo-Saxon Aethelred to return to power. Aethelred came back over to England in 1014 and forced Cnut back to Denmark. Aethelred was now back on the throne.

Edmund and Cnut

Aethelred's return did not last long. Cnut's supporters in England rebelled against Aethelred, and the next few years involved much bloodshed and fighting. At one point, even Aethelred's own son rebelled against him. In April 1016, Aethelred died and his son, Edmund, became king. He was successful in fighting off Vikings, and earned himself the nickname 'Edmund Ironside'. However, in October 1016, Cnut finally got the better of King Edmund and beat him at the Battle of Assandun in Essex. The two men agreed that Edmund would run Wessex, while Cnut would run the rest of the country; and when one of them died, the other would inherit their land. About a month later, Edmund died. Historians believe he was either murdered or died from wounds received at the Battle of Assandun. Now Cnut became king of all England.

How did Britain change under Cnut's rule?

Britain was important to Cnut as it was his richest kingdom: he viewed Britain as his main domain, rather than as a Danish colony. To begin with, King Cnut was tough with those Anglo-Saxons he thought might rebel against him. Early in his reign, he ordered the execution of a number of powerful Anglo-Saxons. Britain was a rich area with a flourishing trade system compared to Scandinavia, and Cnut wanted to have reliable and strong

▼ A Cnut's North Sea Empire

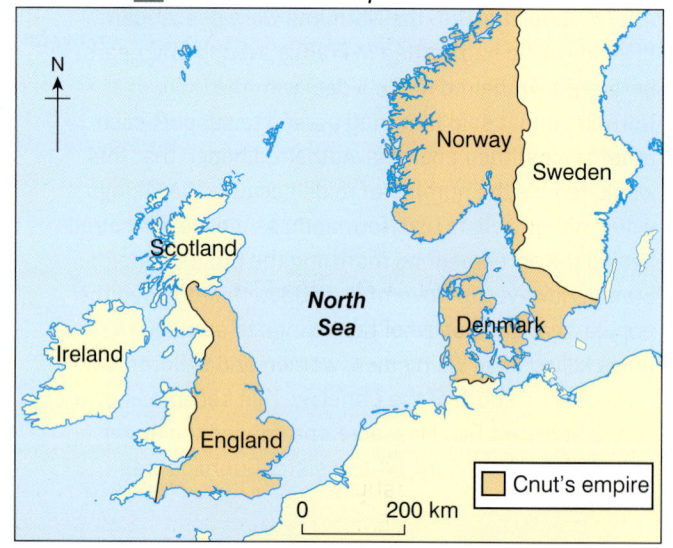

Key Biography

Cnut the Great (reigned as King of England 1016–35)

- Brought in an era of peace that lasted nearly 20 years.
- Was seen as a fair, just and devout ruler, and was popular overall.
- Made expensive payments to fund the part of the Viking army that stayed in England.
- Used money to pay for trusted Danish nobles to move to England to help him maintain order.
- Married Aethelred's widow, Emma of Normandy.
- Died in 1035, and was buried in Winchester.

▼ **INTERPRETATION B** *Adapted from a text by historian Laurence Larson, written in 1912, about the extent of Cnut's North Sea Empire:*

> In the 1040s, Canute was one of the most imposing rulers in Latin Christendom. He was lord of four important realms and the overlord of other kingdoms. Though technically Canute was counted among the kings, his position among his fellow-monarchs was truly imperial. Apparently he held in his hands the destinies of two great regions: the British Isles and the Scandinavian peninsulas. His fleet all but controlled two important seas, the North and the Baltic. He had built an Empire.

▼ **SOURCE C** *Emma of Normandy with her sons*

leaders to help him control Britain. Strong control meant he could transfer the riches back to Denmark to support the Danes. Loyal Danish nobles were given British lands, but some trustworthy English nobles were also left to rule their own areas. Cnut wanted good local leadership – no matter which side of the North Sea they were from.

Despite a brutal takeover of the throne and start to his reign, Cnut's reign was one of peace and freedom from Viking raids. He even sent most of his great battle fleets home. He also worked hard to win over the people of his new kingdom. He was a religious man who established a good relationship with Church leaders, and he brought back many of the popular and fair laws of Edgar the Peaceful. Soon, he inherited the kingdoms of Denmark and Norway from his elder brother, and ruled parts of Sweden too. All this became known as Cnut's North Sea Empire.

Cnut and Emma of Normandy

To bring even greater stability to England, and an improved relationship with the Normans in France, Cnut married Emma of Normandy, widow of Aethelred. They had a son, Harthacnut.

During Cnut's 20-year reign, England was at peace. But his two sons who followed him as king – firstly Harold (Cnut's son by his first wife) and then Harthacnut (his son with Emma) – were hated. Their reigns didn't last long. In 1042, Harthacnut died and the throne passed to his surviving half-brother, Prince Edward. Edward was the son of Emma and Aethlered, and had originally left with his mother and father when Forkbeard invaded many years before. He had been living in Normandy for a large part of his life. King Edward was quickly accepted by ordinary people, but the Anglo-Saxons nobles found that he seemed to prefer his Norman friends to them. He was also a deeply religious man and soon earned himself the nickname 'the Confessor': a name given to a person who lives a very holy life.

Extension

Create your own Key Biography for the life and achievements of Emma of Normandy (c985–1052), the wife of King Athelred and later the wife of King Cnut. She was a fascinating character who, through her marriages and her children, is linked in all sorts of ways to the Anglo-Saxon, Viking and Norman history of this era.

Work

1. Describe King Cnut's time as King of England.
2. Who was Edward the Confessor and why did he become King of England?
3. In what ways are the marriages and children of Emma of Normandy an important part of the history of this period?
4. a What was meant by the term 'North Sea Empire'?
   b Explain why Viking kings such as Cnut wanted to take over Britain. Why was Britain important?
   c How did Britain change under Cnut?

Britain: Migration, empires and the people

2.1 A Norman Kingdom

When Edward became King of England in 1042, he had been living in Normandy, France for many years. He spoke French better than he spoke English, and behaved like a Norman. One of his closest friends was a Norman, too. His name was William, the Duke (ruler) of Normandy, and King Edward spent lots of time in Normandy with him. But Edward had not married a Norman as people expected, and instead married the sister of a powerful Anglo-Saxon called Harold Godwinson. They had no children, and when Edward died in early 1066, the throne of England was up for grabs. With its wealth and land, England was worth fighting for. Who claimed the throne and became England's next king? And what did this mean for the country as a whole?

Objectives

- **Recall** what happened after King Edward's death.
- **Examine** the way in which England became part of a Norman Empire.
- **Explore** the relationship between England and France from 1066 to 1216.

The race for the crown

King Edward died on 6 January 1066. The three main contenders for the English throne were:

- William, Duke of Normandy: As a close friend of Edward, he claimed that he been promised the throne. He also claimed that Harold Godwinson had agreed to support his claim after being rescued from a shipwreck off the coast of Normandy.
- Harald Hardrada: The Viking ruler of Norway; he also said he was King of Denmark. As Vikings had conquered and controlled England for many years, he claimed he should be England's new king.
- Harold Godwinson: By now, Harold was the most powerful man in England; and he was English, unlike the other two. He was a good soldier and the council of the country's most important, powerful nobles (known as the **Witan**) wanted him as king.

The day after Edward's death, the Witan elected Harold as king. He was crowned immediately: but when the other two rivals found out, they planned their invasions. Hardrada the Viking was the first to invade, but was defeated by King Harold at the Battle of Stamford Bridge, near York, in September 1066. A few days later, King Harold heard the news that William of Normandy had landed on the south coast of England. Harold rushed south from Yorkshire to fight him, but was defeated at the Battle of Hastings on 14 October 1066. Over the next few weeks, William faced fierce resistance from the English as they moved from Hastings towards London, but William soon crushed any resistance on his way there, and was crowned as the first Norman King of England on Christmas Day, 1066.

INTERPRETATION A *A fourteenth-century illustration of William killing Harold at the Battle of Hastings*

William completes the conquest

Even though he had been crowned King of England, William couldn't relax. The early years of his reign saw major rebellions up and down the country. These were put down fiercely. The king rewarded his most loyal

Norman followers by giving them important jobs in the Church, and by seizing land from the English and giving it to Normans. Soon, England was divided up between Norman **barons** and lords, each with his own knights and soldiers to keep the peace. This meant that William would have people loyal to him to control the country during the times when he returned to Normandy. These barons and knights built castles to keep them safe from any English rebels who might want to attack them. Soon England had over 500 Norman castles.

▼ **SOURCE B** *A Norman writer, recalling what became known as the 'Harrying (destruction) of the North' in 1070*

> Never had William shown so great a cruelty. He assembled crops, herbs and flocks, food and utensils of every kind and burned them all. Then all sources of life north of the Humber were destroyed. There followed a famine so serious that more than 100,000 of all ages and both sexes perished.

A Norman Kingdom

William was a French prince who had acquired the English kingdom, but he spent more than half his time in France, where he felt at home. It was very important for William to be seen in France because powerful French rivals might take advantage of any absences to seize control of Normandy. But William spared no time in stamping his mark on England too. The Normans became a brand-new ruling class in England. They spoke French and introduced French customs. They built hundreds of new churches, cathedrals and monasteries, and French replaced English as the main language used by the people in power. Hundreds of French words such as soldier, parliament, royal, city, minister and army were soon absorbed into the English language. The English were once again ruled by a foreign power: the land they once owned was taken from them and the taxes they paid went to the Normans. The Anglo-Saxon English became second-class citizens.

Practice Question

How useful is **Source B** to a historian studying the Norman attitude to England? **8 marks**

Key Words

Witan   baron

▼ **C** *The Norman Kingdom; the Normans didn't try to conquer Scotland, but had a strong influence over it*

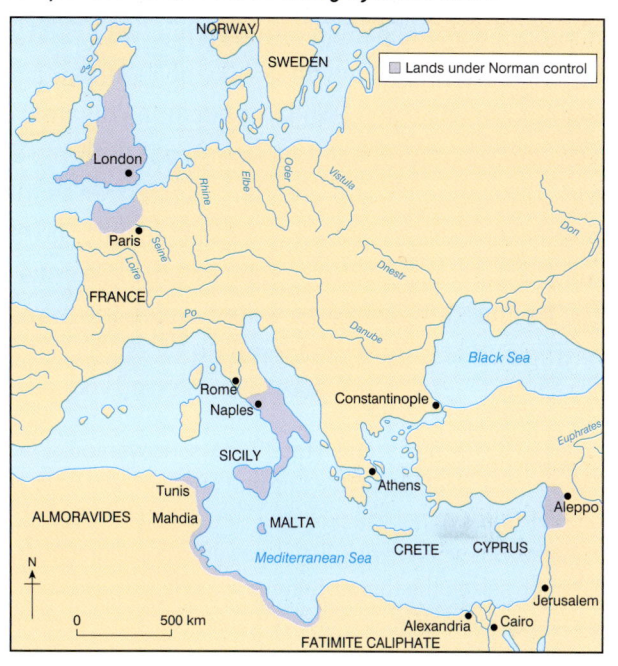

Fact

Like the Vikings, the Normans focussed their efforts on England, but they did have an impact on people from Scotland and Wales. King Malcolm of Scotland raided England in 1070. William's response was violent. He invaded Scotland in 1072 and Malcolm recognised William's power and made peace. William did not attempt to conquer all of Wales, but instructed several Norman barons to seize land there.

Work

1. Explain why you think William, Hardrada and Harold each thought they had a right to be King of England.
2. After becoming king, what did William do with England?
3. How did England change under Norman rule? Make sure you mention: language, castles, the English people.

Study Tip

The provenance says the author is a Norman writer from the time. Does knowing who the author is affect what historians think about the source?

Britain: Migration, empires and the people   189

2.2 Henry II and the 'Angevin' Empire

In 1087, William the Conqueror died and his Norman kingdom was divided up between his two eldest sons. Robert (the eldest) became Duke of Normandy, and William's middle son (William) became William II of England. The youngest son, Henry, got nothing. But in 1100, William II died and Henry took over as King of England. He then went on to defeat his older brother too, and became Duke of Normandy in 1106. So once again the Norman Kingdom was united under one man: Henry I of England and Duke of Normandy.

Objectives

- **Explain** who the 'Angevins' were.
- **Describe** the territory Henry II controlled in Britain and France.
- **Examine** how Henry's territory increased in size during his reign, including the invasion of Ireland.

King Henry ruled peacefully for 20 years. He wanted his daughter, Matilda, to rule England after him when he died. He married her to a powerful French lord Geoffrey of Anjou. But when Henry died, a powerful noble named Stephen seized the throne. Stephen was Henry's nephew and a grandson of William the Conqueror, so many people thought he had a right to the throne. Matilda decided to fight back, however, and for the next 19 years there was a series of battles between the two. Finally, in 1153, an agreement was reached that Matilda's son, Henry, would become England's next king, after Stephen's death. So when Stephen died in October 1154, Matilda's son became King Henry II of England.

Henry II: not just England's king

Henry II was not just King of England: he inherited Normandy from his mother, Matilda, as well other land in France from his father, Geoffrey of Anjou. As a result, Henry II was King of England, Duke of Normandy, Count of Anjou and Count of Maine. In 1152, he married a French duchess, Eleanor of Aquitaine, which meant that he also gained the largest region in his domain: the territories of Aquitaine stretched all the way to Spain. He even bought some areas of France, bullied his way into controlling others, and married his son off to a French duchess so he could acquire Brittany – another powerful, large area of northern France. In fact, Henry II was arguably one of the most powerful rulers in Europe, with land stretching from the Scottish borders to the south of France. He would soon also count Ireland in his empire too.

Invasion of Ireland

Some of the early Norman kings (such as William the Conqueror and Henry I) showed little interest in conquering Ireland. The Irish Sea was rough and difficult to cross, and Ireland wasn't a particularly rich country, so the English felt they wouldn't gain much from taking it over. Ireland was governed by nobles who styled themselves as 'kings'.

But in 1166, 'King' Dermot of Leinster, the leader of Leinster, an area in Ireland, asked Henry II for help. He was fighting

▼ **INTERPRETATION A** King Henry II, shown in a portrait painted in 1620

190 Chapter 2   A Norman Kingdom and 'Angevin' Empire

another Irish king and wanted Henry's assistance. An army of English knights and barons led by the Earl of Pembroke – nicknamed 'Strongbow' – crossed over to Ireland and helped the Irish leader. However, the knights and barons took the opportunity to seize land in Ireland for themselves when Dermot died in 1171 and, within a few years, controlled more land than the Irish. Henry II himself visited Ireland in 1171 and was recognised as the 'overlord' by all the English settlers and the Irish leaders. In fact, this 'deal' became the basis of English sovereignty over the Irish for hundreds of years, up to the 1940s.

Henry's work in Ireland continued as he strengthened existing fortifications there and built new castles, as well as getting investors to develop Dublin as a centre of trade and commerce.

B *The 'Angevin' Empire under Henry II*

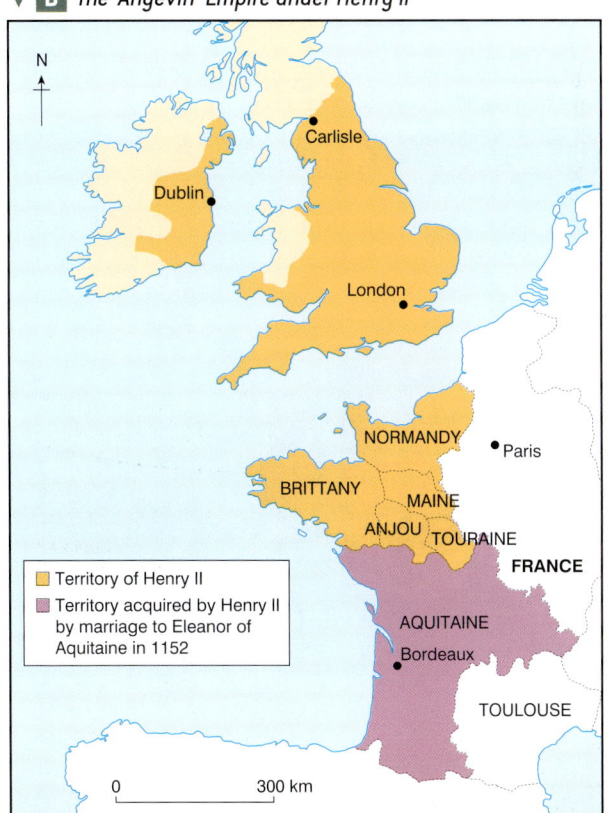

A well-travelled king

At this time, France was not a united country, as it is today. It was divided into areas, each ruled by powerful lords and dukes. France itself was one of these areas, ruled by a king, but other areas included Anjou, Aquitaine, Normandy, and Brittany. Henry II of England ruled over half of these areas, but not France, which was a large, powerful area ruled by King Louis VII. However, Henry II ruled more French land than Louis. With so much land to defend, Henry II spent much of his reign crossing between England and France. It has been estimated that Henry crossed the English Channel up to 30 times in his 35-year reign, prompting Louis VII to remark that Henry 'must fly rather than travel by horse or ship'. There was conflict between Henry II and Louis VII during their reigns too. There was a war in Normandy in 1167, for example, and Louis joined in when Henry's own sons rebelled against him in 1173.

Work

1. Describe the circumstances in which Henry II became King of England.
2. Why is Henry II described as the 'first "Angevin" King of England'?
3. Explain why the first 'Angevin' King of England ruled over more territory than his Norman predecessors.
4. Look at map **B**.
   a. Use the scale to work out how far it is from Carlisle (in the north of England) to Bordeaux (in the south of the 'Angevin' Empire).
   b. How long would it take to travel there by horse, at 50 kilometres a day?
   c. Why might this be a problem for Henry II?
5. Describe how Henry II gradually became 'overlord' of Ireland by 1171.

Fact

The 'Angevins' and the Plantagenets

Henry II (and his brothers who ruled after him) are often referred to as the 'Angevins'. This is because their father Geoffrey came from Anjou in France. Later, the family became known as the Plantagenets because Geoffrey famously wore a yellow plant, *planta genista*, in his hat.

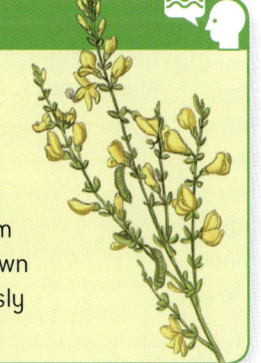

Practice Question

Explain the significance of Henry II's empire. **8 marks**

Study Tip

Refer to Henry II's relationship with Ireland then and Anglo-Irish relations today.

2.3 Why did the 'Angevin' Empire collapse under King John?

When Henry II died in 1189, he was replaced as king by his son, Richard I. Richard spent long periods of his reign in his French lands, or on **crusades** to the Holy Land. As a result, the 'Angevin' Empire became hard to govern. Richard had to return to England to stop rebellions, but he couldn't prevent the French King Philip II from taking large areas of his land in France, including part of Normandy. Richard I died in 1199. His younger brother, John, became the new king, but things got gradually worse. What happened to the 'Angevin' Empire under King John?

Objectives

- **Describe** the losses of territories under King John.
- **Explain** the causes of John's 'Angevin' Empire becoming smaller.
- **Analyse** the impact of losses under King John.

King John's opponents

King John had an opponent waiting to take control of some of his French lands. Powerful lords in Brittany and Anjou wanted John's young nephew, Arthur, as king, and John was drawn into a series of battles against him to defend his land. Arthur also had the support of John's rival, the French King Philip II. But in 1203, Arthur died in mysterious circumstances: many suspected that John stabbed him and threw his body in the River Seine.

King Philip II of France continued his campaign against John, and invaded Anjou and Normandy. In 1204, John's army was defeated in Brittany and began to retreat. Over the next few years, John lost Normandy, Anjou, Maine and other key areas. His military reputation reached such a low point that he was given a new nickname: 'John Softsword'. Soon, John had hardly any land left in France.

SOURCE A *An illustration from c1200 showing King John on a stag hunt*

Timeline

1150	1151	1152	1154	1166–68	1171–72	1189
Henry inherits Normandy from his mother, Matilda, four years before he becomes King Henry II of England	Henry succeeds his father, Geoffrey, as Count of Anjou, Maine, and Touraine in France	Henry marries Eleanor of Aquitaine, and through this marriage he acquires Aquitaine, which includes Gascony, Poitou and Auvergne	Henry becomes King Henry II of England	Henry II invades Brittany	Henry II invades Ireland	Henry II dies and his son becomes Richard I. He goes on a crusade leaving England to be ruled by two justicians (special judges or ministers)

192 Chapter 2 A Norman Kingdom and 'Angevin' Empire

▼ **B** *By 1214, the 'Angevin' Empire had been reduced to only Gascony (the southern half of the Duchy of Aquitaine), Ireland and England*

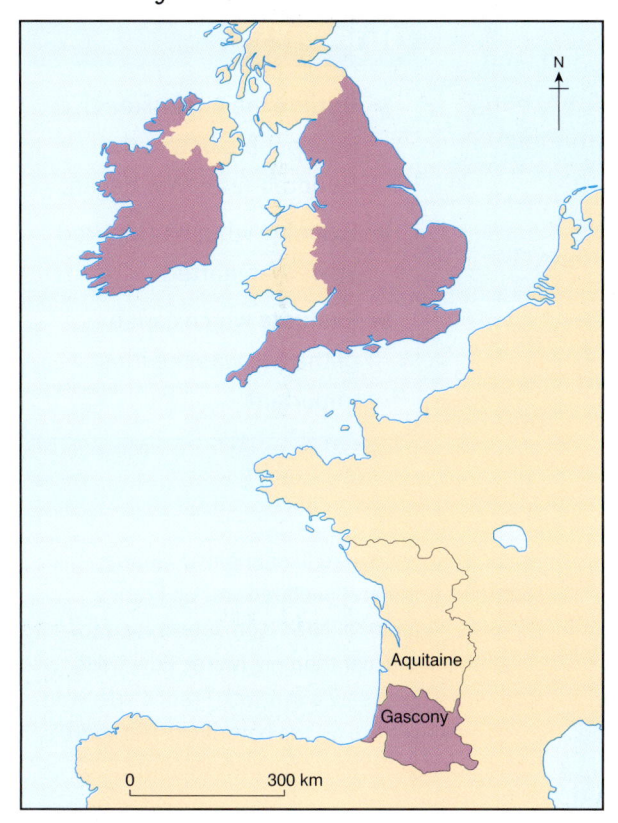

Key Words

crusade   Magna Carta

in France consisted of just one area – Gascony. So the barons rebelled by putting together their own army and marching towards London, to take over. They gave John a choice: change the way he was running the country, or fight the army that was heading towards London. King John gave in and asked the barons what they wanted. John eventually agreed to their demands, set out in a document called **Magna Carta** (Great Charter). He promised, among other things, to respect the rights of the Church and the barons, to stop unfair taxes, and to ensure that trials would be held quickly and fairly.

Work

1. **a** In what ways did the 'Angevin' Empire decline during the reign of Richard I?
   b Can you suggest reasons for the decline?
2. **a** Who was 'John Softsword'?
   b Why do you think he was given this nickname?
3. Create a presentation, poster or write an extended answer that describes the rise and fall of the 'Angevin' Empire. Make sure you use dates, names of territories, and kings in your description. You might want to use maps to give an extra visual dimension to your work.

More losses of territories under King John

After the defeats in France, John went back to England. He attempted to raise an army to invade France and take back the land. But this meant raising taxes to pay for it, which made him very unpopular. After another defeat in France in 1214, the English barons decided to take action against their king. Taxes were higher than ever and French lands such as Normandy, Brittany, Anjou and Maine were no longer under John's control. By now, his land

Extension

How did King John's problems with his 'Angevin' Empire help lead to Magna Carta?

1193–94	1199	1202–05	1204–14	1216
John schemes with King Philip II of France to undermine King Richard; Philip of France invades Normandy and Anjou	Richard I is killed; his brother becomes King John. John and Arthur of Brittany in conflict over land in France; Arthur is murdered	Philip II conquers Normandy, Anjou, Maine and Brittany	King John tries to regain control of Normandy	John dies, and with the loss of Anjou and many other important French lands, this marks the end of the 'Angevin' Empire. King John was an inadequate military leader who did not inspire loyalty. His involvement in the murder of Arthur of Brittany shocked and alienated many of his important subjects. Henry II had been rich, but due to the high cost of Richard I's wars, England was financially exhausted by 1199. King John lost an empire through bad decisions and because he ran out of money at a crucial time

Britain: Migration, empires and the people

3.1 The Hundred Years War

William the Conqueror was both King of England and Duke of Normandy. He spent most of his time up to 1072 in England, and then spent the majority of his time in Normandy. In fact, the early Norman kings of England (who were often based in Normandy) just regarded England as part of an empire they ruled. These kings also brought much of Wales and Scotland under their control and influence. Some kings of England, such as Henry II, were successful in gaining more land from the French. However, most of this land was eventually won back by the French during the reign of King John (1199–1216). By the time Edward III became King of England in 1327, only Gascony and a small part of northern France remained under the King of England's control.

Objectives

- **Outline** the Anglo-French relationship before the Hundred Years War began.
- **Examine** why the Hundred Years War started.
- **Evaluate** which cause of the war was the most important.

Causes of war

SOURCE A *King Edward at his coronation in 1327*

In 1337, King Edward III of England claimed the French throne and declared war on France. He was 24 years old and was determined to be a stronger ruler than his father, Edward II. The young king saw a war with France as a way of achieving glory on the battlefield; but there were other reasons why war broke out:

- England still controlled the Gascony area of France, where a lot of wine was made. When the wine was taken to England it was taxed, and King Edward made lots of money from this. However, the French threatened to take over this wine producing area.
- England sold lots of wool abroad. Areas near France (for example, Flanders) turned this wool into cloth. Both the English and the people in places like Flanders made lots of money doing this. But the French threatened to take over these areas. If the wool trade was stopped, it would make England poorer, and people wouldn't be able to afford to pay King Edward so much tax.
- Edward was closely linked to France. His grandfather had been King of France and his mother was the daughter of a French king. He thought he had a better claim to the throne of France than the French king at the time, Philip VI.
- Edward was in conflict with Scotland at this time. The French promised to help the Scots, which made Edward furious!

194　Chapter 3　The birth of English identity

The Hundred Years War

In 1337, England and France started fighting to gain control of the French throne. Known as the Hundred Years War, the war lasted, off and on, until 1453 (a total of 116 years) and covered the reigns of five English kings. There were battles at sea, but most of the fighting was done on French land. None of the fighting happened in England.

The Hundred Years War can be divided into three distinct phases, separated by truces. The first stage of the war lasted from 1337 until 1360 and it went particularly well for the English. Edward III won important battles at Crécy (1346) and Poitiers (1356) and captured the French port of Calais, the nearest large port to England. Calais remained in English hands for the next 200 years. Edward also captured the French king and held him to ransom. After this, the fighting died down. Edward gave up his demands to the French throne in return for the right to control Gascony, Calais and other minor French territories.

The second stage of the war began in 1370, when the French won back some of the land they had lost. Then the final phase of war began in 1413 when Henry V became England's king. His victory at the Battle of Agincourt in 1415 led to his conquest of much of northern France, including Normandy. But Henry V died in 1422 and was succeeded by his nine-month-old son. Soon, the gains made under Henry V were swept away as the French hit back. Inspired by the leadership of 17-year-old peasant girl, Joan of Arc, the French beat the English forces time and time again. By the end of the war in 1453, the English had lost all their territory in France except for the tiny area around Calais.

▼ **B** *Maps showing the height of English territorial gains during the Hundred Years War (in 1360), and how little territory the English had at the end of the war (in 1453)*

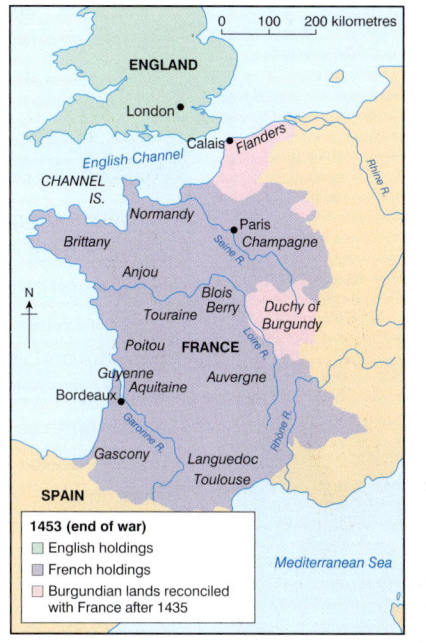

Fact

Every English king between 1199 and 1461 married a French princess or noblewoman, but marriage didn't always bring peace between the two countries.

Work

1. a How many years did the Hundred Years War last?
   b Why do you think it was called the Hundred Years War?

2. Look at the two maps in **B**. In your own words, explain how the French territory under England's control changed between 1360 and 1453.

3. In your opinion, who won the Hundred Years War? Give reasons for your answer.

Extension

Research the reign of Edward II and produce a fact file of his achievements. Why was Edward III determined to be more successful?

Practice Question

Were economic factors the main cause of the Hundred Years War?

16 marks
SPaG: 4 marks

Study Tip

Write about personal reasons as well as economic ones in your answer.

3.2A The impact of the Hundred Years War

The Hundred Years War was not one long war, but a series of battles that lasted from 1337 to 1453. There were many years of little or no fighting, when both sides made peace deals, and times when there were major, aggressive campaigns by one side or another. This war gave both France and England some of their best-known heroes and greatest victories. One of the most notable battles in the later phase of the war occurred on 25 October 1415 near Agincourt, France. It was fought between the heavily outnumbered army of King Henry V of England and that of King Charles VI of France. Why was the Battle of Agincourt so important? And what was the impact of the battle, and of the Hundred Years War, on the birth of English identity?

Objectives

- **Recall** the importance of the Battle of Agincourt.
- **Analyse** the impact of the Hundred Years War for both England and France.
- **Assess** how the war contributed to the birth of English identity.

The Battle of Agincourt

Twenty-five year old Henry V became King of England in 1413. Two years later, he sailed for France, which was to be the focus of his attention for the rest of his reign. Henry was determined to regain the territories in France that former kings of England had lost. Soon after arriving in France, he captured Harfleur, a port in Normandy. But Henry lost half his men to disease and battle injuries, so decided to march his army north to Calais, where he would meet a fleet of English ships and return to England. But the French had no intention of letting Henry get away: at Agincourt, a vast French army of 30,000 men stood in his path.

▼ **INTERPRETATION A** *An interpretation of King Henry V (in the crown) at the Battle of Agincourt, from a book about English history published in England in 1864*

Approximately 11,000 exhausted English archers, knights and foot soldiers were there, and they were outnumbered three to one.

The battle took place in a field that lay between two woods. It had rained heavily before the battle: this, combined with the fact that the field had recently been ploughed, would have a major impact on the outcome of the battle. Fighting began around 11:00am on 25 October 1415. Diagrams B and C show two stages in the battle.

Fact

The archers that fought for Henry used large bows called longbows. They could fire around 12 arrows a minute and could kill a man nearly 200 metres away. The French tended to use crossbows, which were very powerful and accurate, but took longer to load. The archers proved decisive at Agincourt, as they had done at the Battle of Crécy in 1346. The humble, common archer was now more than a match for the powerful knight on horseback.

Chapter 3 The birth of English identity

▼ **B** The first stage of the Battle of Agincourt

▼ **C** The end stage of the Battle of Agincourt

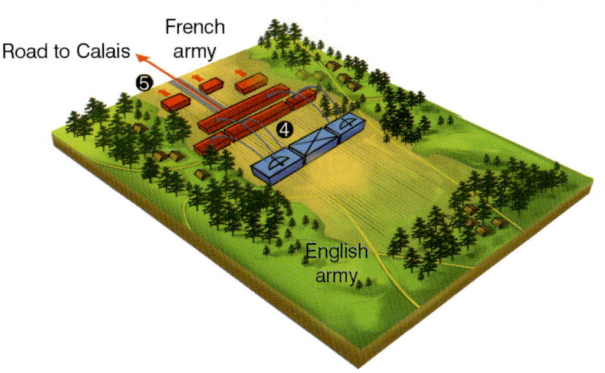

1 English (blue) and French (red) positions at start of the Battle of Agincourt.

2 Henry immediately moved his troops forward and ordered his archers to open fire.

3 The French tried to charge at the English, but a combination of thick mud, heavy armour, and wooden spikes that the English had set up in front of themselves, slowed them down.

4 The French continued to charge, but they were bogged down in the mud and unable to advance. The English archers continued their attack from above and slaughtered the French.

5 The battle was a disaster for the French; the survivors fled.

Consequences of the battle

Estimates suggest that the French lost between 7000 and 10,000 men at Agincourt, while the English lost only a few hundred. After the victory, Henry V went on to conquer Normandy and tighten his grip on France. Many powerful French knights and nobles were killed at Agincourt and, before long, the daughter of the French king had become Henry's wife, as part of the Treaty of Troyes, 1420. The treaty, which was a direct result of English military success, made Henry V heir to the French throne; but he never lived to be king of a united England and France. In 1422, aged just 35, Henry died suddenly of dysentery. Soon after, French fortunes began to turn. Inspired by a French peasant girl called Joan of Arc, who claimed that voices of the saints had called on her to free France from the English, the French gradually began to drive the English out. The English caught Joan of Arc, accused her of witchcraft and burned her to death, but over the next few decades, the French regained most of the territories occupied by the English.

Work

1. Why was there a battle at Agincourt?
2. Look at **Interpretation A**.
   a. What impression do you get of Henry V from this picture?
   b. Consider the provenance (caption). Can you suggest reasons why Henry is portrayed like this?
3. You have been asked to design a page on the battle for a children's history book, aimed at children under 11. Plan out the page on A4 paper and, in under 200 words, write a simple description suitable for children of this age.

Extension

Agincourt is not the only famous battle to take place during the Hundred Years War. Research another famous battle that took place (such as the Battle of Crécy or the Battle of Poitiers), and consider its significance.

3.2B The impact of the Hundred Years War

The legacy of the Hundred Years War

Historians often debate about whether or not an event, individual or issue is significant. When historians see something as significant, it means more than just that it is important. The following criteria are commonly used when assessing historical significance:

- Impact at the time: Was the event, person, development or issue important at the time? How deeply were people's lives affected? How many lives were affected?
- Impact in the long term: For how long have people's lives been affected? Is the event, person, development or issue still relevant in today's world?

So, when exploring the impact of the Hundred Years War, it is important to think about these questions so you can judge whether the war was a significant event, and how significant it is!

Fact

Historians have found it very difficult to put a number on the amount of soldiers and civilians who died during the conflict as a result of battle, disease, and famine. Estimates range from 180,000 to over three million.

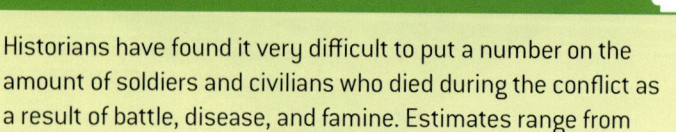

▼ SOURCE A *A painting of the Battle of Poitiers in the Hundred Years War, from* Froissart's Chronicles, *written in the fourteenth century*

Impact on France and England at the time

Some areas of France (for example, Normandy) were devastated during the fighting. Armies on both sides seized crops and animals, and stole whatever riches they could find. If an army was retreating, they might burn all the buildings they left behind so their advancing enemy couldn't use them. Lots of ordinary men fought (and died) on both sides too, although there were fewer battle casualties on the English side. Many English deaths were from dysentery, rather than destruction on the battlefield.

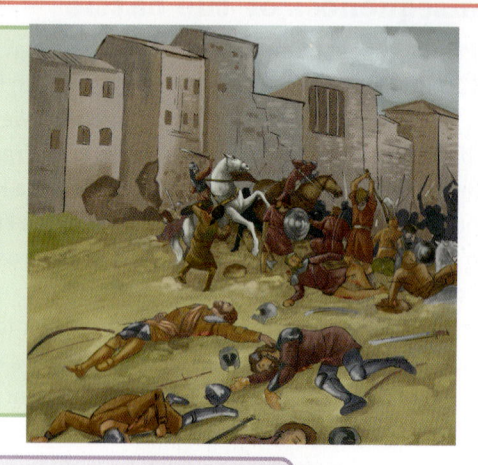

The cost of war

The high cost of weapons, food, armour and horses meant that wars were very expensive. As a result, both the French and English had to pay higher taxes, more frequently, to pay for the war. By the end of the war, England had lost wealthy French regions like Normandy and Aquitaine, so could no longer make money from these areas. However, some Englishmen got very rich from the stolen goods taken from France. Bodiam Castle in Sussex, for example, was built from the proceeds made from the war.

198 Chapter 3 The birth of English identity

The military impact

The war changed the way battles were fought. Before the Hundred Years War, the knight on horseback, fighting as part of the cavalry, was the most effective, powerful and feared part of an army. However, it was the archers, firing thousands of arrows, that led to the great French defeats at Crécy, Poitiers and Agincourt. This spelled the end of the dominance of the knight on horseback. From then on, the power of missile fire, first from the longbow and later from the handgun, was the most effective battle technique. Soon, the ordinary foot soldiers were the key element to an army, rather than the cavalry. The war also saw the increased use of gunpowder, cannons and handguns. And as soon as gunpowder was used regularly, castles proved to be of little use in battles, so they began a long decline.

French unity

France had long been a collection of separate territories – Normandy, Aquitaine, Brittany and Gascony, for example. But a great number of the powerful, important French nobles who controlled these areas were killed during the war. As a result, the King of France emerged more powerful than ever. He was the one central leader of the country, and the French people rallied behind him. The Hundred Years War led to a surge in nationalist feelings among the French: a love of their country and a love of their king! Also, the high cost of paying for the war led the French to set up a better system of taxing the whole country: this was so successful that they were able to pay for the first full-time army in Europe.

The birth of English identity

England and France had been connected since the days when William, Duke of Normandy defeated Harold to become the King of England. The Hundred Years War caused the two countries to forge their own identities. During the course of the war, England stopped using French as its official court language, because it was seen as the 'enemy language'.

After losing its territory in France, England became less involved in relations with the rest of Europe. England began to see itself as 'apart' from Europe, rather than a part of it. A much more unified country developed against the French, Scots and everyone else; and Crécy, Agincourt and other major battles gave the English a sense of pride and a unique identity. With a common language and homeland, a sense of what it meant to be 'English' quickly developed. Kings started to use the English language, and people started speaking of themselves as 'English' – not just from a region of England.

England's outlook and aims changed too: it was now a country looking to conquer lands outside Europe, a country that would soon look to develop an empire in newly found lands.

Work

1. In your own words, explain the impact of the Hundred Years War on the following:
   - England and France at the time
   - the way wars were fought in the future
   - the French monarchy
   - the English language.
2. a What do you think is meant by the term 'English identity'?
   b Why might the Hundred Years War be seen as a major factor in the birth of English identity?
3. In what ways was the Hundred Years War a 'significant' event? Use the criteria on this page to help you with your judgement.

Practice Question

Compare the impact on Britain of the Hundred Years War with the Viking invasions of Britain. In what ways were they similar? **8 marks**

Study Tip

Consider the consequences of both events for different groups of people in Britain.

Britain: Migration, empires and the people 199

4.1 Why did Tudor and Stuart explorers look west?

The age of the Tudor and Stuart monarchs was one of momentous change. Under the Tudors, England and Wales were finally united and large parts of Ireland came under direct English control. The Tudors and the Scottish royal family, the Stuarts, came together through marriage too, and later the two countries united under one king. For many, Britain became a more prosperous place as farming and industry expanded. There was also a surge in overseas trade too, as British explorers and even pirates found new sea routes across the Atlantic and Indian Oceans. These adventurers laid strong foundations for an overseas empire.

Objectives

▶ **Describe** the westward explorations of English sailors.

▶ **Explain** the consequences of this expansion.

The New World: overseas exploration

▼ **A** *Maps of the known world in Tudor and Stuart times, in 1480 and in 1600*

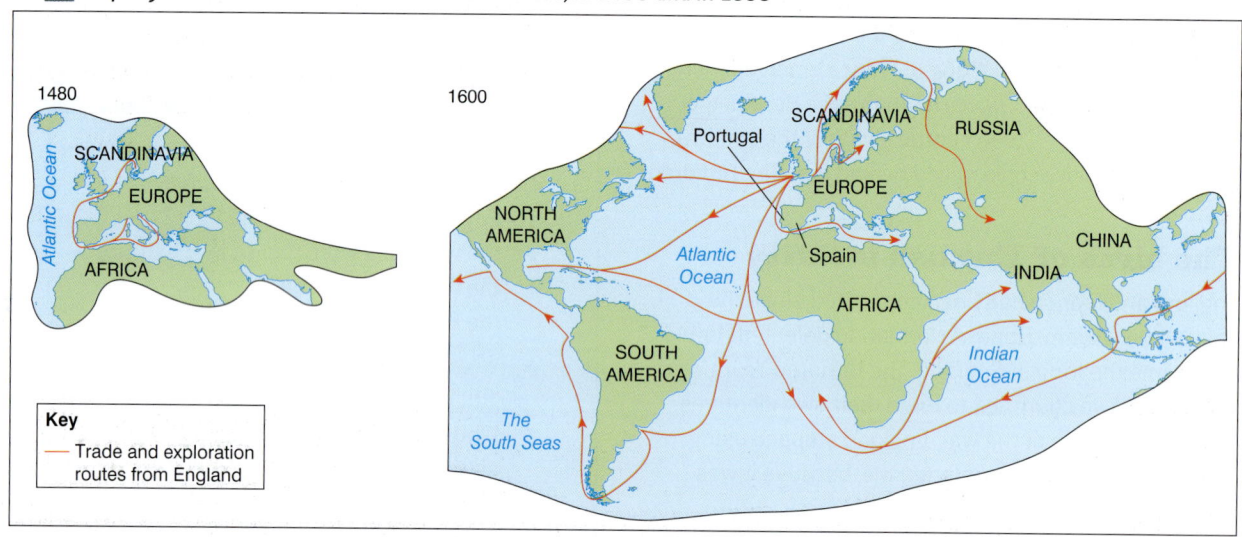

In the late 1400s, improvements in technology for ships and navigation meant longer journeys were possible, and more ships returned from these journeys. In 1492, Christopher Columbus (who was working for the Spanish) set sail across the Atlantic Ocean, hoping to find new routes to India and China by sea. Instead, by sailing west, he 'discovered' a group of islands, later known as the West Indies, which Europeans didn't know existed. In fact, he had found the continents we now know as the Americas. Soon more explorers from Spain, and then Portugal, set sail for the Americas to claim land for their monarchs.

Spain was the first major nation to **colonise** the Americas. The Spanish discovered gold in South America, which made them rich. In 1496, the Tudor King Henry VII joined this age of exploration when he gave the adventurer, John Cabot, the mission of finding new lands.

From the port of Bristol, Cabot sailed westwards across the Atlantic, and landed on the coast of North America in what is now Canada. But there were no great riches or obvious financial gains to be found in this newly discovered place – no silks and no gold – so Cabot returned home. However, Cabot's brief visit marked the start of the British Empire. Over time, British settlers would move out to live in what was named 'Newfoundland', and eventually settle all along the east coast of North America. Establishing a base now meant that other British adventurers, such as Sir John Hawkins and Sir Walter Raleigh, could explore and claim further territory. They could also **plunder** riches from Spanish ships and colonies.

Key Biography

Sir John Hawkins (1532–95)

John Hawkins was the second son of William Hawkins, who sailed in trading expeditions to West Africa in the 1530s. In his youth, John Hawkins' first voyages were to the Spanish Canary Islands in the Atlantic. He became a respected English naval commander, merchant, **privateer** and pirate, and was responsible for building up the Elizabethan Royal Navy.

He was the cousin of another famous explorer, Sir Francis Drake. Hawkins narrowly escaped with his life in a battle with the Spanish at San Juan de Ulua in 1568. He and Drake were surprised by an attack from the Spanish after they thought they had negotiated a truce. Drake and Hawkins swore vengeance for the treachery and the men they lost.

He was also known as the 'Father of the Slave Trade'. To find out more about his role in the development of the slave trade, read pages 204–205.

Key Words

colonise   plunder   privateer   piracy

It is important to note that there was a religious dimension to the competition between Spain and England at this time – Spain was Catholic and England was Protestant. This religious rivalry gave an added edge to the desire of each country's monarch to gain more land and increase their power base.

Piracy and plunder

As Britain failed to find any of its own gold, it used other methods: one of the ways in which countries obtained wealth and riches at this time was simply by taking it from another country's ships or territory. Any sailor with permission from the king or queen – known as a privateer – could attack foreign ships and steal from them. This permission was granted as long as the privateers shared anything they stole with the monarch. Any sailors who didn't have permission, and kept any treasure for themselves, were known as pirates. An estimated 10 to 15 per cent of all Spanish treasure ships were successfully captured by rival countries. Some successful British privateers also took part in **piracy** – keeping the plunder for themselves rather than sharing it with the monarch.

Extension

Research the life of a famous English privateer, such as Sir Francis Drake, Sir Walter Raleigh or Sir Henry Morgan.

Work

1. Describe the circumstances in which Columbus found the Americas.
2. What is the difference between a privateer and a pirate?
3. Why did British invest in privateering and piracy against the Spanish Empire in the Tudor and Stuart eras?
4. Why was Cabot's voyage important?

4.2 Why was piracy replaced by plantations?

Explorers like Drake, Hawkins and Morgan made lots of money for Britain as privateers, by stealing fortunes from Spanish and Portuguese ships. However, by the late 1500s, it became clear that there were other ways to make money out of the **New World** of the Americas. Britain set up colonies there, and by the 1600s, developed huge farms called **plantations**, where crops like sugar and cotton were grown. Where were the plantations set up, and who would do the hard work of farming the crops?

Objectives

▶ **Explain** why Britain moved from piracy and plunder to plantations and colonies in the sixteenth to eighteenth centuries.

▶ **Explore** how sugar and slaves became important in the Caribbean.

Why go the the Americas?

There were a number of reasons (or factors) why people chose to leave Britain for a new life in the New World.

Religious factors

In Britain, there were religious conflicts. Some religious groups such as Puritans and Catholics felt that they were not permitted to worship as they wished in Britain, so they left to settle in a place where they would have greater religious freedom. Find out more on pages 206–209.

Economic factors

Following the establishment of the first successful British colony in America in 1607 (during the Stuart King James I's reign), more Britons were willing to move to the New World to farm and to make money. Homes were built and there was plenty of land to grow new 'cash crops' such as cotton, tobacco, sugar and potatoes. These were grown on farms known as plantations, which can grow specific crops in large quantities. The crops were then exported back to Britain for great profit. This was often the only thing that made the hardship of setting up colonies – with harsh weather, hunger and conflicts with Native Americans or **indigenous** people – worthwhile.

Into the Caribbean

It wasn't just North America where new colonies were set up. British businessmen (or traders) also set up plantations in the West Indies on islands such as Bardados (1625) and the Cayman Islands (1670).

▼ **SOURCE A** *An illustration from 1590 showing English colonists approaching the island of Roanoke in 1585; it accompanied a report that tried to persuade others that there should be more British colonisation in North America*

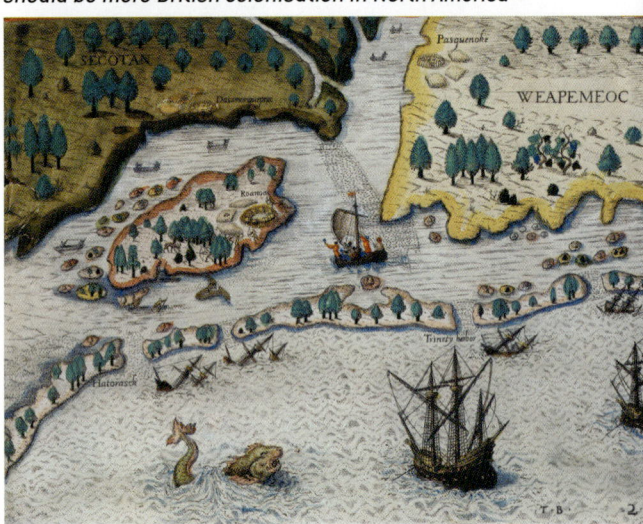

Plantations soon grew in importance: as the Americas were so distant, the colonies depended on successful large-scale farming to survive.

Global trading

British investors were also keen on developing trade in the Americas, because it would help to pay for the growth of the British Empire elsewhere, in India. They realised that they could export crops such as cotton from the New World to Britain, while they could import and sell other goods to the colonies, such as wheat, rice, and coffee. Also, the cotton from American plantations helped supply British fabric factories, who in return would sell the fabric to British colonies for further profit.

Fact

Barbados was an island that the British acquired from the Spanish in 1625. The Stuart King Charles I then allowed the island to be established for tobacco plantations. To begin with, it couldn't compete with the older plantations in North America, but by 1655, it was the largest British slave colony. Plantations soon switched to growing sugar, and by the 1690s, most of the island was covered in successful sugar plantations. Barbados became far more profitable for the British than the mainland America colonies, mainly because it was seen as just a profit-making area, and not as a place to settle.

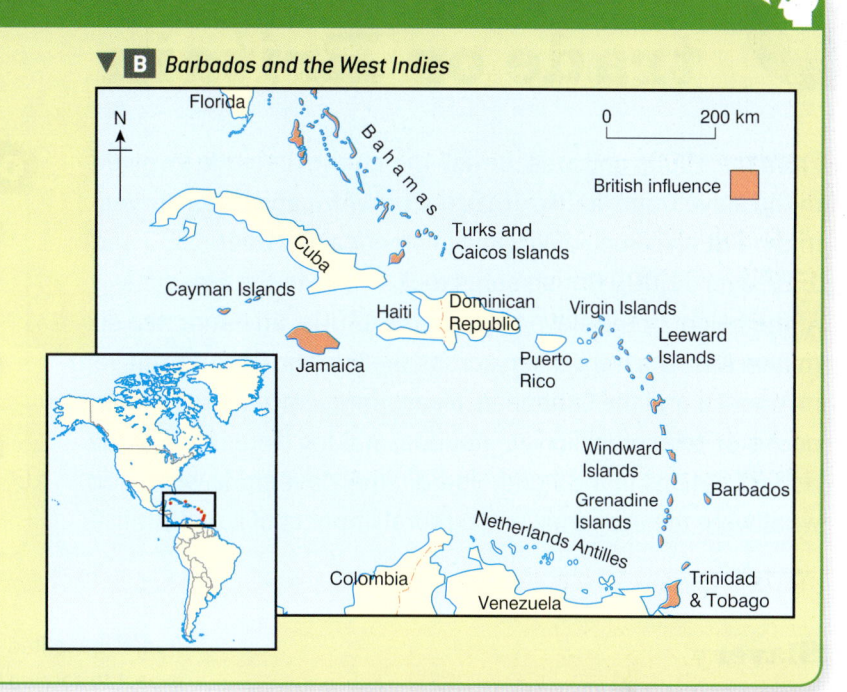

B *Barbados and the West Indies*

Plantation replacing piracy

As Britain's worldwide empire grew in North America (and India), and became increasingly profitable, British monarchs stopped granting privateer permission because there was less need to steal from other nations. The Royal Navy also took increasingly effective anti-pirate measures. This meant that by the 1720s, piracy was rare in the Americas. Pirates were chased out of harbours where they had previously been able to seek safe haven, such as Nassau in the Bahamas. Plantations, not piracy, became the area where huge profits could be made for Britain.

The move to slavery

Many settlers soon found that conditions were hard on plantations: there were new diseases, the weather was too hot, and when crops failed, there were not always enough food for everyone. Not many people were willing to work the farms in these conditions, so the British began using indentured servants for labour. Indentured servants were servants who paid for their voyage to America by being under contract to a plantation owner for a set period of years. Once they had finished their period of service they were then free to work for wages. However, by 1619, African slaves were introduced to British plantations because they were cheaper: plantation owners could buy the slaves outright. Slaves had no legal rights and had to work their whole lives without payment, and any slave children born became slave owners' property too. Purchasing slaves allowed plantations to become more profitable, as the unpaid workforce increased in size.

Key Words

New World   plantation   indigenous

Fact

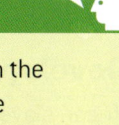

The Spanish were the first to use slaves in the Americas. The British got involved with the slave trade in 1562, when Sir John Hawkins got permission from Queen Elizabeth to transport captured African slaves to Spanish colonies. Hawkins was Britain's first slave trader, and he made a fortune.

Work

1. Why did people leave Britain to settle in the New World?
2. Explain how the settlers hoped to make money in their new colonies.
3. How did the settlers find workers to establish and farm the crops they grew?
4. Why was slavery so profitable?
5. Study **Source A**. How useful is it to a historian studying the reasons for the British colonisation of North America?

Britain: Migration, empires and the people

4.3 The impact of the slave trade on Britain

From the 1560s onwards, British merchants became involved in the slave trade, and in 1619, the first African slaves arrived in the British colony of **Virginia** in America. Between 1690 and 1787, over 11,000 British ships took slaves to the Americas. At the height of the slave trade, in the 1700s, an estimated six million Africans were taken across the Atlantic Ocean to slavery in America and the Caribbean. Meanwhile, British slave traders pocketed tens of millions of pounds, making Britain one of the richest nations in the world. How did the slave trade work, and what were the economic and cultural impacts of it on Britain?

Objectives

- **Outline** the development of the slave trade in the sixteenth and seventeenth centuries.
- **Explain** why the slave trade was so profitable.
- **Evaluate** the economic and social impact of the slave trade on Britain.

Slavery

The idea of slavery is a very old one, but slaves were used in very large numbers in the Tudor and Stuart periods, especially by countries that had started to take over North and South America and the Caribbean. These slaves endured short and brutal lives of hard work and extreme misery: sugar plantation slaves had an average life expectancy of 26, because they often had a poor diet, faced tough punishments, and had no proper medical attention.

Development of the slave trade

African slaves ended up in the Americas and West Indies as a result of a three-part trading journey known as the **slave triangle**.

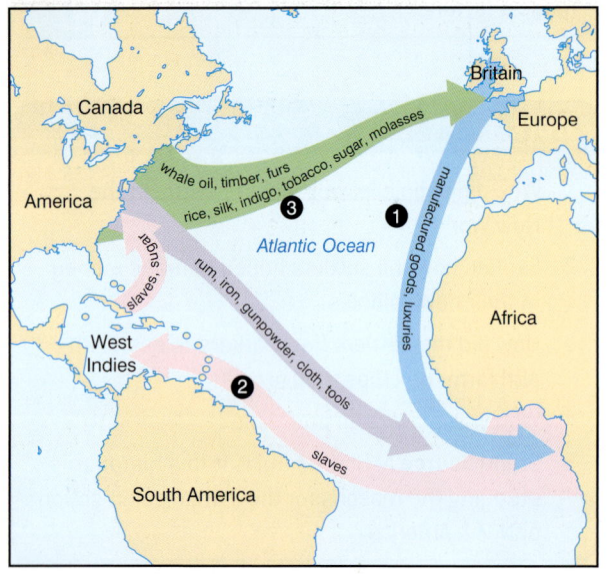

Traders benefited greatly from the slave trade, and could expect to earn up to 800 per cent profit on their investment. They made money not just from selling slaves, but from the other parts of the slave triangle too, and their ships were rarely empty. All they needed was the initial investment to finance the ship, pay a strong crew to control the slaves, and buy the goods they would eventually trade for slaves on the African coast. Slave owners also profited from the slave trade: owners forced slaves to work all their lives, without wages, and in great hardship. The increased slave trading up until the 1800s, and a growing slave population, meant that plantations became more and more profitable. At the same time, as the British Empire grew, the demand for the crops grown in the American plantations and the products made from them grew as well.

▼ **A** *The three parts of the slave triangle*

1 Traders leave Britain and other European ports, headed for Africa, with ships full of goods such as alcohol, guns, and cloth.

2 Traders trade these goods with African tribesmen in return for prisoners from other African tribes, who have already been captured to sell; they also kidnap Africans. The ships are loaded with these slaves and sail across the Atlantic.

3 In the Americas, the slaves are traded to plantation owners and farmers for goods such as sugar, cotton or tobacco. These are loaded onto the ships, which sail back to British or European ports to be sold at great profit.

204　Chapter 4　Sugar and the Caribbean

▼ **SOURCE B** *An illustration from c1840, showing a slave in the French West Indies being whipped while bound to four stakes*

Economic impact

Britain wasn't the only European nation to get involved in slavery during Tudor and Stuart times, but Britain made some of the largest profits. British slave traders didn't just work on their own either: they were supported by investors back in Britain, including monarchs. Queen Elizabeth was a business partner of John Hawkins, and even gave him one of her ships to use for slave trading. King Charles II was a partner in the **Royal African Company**, a large slave-trading business that transported 60,000 slaves from Africa between 1680 and 1688. Many of the slaves were branded with the letters DY when they were captured, after the man who ran the company: James, Duke of York (the future King James II).

In fact, many Britons played a significant part in the slave trade – shipbuilders, ship owners (who allowed their ships to be used), bankers (who lent traders money), investors (who shared in the profits) and importers (who brought in the goods that slaves farmed). Many other Britons were linked in other ways: dockworkers unloading ships full of cotton that slaves had grown; workers turning the cotton into shirts; even the shop owners selling sugar and tobacco from the plantations. Whether directly or indirectly, all these people gained financially from slave trading: the British slave trade industry made approximately £60 million between 1761 and 1808, making Britain one of the richest and most powerful nations in the world.

Key Words

Virginia   slave triangle   Royal African Company

Social impact

Another impact of the slave trade on Britain was that west coast towns and ports such as Liverpool, Glasgow and Bristol grew into large cities during the eighteenth century as they benefited from the shipping trade. Also, many of the fine buildings in these places (and to some extent in London) were built on the profits of slavery: for example, Liverpool Town Hall and the National Portrait Gallery in London were all paid for with the proceeds of slavery. A large number of Liverpool's mayors were slave traders, and in parliament, so were many MPs.

▼ **SOURCE B** *George F. Cooke, a well-known British actor, said the following in 1785:*

> Every brick in the city of Liverpool is cemented with the blood of a slave.

Up until the 1800s, it was not illegal to make money from slave trades. And because slave trading was so widespread, and many British people in power were involved in it, it led to the belief that Europeans were superior to Africans. However, some people at the time felt slavery was wrong, and by the late 1700s a campaign started to get the trade abolished. In 1807, the British parliament abolished the slave trade, and by 1833, it banned slave ownership not only in Britain but also throughout the British Empire.

Work

1. In your own words, describe how the slave trade developed in the sixteenth and seventeenth centuries.
2. Make a list of the ways Britain was linked to the slave trade.

Practice Question

Compare the Vikings and British slave traders. In what ways were they similar? **8 marks**

Study Tip

Consider the 'wealth' which each group extracted from the lands they visited.

Britain: Migration, empires and the people

5.1A British colonies in America

In the sixteenth and early seventeenth centuries, people began to leave different European countries and settle in America. Early British settlers occupied the east coast of North America. These British settlements, or colonies, made up what could be described as Britain's first successful overseas empire. By the mid-1700s there were thirteen successful British colonies. Who were the early settlers, and why did they leave Britain? What were the consequences of British colonisation for the indigenous (Native American) people?

Objectives

- **Identify** different causes of British migration to North America.
- **Examine** the roles of Sir Walter Raleigh and the Pilgrim Fathers in establishing early colonies such as Jamestown.
- **Assess** the impact of the arrival of the British on indigenous tribes.

Why did people leave Britain?

Several causes made people leave Britain at this time. Firstly, economic problems meant that unemployment among farmhands and labourers was high, and wages were low. People struggled to survive, and sometimes faced starvation as a result of failed harvests. As a result, a new start in a new land seemed very appealing.

Secondly, some Christian groups, such as **Puritans**, **Quakers** and **Catholics**, had suffered **persecution** in Britain since the 1530s, when King Henry VIII turned the country from Catholic to **Protestant**. For example, failure to attend **Anglican** Church services was punishable by prison or even execution. As a result, many of these religious groups left Britain to settle in North America, where they set up or joined colonies. Around 80,000 Puritans migrated to America between 1630 and 1641.

Emigration peaked during the British **Civil Wars** and during the time of Oliver Cromwell's rule in Britain (1642–60), partly due to the fact that differences in religious beliefs led to conflicts between religious groups. Furthermore, religious groups in mainland Europe also wanted to escape persecution: some Dutch, French and Germans emigrated from the 1560s onwards. Some religious groups also wanted to emigrate in order to convert the Native Americans to Christianity.

A The 13 American colonies, the goods and crops they produced, and early British settlements

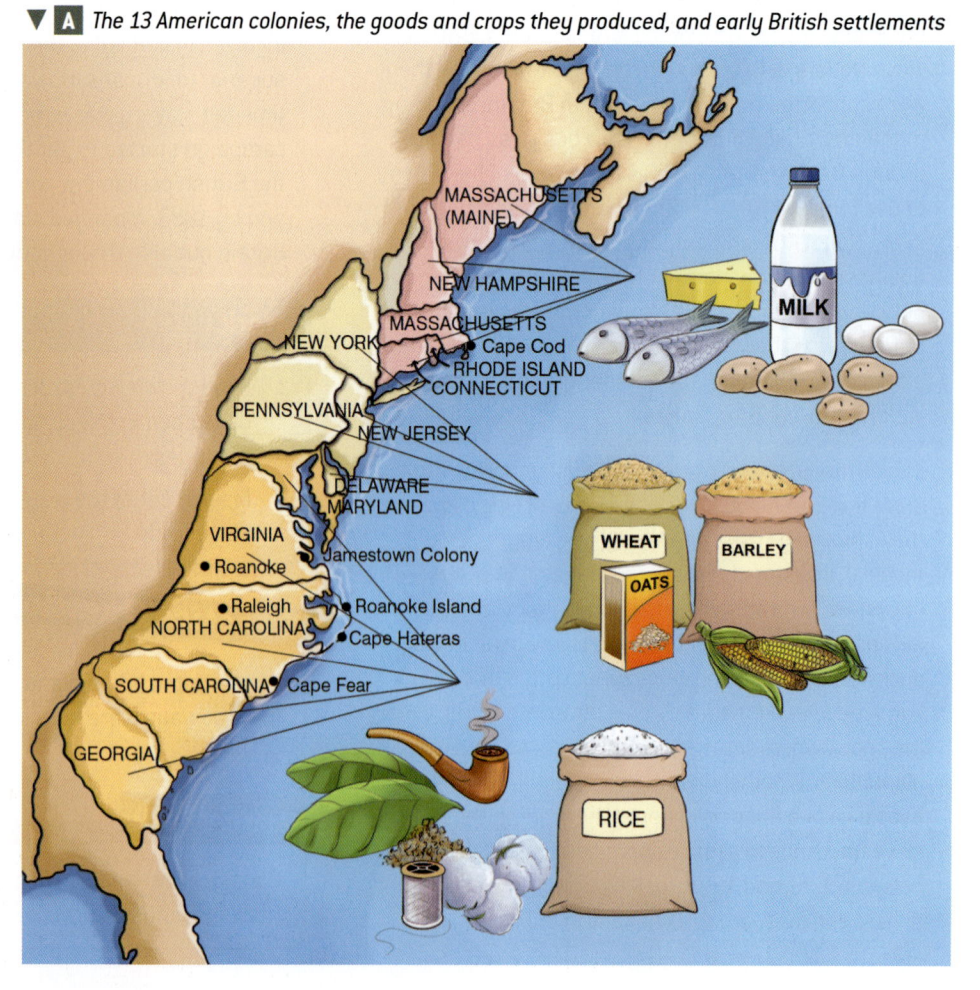

What was attractive about North America?

People from overcrowded British towns were excited by the vast expanse of new land available to settlers in America, and by the chance to make money. People grew crops such as tobacco, corn and cotton, and then transported them back to Britain to sell. Livestock sales were also successful. This drove British businessmen to invest in more voyages. North American seas were stocked with profitable cod, and by the late 1600s, sugar plantations were also bringing in huge profits for Britain.

Early settlers and colonies

Life for the early British settlers in the colonies was not easy to begin with, however. They often faced hardship and failure. Two case studies — Virginia and Massachusetts — highlight how settlers tried to establish colonies.

Extension

Sir Walter Raleigh was in the top 100 'Greatest Britons' in a poll among British people in 2002. Research Raleigh further and explain whether you agree with the title of 'Father of American Colonies', even though those colonies failed.

Case study: Virginia

In the late 1500s, many British people tried to establish settlements in the area known as Virginia, but they failed to survive. In 1606, King James I gave permission for a group of businessmen to sail to Virginia, to establish a new colony called **Jamestown**, to see if the land was fit to grow crops, and to find gold if possible. The colony was founded in 1607, but the settlers faced incredible hardships. At first they had to rely on friendly local tribes to help them find and grow food, but some other tribes massacred numerous early settlers. Also, some of the early settlers were wealthy aristocrats who were unused to doing farm work. Life in Jamestown and other early colonies meant hunger and death for many, but the settlers were determined to stay. With the support of friendly native tribes, the settlers began to farm the land successfully, rather than focus on the search for gold. Tobacco planting in particular led to the success of Jamestown: tobacco was easy to grow and made high profits. This led to more and more British **migrants** seeking their fortune in the New World. Other settlements such as New Plymouth soon sprung up along the East coast of America — eventually developing into **13 colonies**.

Key Words

Puritan   Quaker   Catholic   persecution   Protestant   Anglican   civil war   Jamestown   migrant   13 colonies

Work

1. a List the reasons why Britons migrated to, and built colonies in, North America.
   b Which reason do you think is the most important one? Why?
2. Why did the Jamestown settlers succeed?
3. Describe what Sir Walter Raleigh did to help Britain colonise North America.

Practice Question

Was religion the main factor in causing migration to America?   **16 marks**   **SPaG: 4 marks**

Study Tip

For 'main factor' questions you will need to explain how religion and other factors caused migration (see Chapters 5 and 6). Was religion or another cause the main factor?

Key Biography

Sir Walter Raleigh (c1554–1618)

Sir Walter Raleigh was a sea captain for both Queen Elizabeth and her successor King James I. In 1584, the Queen sent him to start settlements in Virginia. These early colonies faced numerous problems: the settlers were frequently short on supplies, they struggled to grow crops, there were attacks from Native Americans, and they caught diseases like malaria. However, Raleigh is known as the 'Father of American Colonies' for establishing colonies such as Roanoke (in 1584).

Britain: Migration, empires and the people

5.1B British colonies in America

Case study: Massachusetts

One of the most famous groups of British people to settle in America arrived in 1620 on a ship called the *Mayflower*. They were mainly Puritans; strict Protestant Christians who left because they were persecuted by others who did not agree with their religious beliefs. They, and other settlers, set up their own religious colony known as 'New Plymouth', with the aim of fishing and trading with other colonies. Enough of the colonists survived the winter, with help from local tribes, for it to become the first permanent colony (Jamestown eventually became deserted). These settlers became known as the **Pilgrim Fathers**.

▼ **INTERPRETATION B** *A nineteenth-century painting showing the Puritans arriving in America in 1620, with the* Mayflower *sailing away into the distance*

weren't just British **emigrants** looking for quick wealth. In fact, they managed to create religious and democratic rules and traditions that would become the foundation of an American identity.

> **Fact**
>
> Thanksgiving in the USA is a celebration holiday and meal on the fourth Thursday in November. The tradition dates back to a feast held by some of the earliest settlers, the Pilgrims, in 1621 to 'give thanks' for an exceptionally bountiful harvest.

Impact of British colonies on Native Americans

The indigenous (native) tribes in America had been there long before any Europeans. There were many tribes, with different cultures. Most did not have permanent settlements: they lived off the land and established camps where appropriate. As such, the British arrival in North America could be interpreted in different ways. For example, Native American tribes would have seen the British as 'invaders', who took territory by force and wiped out several tribes by passing on diseases that their immune systems could not deal with.

The New Plymouth colony worked very hard, and offshore fishing became the main source of farming: cod was in high demand as one of the few highly nutritious foods in British diets at this time. The settlers wanted peace and order in the colony, so they quickly established **democratic** principles and a **constitution**, to ensure that their Puritan religious beliefs would remain central to colony life. The example of the Pilgrim Fathers led to more religious groups moving to this area: more than 20,000 settlers arrived in Massachusetts between 1629 and 1640. The Pilgrim Fathers are seen by some historians as the first 'real' Americans: they

As in Jamestown and New Plymouth, early settlers' relations with the Native Americans were varied. Good relations initially existed with native tribes such as the Powhatan, and there were some intermarriages. However, in general, the British did not treat them with respect. Massacres were carried out on both sides, over land claims, but some settlers were particularly vicious: they often attacked and destroyed natives' crops and villages. In 1500, there were approximately 560,000 Native Americans in 'British' territories. However by 1700, there were fewer than 280,000. Devastating European diseases such as measles and smallpox, the ill treatment of natives, and British expansion into native territory all had a huge impact on Native

▼ **SOURCE C** *A seventeenth-century drawing of Captain John Smith's encounter with native people in Virginia; Smith was a well-known early British settler who became internationally famous when Disney animated the story of Pocahontas; the drawing appeared in a book published in 1624 by Captain Smith, called* The Generall Historie of Virginia, New-England, and the Summer Isles

Key Words

Pilgrim Fathers   democratic
constitution   emigrant

Americans. Many of them had to find a new way of life, adapt to European ways, or move further inland to avoid the settlers. Today, the Native Americans account for only 0.7 per cent of the total population of the USA.

For the British settlers, however, overall they gained a better life in the 13 colonies, and saw it as a land of opportunity and freedom where British culture and religious beliefs could thrive.

▼ **SOURCE D** *Adapted from a description of the tribes encountered by the Virginian settlers, from the document* Nova Britannia, *written in 1609:*

> It is inhabited by wild and savage people that live all over the forests. They have no law but native. They are easy to be brought to good [Christian ways] but would happily like better conditions.

Work

1. Describe the successes of the Pilgrim Fathers.
2. Identify the advantages and disadvantages about colonisation of North America to: the British; the Native American tribes.
3. a. Study **Source C**. What is happening in the drawing?
   b. Compare **Source C** and **Source D**. Explain how they are similar in their attitudes to Native Americans.
4. What was the British attitude to Native Americans in the sixteenth and seventeenth centuries? Explain your answer.

Practice Question

How useful is **Source C** to a historian studying the impact on the indigenous peoples of the British colonisation of North America? **8 marks**

Study Tip

Use the information about the provenance of the source, as well as what you can see in the image, in your answer.

Britain: Migration, empires and the people   209

5.2 Why did the British fall out with the American colonists?

By the 1760s, the British had gained an overseas empire in North America. They controlled a huge area of land on the eastern coast, stretching back from the Atlantic Ocean to the Mississippi River. Divided into 13 colonies, each had strong ties to Britain. But in 1776, these 13 colonies broke away from Britain and declared themselves to be united as one independent country – the United States of America. How and why did this happen?

Objective
- **Define** the Navigation Acts, the Stamp Act and the Boston Tea Party.
- **Identify** factors that led to American discontentment with Britain.
- **Categorise** reasons why Americans wanted independence from Britain.

Independent minds

The people who lived in the British colonies of North America by the 1760s were tough and independently-minded. Many of them descended from the early Puritans and Quakers who had gone to America to escape religious persecution, or because they were unhappy with the British monarch. During the British Civil Wars in the mid-seventeenth century, Britain did not really have time to deal with the overseas colonies, which meant the people there got used to not having the British intervene with their way of life. The colonies successfully traded products such as bread, clothing, books and guns with each other. Indentured servants and slaves could be bought and sold too, and human trade became a profitable industry. All this meant the colonies had a good economy that didn't rely on British trade. Before long, there were ideas among the colonists that they could exist separately from Britain.

Independent actions

In Virginia and other colonies, the British idea of having a class system of aristocrats (titled nobles) and monarchs was seen as outdated. The people who had succeeded in America were businessmen, mainly due to the plantations. This meant America was full of 'self-made' people, and as a result, many believed in equality – the idea that no matter who you were, it was possible to make a success of yourself. Early colonies such as New Plymouth also set up their own constitutions, which clashed with British rule. So the idea of being governed by men far away in Britain, who had inherited their wealth, started to seem odd. Over time, they began to dislike the control of their colonies by the British, and did not want to be a part of the British Empire. Some negative attitudes towards colonists by the people in Britain didn't help either.

SOURCE A *Adapted from a document called 'On the Plantation Trade', written in 1698 by an English economist and politician who recommended government control of colonial economies:*

> That our subjects in the American colonies are children of the state, and are to be treated as such, no one denies; but it can't reasonably be admitted that the mother country should [ruin] herself to enrich the children, nor that Great Britain should weaken herself to strengthen America.

The Navigation Acts

When the British started to intervene too much in American affairs it caused resentment among the colonists. The **Navigation Acts** of 1651–73 contributed to the colonists' desire for independence from Britain. These acts were introduced to enrich Britain; they were a series of laws which stipulated that American colonies could only import (buy) and export (sell) goods with British ships sailing to and from British ports. This **monopoly** of trade with just the British greatly restricted the type and amount of goods that could be brought to America, which meant competition for products was scarce, and so prices were often very high. When American colonists tried to smuggle in cheaper goods from other countries, the British patrolled the waters and seized the smugglers.

Taxation

If the colonists wanted to buy anything from countries other than Britain, the goods had to go first to Britain, where they were taxed. There was a very high tax on goods such as glass, coffee, wine and sugar. There was also the **Stamp Act** of 1765, which imposed a tax on the paper used for official documents. Colonists were also made to pay taxes to fund the British wars against the French that the colonists felt had little to do with them. Some colonists started to believe that if they were taxed so heavily, then they should have representatives in the British parliament, and have a say in British government.

▼ **SOURCE B** *The Colonies Reduced was published in Britain in 1767; it appeared in colonial newspapers as a protest against the hated Stamp Act. The cartoon depicts Britannia, and she is surrounded by her amputated limbs which are named Virginia, Pennsylvania, New York and New England.*

Key Words

Navigation Acts monopoly
Stamp Act Boston Tea Party

The Boston Tea Party

Colonists had many reasons to complain, and so a conflict began to build. Colonists were especially upset when the British taxed tea: three pence was paid to Britain for every pound of tea sold in America. In protest, a group of Americans boarded British ships in Boston, in December 1773, and dumped 342 crates full of tea (worth around £11,000) into the harbour. The British responded to the '**Boston Tea Party**' by closing Boston port, causing even more anger. When the British also banned all town meetings, the Americans began meeting in secret. In 1774, 56 representatives from the colonies met in Philadelphia to decide what to do. This meeting is known as the 'First Congress' (and even today, the American parliament is still known as Congress). Delegates at the First Congress decided to fight the British: the War of Independence began.

Extension

Research the First Congress of 1774 further to find out who attended and what they agreed. Which of the 13 colonies did not send a representative? Why?

Practice Question

Study **Source B**. How useful is it to a historian studying British involvement in America in the eighteenth century? **8 marks**

Study Tip

Explain the point the cartoonist is making about the consequences of enforcing the Stamp Act.

Work

1. List the reasons why Americans wanted independence from Britain, and how they achieved it. Try to categorise your reasons into 'long-term causes' and 'short-term causes'.
2. Create a timeline, of what happened in American and British relations, with the following dates: mid-seventeenth century, 1765, 1773, 1774.

Britain: Migration, empires and the people 211

5.3 What did losing the American colonies 'cost'?

When discussing the history of the British Empire, historians often mention the 'rise and fall of the British Empire'. The loss of the American colonies at the Treaty of Paris (1783) was certainly a setback. But was it a complete failure for Britain?

Objectives

- **Describe** what happened in the American War of Independence.
- **Explain** why it happened.
- **Analyse** the results of losing the American colonies.

The War of Independence

The British sent soldiers to force the American rebels to stay loyal, but they were met with fierce resistance. In July 1775, the Americans appointed George Washington as the leader of their army – he would go on to become their first President. A year later, in July 1776, Congress met again and formally declared themselves independent from Britain.

SOURCE A *The leader of the British army, Lord Cornwallis, surrendered to George Washington in Yorktown on 19 October 1781*

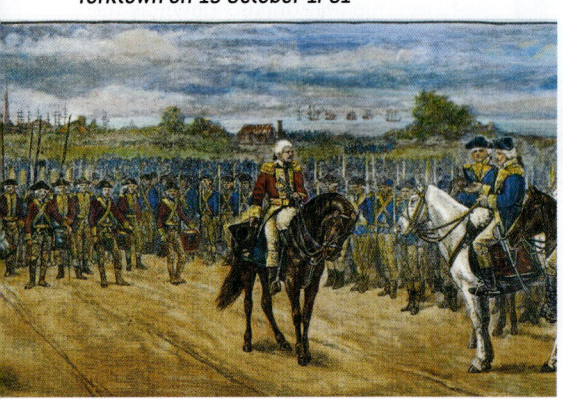

Although the 13 American colonies declared independence in 1776, there was over five years of bitter fighting before the British conceded that they had lost. War officially ended on 3 September 1783, when the Treaty of Paris was signed; but it is the British surrender at the Battle of Yorktown (1781) that was seen as the decisive end of the war. Britain had lost many battles throughout the war, but Yorktown was the most humiliating because the Americans completely surrounded the British and forced Lord Cornwallis, Britain's army leader, to surrender. After Yorktown, Britain realised that victory was impossible and America's ally, the French, increased their support for the Americans further. This meant Britain had little choice but to formally sign the Treaty of Paris, and so this valuable colony was lost to Britain.

Losing America, gaining an empire?

The maps on these pages help us understand the consequences, for Britain and its empire, of losing the American colonies.

B *The British Empire in 1775*

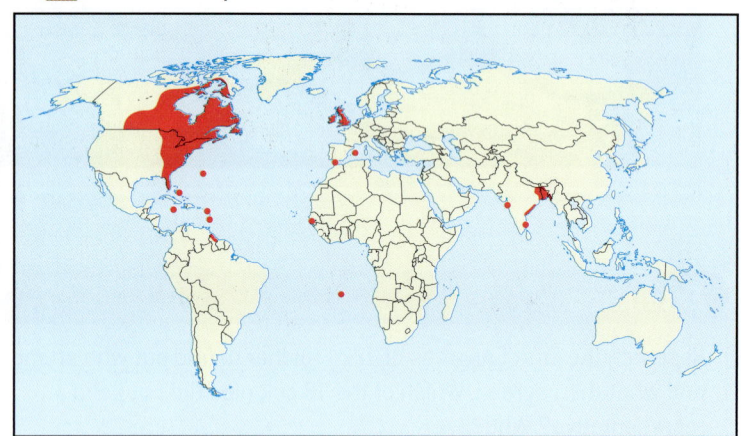

Canada

When America broke away from British rule in 1776, the colonies to the north (now known as Canada) remained part of the British Empire. These huge colonies, such as Quebec, Ontario, New Brunswick and Nova Scotia, remained a key part of the empire for nearly a century, until they achieved 'self-government' (the right to run most of their own affairs) in 1867. America lost 100,000 settlers to Canada, who preferred to emigrate rather than live under a republican government.

Britain

The war cost an estimated £80 million, which increased Britain's debts. However, Britain was rapidly industrialising and was very wealthy. But the human costs were high, with an estimated 10,000 British soldiers dying during battles or from disease, and up to about 20,000 sailors dying.

Britain and America were soon trading again after the war, and by 1785 this trade was back to its pre-war levels. For example, the British slave trade to the Americas continued. As the USA eventually became an ally of Britain's, losing it was not important in the long term. Britain's pride may have been dented, but financially, Britain was still as strong as before – if not more. Since the age of Elizabethan exploration, Britain had had a very strong navy, and by 1813 it had developed into the world's biggest. It helped to defend Britain's existing colonies, gain new colonies, and fight against opponents such as the French. The British Empire stretched from Canada to the Caribbean, parts of Africa (see Chapter 8), and India (see Chapter 7), and Britain was able to focus its wealth and resources in expanding and developing these. The vast territories gained in Africa and India between the 1700s and 1920 meant that Britain controlled a quarter of the world. At that point, the British Empire was the biggest empire the world had ever known.

▼ **C** *The British Empire in 1920*

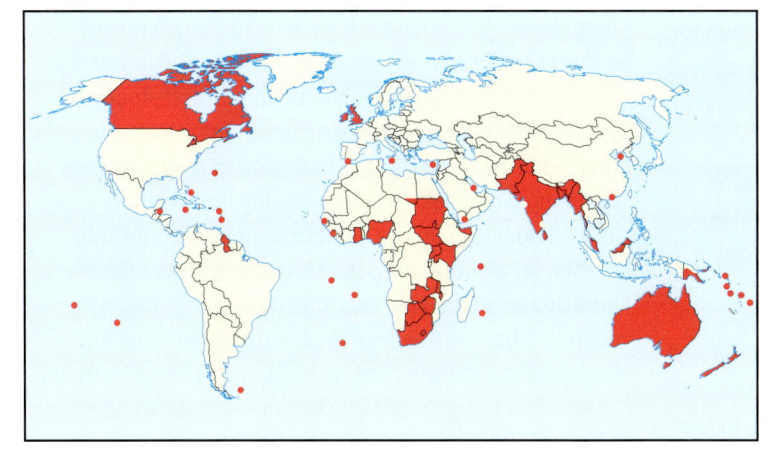

Key Word

republic

The West Indies and South America

Britain colonised parts of the Caribbean and the eastern coast of North America from the 1500s, until American independence in 1776. After that, Britain kept Central American territories (and Canada) until the nineteenth and twentieth centuries. Central American areas such as Anguilla, Montserrat and the Cayman Islands, as well as the Falkland Islands in South America, are examples of countries in the Americas that remained a part of the British Empire.

Australia

After the War of Independence, Britain needed a new place to send criminals, because it was no longer able to send them to America. Australia became the place to send them. Furthermore, like New Zealand and Canada, Australia was a loyal and dutiful colony. It provided willing markets for British goods, and also locations for ambitious or poverty-stricken Britons to emigrate to.

The USA

After beating the British, America was now a **republic** controlling its own political and economic affairs. It was now free to develop and expand as it wished. However, America lost up to 25,000 men during the war, mostly through disease. The impact of the soldiers' deaths on American labour and industry was felt for many years. On the other hand, the result of the war meant that Americans were able to forge stronger links with the French, since they had supported the Americans against the British. However, the cost of helping the Americans fight caused severe problems in France, which developed into their own revolution – the French Revolution – in 1789.

Work

1. Identify three consequences of Britain losing the American War of Independence.
2. Write a short paragraph explaining what you think is the significance of the War of Independence for Britain.
3. Were political or economic reasons responsible for causing the War of Independence in 1775? Explain your answer.

6.1 The first 'refugees': Huguenot migration

While some British people headed to America between the sixteenth and eighteenth centuries, people from other countries migrated to Britain. Immigrants who were escaping religious persecution from France, for example, contributed greatly to British life at this time. However, their migration provoked anti-French and anti-immigration feelings. Were these French Protestants, known as Huguenots, a welcome addition to Britain?

Objectives

- **Identify** the reasons Huguenots emigrated to Britain between the 1500s and the 1700s.
- **Explore** the consequences of Huguenot migration to Britain.

French Protestants arrive in Britain

France was a Catholic country, but it experienced a series of religious civil wars between the 1560s and the 1590s. The ruling French Catholics severely persecuted those who wanted to follow Protestantism. Hostilities reached a peak in August 1572 when tens of thousands of French Protestants were killed in the St Bartholomew's Day Massacre. To escape the killings, French Protestants (or Huguenots) started to emigrate to many different destinations, and neighbouring Britain was an ideal choice. This was because England's King Henry VIII had turned the country from Catholic to Protestant during the English **Reformation** in the 1530s.

French emigration continued when Henry's Protestant children, Edward VI and Elizabeth I, ruled England. They made the country a welcome place of refuge for fellow Protestants. Edward VI, for example, allowed the first French church to be set up, and Elizabeth's ministers invited skilled Huguenot craftsmen to work in England and teach British apprentices their skills. As some Huguenots settled in Britain, more from abroad followed them. Indeed, from Elizabeth's time onwards, Britain experienced an ongoing boom in wealth as the first industrialised nation, and skilled Huguenots played a part in this.

Fact

St Bartholomew's Day Massacre

An estimated 3000 Protestants were murdered in Paris in this massacre in August 1572, and as many as 70,000 throughout France. The massacre started because Catholics believed Protestants were plotting rebellions and war with Spain. This event marked a turning point in the French religious wars, and the Huguenots lost many of their leaders.

Another wave of migration

The number of French migrants fleeing to Britain began to drop as the French religious wars ended by 1598. French King Henri IV issued a bill of rights for the Huguenots called the **Edict of Nantes**, which granted them freedom to practise their religion without fear. However, France became an unwelcome and dangerous place for French Protestants again in the time of Henri's grandson, King Louis XIV. He agreed with his advisers that allowing Huguenots to remain in France meant a threat to his own absolute power as king. He withdrew the privileges Huguenots had been granted since his grandfather's time, and gave Protestant ministers the choice of converting to Catholicism or emigrating. Protestant families faced increasing intimidation. In 1685, Louis tore up the Edict of Nantes: without this written legal protection, the Huguenots were officially **heretics** and faced persecution once more. This time, despite a ban on fleeing the country, up to 200,000 Huguenots fled from France. Many faced risky journeys at sea, including up to 50,000 who escaped to England.

▼ **SOURCE A** *A drawing from 1685, of French Huguenots landing at Dover, fleeing from France when Louis XIV revoked the Edict of Nantes*

Impact of the Huguenots in Britain

The French Huguenots contributed much to British life and had a positive social and economic impact on Britain. As they were largely highly skilled craftsmen, they revitalised British industries such as watch-making, gun-making and bookbinding. Huguenot weavers, merchants and joiners established businesses in communities as far apart as London, Plymouth, Rochester, Norwich and Canterbury.

▼ **SOURCE B** *A painting by Hogarth, from 1738, showing Huguenots (on the right) attending a church in London; on the left are Londoners. Hogarth was a famous English painter who used art to critique society and politics of the time.*

The Huguenots transformed existing British industries, and started up new ones such as paper-making. With no paper mills before the Huguenots arrived, Britain's paper industry relied mainly on imports from France. But by the 1710s, Huguenot expertise meant that Britain boasted 200 paper mills, supplying nearly 70 per cent of Britain's paper market. British banknotes were printed by a Huguenot business from 1712 onwards, for over 250 years. Britain also gained scientists, intellectuals and experts from France that boosted the country's business, arts and crafts.

However, there was some anti-Huguenot feeling in Britain upon their arrival. Some felt that they took jobs away from English people and were full of diseases. They ate strange foods (such as snails) and one Bristol MP even compared them to one of the plagues of Egypt in the Bible. But, in time, the Huguenots merged into English society. They changed or translated their surnames to sound more English (Blanc became White, for example) and married English men and women.

The impact of the Huguenot migration was significant for France too: France lost many talented merchants and craftsmen. Its glassware and hat-making industries were lost, for example. In fact, France was so badly affected that King Louis XIV's ambassador to Britain offered Huguenots cash to return to France! The Huguenots were France's loss and Britain's gain.

Key Words

Reformation   Edict of Nantes   heretic

Work

1. How useful is **Source B** to a historian studying British attitudes towards immigrants to Britain in the 1700s? Explain your answer using **Source B** and your contextual knowledge.

2. Has religion been the main factor in causing migration to and from Britain since 790? Explain your answer with reference to religion and other factors. Look back over your notes from previous chapters to refresh your memory.

Extension

Conduct research to find out more about the impact of Huguenots migrating to cities in Britain. For example, look at the website www.huguenotsofspitalfields.org. What effects have the Huguenots had on London by living in areas like Spitalfields or Soho?

Practice Question

Compare the impact of the Huguenots on Britain with the Pilgrim Fathers on America. In what ways were they similar?   **8 marks**

Study Tip

You will need to refresh yourself with the events of the Pilgrim Fathers migrating to America in Chapter 5. To work out the similarities, you could consider making a list of categories to compare with, such as timescale of the migrations, causes for migration, numbers, locations, and consequences for Britain.

Britain: Migration, empires and the people   215

6.2 What were the Ulster Plantations and the Highland Clearances?

While Huguenots were moving into Britain, there was also a great movement of people out of, and around, the country. In the northern part of Ireland (known as Ulster), English and Scottish Protestants settled on land confiscated from the Irish, while people who lived in the Highlands of Scotland moved to the Scottish Lowlands and other parts of Britain, or emigrated abroad.

Objectives

- **Define** the Ulster Plantations and the Highland Clearances.
- **Explain** the background to these events.
- **Analyse** the impact of Scottish migration to England and emigration abroad.

The Ulster Plantations

The **Ulster Plantations** began in the early 1600s during the reign of King James I of England (and VI of Scotland). He 'planted' the northern part of Ireland (Ulster) from Scotland and England, hoping they would be obedient to him and his government. Most settlers moved hoping to find a new and better life for themselves and their families, but most Irish people resented what they saw as an 'invasion'.

The Ulster Plantations brought big changes. The population grew rapidly as thousands of settlers arrived, and they brought with them new customs and a new religion – Protestantism. Resentment between the Protestant settlers and the mainly Catholic Irish continued for centuries and often spilled over into violence.

▼ **A** *The Ulster Plantations; the settlers were given the name 'undertakers', because they had to undertake certain conditions, including building a house and 'bawn' (fortified barn), and to settle the land with a minimum number of people of the Protestant faith*

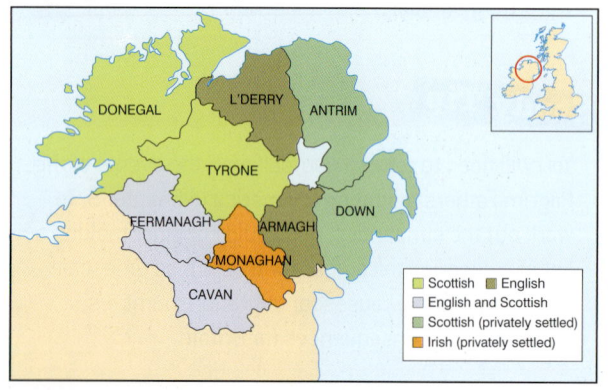

The Highland Clearances

In the early 1700s, over half the people in Scotland lived in the Highlands. Most spoke Gaelic, a language similar to Irish, and the way of life was different from those who lived in Lowland Scotland. Many Highlanders belonged to 'clans' (a type of 'family group', like a tribe). Clan members supported their chief in return for protection and leadership. Most Highlanders were farmers, and families lived on the same small farms for generations. They lived in simple stone cottages called crofts, and made money from selling wheat they grew on the farms. In the Lowlands, the towns and cities were growing, and manufacturers and merchants were becoming wealthy.

The Highlanders were largely Catholics and Jacobites (supporters of the Stuart royal family), and had participated in the Stuart-led **Jacobite Rebellions**. These occurred in 1715 and 1745–46 after the last Stuart monarch, Queen Anne, died in 1714; following her death the German prince George of Hanover had come over to rule the country as King George I. Descendants of the Stuarts tried to regain the throne through the rebellions, but they failed. After they had been finally defeated at the Battle of Culloden in 1746, the English wanted to reduce the power of the Highlanders and their chiefs, since many of them were loyal to the Stuarts, and not to George I.

The English began a brutal policy of removing all potential opposition in the Highlands by eliminating Scottish chiefs who supported the Stuarts, together with their clans. Some chiefs had no choice but to keep the English happy; they did this by supporting English demands to clear the Highlands of its clans, in what became known as the **Highland Clearances**. Laws were passed making life difficult for Highlanders, and bagpipes were banned because they were viewed as 'instruments of war'.

A new type of farming in the Highlands

Much of the land in the Highlands was owned by Englishmen and rented by Highlanders. However, at this time, the English landlords began to prefer the idea of having large sheep farms, rather than renting small strips of land to tenant farming families. Sheep farming made the landlords more money. However, the Highland farmers were usually too poor to buy the large numbers of sheep needed, so chiefs and landlords began to clear the Highlanders away to make way for the more profitable sheep farming. Many were forced to move to towns and cities in the Lowlands to look for work, but many more emigrated abroad.

How were the Highlands cleared?

SOURCE B *A painting by Scottish artist Thomas Faed, called* The Last of the Clan *(1865); Faed was a popular and respected artist in London; the women in the picture are fashionably dressed for peasants*

Different tactics were used to clear the Highlands. From the 1780s to the 1820s, tens of thousands of Highlanders were evicted from their homes. Evictions of up to 2000 families in one day were not uncommon. Highland families were forced onto barren coastal land, or other unworkable land, and many starved to death. Highlanders who refused to leave could be killed. Even the old and dying had their homes burned or were thrown out in the open to die. Many of the chiefs were fully aware of what was going on; and many clans felt betrayed.

Impact on the British Empire

Thousands of Scottish people emigrated during the era of the Highland Clearances, to countries such as Canada, America and England as well as to Scottish cities such as Dundee, Edinburgh and Glasgow.

The word **diaspora** describes the scattering of a group of people across a wide location. The Scottish diaspora contributed greatly to those countries in which the Highlanders settled – and to the empire itself. Many Scots contributed engineering skills to the building of roads, railways and many building schemes in the colonies. Many of the empire's greatest explorers, such as David Livingstone, were Scottish. Some historians argue that the empire didn't really start expanding until England and Scotland stopped fighting and the Scots put their efforts into empire-building. The British Empire was most certainly British, not English.

Key Words
Ulster Plantations   Jacobite Rebellions
Highland Clearances   diaspora

Work

1. a Why were Protestants 'planted' in Ulster by King James?
   b What was the impact of the Ulster Plantations?
2. Who were the Highlanders?
3. Why did the Highlanders rebel against the English during the Jacobite Rebellions?
4. a Suggest two reasons why the Highlands were cleared.
   b How were the Highlands cleared?
5. Compare the Ulster Plantations with the Highland Clearances.

Practice Question

How useful is **Source B** to a historian studying Scottish emigration from the Highlands in the eighteenth and nineteenth centuries?   **8 marks**

Study Tip

Remember that to demonstrate how useful a source is, you should also show that you know what point the source is trying to make. Try to link it to your knowledge of this period and topic.

7.1A How and why did Britain gain control of India?

India today is an independent country in Asia. It's the second most populated country in the world. Over thousands of years, people from all over the world have settled in India, or tried to conquer it. The Persians and Iranians settled there in ancient times. Famous conquerors such as Genghis Khan invaded it – and so did Alexander the Great. The Chinese came to India in pursuit of knowledge and to visit the ancient Indian universities. And then came the French, the Dutch, and finally the British.

Objectives

- **Define** how trade in Indian goods worked in the seventeenth and eighteenth centuries.
- **Explore** who Britain competed with for a hold over India, including the East India Company, Robert Clive and Warren Hastings.
- **Evaluate** how important India was economically to Britain's empire.

What was India like before the Europeans arrived?

India is rich in natural resources – iron ore, silk, copper, gold, silver, gemstones, tea and timber. Spices (which were very valuable in the Middle Ages) are common in India too. This meant that any country that made strong trade links with India could potentially become very rich and powerful.

▼ **SOURCE A** *A British trading station in Bombay (now known as Mumbai) in the 1750s*

Rivalry among nations

In 1497, a Portuguese explorer named Vasco De Gama discovered how to get to India from Europe by sea. Soon many European countries (including Denmark, France and Netherlands) were sending ships to India to trade. At first the ships simply reached an Indian port and bartered with local traders, swapping items such as guns, swords, buttons or shoes for silk, spices, cotton or tea. The European traders then brought these back to their own countries to sell for a big profit.

Fact

India became a valuable source of people – as well as spices, tea and cotton. As a small island, Britain could not always find enough people to help control its growing empire. So, the British created a system to train and pay local Indian people to become soldiers and fight for them. As a result, huge numbers of Indians became the fighting force of the country that had colonised them. In years to come, Indian soldiers would play a significant role in both world wars.

218 Chapter 7 Expansion in India

With the permission of local Indian rulers, the European traders began to set up more permanent bases along the Indian coast. Known as **trading stations**, these large warehouses were surrounded by huge walls and guarded by men with guns. The goods were stored in the warehouses and this was where the trading took place. Sometimes the traders lived there with their families too. There were often workshops or 'factories' within these trading ports that turned some of the raw materials into goods. Cotton cloth, for example, was woven by Indian weavers and exported by the British in huge quantities to supply the demand for cheap, washable, lightweight fabric. Opium, an addictive drug, was also grown and sold by British traders in China at a huge profit.

Key Word

trading station

B *A map of India and the main trading stations, showing the countries that ran them*

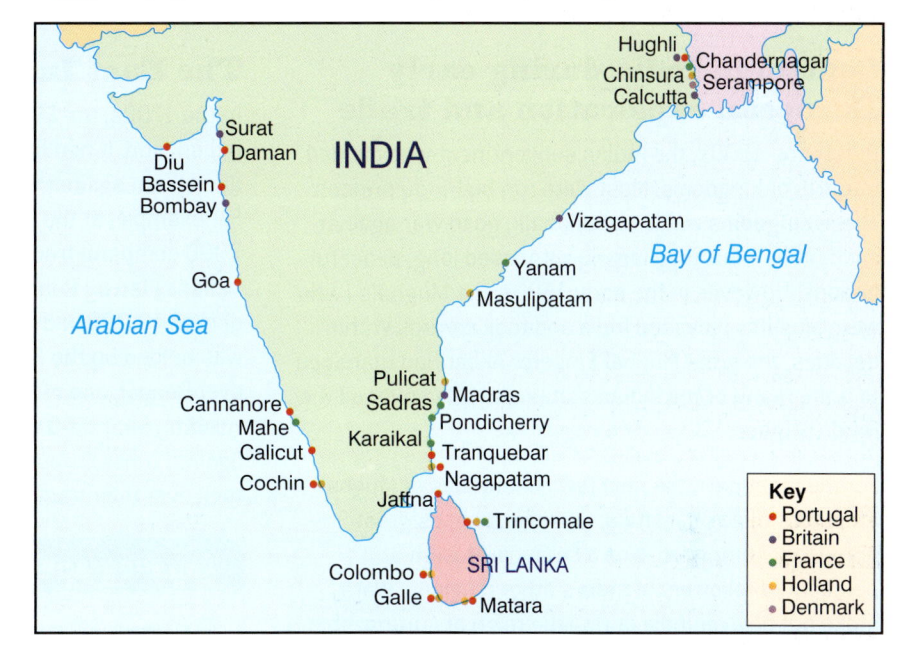

The East India Company

In the early years of European trade with India, the main countries with trading stations were France, the Netherlands and Britain. The British trading stations were run by one company – the East India Company (EIC). It had been trading all over the world since it was set up in 1600. The company's ships carried cheap British goods and exchanged them for goods in countries as far away as Japan and China. They then brought the fine china, silk, coffee and spices back to Britain. As a result, India became a base for some of Britain's growing global trading, and became increasingly important. The businessmen in charge of the company, and the kings and queens to whom they paid taxes, made a fortune from this trade.

The East India Company first set up trading posts in India in Surat (1612), Madras (1638) and Bombay (1668). It had a monopoly in British trade in India to begin with, but this ended in 1694. However, by then the EIC was so powerful, with its own army and navy, that it continued to be the major force in trade in India for the next century.

Work

1. Why do you think European nations took such an interest in India?
2. Look at **Source A** and map **B**.
   a. What is a trading station?
   b. List the countries that set up trading stations in India in the 1600s.
3. What was the East India Company?
4. Explain how the East India Company made such huge profits from trading in India. You could present your ideas as a diagram, poster or leaflet.

Extension

Research the history of the East India Company. When was it formed, and by whom? What goods did it trade in most often? How successful was it? Did it trade in places other than India? What happened to the company?

Practice Question

Compare British actions in India with those in North America in the seventeenth century. In what ways were they different? **8 marks**

Study Tip

Consider how India and North America were different at that time.

Britain: Migration, empires and the people 219

7.1B How and why did Britain gain control of India?

Control in India during early European exploration and trade

Before the 1500s, the Indian subcontinent was divided into lots of kingdoms. Most were run by Hindu princes. These kingdoms would occasionally go to war against each other – but they largely witnessed long, peaceful periods. However, in the early 1500s, the Mughals (who were Muslims) invaded India and took control. Within decades, the great Mughal Emperor Akbar had managed to unite many of the Indian states and ruled over all the Hindu princes.

For the most part, the next few generations of Mughal Emperors ruled peacefully. However, Akbar's great-grandson, Aurangzeb, was a fanatical Muslim and persecuted followers of India's other religions. Wars broke out all over India during the reign of Aurangzeb (1658–1707), and the Mughals began to lose control of the country by the late 1600s and early 1700s. It was at exactly this time, when much of India was at war, that some European nations – and powerful trading companies such as the East India Company – began to take advantage of the situation.

European invasion in the seventeenth and eighteenth centuries

Control over the goods coming out of India wasn't the only thing that attracted the Europeans: India was a good place in which to sell their own goods to the many millions of Indians in their territory. Furthermore, Dutch, French and British companies realised that by helping certain Hindu princes (by providing them with weapons and soldiers, for example), they could affect the outcome of the wars, and help the princes to beat their enemies. They could then demand rewards from the princes they had supported – perhaps land or goods. Furthermore, if they ever fell out with a prince, and fought against him, they could win and take his territory!

The East India Company expands

In the 1700s, the EIC began to take more and more Indian land. It had its own private army and navy, and used them against various regional rulers of India. For example, at the Battle of Plassey in 1757, around 3000 company troops (2200 of whom were local Indians) led by Robert Clive defeated an Indian army of over 40,000, led by local prince Siraj-ud-Daula (who was helped by the French). This allowed the EIC to take over Bengal, one of the richest parts of India formally ruled by Siraj-ud-Daula. The company also fought against other European nations, such as the Dutch, and took over their trading posts.

> **Key Biography**
>
> **Robert Clive (1725–74)**
> - Born in Shropshire to a wealthy family.
> - Moved to India, aged 18, to work as an office clerk for the EIC.
> - Joined the company's army and quickly proved to be a great leader.
> - Best known for his victory at the Battle of Plassey in June 1757. Victory enabled the company to progress further across India.
> - Returning to England, was elected to parliament in 1761 and given an Irish barony.
> - In 1763, returned to India as Governor and Commander-in-Chief of the East India Company's army.

SOURCE C *A painting of the Battle of Plassey in June 1757; Colonel Robert Clive's portrait is at top left*

Over the following decades, more and more of India came under the rule of the East India Company. However, despite making huge profits in India, the EIC was losing money elsewhere, mainly as a result of a decline in trade with America at this time. So the British government decided to step in and help out with the company's financial problems. After all, the government didn't want this British company (that paid a fortune in taxes) to go bankrupt and lose control of large parts of India. So in 1773, the Government of India Act stated that both the British government and the East India Company controlled the territory in India jointly. A Governor General was appointed to control the territory, and Warren Hastings was given the job.

After Britain lost the valuable American colonies in the late 1700s (see pages 210–213), India became an even more important part of the empire. The British government became increasingly involved in India and gradually took more control of the EIC's affairs. By the mid-1850s, much of India was controlled by the British, but a major rebellion, one that would shock the world, was just around the corner.

Key Biography

Warren Hastings (1732–1818)
- First Governor General of India (1773–85).
- Best known as a reformer: reorganised tax systems, tightened anti-corruption laws, wiped out thieving gangs who were running wild in the countryside.
- Tried to preserve existing Indian traditions and systems too.
- Despite ending his career in a controversial way – Hastings was falsely accused of 'high crimes and misdemeanours' by his political enemies – he is regarded as one of the key figures in establishing India as part of the British Empire.

▼ **INTERPRETATION D** *Adapted from* The British Empire, 1815–1914 *by Frank McDonough:*

> Robert Clive, who became known later as 'Clive of India', brought Calcutta and Bengal under the control of the company, negotiated important trade agreements with the numerous independent regional princes, pushed the French out of India, and persuaded the Mughal Emperor to grant monopoly trading rights to the East India Company. By the late eighteenth century the East India Company had also emerged as a major political power in India with responsibilities for law, order, administration, trade, defence and diplomacy. By this time the company – run by London merchants – resembled a state more than a private company.

Work

1. Who were the Mughals?
2. Explain how European nations and trading companies exploited wars in India to increase their power.
3. Read **Interpretation D**. Explain in your own words what the author is saying about how powerful the East India Company became.
4. How did Robert Clive and Warren Hastings each contribute to the growth of British control in India?
5. Suggest reasons why the British government took away more control of India from the EIC in the late eighteenth and nineteenth centuries.

▼ **E** *India 1600–1773: How more and more of India gradually came under British control*

Timeline

1600	1612	1638	1658	1668	1707	1757	1763	1773
East India Company is founded	First East India Company trading post is set up in Surat	East India Company trading post is set up in Madras	Aurangzeb becomes the ruling Mughal Emperor	East India Company trading post is set up in Bombay	Aurangzeb dies; Mughal control is weak	Battle of Plassey; East India Company takes control of Bengal	Robert Clive becomes Governor and Commander-in-Chief of the East India Company's army	Government of India Act; Warren Hastings becomes Governor General of India

7.2A The Indian Rebellion of 1857

By the 1850s, most of India was ruled by a British company – the East India Company. Many of the British people who worked for the EIC lived in great luxury in India and made huge fortunes. To help 'protect' them in India – and to make sure things ran smoothly – British soldiers were stationed there. The army also recruited local Indians as soldiers. However, on 10 May 1857, Indian soldiers (called **Sepoys**) working for the British in Meerut, northern India, shot dead a number of British soldiers who worked alongside them. Soon, the whole of northern India was engulfed in a ferocious fight between the British and the Sepoys, lasting over a year, until June 1858. This was the Indian Rebellion … or the War of Independence! What caused the fighting, and why does the same event have different names?

Objectives

▶ **Explain** the causes and consequences of the Indian Rebellion.

▶ **Explore** how the events of 1857–58 can be interpreted differently.

Sepoys and rebellion

According to Queen Victoria (reign: 1837–1901), the aim of the British Empire was to 'protect the poor natives and advance civilisation'. It was clear, then, that there was more to the empire than just the financial benefits. British empire-builders felt they were superior to the native people who lived in the colonies, who were a different colour and worshipped in a different way. In India, the British claimed that they were improving the country, by building railways, roads, schools and hospitals, rather than exploiting it.

However, in the army, the Sepoys were very unhappy. They felt that they weren't treated very well, had little hope of promotion and were often the first to be sent to the most dangerous places. Some Sepoys also felt that they were being pressured into converting to Christianity.

This build-up of anger boiled over into rebellion in 1857, when new rifles were delivered to the troops with a new method of loading the bullets. And it was these new

SOURCE A *The image from the cover of* Lloyd's Sketches of Indian Life, *published in 1890, showing an Indian soldier waiting on a British woman*

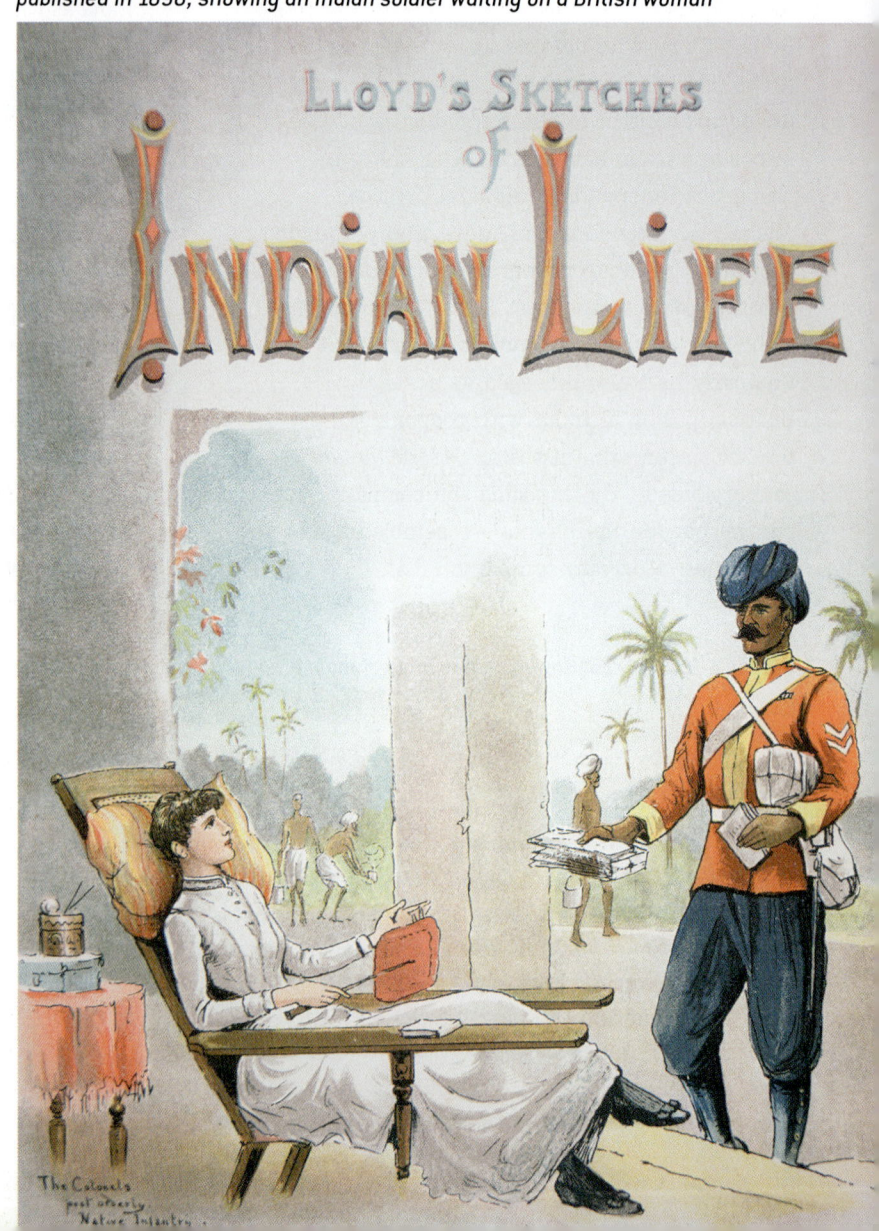

> **Key Word**
>
> Sepoy

bullets, and the cartridges that held them, that led to the start of one of the British Empire's bloodiest rebellions.

The spark

In January 1857, a new Enfield rifle was given to each Indian soldier. The bullet (which fired from the rifle) and the gunpowder that fired it, were neatly packaged together in a cartridge. Loading the cartridge was rather complicated: it involved biting off the top of the cartridge, pouring the gunpowder into the gun and then ramming the rest of the cartridge with the bullet inside down into the gun. The problem for the Hindu and Muslim Sepoys was that the new cartridges were covered in grease to make them slide down easily. Because the soldiers had to bite off the top of the greasy cartridge, it meant that they got grease in their mouths. It was rumoured that the grease was made from animal fat, probably (but not definitely) a mixture of pork and beef fat. This was the worst possible mixture for Hindus and Muslims — Hindus don't eat beef because cows are sacred to them, and Muslims are forbidden to eat pork.

The Sepoys objected to the new cartridges, but they were largely ignored. When 85 Sepoys refused to use the cartridges in Meerut on 9 May 1857, they were arrested and sent to jail for ten years. The day after, a group of Sepoys broke into revolt in Meerut. They killed British officers, freed the imprisoned Sepoys and set fire to army barracks and the homes of British civilians living in the area. Other Sepoys rioted in support, and soon the whole of northern India was engulfed in rebellion.

▼ **B** *A cross-section diagram showing the new Enfield rifle cartridge*

▼ **INTERPRETATION C** *An illustration from* The Heroes of History, *published in the twentieth century. It shows the Siege of Lucknow, when British soldiers were surrounded and attacked by Indian rebels on 1 July 1857. The siege ended in November when support for the British arrived.*

India at war

The main battles were fought in Delhi, Cawnpore and Lucknow. The massacre of 200 British women and children at Cawnpore (July 1857) outraged the British. Back home in Britain, crowds cried for blood. Even Queen Victoria was horrified. Soon, 70,000 fresh troops were sent to India armed with the latest Colt revolvers made in America. Revenge was violent, bloody and swift.

> **Work**
>
> 1 a What is a Sepoy?
>   b Why were some Sepoys unhappy at this time?
> 2 a Study diagram **B**, the Enfield rifle cartridge cross-section. Write a short explanation of what a cartridge is.
>   b Explain what caused the 1857 rebellion. You need to include what the British did in January 1857 — and why Hindu and Muslim Sepoys objected so strongly.

Britain: Migration, empires and the people   223

7.2B The Indian Rebellion of 1857

When some Muslim **mutineers** were captured, they were sewn into pig skins before they were hanged. One British soldier wrote of a giant tree with 130 Sepoys hanging from its branches. An equally horrible punishment was to strap the rebels across the barrel of a gun, which was then fired.

▼ **SOURCE D** *A poem about the reaction to the massacres in India, written by British poet Martin Tupper in 1857 at the time of the rebellion:*

> And England, now avenge their wrongs by vengeance deep and dire,
> Cut out their cancer with the sword, and burn it out with fire,
> Destroy those traitor regions, hang every pariah hound,
> And hunt them down to death, in all hills and cities around.

▼ **SOURCE E** *This cartoon appeared in* Punch *magazine in August 1857 and is called 'The British Lion's Vengeance on the Bengal Tiger'. It shows a British lion (representing Britain) attacking a Bengal tiger (representing India) that had attacked an English woman and child. The cartoon received much attention at the time.*

Fact

The majority of Sepoys took part in the rebellion – but not all of them. Thousands, including the Gurkhas, the Sikhs and the Pathan regiments, remained loyal to the British. Even today, the Gurkhas who fight in the British army have a long-standing reputation for loyalty to it. The very large Bengali element in the British army in India were thought to be responsible for the rebellion. Subsequently recruitment came from the Punjab, Sikhs, and Gurkhas – the groups that the British felt made the best soldiers.

The end and aftermath

Peace was finally declared on 8 July 1858, but the rebellion had shocked the British. For a long time it had looked as if the British might be defeated by the Sepoys, and politicians were taken aback by the ferocity of feeling that had been shown in India against the British.

After the events, the British were a lot more careful about how they governed India. They still wanted India as part of the British Empire of course, but the running of the country was taken away from the East India Company and replaced with direct rule by the British government. A new government department (the India Office) was set up, and a **viceroy** was put in charge of India on behalf of Queen Victoria.

Before the rebellion, the British policy in India had been to introduce British ideas about religion and education, which threatened the Hindu, Muslim and Sikh ways of life. After 1858, the British tried to interfere less with religious matters, and started to allow Indians more say in the running of India by allowing them jobs in local government. Although the number of Indians gaining jobs in local government was on a limited scale, a new, professional middle class of Indian citizen emerged: they were able to use English in addition to their own language, and to learn about new technology and methods of organisation that the British were bringing

▼ **SOURCE F** *Adapted from Queen Victoria's Proclamation to India, November 1858, in which she commented on the new way of running India:*

> We hold ourselves bound by the same obligations of duty which bind us to our other subjects, so it is our will that our subjects of whatever race or creed, be freely and impartially admitted to offices in our service, the duties of which they may be qualified by their education, ability and integrity, duly to discharge.

▼ **INTERPRETATION G** *Adapted from a BBC interview with historian and author William Dalrymple, September 2006:*

> 1857 was a pivotal point in Indian history. The better educated Indians who emerged from English-speaking schools in India, and who had learned about political parties, strikes and protest marches when they were in these schools, used these new methods against the British to gain their freedom. Had 1857 not happened, modern Indian history might have taken a quite different course.

into the country. In time, the Indian Universities Act created universities in Calcutta, Bombay and Madras. This was to have a major long-term impact on Britain's relationship with India.

Mutiny, rebellion or war of independence?

Historians often give names to different events (the Peasants' Revolt, the English Civil War and so on) – but there is no universally agreed name for the events of 1857–58. At the time in Britain, it was known as the 'Indian Mutiny' or the 'Sepoy Rebellion'. It is often still called this in Britain today. However, for Indians today, it is most often referred to as the 'War of Independence' or the 'Great Rebellion'. It is looked upon as the first episode in the great struggle against the British for an independent India. Indeed, in 2007 the Indian government celebrated the 150th anniversary of it with special events and ceremonies.

Practice Question

Explain the significance of the Indian Rebellion on the development of the British Empire. **8 marks**

[Taken from AQA 2016 Paper 2 specimen material]

Key Words

mutineer   viceroy

▼ **INTERPRETATION H** *Adapted from a quote in a section entitled 'The Indian Freedom Struggle', from the official Indian government website, india.gov.in. The website was set up in 2005 (and updated in 2012) to celebrate the Great Rebellion of 1857–58:*

> The Hindus, Muslims and Sikhs and all the other brave sons of India fought shoulder to shoulder to throw out the British.

Work

1. Why do you think the punishments given to the Indian rebels by the British were so brutal?
2. Read **Source D**. Do you think Martin Tupper was a supporter of the Sepoys or a supporter of the British? Give reasons for your answer.
3. Look at **Source E**.
   a. Describe what is happening in the cartoon.
   b. What point do you think the cartoonist was trying to get across?
4. How did the British change the way India was governed as a result of the events of 1857?
5. How useful are **Sources E** and **F** to a historian studying the British reaction to the Indian Rebellion of 1857?

Extension

Read **Interpretation G**. What is the author saying about the long-term impact of the Indian Rebellion? You may wish to read ahead to Chapter 10 about events in twentieth-century India to help you answer this question.

Study Tip

Why do you think the events of 1857 are given different names?

Britain: Migration, empires and the people   225

7.3A What was the impact of empire on Britain and India?

India was the largest and richest of all the territories in Britain's empire. In 1858, a viceroy appointed by the British was put directly in charge of the country and ran it on behalf of Queen Victoria. The queen even gave herself an extra title, Empress of India, in addition to her traditional title of Queen of Great Britain and Ireland. Indeed, India was the colony that many people in Britain treasured most — even calling it 'the jewel in the crown'. So what impact did the British make on India? What was British rule like for Indians? And what impact did the British rule of India have on Britain itself?

Objectives

- **Examine** the different factors that affected the British Empire in India in the nineteenth and early twentieth centuries.
- **Assess** ways in which the British takeover of India could be viewed both positively and negatively.

There is little doubt that the British made a huge impact on India. However, there is much debate over whether the British had a positive or a negative overall influence. Some argue that any foreign interference in another country is a bad thing, while others would say that it is a good thing if a nation's rule of another country brings improvements. Below are some insights into British rule in India that will help you assess the impact that Britain had.

India's economic resources

India gave British businessmen, merchants and traders the opportunity to make lots of money. They used India to build up personal fortunes, making some of them the richest people in the world. They would buy (or take) raw materials from India (such as tea, coffee, sugar cane, gemstones, gold, silver, silk and spices) and sell them for a high price in Britain. In the mid-1800s, the tea trade alone was worth £30 million a year! Trading in goods not only made money for the traders, but created jobs for both Indians and the British in shipping, transportation and sales. However, the British improved things too: they introduced an irrigation programme in the countryside, which increased the amount of land available for farming by eight times. Also, they developed coal mining, something that had not existed before. It is important to consider that these innovations and developments were paid for by British investors, whose priority was to make a profit for themselves rather than improve the life of Indian people.

▼ **SOURCE A** This engraving was published in a London news magazine in 1853, depicting a shipment of Indian gold being unloaded in the East India Docks, London. Note the police guarding the area.

Building factories

Many areas in India became industrialised in the same way that British towns and cities were in the 1800s. Factories were built there, producing goods such as cotton and woollen cloth, and flour. British businessmen owned the factories and mills, but provided work for local Indians. India was also a place where British-made factory goods could be sold, too. It was common for Indian-grown cotton to be shipped back to Britain, made into something (such as a shirt or trousers) in a British factory – and then taken back to India to be sold there.

Communications: railways and transport

The British built over 30,000 kilometres of railways and 130,000 bridges all over India. This was important for the development of India, as goods and people could travel quickly over vast areas and distant parts of the country could be linked together. The total British investment in India amounted to more than an estimated £400 million by 1914. This included not only railways, but also canals, roads, factories, mines and farms. Some argue that this was done simply to exploit the country and make huge profits, which were taken back to Britain. Others say that the investment created a legacy that still survives today.

▼ **SOURCE B** *This railway station was built in Bombay (now Mumbai) in 1897. It was known as Victoria Station until 1996, when it was renamed after a seventeenth-century Hindu king. Today, Indian Railways is one of the world's largest employers, with an amazing 1.6 million employees.*

Improved health?

The British made an impact on health in India too. They introduced a vaccine and treatment programme to fight killer diseases such as malaria and smallpox, and improved sewage systems and water supplies. As a result of these changes, life expectancy increased. However, there were devastating famines that struck India in the late 1800s. Millions died of starvation. Many blamed the British for helping to cause the famines because they had forced Indian farmers to replace food crops such as rice and wheat with high value crops that the British could sell in Britain, such as cotton, tea and oil seeds.

Culture and society: the law and education

The British created a legal system based on the one in Britain. They felt that their legal system was the most advanced in the world and should be used as a model for other nations where possible. High courts were set up in Madras, Calcutta and Bombay and parts of Indian law were built into the new legal code. Hindu and Muslim judges made sure that the British did not forget about Indian traditions and customs when dealing with legal matters. The British also had a major impact on education. Thousands of schools and colleges were opened, English language learning spread, and western education meant that Indians adopted more modern, democratic, liberal views. New knowledge in science, humanities and literature were opened up to Indians too, as well as the opportunity to study in Britain.

Work

1. Write a sentence or two explaining the following terms: viceroy; Empress of India; 'the jewel in the crown'.
2. Make two lists: one of the positive things that British rule brought to India, and one of the negative things about British rule.

7.3B What was the impact of empire on Britain and India?

The impact of British Raj on Britain

Arguably the greatest impact of British rule in India was the boost it gave to British industry and wealth. India provided a steady supply of raw materials into Britain, which were converted into finished products in British factories and then sold back to countries in the British Empire, including India itself. This created jobs for British businessmen and merchants, sailors, dockworkers, factory workers, shopkeepers and so on. By the late 1800s, for example, it has been estimated that around a quarter of Britain's total exports went to India – and by the early 1900s these exports were worth nearly £140 million!

> **Fact**
>
> The term 'British Raj' was used to describe the period of British rule in India between 1858 and 1947. The word 'raj' is Hindi for 'rule'. The British Raj had its own flag.

British rule in India brought other benefits to Britain, most notably, the Indian army. This army was used in all parts of the British Empire, and fought bravely and decisively in both the First and Second World Wars. It is notable that in the First World War, by December 1914, one in every three soldiers fighting for Britain in France was from India.

▼ **SOURCE C** *The British viceroy of India, Lord Curzon, wrote the following to the Conservative MP (and future Prime Minister) Lord Balfour, indicating that the Indian army was viewed as vital to Britain's power on the world stage:*

> As long as we rule India, we are the greatest power in the world. If we lose it we shall straightaway drop to a third rate power.

There were also some more subtle impacts in Britain. Indian tea became a popular drink and Indian food became more and more common in people's homes. Queen Victoria employed an Indian secretary to teach her Hindi and Urdu, and had Indian dishes on most of her dinner menus. Indian words, such as 'bangle', 'shampoo', 'pyjamas' and 'cash' became commonly used, and many grand buildings (like the Royal Pavilion in Brighton) were built in an Indian style.

▼ **INTERPRETATION D** *Adapted from* Pax Britannica, *written by modern historian James Morris in 1968. At the time he wrote, Ceylon (now Sri Lanka) was classified as part of India and was under British rule:*

> Ceylon was unified under British rule in 1815. Over the next 80 years, the British built 3700 kilometres of road and 4600 kilometres of railway. They raised the area of land used for farming from 160,000 hectares to 1.3 million hectares, the livestock from 230,000 to 1.5 million, the post offices from 4 to 250, the telegraph lines from 0 to 2500 kilometres, the schools from 170 to 2900, the hospitals from 0 to 65, the annual amount of goods shipped abroad from 68,000 tonnes to 6.3 million tonnes.

Divided opinions

The issue of British control and influence in India has always been controversial and has often been interpreted differently. Some argue that India benefited from British influence in some ways. By 1900, the British had built nearly 80,000 kilometres of road, as well as railways, schools and hospitals. They built dams and dug nearly 12,000 kilometres of canal. They also introduced a new legal system and helped settle ancient feuds between rival areas and regions – whether the Indians wanted these things or not. It cannot be denied that the British invested a lot of money into India, but they made an enormous amount of money too.

Furthermore, India suffered greatly in many ways. British customs were forced onto people, and local traditions, cultures and religions tended to be ignored. Indian workers were often exploited, the country's raw materials were taken back to Britain, and native lands were seized. If there was ever any resistance, the British army usually came down very hard on the rebels.

SOURCE E *The view of Pandit Nehru, who became India's Prime Minister after the country gained its independence from Britain in 1947:*

> I hate the British for the wrong they have done in India. Their parliament makes laws for us and they appoint a viceroy to rule over us. The British are arrogant, despising our brown skins. Worst of all, the British have kept us poor. Our people toil for slave wages in British-owned cotton mills and on British tea plantations.

SOURCE F *An illustration from a French newspaper about the Indian famine of the late 1800s; approximately six million Indians died – and many Indians blamed the British for not doing enough*

SOURCE G *Florence Nightingale, the famous British nurse, said in the late 1800s about the Indian famine:*

> We do not care enough to stop them dying slow and terrible deaths from things we could easily stop. We have taken their land, and we rule it, for our good, not theirs.

SOURCE H *Adapted from* Indian Home Rule, *written by Mohandas K. Gandhi in 1938:*

> India has become impoverished by their [Britain's] government. They take away our money from year to year. The most important jobs are reserved for themselves. We are kept in a state of slavery. They behave insolently towards us and disregard our feelings.

Work

1. Create a poster called 'The British in India'. Using no more than ten words show both the positives and the negatives of British rule there.
2. Suggest reasons why the British rule of India divides opinions, even today.
3. a What point does **Source E** make about British rule in India? What about **Source H**?
   b How useful is **Source F** to a historian studying British rule in India?

Extension

The English language has absorbed many Indian words, such as 'bangle', 'cash' and 'shampoo'. Research other Indian words that are commonly used in English today. What about other countries within the British Empire? What words are used from Africa, Australia or Native America?

Practice Question

Have the economic benefits been the main consequence of British rule in India? **16 marks** **SPaG: 4 marks**

Study Tip

Consider the social and cultural consequences of British rule as well in your answer (see pages 226–229).

Britain: Migration, empires and the people 229

8.1 The scramble for Africa

Until the 1800s, European countries weren't really interested in Africa – unless it was to make use of people from the west of Africa as slaves. Between 1562 and 1807 (when Britain stopped slave trading), British ships took around three million Africans into slavery in America and the Caribbean. But even as late as 1870, only ten per cent of Africa was controlled by European countries. Yet by 1900, European nations controlled over 90 per cent of Africa – and Britain was one of the nations that took the most land: 16 colonies were added to the British Empire between 1870 and 1900. Why did this happen?

Objectives

- **Define** the 'scramble for Africa'.
- **Explain** why Britain joined in the scramble for Africa in the late 1800s.
- **Examine** trade and missionary activity in Africa in the nineteenth century.

Why were European countries interested in Africa?

By the 1860s, France, Germany and the USA had all become powerful nations. They each had huge armies and navies, and their factories produced goods that were sold all over the world. Until then, Britain had been the world's leading power in both industry and trade, but now there were some serious rivals.

Explorers and missionaries (such as Britain's David Livingstone) brought back tales of African gold, diamonds and ivory – as well as 'cash crops' such as rubber, coffee and timber – so some of the world's richest countries looked to Africa as a way of getting even richer. They thought that if they could take over huge areas of Africa, they could sell their goods to the people who lived there, and could also take valuable raw materials from the land. This was an era when some of Europe's major nations were rivals and went 'empire-building' in order to become richer than their neighbouring countries. Between 1880 and 1900, there was a race to grab as much of Africa as each nation possibly could before another country got there first, and this became known as the 'scramble for Africa'.

Christian missionaries also felt it was their duty to convert Africans to Christianity. They travelled through Africa preaching the benefits of Christianity, as well as setting up schools and hospitals. Europeans often referred to Africa as the 'dark continent', and missionaries felt it was their role to 'enlighten' it.

The scramble begins

In the late 1870s, several European nations started to 'claim' land in Africa. The French and Belgians began to colonise much of the west of Africa, while the Germans and the British were interested in the east and the south. Portugal, Italy and Spain joined in the land grab. To prevent a war erupting between the European powers, their leaders held a conference in Berlin, Germany during the winter of 1884, to decide which nation could take which areas. Little attempt was made to understand the wishes or needs of the Africans themselves, so differences in race, language, culture and traditions were ignored as the European nations grabbed what they could.

▼ **SOURCE A** *British politician Lord Rosebery, who became Prime Minister in 1894, made a speech in 1893, during the 'scramble for Africa'. He stated:*

> It is said that our empire is already big enough and doesn't need extension. That would be true if the world were elastic, but it is not. At present we are 'pegging out claims for the future'. We have to remember that it is part of our heritage to make sure that the world is shaped by us. It must be English-speaking. We have to look forward to the future of our race. We will fail in our duty if we fail to take our share of the world.

▼ **SOURCE B** *A well known African saying; its origins are unclear but it has been said by both Jomo Kenyatta, independent Kenya's first Prime Minister (1963–64) and first President (1964–78), and Archbishop Desmond Tutu, a South African social rights activist and bishop:*

> When the missionaries arrived, the Africans had the land and the missionaries had the Bible. They taught us how to pray with our eyes closed. When we opened them, they had the land and we had the Bible.

C *Africa in 1900, after the 'scramble', showing the areas controlled by various European countries*

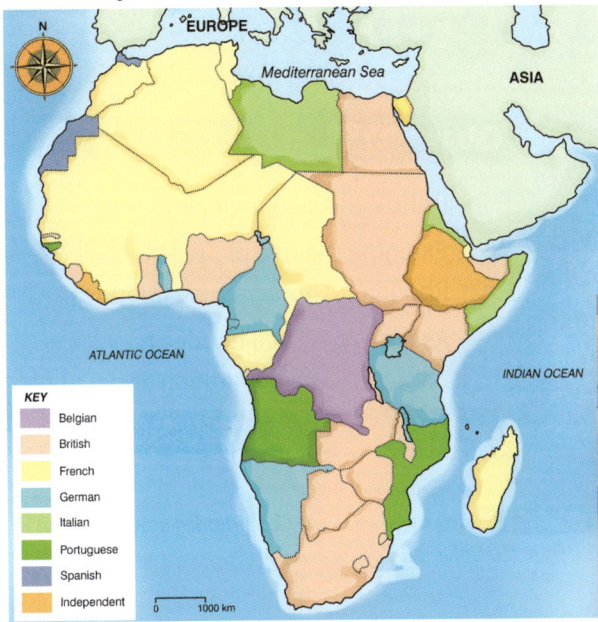

KEY
- Belgian
- British
- French
- German
- Italian
- Portuguese
- Spanish
- Independent

The British scramble
Britain took over 16 huge areas of land (or colonies) in Africa during the 'scramble', including Sudan, Nigeria, Kenya, Egypt and Northern and Southern Rhodesia (now Zimbabwe and Zambia). In fact, Britain's land ran in an almost unbroken line from Egypt in the north of Africa to South Africa in the south. In total, the British had claimed 32 per cent of Africa by 1900. Britain's control of key areas of African land (in southern Africa, for example) was important because it lay along part of Britain's sea route to India.

African resistance
African people fought fiercely at times to defend their lands, but the invention of the Maxim gun (a type of machine gun) gave the European armies a major advantage over the Africans, who were mainly armed with spears and swords. Sometimes, African tribes scored major victories over European countries (such as in the Zulu War of 1879), but more often than not the European invaders wiped out the African forces. After they were defeated, many Africans suffered hardship and hunger as their traditional way of life was destroyed. Some were forced to work as cheap labour in mines or on huge British-owned farms growing tea, coffee, cotton or cocoa for export back to Britain.

SOURCE D *A cartoon from 1911, called 'The Sleeping Sickness'; it shows an African man asleep against a tree while European countries plant flags labelled England, Portugal, Belgium, Turkey, Italy, Germany, Spain, and France all around him*

Fact
One of the reasons that Europeans had not ventured into Africa before the 1870s was that they lacked resistance to diseases they encountered there. After 1870, treatments for combating diseases such as malaria had been invented, meaning that Europeans could explore, and conquer, Africa.

Work
1. In your own words, explain what is meant by the term 'scramble for Africa'.
2. Why do you think Britain was so keen to take part in the 'scramble'?
3. Explain how each of the following contributed to the 'scramble for Africa': political factors (rivalry between nations); economic factors (trade); religious factors (Christianity); explorers; technology; medical progress.
4. Look at **Source A**. According to this source, what are the reasons for Britain's expansion into Africa?

Practice Question
How useful is **Source D** to a historian studying attitudes to European expansion in Africa? **8 marks**

Study Tip
What does the caption and the picture suggest about European motives for expansion?

8.2 Why is Cecil Rhodes such a controversial figure?

Cecil Rhodes is regarded as one of Britain's greatest empire-builders. Streets, schools, and even two African countries – Southern and Northern Rhodesia (now Zimbabwe and Zambia) – were named after him. When he died, statues of him were erected all over the world. However, in 2015, a Cecil Rhodes statue was removed from the University of Cape Town in South Africa. Why have opinions of Rhodes changed over the years?

Objectives

- **Define** 'social Darwinism'.
- **Examine** the role played by Cecil Rhodes in the 'scramble for Africa'.
- **Assess** why Cecil Rhodes has attracted both admiration and hatred.

SOURCE A The removal of the Cecil Rhodes statue, in April 2015, from the University of Cape Town

What did Rhodes think about the British Empire?

Rhodes was an **imperialist**, and believed that Britain should extend its power and influence over other parts of the world by any means possible. He believed he could take Darwin's theory of evolution, which said that weaker animals would die out and stronger ones would evolve and survive, and apply it to countries or peoples. Darwin's theory made Rhodes think it was right for the stronger (and therefore 'superior') Britain to take over weaker countries. This belief – called **social Darwinism** – was frequently used to justify European imperialism in Africa and other areas of the world.

Key Biography

Cecil Rhodes (1853–1902)

- Born in Bishop's Stortford.
- In 1870 went to Cape Colony, the southern part of Africa controlled by the British, to work in gold and diamond mines. Soon made a fortune.
- In 1881 was elected to the Cape Colony parliament, and in 1890 became its Prime Minister.
- In 1888 he formed a company, De Beers, which owned most of the gold and diamond fields in southern Africa. He then used his money and political skills to gain control of more land. When gold and diamonds were discovered in the Transvaal, an area controlled by Dutch settlers known as **Boers**, Rhodes was refused permission to mine there. He tried to get rid of the Boer leader, Paul Kruger, by force, but failed, and Britain was dragged into wars with the Boers. The British eventually won and gained more territory, but Rhodes died in 1902, a few months before the wars ended.

SOURCE B Adapted from an essay written by Cecil Rhodes in Confessions of Faith, 1877. When Rhodes writes 'Anglo-Saxon' he means 'British', and he thought of the British as a 'master race', many years before the term became associated with Adolf Hitler and the Nazis:

> I contend that we are the finest race in the world and that the more of the world we inhabit the better it is for the human race. What an alteration there would be if Africans were brought under Anglo-Saxon influence.

Chapter 8 Expansion in Africa

Assessing Cecil Rhodes

Rhodes was a controversial figure when he was alive, as well as today. He attracted criticism when his actions in the Transvaal led to the wars in which thousands died. While a politician, he introduced an act that pushed black people from their lands and increased taxes on their homes. He also made it harder for black people to vote.

Undoubtedly, though, Rhodes had many supporters, who argued that he brought vast wealth to Britain and made the southern part of Africa into a more stable and developed place. When he died, he left money in a scholarship fund that allowed overseas students to study at Oxford University, and many institutions, including the University of Cape Town, benefited from his generosity.

Some would argue that Rhodes was a man 'of his time' and that we shouldn't judge his actions and beliefs by today's standards. Ideas like social Darwinism were widely accepted at the time, and Rhodes was simply doing what lots of people and countries were doing. However, others argue that there should be no excuse for a person's actions and beliefs, no matter when they lived. We look at Rhodes differently today because we have contrasting views about empire and race to those that were common in previous centuries.

SOURCE C This cartoon appeared in Punch magazine in 1892, next to an article about Rhodes's plan to extend an electrical telegraph line from Cape Town in the south to Egypt's capital city Cairo in the north. Both Cape Colony and Egypt were under British control.

Key Words

imperialist   social Darwinism   Boer

INTERPRETATION D Adapted from an article called 'Cecil Rhodes' colonial legacy must fall – not his statue', which appeared in The Guardian in March 2015, written by Siya Mnyanda, a politics and philosophy graduate from the University of Cape Town (UCT):

> Dr Max Price, vice chancellor of UCT, summed up the contradictions by saying that although Rhodes was considered a 'great man', the attitudes and means he used 'were not right'. He said, 'Rhodes was racist. He used power and money to oppress others. So on balance he was a villain.'
>
> But as a black UCT student, who walked past that statue for four years, I think Rhodes should be left exactly where he is. Removing him omits an essential part of the university's history that has contributed to everything good, bad and ugly about it – and arguably the country too.

Extension

Read **Interpretation D**. Describe the two views of Rhodes that Dr Max Price describes. Why does the writer of the article think the statue of Rhodes should stay? Why do you think there are different views of Cecil Rhodes?

Work

1. Make a list of things that Rhodes either said or did that shows him to be: an imperialist; a social Darwinist.
2. Do you think the students of the University of Cape Town were right to vote for the removal of the statue? Discuss with a partner, and give reasons for your answer.
3. How useful is **Source C** to a historian studying the aims of Britain in Africa?

Practice Question

Explain the significance of Cecil Rhodes for the development of the British Empire in Africa.

8 marks

Study Tip

Remember the definition of 'significance' here. A significant person was not only important at the time, and affected many people's lives deeply, for a long time, but they are also still relevant in today's world.

Britain: Migration, empires and the people

8.3 Why did Britain get involved in Egypt?

Look at map **A** and **Source B**. They show the Suez Canal in Egypt, an important trade link between the Mediterranean Sea and the Indian Ocean. The 164-kilometre-long canal is in northern Africa. Its opening in 1869 meant that countries who wished to trade with India (and other eastern countries) did not have to sail their ships all around the vast continent of Africa. This was safer and faster, so goods could travel much quicker. Britain took no part in the building of the canal, and yet by 1882 it had managed to gain control of both Egypt and the Suez Canal. How did Britain gain control of this important canal? How and why did Britain get involved in this area of Africa?

Objectives

- **Examine** how Britain gained control of both the Suez Canal and Egypt.
- **Assess** the extent to which Britain's control of Egypt enhanced the British Empire.

The Suez Canal: a new route

▼ **A** *A map of the Suez Canal, and the different shipping distances from London to Mumbai. The canal reduces the journey distance by over 4000 nautical miles, making the journey around two weeks shorter.*

▼ **SOURCE B** *The opening of the Suez Canal in November 1869. It was funded and built jointly by France and Egypt. Initially Britain saw the building of the canal as a threat to its global maritime empire.*

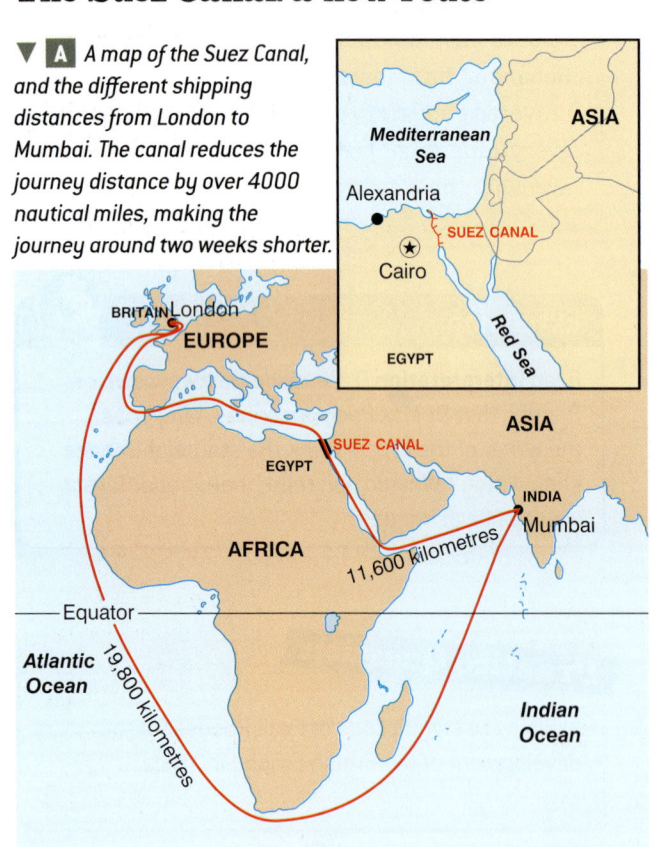

The British government took no part in paying for the Suez Canal, or its construction. However, the route was vital for Britain's trade with India as it meant that ships could take a short cut. Within a few years of the canal opening, around 80 per cent of the ships using the canal were British. Furthermore, in the event of another rebellion in India, or problems in other British colonies in the area, the time saved by using the canal could be vital. So to secure the route, the British government bought a controlling share in the canal from the Egyptians when they got into financial difficulty. The deal to buy this share of the canal was organised by British Prime Minister Benjamin Disraeli, who arranged for the government to borrow £4 million from a famous banker and politician, Lionel de Rothschild. When Disraeli heard the news that the sale had gone through he said to Queen Victoria, 'It is settled; you have it, madam. Four million pounds!' Lord Curzon, who was Viceroy of India between 1899 and 1905, described the canal as 'the determining influence of every considerable movement of British power to the east and south of the Mediterranean.'

Egypt in trouble

Just a few years after receiving money from the sale of their shares in the canal, the Egyptian government was again in economic difficulties. The British, in partnership with the French, gave money to the Egyptians in return for control over much of their trade, railways, post offices and ports. But in 1882, the Egyptians rebelled against this British and French 'interference'. In one riot in Alexandria, a number of British people were killed, and the British responded by ordering the navy to bomb the city. The French, however, refused to get involved.

Occupying Egypt

A few days after the bombing of Alexandria in July 1882, 24,000 soldiers from Britain and 7000 soldiers from British India entered Egypt. They began taking control of major towns and cities, including the capital, Cairo. Over 40 navy warships secured the Suez Canal.

So, by 1882, Britain had gained control of another African country. Thousands of soldiers were permanently based in Egypt and British navy warships defended the Suez Canal. Control of Egypt also gave Britain responsibility for Sudan – a country that the Egyptians controlled. In 1884, a religious leader known as the Madhi led an uprising in Sudan against the British and Egyptians. The rebels killed the British commander, General Charles Gordon, and held out for many years. However, between 1886 and 1888 the British, under Lord Kitchener, led a series of brutal military campaigns against supporters of the Madhi. Eventually, in 1899 Sudan, like Egypt before, came under British control.

Extension

Look at the famous *Punch* political cartoon in **Source C**, called 'The Lion's Share'. The man on the left giving money to the Egyptian leader is Benjamin Disraeli, the British politician who organised the sale of the shares. Why do you think the cartoonist has drawn the lion holding a key? Why is the cartoon called 'The Lion's Share'?

▼ **SOURCE C** *A* Punch *cartoon from 1876 called 'The Lion's Share'. It is commenting on the sale of shares in the Suez Canal.*

THE LION'S SHARE.
"GARE À QUI LA TOUCHE!"

Work

1. What is the Suez Canal?
2. Why do you think the Suez Canal was constructed?
3. Why do you think the British were particularly interested in the Suez Canal?
4. In your own words, explain how Britain gained control of both Egypt and Sudan.
5. Conduct research to write a news article titled 'The Suez Canal: then and now' to report on what has happened to the Suez Canal since the 1800s. Is it still under British control? If not, how did the British lose control? How important is the Suez Canal today?

8.4A The Boer War of 1899–1902

In the 1800s, two groups of Europeans competed for control of land in southern Africa – the British and the Boers. The Boers were descendants of Dutch settlers who had gone to southern Africa in the 1650s. They were mostly farmers (*boer* is the Dutch word for farmer) and their colony was named Cape Colony. In 1806, the British invaded Cape Colony and it soon officially became part of the British Empire. The Boers resented British control and left Cape Colony to head north. They set up two new colonies named the Transvaal and the Orange Free State.

Objectives

▶ **Identify** why the British fought wars against the Boers in South Africa.

▶ **Assess** the consequences of the wars, in particular the Boer War of 1899–1902.

▼ **A** This map shows the two Boer colonies – the Transvaal and the Orange Free State. Their flags are based on the red, white and blue of the Dutch flag. The map also shows the British-controlled lands of Cape Colony and Natal.

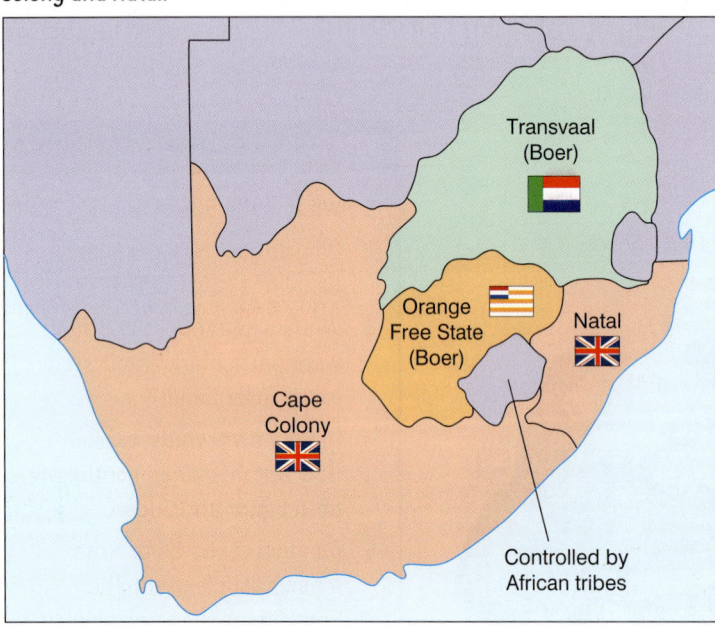

First Boer War breaks out: 1867–81

In 1867, diamonds were discovered in the new Boer states. The British government tried to get the Boers to unite their states with the British ones (Cape Colony and Natal), but the Boers refused. British troops were sent in to try to force the Boers to accept British rule, but the Boers fought back brilliantly. At the Battle of Majuba Hill in February 1881, the British suffered a heavy defeat and put their takeover plans on hold.

In 1886, gold was discovered in the Boer states. British businessman Cecil Rhodes (who lived in Cape Colony) saw this as an opportunity and opened dozens of mines inside Boer territory. Thousands of British workers flooded into the area and soon the Boers felt their land was under threat. The Boer leader, Paul Kruger, refused to give the British workers any political rights. Tensions reached breaking point when Cecil Rhodes sponsored a plan to overthrow Kruger and replace him with a British ruler. Rhodes' plan failed – and relations between the British and the Boers got worse. The British began to send more troops to Cape Colony, and placed them along the borders with the Boer states. In 1899, another war broke out.

The Second Boer War, 1899–1902

Early on in this war, known as the Second Boer War, the small Boer army stunned the British with a series of victories. The British had completely underestimated the Boers, who were highly skilled fighters, armed with modern guns, who knew the terrain well.

236 Chapter 8 Expansion in Africa

B *Boer soldiers adopted brilliant military tactics against the British forces*

No military uniform, so they easily blended in with local settlers

Armed with the latest German-made military rifles and artillery

All fighters were mobile, on horseback; unlike the British, there were no **infantry** soldiers to slow down the unit

Fighters often 'lived off the land' by foraging for food or capturing enemy supplies; the British needed long supply chains to keep their vast groups of soldiers fed and armed

Mainly fought in small groups (5–12 fighters), so units were hard to detect and moved around easily, capturing supplies and attacking troops and communication lines when least expected; these tactics were known as **guerrilla** (Spanish for 'little war') tactics

Key Words

infantry   guerrilla

SOURCE C *Three generations of Boer War soldiers in 1990; (from left to right) P. J. Lemmer (age 65), J. D. L. Botha (age 15), and G. J. Pretorius (age 43)*

Work

1. **a** Who were the Boers?
   b Why did the Boers leave Cape Colony?
2. Why do you think the British become interested in the new Boer colonies?
3. Why did war break out in southern Africa in 1899?
4. Look at diagram **B**. Use it to help you explain why the Boer fighters were so successful against the British forces in the early stages of the war.

Britain: Migration, empires and the people   237

8.4B The Boer War of 1899–1902

The British fight back

In January 1900, the British responded to their losses by sending half a million troops to fight approximately 50,000 Boer soldiers. The British army used all the hi-tech weaponry they had – machine guns, modern rifles and high explosive shells. Yet the Boers refused to surrender and carried out dozens of small raids on British camps, railways and mines. The British responded savagely.

The British commander during the Second Boer War, General Kitchener, decided that the only way to get the Boers to surrender was to introduce a **scorched earth** policy. This meant that British soldiers were instructed to burn down Boer farms, kill the animals, destroy crops and poison drinking wells. Then Boer men, women, children, and their black servants were rounded up into 'concentration camps'. Out of 116,000 Boers put in these camps, 28,000 (mainly children) died, largely due to disease and illness brought on by poor conditions.

Peace at last

By 1902, both sides were exhausted after years of brutal fighting. Eventually the Boers were forced to surrender, and peace talks began. It was agreed that the Boer states would become British colonies, but the Boers were promised that they could make many of the key decisions in running their lands. In 1910, the Boer states joined with Cape Colony and Natal to form the Union of South Africa, part of the British Empire. However, this Union (commonly known as South Africa) was classed as a **dominion**, rather than a colony, and ran its own affairs.

Consequences of the Boer War of 1899–1902

The Boer War was Britain's biggest twentieth-century 'empire war'. At first in Britain, there was great support for the war and thousands of men volunteered to fight, but enthusiasm for the war was short lived. Around 450,000 British soldiers fought in the war, and nearly 6000 died in battle. A further 16,000 died from illness and wounds sustained in battles. The Boers lost around 7000 of their 90,000 soldiers, and over 28,000 civilians. The war showed how determined the British were to hold onto their empire – at whatever cost.

SOURCE D *An Illustration from French newspaper* Le Petit Parisien *from January 1901, showing Boer prisoners in a British camp in the Transvaal. The British soldiers are outside in the white helmets.*

The Boer War also had an unexpected consequence. Young British men had volunteered to fight in their thousands, but over a third of them were classed as 'unfit for duty'. This worried the government. Unless something was done, how was Britain going to fight its wars in the future?

Around the same time, several special investigations into the lives of the poor started to make headlines. One report found that around 30 per cent of Londoners were so poor that they didn't have enough money to eat properly, despite having full-time jobs!

Finally, in 1906, the government decided to act. One of the first moves was to introduce free school meals for the poorest children. Other measures over the next five years included free medical checks and health treatments in schools. The government also encouraged the teaching of 'domestic science' in schools, which was the study of nutrition, food, clothing, child development, family relationships, and household skills. This was a direct result of the fact that so many young people who volunteered to fight in the Boer War were so physically unfit for military service.

After helping children, the government moved onto other sections of society. They introduced unemployment benefit (the 'dole'), sickness pay and old age pensions. They even built Britain's first job centres. Indeed, it seems that a distant war in southern Africa led to many of the ideas that still help the most vulnerable people in our society today.

Practice Question

Were ideas such as imperialism and social Darwinism the main factor driving British involvement in Africa in the nineteenth century?

16 marks
SPaG: 4 marks

Study Tip

Try to write a paragraph about at least one other factor, such as trade or wealth, in your answer.

Key Words

scorched earth   dominion

Extension

One of the most famous battles of the Boer War was fought at a place called Spion Kop in January 1900. Many football clubs named stands in their football grounds after this battle. Find out which clubs have used the word 'kop' when naming one of their stands. Why do you think football clubs would choose to name parts of their ground after this battle?

Fact

The wars in southern Africa in the nineteenth century have many names. For the British they were the Boer Wars – but for the Boers they were the Wars of Independence. Today, most South Africans refer to them as the Anglo-Boer Wars.

Work

1. Explain the following terms:
    a. scorched earth policy
    b. concentration camp
    c. Union of South Africa.
2. Look at **Source D**.
    a. In your own words, describe what you can see in the image.
    b. At the time this illustration appeared, the French were Britain's rivals in trying to conquer areas of Africa. Do you think this might have had an impact on the way this image was drawn?
3. In your own words, assess the impact of the Boer Wars on British society. Consider the social and political results of the wars in Britain and South Africa.

Britain: Migration, empires and the people

8.5 Celebrating the British Empire

In 1887, Queen Victoria celebrated 50 years as queen. The event was marked by special celebrations, and Queen Victoria was cheered by thousands of people as she travelled to a special service at Westminster Abbey, London. The public enthusiasm for her Golden Jubilee resulted in the production of a huge range of souvenirs. Commemorative plates, teacups, biscuit tins, spoons, special coins and pictures were produced and bought by members of the public. These souvenirs form part of what we can call **imperial propaganda**. But what is 'imperial propaganda', and how did it help to spread ideas about Britain and its empire?

Objectives

▶ Define 'imperial propaganda'.
▶ Examine the variety of methods used to promote the British Empire.

Queen and empire

The British Empire expanded rapidly during the reign of Queen Victoria (reign: 1837–1901). The British government, and the queen herself, knew that a large empire brought trading benefits to Britain and made the country richer. There was also the belief the British had a 'right' to the land and were helping people in conquered nations by teaching them a new, Christian way of life. Even Queen Victoria said that one of the aims of the British Empire was to 'protect the poor natives and to advance civilisation'. This was a time when most people were very loyal to their queen and their country, and patriotic pride was encouraged – the government realised that if people's enthusiasm for the empire remained high, then it would have their full support when taking over more land abroad.

Books and newspapers helped to fuel people's enthusiasm for the empire. Magazines for young people had such titles as *Union Jack* and *Young England*, and the popular magazine for teenagers, *Boy's Own Paper*, was filled with stories of brave soldiers 'doing their duty' while fighting enemies on behalf of the queen. Newspapers wrote vivid accounts of successful battles overseas, and the spread of the telegraph communication system meant that stories could appear within a day of the event. This certainly made an impact on people: for example, during the Boer War, huge crowds gathered at fairgrounds and music halls to see film clips from the battle front on the newly invented cinema screen.

▼ **SOURCE A** *A Pears' Soap advert from 1880. Soap was first used widely in the Victorian period and became a symbol of how clean, civilised and racially superior the British were. This advert links the idea of 'cleanliness', 'whiteness' and 'superiority' together. The white child is 'helping' the black child by making him cleaner – and whiter. It plays on the racist idea that 'white is better'.*

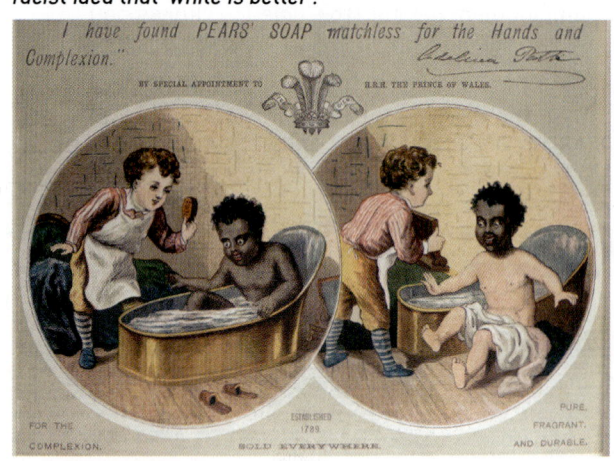

Imperial propaganda

The commemorative plate shown in **Source B** does not just commemorate Queen Victoria's Golden Jubilee, it also celebrates the size and power of Britain's empire. A map is included on the plate, highlighting (in red) the areas of the world controlled by the British. Four of those areas are specifically mentioned: Australia, Canada, Cape Colony in southern Africa and India. The plate also shows the amount of goods sold abroad (exports) and goods bought into Britain (imports). The total population of the British Empire is also written. In fact, at this time, pride in the British Empire was at its height, and companies took advantage of that pride to make money.

▼ **SOURCE B** A commemorative plate celebrating Queen Victoria's Golden Jubilee

All sorts of products, from bars of soap to tins of chocolates, were covered with images relating to the glory of the empire. Posters, school books, exhibitions and parades all conveyed the empire's positive aspects. This was a type of imperial propaganda, in which the positive aspects, ideas and information about the empire were spread in order to influence public opinion and beliefs.

In schools, textbooks were filled with stories of Britain's great empire-builders, such as Cecil Rhodes, and students were taught that a huge empire was Britain's destiny. Poems and music hall songs celebrated the power of Britain and its armed forces, and even nursery rhyme books sometimes had an empire theme. Furthermore, two new societies were formed (the British Empire League and the British Colonial Society) to support the idea of imperialism and to promote loyalty to the British Empire. Although the impact that organisations like these, and imperial propaganda in general, had on the ordinary British citizen is unclear, there is little doubt that they could not escape the promotion of patriotic pride at this time.

▼ **SOURCE C** A well-known poem from the 1870s; it introduced a new word to the English language – **jingoism** – to define an aggressive attitude towards foreign nations. In the song, the word 'jingo' was used instead of 'Jesus', which was viewed as an inappropriate word to use in a song at the time:

> We don't want to fight,
> But by jingo if we do,
> We've got the ships,
> We've got the men,
> We've got the money too!

Key Words

imperial propaganda   jingoism

▼ **SOURCE D** From an 1899 nursery rhyme book called ABC for Baby Patriots. It makes reference to the belief that the British thought they were justified in taking over other nations:

> C is for colonies, rightly we boast,
> That of all the great nations
> Great Britain has most.
> [...]
> F is the flag; which wherever you see,
> You know that beneath it; you're happy and free.

Work

1. Look at **Source A**.
   a. Describe what is happening in the two images in the advert.
   b. Can you suggest reasons why the white boy has been drawn standing up and the black boy sitting down?
   c. Why do you think the black boy's body has changed colour, but his head hasn't?
2. Look at **Source B**.
   a. In your own words, describe the plate.
   b. Suggest two reasons why someone might buy one of these plates.
3. a. Explain what is meant by the term 'imperial propaganda'.
   b. Make a list of methods used to spread positive ideas and messages about the British Empire.
   c. Why do you think the British government was so keen to spread these positive ideas and messages about the British Empire?

Practice Question

How useful is **Source A** to a historian studying attitudes to the British Empire in the late nineteenth century?   **8 marks**

Study Tip

Consider how the source relates to the motives for gaining an empire. What does it suggest about different races? Why would Pears use these ideas in their advertisements?

Britain: Migration, empires and the people   241

9.1 Irish migration to Britain

People, or groups of people, have always moved between different countries. Some move because they want to (known as **voluntary migration**), while others move because they have no choice and are forced to (called **forced migration**). One of the largest groups to come to Britain in the last few hundred years has been the Irish. There were a number of reasons why they came – and their impact was important. Why did the Irish move? How did people react to their arrival, and what impact did they have?

Objectives

- **Examine** reasons why many Irish migrants came to Britain.
- **Analyse** the experiences of Irish immigrants.
- **Assess** the impact of Irish migration.

Why did the Irish migrate?

From the late eighteenth century onwards, large numbers of Irish people migrated to Britain, mainly through the ports of Liverpool and Glasgow. Thousands stayed in those cities, and there are still large Irish communities there now. Most came to escape the extreme poverty in parts of Ireland, and to find better paid work. Many found jobs around the country as **navvies**, building the many new canals, roads and later railways: one third of the navvies who worked on the railways were Irish. They also worked in mines and in cotton mills, in Britain's quickly expanding towns and cities.

There was a great surge in Irish immigration after 1846, when a disease called 'potato blight' ruined the Irish potato harvest. Potatoes formed a major part of the Irish diet at this time, so many people starved. Around one million people (or one eighth of the population) died during famine, either from starvation or from illnesses that their weakened bodies couldn't fight. Hundreds of thousands fled to Britain, peaking in the 1840s and 1850s, when over one and a half million Irish people left their homeland.

Fact

Britain was not the only destination for the Irish – nearly a million travelled to the USA. Today, large communities with Irish ancestry can be found in many US cities including Philadelphia, Chicago and Boston. Many places across the country have annual St Patrick's Day parades; the one in New York is one of the world's largest parades.

▼ **SOURCE A** *A picture during the potato famine showing a Catholic priest blessing a group of emigrants as they leave Ireland for a new life abroad*

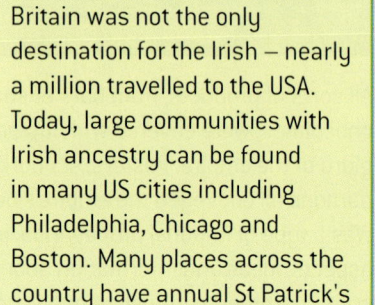

By 1861, there were around 600,000 Irish-born people in Britain. Like many migrant groups, before or since, the Irish tended to live close together in towns and cities. Despite getting work, they were not wealthy, and often ended up in the poorest quality housing in the worst parts of town.

How did the British react to the Irish?

▼ B *At the time, many people did not like their new Irish neighbours*

Key Words

voluntary migration   forced migration   navvy

Religious differences

Most of the Irish were Catholic – and Britain was a strongly Protestant country. This was a time when religious differences could lead to violence, and on several occasions angry Protestants marched through Irish areas and destroyed property.

Disease

The Irish lived in terrible conditions so disease was common. As a result, people would blame the Irish for causing the disease in the first place. The fact that disease was just as common in other places seemed to go unnoticed. Typhus – a deadly infectious disease common in crowded, unsanitary conditions – was even nicknamed 'Irish fever'.

Crime

The Irish were blamed for high crime rates in many towns and cities. The navvies tended to drink a lot and this would sometimes lead to violence. In 1847, *The Times* newspaper described the Irish as 'more like squalid apes than human beings'.

Jobs

The Irish were accused of taking jobs that the British could have done. There were anti-Irish protests; in some places people with Irish accents (or even Irish names) were barred from jobs. As a result, there were times when the Irish couldn't always find regular work – so they were accused of being lazy too.

British reaction to the Irish

Impact of Irish migration on Britain

Despite the difficulties, the Irish settlers continued to arrive in Britain, especially in the 1930s, 1950s and 1960s, when people came looking for work in Britain's expanding cities. Over the years there were fewer problems between the Irish and the British as they intermarried. The Irish roots remain strong in places like Liverpool and Birmingham that had a high Irish population in the 1800s. In fact, according to the 2001 census, six million people (ten per cent of the total British population) had Irish parents or grandparents.

The Irish, therefore, have made a huge impact on Britain. Britain's canals, roads and railways could not have been built without the Irish navvies, and in the early 1800s, as many as 40 per cent of soldiers in the British army were Irish. Irish dancing, music and bars have become part of British culture. Famous Irish-born people include writers Oscar Wilde and C. S. Lewis, explorer Ernest Shackleton and the military hero, the Duke of Wellington.

Extension

Carry out some additional research into the impact that Irish immigration has had on Britain. Which famous Britons have Irish ancestry? In what ways have the Irish influenced British culture?

Work

1. **a** Explain the difference between voluntary and forced migration.
   b Do you think the Irish migrants to Britain experienced voluntary or forced migration, or a mixture of both? Explain your answer carefully.
   c Why did so many people leave Ireland in the 1800s?
2. **a** Make a list of all the problems blamed on the Irish when they arrived in Britain.
   b Why do you think so many British people were so keen to blame the Irish for their problems?

Practice Question

Compare the Huguenot migration to Britain and the Irish migration to Britain. In what ways were they similar?   **8 marks**

Study Tip

Try to write about the contribution each group made to Britain after they arrived.

Britain: Migration, empires and the people   243

9.2 Jewish migration to Britain

In 1290, King Edward I expelled all the Jews from England. It was over 350 years until England's leaders allowed Jews back in. There were only about 400 Jews living in England in 1690. However, by 1850 the number of Jews had grown to about 40,000 (out of a population of 18 million). As the Jewish communities prospered, their contribution to British life grew. Why does Britain have a large Jewish community? And what is their contribution to British society?

Objectives

- **Explain** why there was an influx of Jews into Britain in the late 1800s.
- **Examine** how Jews were received in Britain at that time.
- **Assess** the Jewish contribution to the British way of life.

By the mid-1800s, Jewish people had made important contributions to Britain. By then, of course, many Jews regarded themselves as British. The vast majority had been born in Britain, spoke English and lived typical British lifestyles. The first Jewish Mayor of London took office in 1855, and shortly afterwards Lionel de Rothschild became the first Jewish MP. As well as his role as a politician, Rothschild was a banker who famously lent money to the British government to buy a controlling share in the Suez Canal from Egypt. Since then, the British parliament has never been without Jewish politicians. In 1874, Benjamin Disraeli became Britain's first Jewish Prime Minister.

Key Biography

Benjamin Disraeli (1804–81)

- Born Jewish, but was baptised as a Christian in 1817.
- Became Prime Minister of Britain twice (in 1868 and again in 1874).
- Arranged for Queen Victoria to be officially titled 'Empress of India' in 1877.

SOURCE A *Disraeli and Queen Victoria, painted in 1887*

New Jewish migration

In the 1870s and 1880s, there was a new influx of Jews from Eastern Europe, mainly from Russia. Jews had been wrongly blamed for the assassination of the Russian emperor Tsar Alexander II in 1881, and from 1882 a series of laws against them were strictly enforced. There were restrictions placed on the number of Jews allowed in schools, for example, and in some cities like Moscow (in 1891) Jews were expelled altogether. Religious attacks, called **pogroms**, were common too. In 1903, for example, a pogrom in Kishinev (then part of Russia) left 49 Jews dead, 500 injured and hundreds of homes and businesses destroyed. As a result, between 1881 and 1914 around 120,000 Jews arrived in Britain, mainly fleeing from extreme persecution like this.

However, apart from their faith, these new **refugees** had little in common with the Jews already living in Britain. They looked different, were largely uneducated and didn't speak any English. They worked hard but generally lived in the poorest areas. They were badly paid but were charged high rents for their overcrowded, disease-ridden rooms. As more Jews arrived, anger and hostility towards them grew, mainly because they were accused of taking jobs from British workers. This has been a familiar theme with any new immigrant group.

The new immigrants mainly took on three kinds of work – making clothes, shoemaking or furniture-making. These jobs mainly took place in small, back-street workshops, known as 'sweatshops' because of the warm conditions and long hours. But the Jews did very well in their new trades.

Within a few decades, Jewish communities gained a reputation as hardworking, law-abiding citizens with ambition and keen business sense. One immigrant called Michael Marks opened a market stall in 1894. His business partner was Tom Spencer, an Englishman. By 1900, Marks & Spencer had 36 outlets, and it is now one of the best known high street stores in the world. Jack Cohen, the son of Jewish immigrants from Poland, set up a business selling (among other things) tea from a supplier called T. E. Stockwell. He soon created a brand name for his business by using part of his surname and the initials of his main supplier, and TESCO was born.

▼ **SOURCE B** *An engraving of Wentworth Street in Whitechapel, a poor area of London, in 1872. It shows not only poor Jews, but other immigrants – Irish, Indians and Germans, for example.*

Fact

Many people were concerned about the influx of Jews from Eastern Europe. A campaign to stop Jewish immigration began in the late 1800s and continued for many years, despite the fact that many Jews worked incredibly hard and set up shops and businesses in Britain. A number of key politicians supported the campaign, and in 1905 the first Aliens Act was passed by parliament, limiting the number of Jewish immigrants.

Key Words

pogrom   refugee   chain migration

Our 'oldest ethnic minority'

The Jewish community is now a successful and important part of British society. Jews live all over Britain but have particularly large communities in London, Manchester, Leeds and Glasgow. In 2006, during commemorations of 350 years since Jews were re-admitted into Britain, the then Prime Minister Tony Blair said that the Jewish communities of Britain have shown that 'it is possible to retain a clear faith and a clear identity and, at the same time, be thoroughly British'.

British Jews who today continue to excel in the world of business include Lord Alan Sugar and Philip Green (owner of Topshop and Miss Selfridge). Many British Jews have been successful in show business too, including Daniel Radcliffe, Orlando Bloom and Matt Lucas. Many Jews have fought for Britain, including poet and soldier Siegfried Sassoon, and six British Jewish soldiers have received the Victoria Cross, the highest award for bravery.

Fact

In many cases, young Jewish men emigrated first, then were followed by their wives and children once they had established a home and a place to live. Older relatives followed later. This is known as **chain migration**.

Work

1. For what reasons did large numbers of Jews arrive in Britain in the 1870s and 1880s?
2. a Describe how the new Jewish immigrants were treated.
   b Can you think of reasons why they were treated this way?
3. a Look carefully at **Source B**. Describe what you see – and then try to explain what you think the artist thought about immigrants.
   b Discuss in pairs: How useful is **Source B** to a historian studying attitudes towards new immigrants in the late 1800s?

Britain: Migration, empires and the people

9.3A People on the move in nineteenth-century Britain

In the eighteenth and nineteenth centuries, many millions of people moved around the British Empire for different reasons. But it wasn't just within the empire that this migration happened — millions of people moved around Britain too. So where did people move to, and why did people move around Britain so much? How did the British Empire affect migration?

Objectives

▶ **Explore** how the British Empire affected migration, including the migration of Asians to Africa.

▶ **Discover** how Australia became an important part of Britain's justice system.

▶ **Examine** why people moved from rural to urban settings between 1750 and 1900.

During the era of the British Empire, millions of people migrated huge distances across the globe. Some of these people had no choice but to move and were forced to go. Others willingly migrated as they looked for fresh challenges and new opportunities.

Forced migration

Case study: Africa and Asia

The most obvious example of forced migration was the transport of millions of Africans as slaves to work on sugar, tobacco and cotton farms in the West Indies and North America. The **transportation** of prisoners to America and Australia in the 1700s and 1800s is another example of forced migration.

When slavery ended in the early 1800s, the British needed another way to get large amounts of people to work on their plantations, estates and farms in various parts of the empire. The **indenture system** was created, meaning that migrants would agree to work for a period of five years in return for a basic wage and transport to their new workplace. The worker was to be returned at the end of the period of service to the port of departure. Around half of the immigrants to the American colonies in the sixteenth and seventeenth centuries went there under this system, as did millions of Tamils from South India who went to pick tea on estates in Sri Lanka, or tap rubber in Malaya. It has been estimated that, between 1841 and 1910, around 150,000 people per decade moved around the empire under this system. In the British African colonies of Kenya and Uganda, for example, over 30,000 Indians moved there under the indenture system to help build railways, bridges and roads. Some came home when the work was done, but thousands stayed and they and their descendants went on to play a vital part in the African economies as businessmen, bankers, shopkeepers and professionals. By the late 1960s there were about 180,000 'Kenyan Asians' (as they were known) and around 60,000 'Ugandan Asians'.

▼ **SOURCE A** *The 1000-kilometre-long Uganda Railway in British East Africa was built mainly by indentured workers from India, like the ones pictured here*

246 Chapter 9 Migrants to, from and within Britain

Fact

It is important to note that lots of migrants flooded into Britain in the nineteenth century too. Irish migrants and Eastern European Jews are covered on pages 242–245, but there was also an influx of Chinese migrants, central European migrants (such as Germans), and ex-slaves into Britain at this time.

Key Words

transportation
indenture system
Aboriginal

Case study: Australia

In April 1770, a British explorer named James Cook claimed the east coast of Australia for Britain and named it New South Wales. The British government then sent naval commander Captain Arthur Phillip to set up the first colony on Australian soil. The government also wanted him to transport convicts from Britain's overcrowded jails to help him do it: it was hoped that these prisoners would never return to Britain. In May 1787, 11 ships left Portsmouth heading for the new British colony. There were over 1300 people on board the ships, including 736 convicted criminals.

The convicts began to build the settlement. Each convict was assigned a master. The master decided what work each convict would carry out. Good, hardworking convicts earned themselves an early release, while bad behaviour ended in a whipping or an extended sentence. Over the next 20 years, British courts transported over 20,000 more convicts to join them. But life in the new settlement was tough. Few of the convicts – or their masters – knew about farming or carpentry, two of the most important skills needed in the new colony.

Australia was first used mainly as a place to dump Britain's criminals, but things soon started to change. The majority of convicts decided to stay in Australia at the end of their sentences. Many became sheep or wheat farmers. Britain would eventually claim the whole of Australia as part of the British Empire.

Fact

Transportation became a very common punishment. It not only removed the criminal from Britain, but it was also quite cheap: the government only had to pay the cost of a one-way journey. The punishment began in the 1600s when the British colonies in North America began to receive transported British criminals. This stopped when the American War of Independence broke out in 1775; Australia then became the favoured alternative destination after 1787.

▼ **SOURCE B** *The first British colony in Australia, pictured around 1835. It was named Sydney after a British politician. Note the Aboriginal Australians fishing in the bay. The term 'Aboriginal' is from the Latin* ab *(meaning from) and* origo *(meaning beginning).*

Work

1. What is the difference between 'forced migration' and the 'indenture system'?
2. What work did people who were forced to migrate to Africa and Australia do?
3. What happened to them and their descendants?

Extension

Try to find out what happened to some of Australia's convicts. For example some, upon their release after their sentences, became famous artists, architects and merchants. One former convict earned enough money to help pay for the building of one of Australia's most famous schools.

9.3B People on the move in nineteenth-century Britain

Leaving home

It has been estimated that over 22 million people left Britain between 1815 and 1914, the vast majority going to North America, South Africa, Canada, Australia and New Zealand. They left hoping to make a better life for themselves in a country where they felt they had more opportunities. They did all sorts of jobs when they got to their destinations. Most men found work in building, engineering, farming or mining, while women took up jobs as tutors or maids. Thousands were lured to North America and South Africa to hunt for gold and diamonds. In the late 1700s, the first 'free settlers' began to arrive in Australia from Britain, attracted by the idea of a new life in another part of the world. They brought the supplies and skills needed to help the settlement survive and grow.

Emigration was also seen as a solution to the growing problem of crime and poverty in Britain. The government gave local councils money to create schemes that encouraged the poorest people in an area to emigrate. Other schemes took young criminals away from their families and set them up in new lives in Canada or Australia.

Moving around Britain

Migration is not just about leaving one country to go to another. A person can also migrate *within* their own country. This is sometimes called **internal migration**. This took place in Britain, more rapidly than at any other time, between the years 1750 and 1900.

During this period, the population of Britain rose quickly. Better medical treatments, improved food supplies and improved sanitation are among some of the many reasons why more people survived childhood and lived longer lives. In fact, Britain's population went from around 10 million in 1801 to about 37 million in 1901.

The amount of people in towns and cities (**urban** areas) grew much faster than in country (**rural**) areas at this time, particularly in London and the large industrial towns in the North and the Midlands. In 1750, for example, around 80 per cent of people lived and worked in the countryside. By 1825, this had dropped to 60 per cent, and by 1901 around 75 per cent of people lived and worked in towns and cities. We call this process **urbanisation** – the increase in the proportion of people living in urban areas. There were several reasons why towns and industrial areas grew more rapidly than country areas:

- Immigration from abroad: immigrants were attracted to jobs in urban areas. Many workers came from Ireland, for example, to find jobs in the cotton mills of Lancashire and Yorkshire. By 1851, 10 per cent of the population of Manchester and 15 per cent of the population of Liverpool were of Irish origin. In Coatbridge, a mining town near Glasgow, the Irish proportion of the population was 49 per cent.
- Rural to urban migration: farm machinery became more common, so fewer workers were needed on farms. Farming is also very seasonal, whereas factory work isn't, so workers in the countryside poured into urban areas to find work. The larger the towns became, the more jobs this created in shops, businesses, building work and so on.

▼ **C** *Population of two English counties (in thousands)*

County	Main job type	1701	1751	1781	1801
Lancashire	Industrial	239	318	423	694
Suffolk	Farming	161	159	188	217

Extension

Research what the 'push' and 'pull' factors of migration are. Then carry out a survey of the people in your class to establish the levels of internal migration and immigration. What were the push and pull factors in each case? How do the push and pull factors from those moving *around* the UK (internal migration) compare to those moving *into* the UK (immigration)?

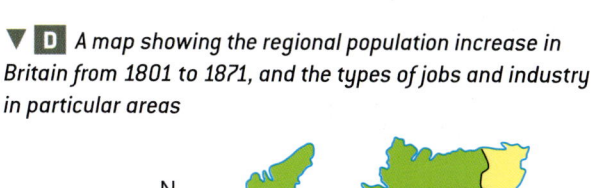

▼ **D** *A map showing the regional population increase in Britain from 1801 to 1871, and the types of jobs and industry in particular areas*

Key Words
internal migration
urban
rural
urbanisation

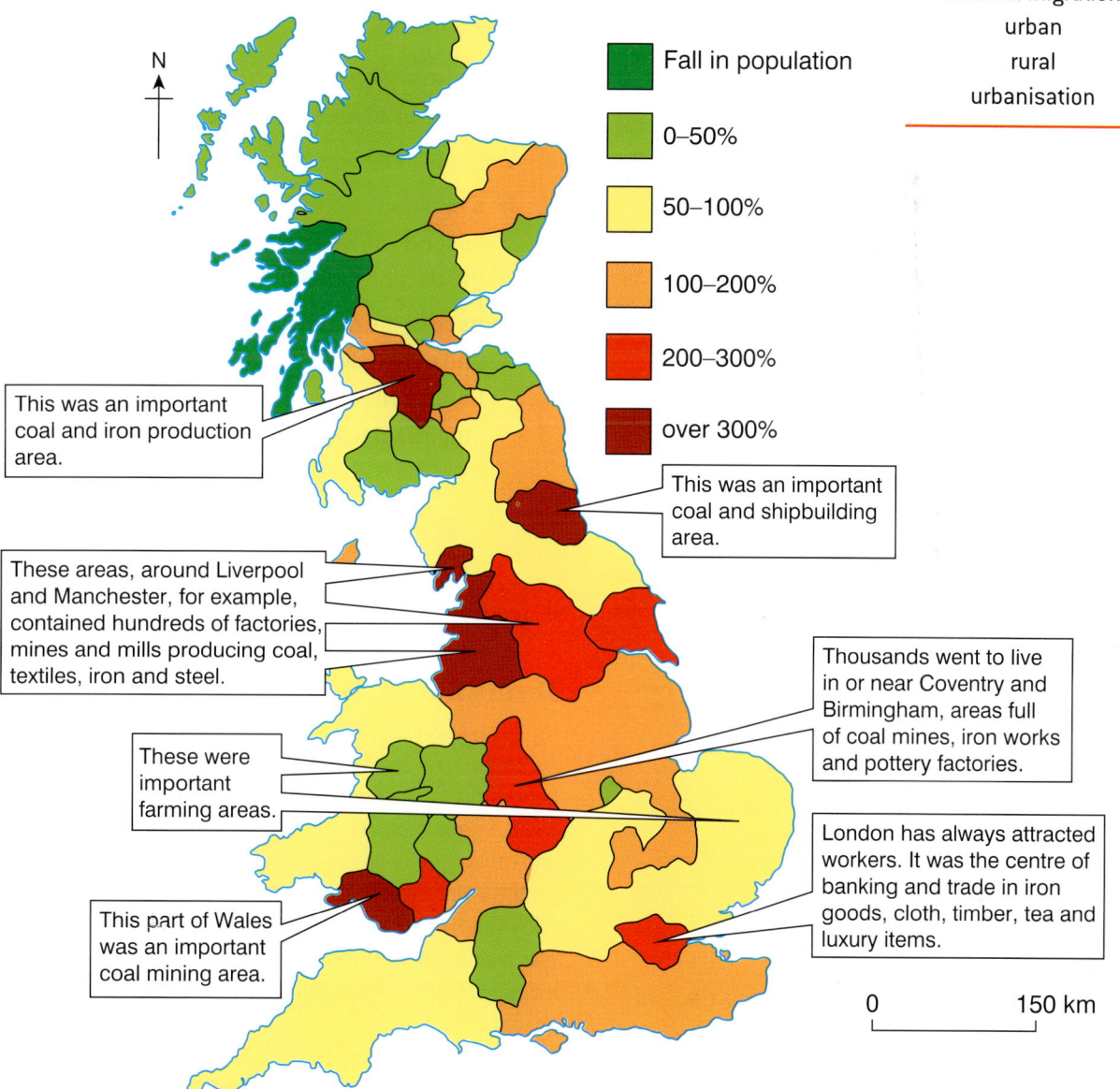

Map legend:
- Fall in population
- 0–50%
- 50–100%
- 100–200%
- 200–300%
- over 300%

Map annotations:
- This was an important coal and iron production area.
- This was an important coal and shipbuilding area.
- These areas, around Liverpool and Manchester, for example, contained hundreds of factories, mines and mills producing coal, textiles, iron and steel.
- Thousands went to live in or near Coventry and Birmingham, areas full of coal mines, iron works and pottery factories.
- These were important farming areas.
- London has always attracted workers. It was the centre of banking and trade in iron goods, cloth, timber, tea and luxury items.
- This part of Wales was an important coal mining area.

0 — 150 km

Work

1. Give three examples of how different people might have moved around the British Empire.
2. a Explain what is meant by the term 'urbanisation'.
   b What were the main causes of urbanisation between 1750 and 1900?
3. Look at table **C**. Why was the population increase so much greater in one county than the other?
4. Look at map **D**. Explain why the populations of Manchester and Liverpool increased far more rapidly than the populations of mid-Wales.

Practice Question

Has industrialisation been the main factor causing changes in the population of Britain in the nineteenth century?

16 marks
SPaG: 4 marks

Study Tip

Consider the push and pull factors involved in causing people to move.

Britain: Migration, empires and the people 249

10.1A How did the British lose their empire?

Map **A** below shows the British Empire at its largest, in the early 1920s. At that point it was the largest empire the world had ever known. It contained around 450 million people (approximately one quarter of the world's population) and it covered about one quarter of the world's total land area. Today the British Empire (now called the British Overseas Territories) is very small, consisting of a few small areas, mainly islands, dotted around the world. At its height, the empire covered around 34 million square kilometres. Today, it covers around 1.7 million square kilometres. What happened to the British Empire?

Objectives

- **Recall** how Britain gradually lost its empire
- **Evaluate** the impact of the First and Second World Wars and the Suez Crisis on the decline of the British Empire.
- **Assess** the importance of independence and nationalism, as well as the roles of Gandhi, Nkrumah and Kenyatta, in the empire's decline.

▼ **A** *The British Empire at its territorial peak in 1921*

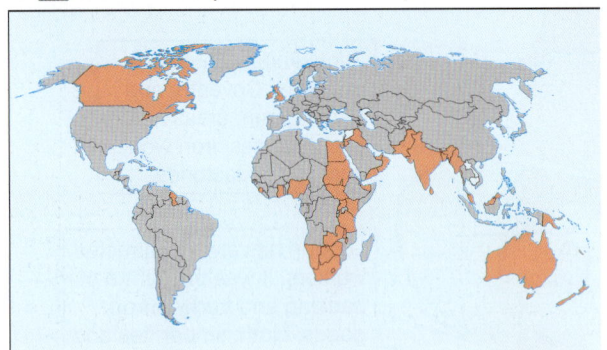

The impact of the world wars

Before the First World War, Britain was one of the richest countries in the world, with its mighty industrial power and vast empire. However, after four years of fighting, Britain's wealth was nearly all gone: it was now in debt because it had borrowed money, mainly from the USA. Also, during the war many countries had been cut off from the supply of British goods so had been forced to build up their own industries. They were no longer reliant on Britain, and directly competed with it instead. The First World War changed Britain's status in the world: it was no longer the world's economic superpower.

After the war, Britain recovered some of its strength, but it was then completely bankrupted by the Second World War. Britain's economy was also beginning to change. Its trade with Europe and the USA became far more important than its trade with countries of the empire. Britain was also no longer as important on the world stage. It was now overshadowed by the political and financial might of the USA and the Soviet Union.

Demanding independence

By 1914, several of Britain's colonies – such as Canada, Australia, New Zealand and South Africa – had already been running their own affairs for several years. In 1922, Egypt became independent too. These countries, and others in the empire, played an important role in Britain's victory in both world wars by supplying troops and materials. However, by the end of the Second World War, many other British colonies were demanding independence, or the right to rule themselves. Britain no longer had the military strength or the wealth to hold onto them. Also, many British people felt that rebuilding Britain after the war was far more of a priority than holding on to distant colonies.

There were several reasons why there was an increasing demand for independence:

- The British-style education systems in some of the colonies (such as India) meant that many people there were now becoming teachers, lawyers and doctors. They learned about political ideas, like democracy and freedom, and wanted this for their own countries.
- The Africans and Indians who had fought for Britain felt they were fighting to defend freedom, and were getting increasingly frustrated that their own countries were not yet free. They thought it was wrong that they should fight to stop the Nazis occupying other countries, but not fight to stop Britain occupying theirs.

- Researchers, historians and scholars were showing how important the cultures and achievements of Africa and Asia had been before the Europeans had taken over. Many people in the colonies were very **nationalistic** and wanted to revive their old traditions, and this could only be done if the British left.
- Some critics of British rule argued that Britain seemed happier to allow self-rule in countries that contained a majority of white settlers (such as Australia and Canada) rather than 'non-white' colonies such as India or in Africa. They suggested that the British thought people of European descent (such as in Australia and Canada) were superior to non-Europeans. The demand for independence from the 'non-white' colonies began to grow.

After the Second World War, Britain lost its empire very quickly. It had taken centuries to build up, but only decades to lose.

Key Words

nationalistic   Indian National Congress   Muslim League   partition

Work

1. Compare the British Empire at its height with the British Overseas Territories today.
2. Why did some colonies begin to demand their independence from Britain?
3. Why do you think some critics of the British Empire accused the British of racist attitudes when it came to allowing some countries to rule themselves?

Case study: independence for India

The campaign for Indian independence began with the founding of the **Indian National Congress** in 1885, which held meetings and organised demonstrations, although the British largely ignored their demands. In 1919, after India's great contribution in the First World War, the British made slight changes to the way India was governed. Law-making councils were set up in each province and over five million wealthy Indians were given the vote. However, the British government in London still controlled taxation, the armed forces, education and much more.

In the 1920s, the Indian independence movement gained more support under the leadership of Mohandas Gandhi, a Hindu and former lawyer. He led a series of non-violent protests against the British. Eventually, in 1935, the Government of India Act gave Indians the right to control everything except the army. But India was still part of the British Empire and was still ruled by a viceroy. Many Indians, like Gandhi, continued to demand complete independence. By now, Muslims in India had formed their own independence group (the **Muslim League**), and their leader called for a new separate country for Muslims.

After the Second World War, Britain wasn't strong enough to hold on to a country so desperate to rule itself. In 1946, Britain offered independence to India – but Muslims did not want to live under a Hindu majority and terrible violence broke out. Indian and British leaders finally agreed to **partition** British India into two states – Hindu India and Muslim Pakistan. Pakistan became independent on 14 August 1947, and India the next day. Immediately, over seven million Muslims fled to Pakistan, and the same number of Hindus and Sikhs to India, and violence occurred. Sadly, troubles at the start of the two new, independent nations continue to this day.

SOURCE B *Gandhi standing in front of 10 Downing Street with British Prime Minister Ramsay MacDonald, 1931*

Extension

Mohandas Gandhi (1869–1948) was a famous leader who used non-violence as a means to make a difference. Conduct research into his life and write a short 'Key Biography' of his achievements.

10.1B How did the British lose their empire?

The Suez Crisis

After Indian independence, the next blow to Britain's empire was the Suez Crisis. In 1956, Egypt's President Nasser took control of the British and French-owned Suez Canal. The canal was valuable to Britain as a gateway to the Middle East. When talks failed, British and French troops landed in the canal zone and Israel, an ally of the two countries, attacked Egypt overland. The whole world was shocked, and both the USA and the United Nations condemned the invasion. The troops were forced to withdraw and Britain's Prime Minister resigned in humiliation.

The impact of the crisis was clear — Britain could no longer go to war to preserve their interests if the rest of the world disapproved. As a result, the British decided to allow independence in colonies they felt were stable and prosperous enough. They hoped that by freely granting independence, they were more likely to have a successful relationship with the newly formed countries.

Case study: independence along the African Gold Coast

Europeans had been trading both gold and slaves along the west coast of Africa since the 1500s. Because of its gold mines, the area became known as the Gold Coast. In 1874, the British officially took control of the Gold Coast during the 'scramble for Africa'.

In the 1920s, an independence campaign began in West Africa. A number of educated West Africans created the **National Congress of British West Africa** and asked the British government for more control of their own affairs, but the request was rejected. By the 1940s, there were large independence movements in several African nations including Nigeria, Gold Coast, Sierra Leone and Gambia.

After the Second World War, the British were not against the idea of independence for West African countries, but they wanted any new countries in the region to be stable and democratic.

The key independence leader in the Gold Coast, Dr Kwame Nkrumah, felt his country was ready. Indeed, it was one of the most stable and prosperous countries in the region. Nkrumah campaigned hard for the British to leave and was thrown in jail several times. In the 1951 Gold Coast elections, Nkrumah won, even though he was still in jail. He was let out of prison and allowed to become Prime Minister — but the Gold Coast remained part of the British Empire. In 1956, he was re-elected, and the British took this as a sign that they should leave. The Gold Coast became the independent state of Ghana in March 1957.

Key Biography

Kwame Nkrumah (1909–72)

- Spent time studying at universities in both the USA and Britain.
- Returned to the Gold Coast to begin his political career in 1946.
- Wrote his first book on independence in Africa in 1947, called *Towards Colonial Freedom*.
- Had a troubled time as Ghana's leader. Ghana became a republic in 1960, and Nkrumah was elected President. There were fierce rivalries between him and other political leaders and there was an attempted assassination in 1962.
- He dealt harshly with groups that opposed his rule. The economy declined in the early 1960s and the army and the police seized control in 1966. Nkrumah fled to nearby Guinea and later Romania.

SOURCE C *Kwame Nkrumah visiting Balmoral Castle in Scotland in August 1959, pictured with Queen Elizabeth and Princess Anne*

Case study: independence in Kenya

In Kenya, a number of groups formed to fight for self-rule in the 1940s. One group, the **Kenya African Union** (KAU) and its leader Jomo Kenyatta, campaigned for both independence and access to white-owned land. Another group, known as the Mau Mau, favoured violence against the white settlers who controlled large areas of land. In the 1950s, the British fought the Mau Mau with their own violent campaign and hundreds were killed. Many Kenyan independence leaders (including those with no connection to the Mau Mau, such as Kenyatta) were arrested and jailed. Many white settlers later chose to leave Kenya.

The **Mau Mau Rebellion**, as it was known, lasted for over eight years and eventually persuaded the British that reforms were necessary. On 12 December 1963, Kenya gained its independence from Britain and Kenyatta, who had been released from prison in 1961, became Prime Minister.

Key Words
National Congress of British West Africa
Kenya African Union   Mau Mau Rebellion

Key Biography

Jomo Kenyatta (1891–1978)
- After working as an apprentice carpenter, became involved in the Kenyan independence movement.
- In 1947, was elected President of the Kenya African Union (KAU) and campaigned for independence.
- Was accused of being a member of the Mau Mau and imprisoned from 1953 to 1961.
- Became Kenya's Prime Minister (1963) and later President (1964). He dealt harshly with groups that opposed his rule – and eventually banned opposition parties.

▶ **SOURCE D** *Jomo Kenyatta celebrating Kenya's independence from Britain in 1963*

Work
1. a Describe the Suez Crisis
   b What was the impact of the Suez Crisis on Britain and its empire?
2. Look again at the Gold Coast and Kenya case studies. Make a list of similarities and difference between the ways these nations gained independence.

Practice Question

Were the two world wars the main factors in causing Britain to lose much of its empire in the twentieth century?

16 marks
SPaG: 4 marks

Study Tip

Plan your answer to have at least two paragraphs. One should be on the world wars and a second on another important factor.

Britain: Migration, empires and the people   253

11.1 Why did immigrants come to Britain after the Second World War?

There were two main reasons why large groups of immigrants came to Britain after 1945. Some came as refugees from war-torn Europe. Their homes and livelihoods had been destroyed so many looked for a new life and new opportunities in Britain. Other migrants came from parts of the British Empire to find work. The government encouraged migration because there was a shortage of workers, particularly in mining, building, transport, healthcare and farming. The map on these pages outlines some of the main areas where these immigrants came from in the years immediately after the war. It also details locations where people have moved from in later years.

Objectives

▶ **Explain** where the majority of immigrants to Britain after the Second World War have migrated from.

▶ **Examine** the reasons why these people migrated to Britain.

Ireland
Many generations of Irish people had come to Britain before 1945. There were further surges of Irish immigration in the 1950s and 1960s. Some came to join their families in existing communities, and others came to look for work in Britain's expanding cities, and to escape poverty and hardship in Ireland. By the 1960s, the number of people of Irish origin in Britain had risen to nearly one million. And by 2001, around six million people (ten per cent of the total British population) had Irish parents or grandparents.

West Indies
During the Second World War, thousands of West Indians moved to Britain to help with the war effort, although most returned home when the fighting ended. From 1948 to 1970, a new wave of immigrants (around half a million) from the colonies of Jamaica, Barbados, and Trinidad and Tobago were encouraged to come to Britain because of the labour shortage. Many came because of unemployment and poverty at home too.

Cyprus
Cyprus became a British colony after the First World War. Both Turkish and Greek people lived on the island. They had different cultures and languages and there was often tension and violence between the two groups. Thousands of Cypriots fled the violence (as well as poverty and hardship) to start a new life in Britain in the 1950s. The island became an independent country in 1960, but when Turkey invaded and divided the island in two in the 1970s, there was a further wave of emigration when around 70,000 Cypriots left to make their home in Britain.

Europe

By the start of the twentieth century, around 200,000 Eastern European Jews had fled persecution and settled in Britain. In the 1930s, around 60,000 German Jews came to Britain when the Nazis gained power. When fighting broke out in 1939, thousands of Poles sought safety in Britain, and when the war ended around 114,000 of them decided not to return to Poland. By 1950, around 100,000 Hungarians, Ukrainians, Yugoslavs, Estonians, Latvians and Lithuanians who had fled from Russian rule had also settled in Britain.

Far East Asia

People from the Far East began to move to Britain during the 1950s and 1960s. Most came from the poorest areas of the British colony of Hong Kong, but others came from British-controlled Malaysia and Singapore. By 1961, there were around 30,000 people from the Far East living in Britain. In 1997, Hong Kong stopped being a British colony and became part of China. Around 50,000 people from Hong Kong were given British passports at this time. Today there are around 400,000 British Chinese people.

South East Asia

When India gained independence from Britain in 1947, it split into different countries: India and Pakistan. This partition led to fighting, as whole populations moved across the dividing lines. Some came to Britain to escape this violence. By 1955, around 10,000 people had moved to Britain, hoping to find work and better education opportunities. Many started their own businesses or worked in industries like textiles or steel making. Today around four million people of South Asian descent live in Britain.

Extension

People don't just move *into* Britain. British people also move abroad. Research the most popular destinations for British people moving abroad today.

West Africa

The countries of British West Africa (now Nigeria, Gambia, Sierra Leone and Ghana) made a huge contribution in the Second World War. They provided soldiers, raw materials and air bases. After 1948, many West Africans went to Britain to find employment and to get a better standard of education than was available in their own countries.

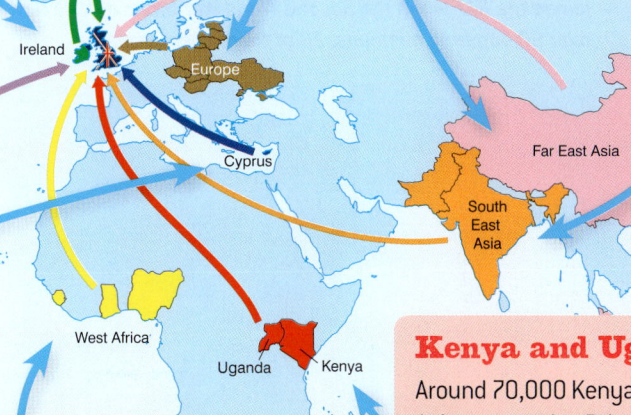

Kenya and Uganda

Around 70,000 Kenyan and Ugandan Asians moved to Britain from their homes in Africa in the 1960s and 1970s. They had originally moved to Africa from India and Pakistan, when these nations were part of the British Empire, to build railways and roads. Most stayed, and made strong communities. By the twentieth century, they played a vital part in the economies there, as shopkeepers and professionals. But when Kenya and Uganda became independent from Britain, the new governments decided to drive them out, so many came to Britain to escape racist attitudes and intolerance. In Uganda, President Idi Amin told Ugandan Asians to leave the country, after he claimed he'd had a dream in which God told him to expel them! Jomo Kenyatta, the Kenyan leader, introduced a law that banned Kenyan Asians from trading in certain areas. Around 44,000 Asians from Kenya and 26,000 from Uganda came to Britain at this time.

Work

1. Make a list of all the reasons why different groups have moved to Britain. You might want to divide your list into 'push' and 'pull' factors: push factors are reasons why people are driven away from their own countries, and pull factors are reasons why people are attracted to life in Britain.

2. In groups or in pairs, discuss what you think were the most common reasons why people came to Britain.

3. Can you make a link between immigration to Britain and the British Empire? Explain your answer.

Britain: Migration, empires and the people   255

11.2A Empire Windrush and the Caribbean migrants

On 22 June 1948, a ship named *Empire Windrush* arrived at the London docks. The ship was returning to London from Australia and had stopped off in Kingston, Jamaica, to pick up British soldiers who were there on leave. But it wasn't just soldiers who got on the ship in Jamaica: 492 other people did too, most of them young men, who were travelling to Britain to start a new life. This was an event that would change the face of British society forever. Why did these newcomers move to Britain in the first place? How were they, and others who followed in later years, treated?

Objectives

- **Define** the 'Commonwealth' and consider why Commonwealth migrants from the West Indies decided to move to Britain.
- **Discover** what life was like for the 'Windrush generation' when they arrived in Britain.
- **Assess** the impact of the Windrush generation, including the role of Claudia Jones.

SOURCE A *The* Empire Windrush *at Tilbury docks, London; the first black immigrants to arrive in Britain from the West Indies after the Second World War became known as the 'Windrush generation'*

At the time of the Second World War, many islands in the Caribbean Sea (known as the West Indies) were part of the British Empire, including Jamaica, Barbados, and Trinidad and Tobago. These islands had supplied over 10,000 men for Britain's army, navy and air force, and they had been proud of their role in helping Britain. However, soon after the fighting ended and they returned home, they found they had little to celebrate. Life was very hard in the Caribbean in the 1940s. Jamaica had been devastated by a hurricane in 1944, and poverty and hardship were common. The Caribbean had not yet developed a tourist industry to provide jobs, and the price of sugar — the Caribbean's main export and source of income — was at an all-time low. To ambitious men seeking better opportunities and wanting to see the country they had been fighting for, it was clear that their future lay abroad in Britain, the 'mother country'.

SOURCE B *Ulric Cross was one of 250 Trinidadians who joined the RAF when the Second World War broke out; he flew over 80 bombing missions, 20 of them over Germany*

The Commonwealth

In 1948, the British parliament passed the British Nationality Act. This meant that all people who lived within the British Empire — now commonly referred to as the **Commonwealth** — were British passport holders and therefore entitled to live and work in Britain. Many West Indians saw this as a great opportunity. Having

256   Chapter 11   The legacy of the British Empire

been brought up speaking English, named after British heroes, and educated to believe in 'king and country', many West Indians felt very 'British'. And at the time, Britain was short of workers, for example in transport, healthcare and building.

Fact

Nearly all former colonies of the British Empire now belong to an organisation called 'The Commonwealth of Nations'. It promotes democracy, human rights, good government, fair laws and world peace in the nations that were formerly controlled by Britain. There are currently 54 member countries (containing 1.7 billion people – 30 per cent of the world's population), each with close cultural, trade and sporting links to Britain.

▼ **SOURCE C** *Adapted from an article in* The Guardian *newspaper, 23 June 1948:*

> What manner of men are these the *Empire Windrush* has brought to Britain? This morning, on the decks, I spoke with the following: an apprentice accountant, a farm worker, a tailor, a boxer, a mechanic, a singer, and a law student. Or thus they described themselves.
>
> And what had made them leave Jamaica? In most cases, lack of work. Most of the married men have left their wives and children at home, and hope to send for them later.
>
> They are, then, as mixed a collection of humanity as one might find. Some will be good workers, some bad. No doubt the singers will find audiences somewhere. Not all intend to settle in Britain; a 40-year-old tailor, for example, hopes to stay here for a year, and then go on and make his home in Africa.
>
> But the more world-wise among them are conscious of the deeper problem posed. In the past Britain has welcomed displaced persons who cannot go home. 'This is right,' said one of the immigrants. 'Surely then, there is nothing against our coming, for we are British subjects. If there is – is it because we are coloured?'

Key Word

Commonwealth

▼ **SOURCE D** *Prize-winning student nurses at the Dreadnought Seaman's Hospital in 1954: C. S. Ramsay of Jamaica (left), C. Bishop of England (centre) and J. E. Samuel of Trinidad (right)*

Work

1. a List reasons why many people wanted to leave the Caribbean at the end of the Second World War.
   b List reasons why people from the Caribbean may have chosen to come to Britain.
2. What was the British Nationality Act?
3. a What was the *Empire Windrush*?
   b Find at least two reasons contained in **Source C** that explain why some of the passengers on the ship came to Britain.

Practice Question

How useful is **Source C** to a historian studying the reaction in Britain to Caribbean migrants?

8 marks

Study Tip

What do you think is the attitude of the journalist to the migrants?

Britain: Migration, empires and the people 257

11.2B Empire Windrush and the Caribbean migrants

Impact of *Empire Windrush*

The voyage of the *Empire Windrush* made headlines before the ship had even arrived. Thousands of immigrants from Europe had been coming to Britain ever since the Second World War finished, but it was the arrival of this ship of English-speaking, Christian, British citizens that made the headlines. Newspapers were full of stories of the 'colour problem' that was heading towards Britain, and some politicians demanded that the ship should be turned around and sent back. When the ship finally docked, the smartly dressed West Indians smiled nervously at the journalists, and one of them sang a song called 'London's the Place for Me'. Soon, most had found jobs – and their friends and relatives followed in search of work.

SOURCE E *Some of the men from the* Empire Windrush, *dressed in their best suits, photographed on arrival in London on 22 June 1948; pictures like these have come to symbolise the beginning of Britain's modern multicultural society*

The British experience

Not all white Britons welcomed Britain's newest citizens. Many West Indians found that their skin colour provoked hostile reactions. Some immigrants found good jobs, but many – whatever their qualifications – ended up working in low-paid jobs as cleaners, ticket collectors and hospital porters. They also experienced difficulties finding decent places to live. Often, they would be faced with openly racists words on house rental signs specifying 'No Irish, No Blacks, No dogs'. These racist attitudes that prevented black and other minority ethnic groups from renting houses and getting jobs became known as the '**colour bar**'.

SOURCE F *Jamaican men in a street in Brixton, south London in the 1950s; the graffiti on the wall stands for 'Keep Britain White'*

SOURCE G *Sam King, one of the passengers on the* Empire Windrush, *had fought in the RAF during the Second World War and later became the Mayor of Southwark, London. His family sold three cows to buy his ticket for the ship, which cost £28.10s at the time (around £600 today). King said:*

> The second day in Britain I was offered five jobs. If someone wants to leave, let them leave, but I have been here during the war fighting Nazi Germany and I came back and helped build Britain. People said that we would not stay longer than one year; we are here, and I and my people are here to stay.

SOURCE H *John Richards, one of the passengers on the* Empire Windrush *said:*

> I knew a lot about Britain from schooldays, but it was a different picture when you came face to face with the facts. They tell you it is the 'mother country', you're all welcome, you're all British. When you come here you realise you're a foreigner and that's all there is to it.

In the 1940s, Caribbean arrivals in Britain numbered around 500 to 700 each year. By 1953, the figure had increased to around 2200 per year. By 1960, there were around 40,000 West Indian immigrants arriving each year. This outnumbered all other immigrants from other areas of the world. The newcomers settled in industrial areas such as Liverpool, Manchester, Birmingham and Nottingham. Most, however, stayed in London.

On occasions there were outbreaks of violence in areas where large numbers of West Indians lived. In 1958, in Nottingham and in Notting Hill, London, there were several weeks of violence when white youths attacked black youths on the streets, at nightclubs, and in their homes. In fact, the Notting Hill Carnival (which now attracts over one million visitors each year) began as a gesture of defiance by the black community against the widespread racial attacks of the time. In 1962, the government made an attempt to slow down the number of black and Asian people entering Britain by passing an Immigration Act. This said that any black or Asian person wanting to enter the country must have a skilled job already lined up – and a limit was put on the number of immigrants allowed in. However, no limits were put on Irish immigrants or any other white minority ethnic groups, such as Australians. In 1968, when the government feared a large influx of Kenyan Asians into Britain, the Commonwealth Immigration Act was created. This said that Kenyan Asians with British passports were no longer allowed to enter the country – but white Kenyans with British passports were! These policies divided the country. They were welcomed by those who were not happy with the large number of immigrants coming into the country, while others felt that that the laws were racist. Yet despite the discrimination, the racial tension and other obstacles, thousands of West Indians decided to make Britain their home.

Key Words

colour bar   asylum

Work

1. Why might people from the Caribbean believe they had a right to move to Britain?
2. Use all the information and sources on pages 256–259 to answer the following question: Who were the 'Windrush generation' and what was life like for them in 1940s and 1950s Britain?
3. The West Indians on the *Empire Windrush* moved to a completely new country, with a different climate and culture. How might they have felt about moving and what do you think they would like or dislike about their new home? Discuss with a partner your own experiences of moving to a new house, or starting a new school. Do you think our experiences help us to understand the experiences of the *Empire Windrush* immigrants?

Key Biography

Claudia Jones (1915–64)

- Born in Trinidad, moved to New York aged nine.
- Worked on a variety of newspapers and magazines; made speeches about the importance of democracy, equal rights for African Americans, and safe working conditions.
- Was considered an extreme radical in America because of her views on civil and human rights issues; was deported from the USA and gained **asylum** in Britain in 1955.
- In 1958, became founder and editor of the first black British weekly newspaper, *The West Indian Gazette*.
- Following the Notting Hill and Nottingham riots in 1958, she helped launch an annual 'Mardi Gras' event in 1959, aimed at showing the culture of the Caribbean to the people of Britain. She said she wanted to 'wash the taste of Notting Hill and Nottingham out of our mouths'. This later became the Notting Hill Carnival, one of the largest street festivals in the world.

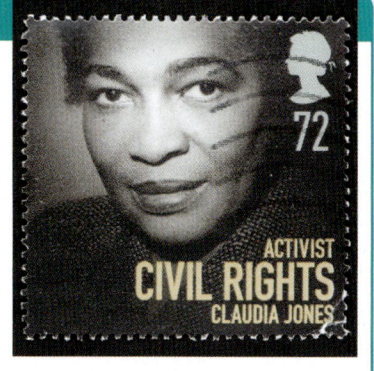

Extension

Carry out your own research on Claudia Jones. Spend some time finding out about her early life, focussing on the things that might have influenced her in her younger years. Then think about this question: What is the significance of Claudia Jones on the legacy of the British Empire?

11.3 What was the significance of the Falklands War?

Over the last hundred years, the British Empire has gradually got smaller as more countries have begun to rule themselves. However, several small colonies dotted around the world did not leave and remain part of the British Empire. One of these colonies is a group of islands in the southern Atlantic Ocean, off the east coast of Argentina, called the Falkland Islands. In 1982, Britain fought a war to defend these islands when Argentina invaded. Why did the war happen, and what were the key events? What impact did the war have on Britain and its position on the world stage?

Objectives
- **Outline** the causes of the Falklands War.
- **Examine** the key events of the war.
- **Evaluate** the impact of the war.

The Falklands are located about 300 miles off the coast of Argentina. They are a collection of over 700 islands, but most people live on the two main islands, East and West Falkland. Britain first claimed the islands in 1765, but the Spanish later took them over and named them the Islas Malvinas. When Spanish rule ended in 1806, the islands were claimed by Argentina. Up to this point, the islands were uninhabited. Britain seized the islands from Argentina in 1833, and British settlers began to live there. As a result, the majority of the population of around 2000 are of British descent. From the time that Britain took control of the islands there has been a long, heated argument between Argentina and Britain over who should control them.

What caused the Falklands War in 1982?

In the early 1980s, Argentina was controlled by the army and its leader, General Galtieri. Argentina's economy was having severe problems at this time – unemployment was high, banks were failing and prices were rising quickly. Galtieri hoped that a quick, successful war that ended with the return of the Falklands to Argentina would take peoples' minds off their problems and restore their belief in him.

On 2 April 1982, Argentine troops invaded the islands. About 12,000 soldiers arrived, and they quickly took control. Most South American countries (except Colombia and Chile) supported Argentina's invasion and its claim to the islands. However, most of Argentina's troops were new recruits who were poorly trained.

Britain's Prime Minister, Margaret Thatcher, responded quickly and defiantly to the invasion. She said, 'We have to recover those islands. We have to recover them for the people on them are British and British stock and they still owe allegiance to the Crown and want to be British.' She received near universal support from politicians and the British public, and plans to re-take the Falklands were up and running very soon.

Britain sent a **task force** of over 100 ships and around 28,000 troops to the islands, and declared a 320-kilometre **exclusion zone** around them. This meant that the British would, without any warning, open fire on any ship or aircraft from any country entering the zone. Britain and Argentina were now at war, which ended on 14 June when the Argentines surrendered. In total, about 750 Argentines and 255 British troops were killed during the war.

▼ **SOURCE A** *British soldiers flying the British flag at Port Howard, West Falkland, June 1982; at the same time another flag was flown at Port Stanley, signifying the end of the war*

SOURCE B *The route of the British task force and the exclusion zone.* HMS *Sheffield was a British ship, and the* General Belgrano *was an Argentinian ship. As well as the Falklands, Argentina also attacked the British-controlled islands of South Georgia and the South Sandwich Islands.*

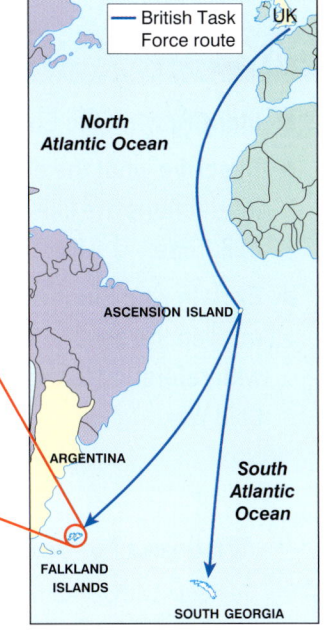

Key Words

task force
exclusion zone

resign, paving the way for a new, democratic government.

However, the war did not end the dispute between the two countries. Argentina continues to claim the islands, but Britain maintains that this is not open to negotiation. To this day, the Argentinians always refer to the islands as Islas Malvinas. Around 1000 British troops are posted there and are involved in patrolling the islands, as well as road building and monitoring the huge quantity of explosive mines that were planted there by Argentine forces during the conflict.

The impact of the Falklands War

The war cost Britain the lives of 255 men, six ships (ten others were damaged), 34 aircraft and over £2.5 billion. Politically, the war was a huge boost to the popularity of the British Prime Minister, Margaret Thatcher, and the war played a role in her re-election in 1983. The relationship between Britain and the USA became stronger during the conflict too, with US President Ronald Reagan even offering to loan Britain a US warship if a British aircraft carrier was sunk. This 'special relationship' between Britain and the USA has remained in place ever since.

There was also a boost in patriotic feeling among British citizens, who were proud of their country's defence of one of its last colonies. Foreign politicians reported that there was an increase in international respect for Britain, a country that was regarded as a fading power after the failure of the 1956 Suez campaign and the loss of its colonies. Still today, the victory is looked upon with pride by many who remember the war, or even fought in it. In 2012, a commemorative service was held to mark the thirtieth anniversary of the start of war. The British Prime Minister, David Cameron, said, 'We are rightly proud of the role Britain played in righting a profound wrong. And the people of the Falkland Islands can be justly proud of the prosperous and secure future they have built for their islands since 1982.' The war even had a positive effect in Argentina. After the country's humiliating loss, President Galtieri was forced to

Work

1. Why did Argentina invade the Falklands? Try to think about both long-term and short-term reasons in your answer.
2. Look at **Source A**. Why do you think this image appeared in newspapers across the country – and the world – shortly after Britain's victory?
3. In your own words, explain the impact of the war on: Margaret Thatcher; Britain's relationship with the USA; Britain's status in the world; Argentina.

Practice Question

Compare Britain's reaction to the invasion of the Falklands with the seizure of the Suez Canal. In what ways were they different? **8 marks**

Study Tip

Read pages 252–253 to recall what happened with the Suez Canal crisis. You could consider in your response how the outcome of each event was different.

Britain: Migration, empires and the people

12.1 What is Britain's relationship with Europe?

During the first half of the twentieth century, Western Europe was devastated by the two world wars. During the second half of the century, Europe witnessed increased stability and wealth, and closer cooperation than ever before. Why did Europe become largely peaceful? What are the advantages and disadvantages of European unity and cooperation for Britain?

Objectives

- **Identify** what the European Union is.
- **Describe** what the economic, social and cultural interactions are like between Britain and the rest of Europe.
- **Explain** why European countries have cooperated more in the second half of the twentieth century, with reference to the Second World War and the Cold War.

After the horrors of the Second World War, when European neighbours were enemies, European leaders saw that things had to change. They were determined to avoid another large-scale war, and felt that future peace was far more likely if differences in language, culture and history were put aside, and countries worked together. Rather than compete as rivals, they would join forces where possible to develop Europe peacefully. Also, it was thought that a strong, unified Europe might become a powerful trading group and a competitor for the increasingly powerful and influential USA.

The early years

To begin with, Britain didn't join either the **European Coal and Steel Community (ECSC)** or the **European Economic Community (EEC)**. At this time Britain had strong ties with countries that were still part of the British Empire, and also with those that had gained independence. Britain was also closely linked with the USA. However, in the early 1960s, things began to change. Many more countries began to gain their independence from Britain and it was clear that the EEC was becoming an economic success. Britain's first

Timeline

1951	1957	1968	1973	1975	1993	2016
Six countries (France, West Germany, Italy, Belgium, the Netherlands, and Luxembourg) join their steel and coal industries together; forming the ECSC. These countries also agree never to build up armed forces on their own, and without the others knowing	The ECSC group is renamed the EEC. Member countries further agree to cooperate with each other in producing nuclear power	The EEC begins to trade with other countries as a single group, to form the biggest trading organisation in the world	Britain, Denmark and Ireland are admitted into the EEC	A UK **referendum** is held to decide whether Britain should remain part of the EEC. The result is two to one in favour of staying in	The EEC becomes the European Union (EU)	A UK referendum is held again to decide whether Britain should remain part of the EU

Chapter 12 Britain's relationship with Europe

few applications to join the EEC were blocked by France, as they were suspicious of Britain's relationship with the USA, and of its trade links with Commonwealth countries.

The impact of the Cold War

At the same time, the USA and the USSR became the world's superpowers after the world wars. They became rivals and each tried to prevent the other from gaining too much power. This period of tension was known as the Cold War. Other countries also supported the rivalry: for example, the USA built a very close relationship with Britain, while the USSR forged very strong links with countries in Eastern Europe such as Hungary and Poland.

In the meantime, Britain was finally admitted into the EEC in 1973; Denmark and Ireland joined on the same day. And in 1979, the European parliament was created and **MEPs** (Members of the European Parliament) were elected by EEC citizens. At first, the European parliament could just advise, but now it can pass laws that apply to all member countries. In the 1980s, three more countries joined the EEC, and a **single market** was created. This meant that goods, services and people could move freely between all 12 EEC countries.

In the early 1990s, the Maastricht Treaty was signed, and the EEC became the **European Union (EU)**. All countries agreed to extend cooperation even further to include foreign affairs. Another three countries became members, and the EU agreed to accept more members in the future.

The early 1990s also marked the end of the Cold War, when the USSR's influence and control over many countries in Eastern Europe stopped. Many of these newly independent nations wanted to become EU members, and in 2004, eight of them joined. Two more joined in 2007, and Croatia joined in 2013, bringing the total number of EU member countries to 28.

In 1999, 12 member countries adopted the Euro as their currency. Soon, around 300 million Europeans were carrying the same coins and notes in their pockets. However, Britain refused to adopt the Euro, which is now used in 19 of the 28 member countries.

A divided Britain

The British public has been divided over its EU membership since it joined. In 1975, for example, 26 million people voted in a referendum, which asked whether Britain should remain part of the EEC. The result was two to one in favour of staying in. Those in favour of Britain remaining a part of the EU believe that the country benefits from the strong trade links and 'collective security' of its membership. These people are known as **pro-Europeans**. However, those against it argue that Britain is different from other European countries. They feel that Britain's unique history, traditions and culture should be preserved and not changed in any way to 'fit in' with the rest of the EU. They worry that Britain is losing its independence and identity, and should be free to make its own decisions. These people are called **Eurosceptics**.

Key Words

European Coal and Steel Community (ECSC)
European Economic Community (EEC)
referendum   MEP   single market
European Union (EU)   pro-European   Eurosceptic

▼ **A** *The evolution of the European Union, showing membership by decade*

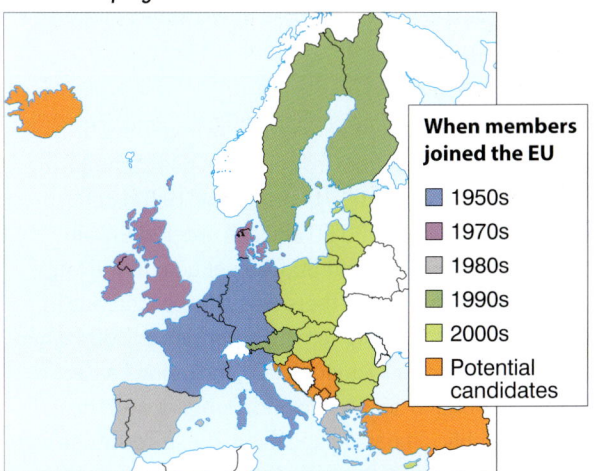

Work

1. Explain why many European countries wanted to increase cooperation between themselves in the 1950s.
2. Why did Britain decide not to join in the beginning?
3. Why do you think Britain eventually joined?
4. How did the Cold War affect the EU?
5. What different beliefs are held by pro-Europeans and Eurosceptics?

12.2 Migration in Europe

If you live in a European Union (EU) member state, you have the right to live and work in any of the other member states. EU countries cannot stop any citizen from another EU country from living and working there. This means that, every year, numerous Europeans move between European countries. Europe is also a popular destination for people who do not live in the EU: with non-EU citizens, individual countries can decide how many they will admit. How many people leave Britain to go and live and work in other places? How have the people of Britain and Europe responded to migration in recent years?

Objectives

- **Define** the different policies relating to EU and non-EU migration.
- **Examine** statistics relating to EU and non-EU migration into Britain.
- **Assess** how migration has affected Britain and Europe.

Migration within the EU

Fact

Around 11 million EU citizens currently live and work in another EU country.

Around 3.4 million EU citizens move to another EU country every year.

There is a huge amount of migration within the EU. In Britain, immigration from EU countries has steadily increased over the last 50 years. In the 1970s, for example, around 20,000 EU citizens entered Britain every year, rising to about 60,000 per year in the late 1990s and early 2000s. There was a huge increase in immigration into Britain from EU countries in 2004 when eight more countries joined the EU, including Eastern European nations such as Poland, Hungary and the Czech Republic. Generally speaking, these countries were poorer than many of the existing EU countries, so the wealthier countries such as Britain, Germany and France attracted people from the new EU member countries. As a result, between 2004 and 2006, around 600,000 Eastern European immigrants came to Britain. Many found jobs in the construction and retail industries, earning five times as much as they did in their home countries.

What are the impacts of migration?

When the EU was expanded in 2004, the largest group of new EU migrants into Britain were from Poland. Using Poland as an example, table A outlines the impacts of this migration on both Britain and Poland.

▼ **A** The impacts of Polish immigration to Britain on both Britain and Poland

Impacts on Britain (the host country)	Impacts on Poland (the source country)
Many immigrants are young, hard working and motivated.	Money sent back to Poland (almost £4 billion in 2005/6) helps the Polish economy.
Many fill shortage jobs in farm work, building and healthcare.	There are fewer unemployed people in Poland.
Local services such as schools and housing can sometimes be strained in some communities.	There are fewer skilled workers in Poland (such as dentists and plumbers).
Local and national economy benefits because of the immigrants renting houses, buying goods and services, and paying taxes.	Poland's population is ageing because so many younger workers are leaving. This also means the Polish government does not receive tax from these people.

Migration from outside the EU

After the Second World War, immigration was encouraged by the British government. Immigrants came mainly from current or former countries of the British Empire. Britain tightened immigration controls in the 1970s, but many thousands of non-EU migrants still come to Britain.

Britain operates a points-based system for non-EU immigrants. Applicants are awarded points depending on their skills, education, income and age. If an applicant reaches a certain total of points, then they are given a **visa** to allow them entry into Britain for work, especially if there is a shortage of labour in that sector. Britain also gives permission for thousands of non-EU citizens to come into the country to study at colleges and universities. Some of the most common non-EU countries where immigrants come into Britain from are India, Pakistan, the Philippines, Australia, China, the USA and Bangladesh.

What is net migration?

There are roughly the same amounts of EU citizens moving into Britain as there are non-EU citizens, but people also leave Britain too. People emigrate for all sorts of reasons – including a better job, a better climate or more opportunities.

Net migration is the final change in population after all the people leaving Britain (emigrating) and all the people moving into Britain (immigrating) have been taken into account. Graph B below shows Britain's net migration figures from 2005 to 2015. The figures clearly fluctuate a lot, but overall, net migration has remained roughly the same.

People have different opinions about the impact of migration on Britain. Some believe that immigration damages community relations, and that there is great public anxiety over issues such as pressure on public services. Others argue that most immigrants are young and able, so they work and pay more in taxes, use less of the public healthcare and education services, and help with the economic growth of the country.

▼ **B** *Immigration to and emigration from Britain, 2005–15*

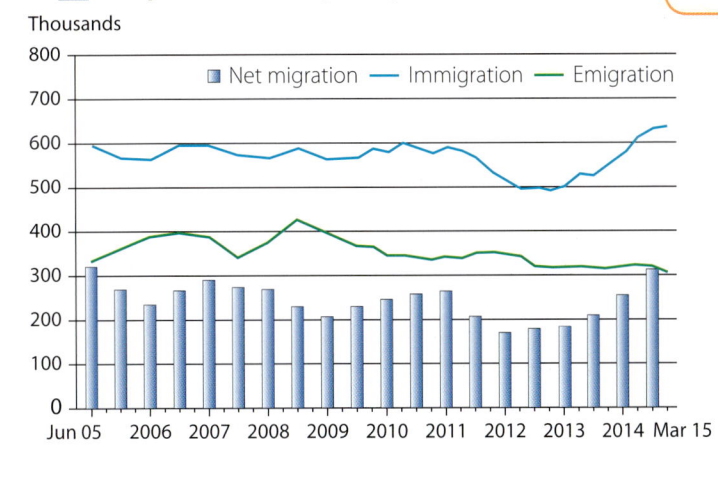

Key Words

host country   source country   visa
net migration

Fact

In recent years, there has been a growing number of refugees looking to come into the EU from war-torn countries like Afghanistan, Iraq and Syria. Many governments (including in Britain) have made it harder to gain entry into their countries, but the EU is working hard to agree on a new, long-term humanitarian approach on migration for asylum seekers.

Extension

Poland and Britain have a long tradition of friendship going back to the start of the Second World War. Research the links between Poland and Britain, and Polish communities in Britain since the Second World War.

Practice Question

Have governments been the main factor in population movements in the twentieth century?

16 marks
SPaG: 4 marks

Study Tip

In your answer consider the influence of government and other factors such as the desire for a better standard of living.

Work

1. Why did immigration to Britain increase after 2004?
2. In what ways can immigration affect: the host country; the source country?
3. In what way is it different for an EU citizen to gain entry into Britain, in contrast to a non-EU citizen?
4. Look at graph **B**. What does it show?

Britain: Migration, empires and the people

How to... analyse significance

In your exam, you will have to deal with a question about the significance of something, such as an event, an issue or a person.

Practice Question

Explain the significance of Cecil Rhodes in relation to the British Empire. **8 marks**

Study Tip

Judging the significance of a person is about looking at the impact that the person had *at the time*, how they affected people *in the long term*, and whether they are still *relevant today*.

Over to you

When we say an event, idea or person is significant, we mean more than just that it is important. Judging the significance of an event, idea or person is about looking at the impact that it had at the time and how it affected people, and whether it had long-lasting effects or caused important change. You should also consider whether the event, idea or person is still relevant to the present day. Now, work through the following questions.

1. Start by planning out your response: what do you know about Cecil Rhodes? Try to make notes about what Cecil Rhodes did *at the time*.

2. Consider Rhodes's role in the British Empire and his *impact during his lifetime*. Write about his thoughts and theories – and also his actions in relation to the British Empire.

3. After you have written about Rhodes's impact at the time, move on to consider how he might have made an impact *in the long term*.

4. Lastly, does Rhodes affect our world *today*? Is his impact still recognised, remembered or debated? Does he still cause controversy perhaps, as he did in his lifetime? Remember that the significance of an event, idea or person can change over time.

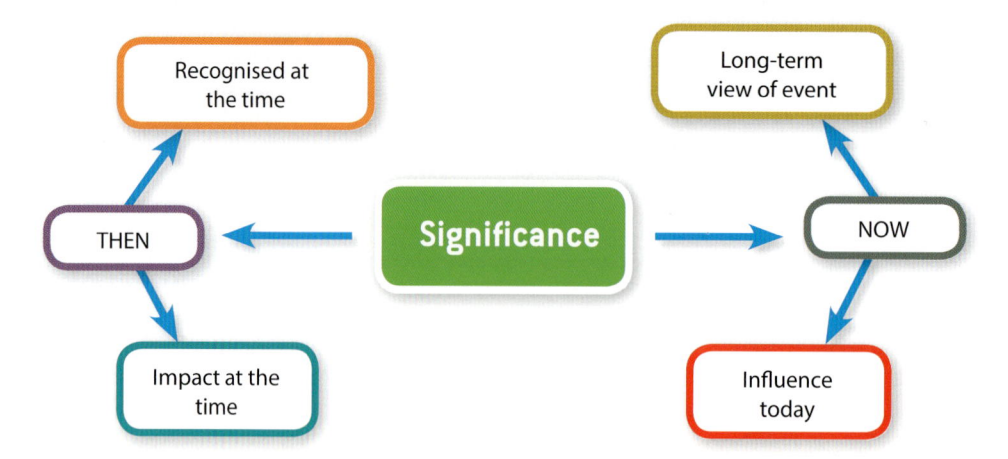

Recognised at the time

Long-term view of event

THEN ← **Significance** → NOW

Impact at the time

Influence today

5 Read the following response. Can you identify where the answer explains about Cecil Rhodes being recognised at the time, his immediate impact as well as his long-term impact, and his relevance today?

> Cecil Rhodes was significant for his achievements. He made an enormous amount of money from diamonds and later gold and his De Beers diamond company is still important today. Scholarships to university are still paid for by money from his estate. He was responsible for establishing British influence in the southern half of Africa. He established a private empire in Southern and Northern Rhodesia, countries that were named after him. However, he never achieved his imperialist ambition to link the north and south of Africa, from Cairo to the Cape. Nevertheless he was inspired as an imperialist by a belief that the English race was superior and destined to rule. He thought that it was right to use military force for this aim. Today Rhodes is significant because he is seen by many people to represent everything that was bad about the British Empire in Africa — its arrogance and greed. At the time Cecil Rhodes was significant because he made sure that Britain did well out of the 'scramble for Africa'.

6 Now try to answer the Practice Question yourself!

How to... analyse sources

In your exam, you will have to deal with a question about the usefulness of a source to a historian studying that particular part of history. You will be asked a question that directly relates to a source.

▼ **SOURCE A** A painting by Scottish artist, Thomas Faed, called *The Last of the Clan, painted in 1865. The painting focuses on people who are left behind (those too old or too young to leave) as Scots emigrate to foreign countries during the time of the Highland Clearances. The viewer's vantage point is the deck of a departing ship, looking at the last images an emigrating Scot might ever have of his homeland and his clan.*

Study Tip

Ask yourself, 'What is this source?' In this case it is a painting. The provenance (such as the date of publication, the type of source, and the title) will help you to assess the usefulness of the source. What do you know about the topic that you can link with the information from the provenance?

Study Tip

With all visual sources, try to think of three Cs:

Context: what was going on at the time the source was created?

Content: what does the source show? What is happening? What can you see?

Comment: what point is the artist trying to make about the events portrayed?

Practice Question

Study **Source A**. How useful is **Source A** to a historian studying Scottish emigration from the Highlands in the eighteenth and nineteenth centuries?

8 marks

Over to you

The usefulness of a source is what it tells you about the history of the time. A source might be useful because it reveals something new, why events turned out the way they did, or why people acted or thought in a particular way at that time. This question suggests that the source has a use: remember this as you work through the following questions.

1. Start by analysing the content of **Source A**. What is the author trying to say about the Highland Clearances? And what does it tell us about the topic that makes it useful or not? The content of the source should be checked against your own knowledge of the topic.

2. You should also consider the provenance of **Source A**:
   a. What does it tell you about how useful, or not, the source might be? Provenance could mean who produced the source, why it was produced, who it was produced for, where and when it was produced.
   b. What was the context of the time in which the source was created? Remember that to answer a question about the usefulness of a source, the provenance of a source is just as important as the content.

3. Recall the actual question: it asks about a historian studying the Highland Clearances. In **Source A**, the artist has painted a number of different things in the scene. Do you think he is trying to make you feel a particular way about the clearances? Why might this be?

4. Now try to answer the Practice Question yourself! You could use some of these sentence starters to help you compose your answer.

> The source is useful because it comes from the time of the Highland Clearances, so it shows what some people (in this case, the artist) were thinking about the clearances. The painting shows...
> The artist is trying to get the viewer of his painting to...
> I know from my own knowledge that...
> However, despite this painting being useful, it is one man's view or interpretation of the clearances so...

How to... compare similarities

In your exam, you will have to deal with a question about comparing the similarities of two things, such as two events or developments.

Practice Question

Compare Huguenot migration to Britain and Irish migration to Britain. In what ways were they similar?

Explain your answer with reference to both migrations.

8 marks

Study Tip

With compare questions, it is important to think about the *similarities* between the two topics or aspects of history you have studied, and not the *differences*.

Over to you

This style of question asks you to compare what you know about two topics or aspects of the history you have studied. You are looking for similarities between the two events: remember this as you work through the following questions.

1 Start by planning out your response: what are the similarities between Huguenot migration to Britain and Irish migration to Britain? Make a list or a mind-map to help you analyse the similarities. For example, when comparing the two events, consider:
   a causes: why did the event happen?
   b development: how did the event develop?
   c consequences: events will have results.

2 Try to organise your response in three sections, covering causes, development and consequences. Remember that you will need to show how well you have understood both events by explaining the similarities that you can find.

3 Read the following response. Can you identify where the answer explains about similarities in terms of causes, development and consequences?

> There are a number of similarities between both the Huguenot migration to Britain and Irish migration to Britain. For example, both the Huguenots and the Irish left their own countries because they felt that they could no longer lead the sorts of lives they wanted. Both groups of people were pushed out of the place where they were living. The Huguenots were pushed out because of persecution for their religion after the Edict of Nantes was withdrawn in 1685. The Irish were pushed out because of hunger caused by the potato famine and the failure of the potato crop in the mid-nineteenth century. Although many French Huguenots and the Irish both found work and a new life in North America, they are similar in that both groups came to Britain. The Irish found work in the factories of the big cities, and the Huguenots used their weaving and silk skills in the textile industry.

4 Now try to answer the Practice Question yourself!

How to... evaluate main factors

In your exam, you will have to deal with a question that asks you to evaluate factors.

Practice Question

Were the two world wars the main factors in causing Britain to lose much of its empire in the twentieth century?

Explain your answer with reference to the two world wars and other factors.

16 marks
SPaG: 4 marks

Study Tip

During your study of migration, empires and the people, you may have noticed a number of factors appearing time and time again. These factors are important because historians not only just describe events that happened in the past, they also explain why they happened. These factors are the causes that have made things happen during your thematic study. This question suggests that war might be the main factor.

Over to you

Different factors have affected your migration, empires and the people thematic study over a long period of time. Those factors are war, religion, government, economic resources, science and technology, ideas such as imperialism, social Darwinism and civilisation, and the role of individuals. Frequently, factors worked together to bring about particular developments at particular times. This question is asking about one particular factor and its influence compared with other factors: remember this as you work through the following questions.

1. Start by writing about the factor that has been named in the question: in this case, it is about the two world wars. Think carefully about these two wars and recall how they might have contributed to the decline of the British Empire in the twentieth century. The factor you are addressing might sometimes have *helped* and sometimes *hindered* the development of the British Empire – make sure you make a note of this.

2. Next, consider other factors that have influenced the break-up of the British Empire in the twentieth century. Choose two or three other factors from your study and explain, with examples, how those factors might have contributed to the decline of the British Empire.

3. Lastly, you will have to deal with the *judgement* in the question. The question picked out that war was the main factor. You have to say whether or not you agree with this. Try to weigh up or assess the factor of war against any other factors you have mentioned, and say which was more important. To back up your conclusion, you should also explain *why*, with supporting evidence.

4. Read the following essay conclusion to the question. Can you identify: the given factor (the two world wars) and two others factors? The supporting points about each factor? An assessment or judgement about which is the main factor?

> The twentieth-century world wars were a factor that exhausted Britain financially and militarily. When Britain gained its colonies, military power had been used to establish control. After 1945, when Britain's 'authority' was challenged, there was no longer any military power to back it up. And the empire was too big and Britain too poor to do anything about it. But Britain's authority was challenged by nationalist independence movements in the empire. They won the argument for world opinion and were the main factor.

5. Now try to answer the Practice Question yourself!

Practice Questions for Paper 2: Britain: Health and the people: c1000 to the present day

The examination questions on the Thematic Studies will be varied but there will be a question on a source (AO3), a question on significance (AO1 and AO2), a comparison question (AO1 and AO2), and an extended writing question using factors (AO1 and AO2). Below is a selection of these different kinds of questions for you to practise.

Answer **all four** questions. You are advised to spend 50 minutes on these four questions.

Source A A cartoon from the satirical* magazine *Punch*, 1948. It shows the Minister for Health, Aneurin Bevan, giving doctors their NHS medicine. The title of the cartoon is 'It still tastes awful'.

DOTHEBOYS HALL
"It still tastes awful."

*satirical = critical and humorous

1 Study **Source A**.

   How useful is **Source A** to a historian studying the creation of the NHS?

   Explain your answer using **Source A** and your contextual knowledge. **8 marks**

2 Explain the significance of penicillin in the development of medicine. **8 marks**

3 Compare surgery in the Middle Ages with surgery at the time of John Hunter.

   In what ways were they similar? Explain your answer with reference to both times. **8 marks**

4 Has science and technology been the main factor in understanding the causes of disease in Britain?

   Explain your answer with reference to science and technology and other factors.

   Use examples from your study of Health and the people. **16 marks**
   SPaG: 4 marks

   [All questions are taken from AQA 2016 Paper 2 specimen material.]

Practice Questions for Paper 2: Britain: Power and the people: c1170 to the present day

The examination questions on the Thematic Studies will be varied but there will be a question on a source (AO3), a question on significance (AO1 and AO2), a comparison question (AO1 and AO2), and an extended writing question using factors (AO1 and AO2). Below is a selection of these different kinds of questions for you to practise.

Answer **all four** questions. You are advised to spend 50 minutes on these four questions.

Source A   A poster printed by suffragettes in 1912. The poster was produced by a group of artists founded in 1909 with the aim 'of encouraging artists to promote the women's movement and particularly votes for women, by means of images'.

1 Study **Source A**.

   How useful is **Source A** to a historian studying votes for women?

   Explain your answer using **Source A** and your contextual knowledge.

   8 marks

2 Explain the significance of the trial and execution of Charles I for royal authority.

   8 marks

3 Compare the campaigns for workers' rights in the nineteenth century with protests for the rights of ethnic minorities in the twentieth century.

   In what ways were they similar? Explain your answer with reference to both periods.

   8 marks

4 Has war and violence been the main way in which royal authority and governments have been challenged?

   Explain your answer with reference to war and violence and other ways.

   Use examples from your study of Power and the people.

   16 marks
   SPaG: 4 marks

   [All questions are taken from AQA 2016 Paper 2 specimen material.]

Practice Questions for Paper 2: Britain: Migration, empires and the people: c790 to the present day

The examination questions on the Thematic Studies will be varied but there will be a question on a source (AO3), a question on significance (AO1 and AO2), a comparison question (AO1 and AO2), and an extended writing question using factors (AO1 and AO2). Below is a selection of these different kinds of questions for you to practise.

Answer **all four** questions. You are advised to spend 50 minutes on these four questions.

Source A A seventeenth-century drawing of Captain John Smith's encounter with native people in Virginia; Smith was a well-known early British settler who became internationally famous when Disney animated the story of Pocahontas. The drawing appeared in a book published in 1624 by Captain Smith, called *The Generall Historie of Virginia, New-England, and the Summer Isles*.

1. Study **Source A**.

   How useful is **Source A** to a historian studying the impact on the indigenous peoples of the British colonisation of North America?

   Explain your answer using **Source A** and your contextual knowledge.

   8 marks

2. Explain the significance of Cecil Rhodes for the British Empire.

   8 marks

3. Compare England's loss of European land in Medieval times with the loss of the British Empire in the twentieth century.

   In what ways were they similar? Explain your answer with reference to both periods.

   8 marks

4. Has the economic factor been the main cause of people migrating **from and within** Britain?

   Explain your answer with reference to the economic factor and other factors.

   Use examples from your study of Migration, empires and the people.

   16 marks
   SPaG: 4 marks

   [All questions, with the exception of question 1, are taken from AQA 2016 Paper 2 specimen material.]

Glossary

13 colonies thirteen British colonies in America that would eventually become the United States of America

Aboriginal inhabiting or existing in a land before the arrival of colonists

alternative medicine term used to describe any other way of treating an illness or health condition that doesn't rely on mainstream, doctor-dispensed scientific medicine, or on proven evidence gathered using the scientific method; it contains a wide range of practices and therapies

anaesthetic substance that removes pain

anatomy science of understanding the structure and internal organs of the body

Ancient World period in Western history when Greek and Roman cultures and civilisations were at the heights of their power, from around 700BC to AD500

Anglican relating to the Church of England or any of the Churches related to it in origin

anti-contagionism belief that infection was caused when infectious matter interacted with the environment and created the disease, which affected weak individuals

antibiotic medications used to cure, and in some cases prevent, bacterial infections; they are not effective against viruses such as the common cold

antiseptic chemical applied to a wound to prevent the growth of disease-causing microbes; also applied to surgical instruments

aristocratic being part of the ruling class or the nobility

aseptic state of being completely free of harmful microbes; sterilising to create a contamination-free environment

astrology study of the stars and planets

asylum protection given by a country to someone who has left their home country

autocrat ruler who holds all the power

autocratic relating to a ruler who holds all the power

bacteria microorganisms that live in water, soil, plants and animals and that can cause diseases

bacteriologist someone who studies bacteria

ballot slip of paper used to register a vote, completed in secret

barber-surgeon Medieval barber who practiced surgery and dentistry

baron man who had been given high rank by the king; the title came with land

bill proposed law presented to parliament for discussion and consideration

bloodletting Medieval medical treatment of removing some blood from a patient by opening a vein or using leeches to suck it out

Boer South African person of Dutch descent

Boston Tea Party violent demonstration in 1773 by American colonists prior to the American War of Independence

bubonic plague plague spread by the bite of a flea; buboes are lumps

burgess person who owned land or a house in a burgh; like peasants they were bound to their Lord

Caliph ruler of the Islamic Empire

catapult device used to launch stone balls or other missiles from far away

catechism fixed questions that are used for religious instruction; common in the Catholic Church

Catholic Christian who remains loyal to the Catholic Church

cauterisation using a heated iron to stop bleeding and seal a wound

cavalry soldiers on horseback

cesspit pit for the disposal of liquid waste and sewage

chain migration process by which immigrants follow family members to a new place; often, laws allow immigrants to reunite with family in the new destination

chancellor in Medieval times this was the person who wrote all the paperwork for new laws and produced other official paperwork

Chartist movement nineteenth-century campaign to gain political representation and rights for working-class people

cholera infectious and often fatal bacterial disease, usually contracted from infected water supplies and causing severe vomiting and diarrhoea

civil war war between different groups in one country

coal seam bed of coal underground

colonise send settlers to a place and establish control over it

colonist settler in or inhabitant of a colony

colony country or area under the full or partial control of another country and occupied by settlers from that country

colour bar segregation of people based on colour or race, especially any barrier to black people participating in activities

Commonwealth voluntary association of independent nations and dependent territories linked by historical ties (as parts of the former British Empire) and cooperating on matters of mutual concern, especially regarding economics and trade

communism political ideology which promotes the common ownership of industry and production with no private owners

Congress national legislative body in the USA that makes laws

constitution written document stating how a country or state is to be governed

contagionism belief that infection was caused by contact with an infected person or germ

contagious spreadable

crusade holy war fought in the Middle Ages between Christians and Muslims

crusading order military monks who fought to gain control of the land of Christ's birth from Muslim rulers

Danegeld land tax levied in Anglo-Saxon England to raise funds for protection against Danish invaders

Danelaw part of northern and eastern England occupied and controlled by Danes from the late ninth century until after the Norman Conquest

democracy system of government which gives everyone a say by allowing them to vote for people to represent them in parliament

democratic system of government where people elect their representatives; belief in social equality

depression long-term downturn in the economy that can see businesses fail and, in the extreme, people starving

diagnosis identification of a disease

diaspora group of people from a small geographical area scattered across different countries

dissection methodical cutting up of a body or plant in order to study its internal parts

divine right idea that a person (such as a king) has been appointed by God, and has the right to make any decision and not be questioned, as they are God's representative on earth

DNA (deoxyribonucleic acid) molecules that genes are made from

dominion semi-independent country that was part of the British Empire but had its own government

Edict of Nantes agreement granting Protestants civil rights in France in 1598; revoked in 1685 by Louis XIV of France

emetic substance that makes a patient vomit

emigrant people who move out of a country

empire collection of tribes, regions, territories, states or countries that are ruled over and controlled by one leader or 'mother country'; the areas controlled are usually called colonies (although sometimes dominions or dependencies); the mother country makes many of the key decisions to do with the places it rules over

enema fluid injected into the bowel to clean it

epidemic spread of a disease to a large number of people

European Coal and Steel community (ECSC) group of six countries (France, West Germany, Italy, Belgium, the Netherlands and Luxembourg) who joined together their steel and coal industries in 1951

European Economic Community (EEC) new name for the ECSC, created in 1957; the group also agreed to cooperate with each other in producing nuclear power

European Union (EU) group of European countries that participates in the world economy as one economic unit

Eurosceptic person opposed to Britain's role in the EU

exclusion zone area into which entry is forbidden, especially by ships or aircraft from particular nations

feudal system Medieval system of land holding and distribution in which the use of the land is paid for by performing services and work for the owner

forced migration when migrants move because they have no choice and are forced to

foreign competition when other countries produce the same product but at a more competitive price or more quickly

free trade trade that is not restricted by governments

freeman peasant in the feudal system who rented land from a landowner for an agreed fee; different from unfree peasants who had to provide services to the landowner in exchange for the land that they used

general strike strike where different industries engage in strike action at the same time

Germ Theory theory that bacteria (germs) cause disease

gong farmer person who cleaned out privies or cesspits in Medieval times

groat silver coin worth four English pennies

guerrilla member of a small group of soldiers who do not belong to a regular army; they usually fight as independent units and wage small-scale attacks on their enemies

guild group of skilled tradesmen who organised pay and conditions

health visitor qualified nurse or midwife with additional training and qualifications in public health; they assess the health needs of individuals, families and the wider community to promote good health and prevent illness

heretic non-believer, or believer in an opposing religion

Highland Clearances forced eviction during the eighteenth and nineteenth centuries of a large number of people from land they farmed in the Scottish Highlands

host country country that takes in immigrants

Human Genome Project international project to de-code and identify human genes

humours the theory of the four humours is based on the idea that everything was made of the four elements of fire, wind, earth and water; and that elements exist as different liquids in the body

Hundred Years War series of wars between England and France, lasting from 1337 until 1453

hunter-gather person who lives by gathering food, like nuts and berries, and kills wild animals for meat and fur

immigrant people who move into a country

imperial propaganda a government's attempts to spread a set of ideas and beliefs about empire and conquest

imperialist person who practices or supports imperialism, which is a set of ideas and beliefs about empire and conquest

indenture system labour system in which people paid for their passage to a new country by working for an employer for a fixed term of years

indentured servant servant who paid for their passage to a new country by signing a contract stating that they would work for a certain number of years for their master

Indian National Congress political organisation that led the campaign for Indian independence

Indian subcontinent large area of land that consists of India, Pakistan and Bangladesh

indigenous originating from a particular place; native

infantry soldiers who fight on foot

inherit gain something from a family member, normally parents; this can be genetic or material, for example money

inoculation using weakened but live germs of a disease in a healthy person to build up an immunity (resistance) against the stronger form of the same disease

internal migration refers to people within a country moving to another location within its borders

Jacobite Rebellions rebellions in the 1700s that aimed to help the Stuarts regain the British throne; 'Jacobus' is Latin for James, the first Stuart king of England

Jamestown early British colony established in the name of King James I

jingoism feeling or belief that a person's country is always right; jingoism means being in favour of aggressive acts against other countries

Justice of the Peace local official appointed by the king, responsible for law and order

Kenya African Union political group that campaigned for both independence for Kenya and access to white-owned land

keyhole surgery modern surgical technique in which operations are performed inside the body using cameras and instruments inserted through small incisions on the skin

knight in the Middle Ages, a man who served his feudal lord as a soldier on horseback

laissez-faire French words meaning 'leave alone'; in the nineteenth century many people felt that this was what the government should do: not interfere, not force people to change, and allow things to take their own course

Laudian something done by William Laud

lavatorium communal washing area for monks

lay people ordinary people who were not monks or priests

leech blood-sucking worm-like insect

legislation laws that have been passed by parliament

leprosy contagious disease that ate away parts of the victim's body, which would then become horribly deformed

liberal not as strict and more inclusive of different groups

Magna Carta document written in 1215 that recognised people's rights to certain basic liberties

martyr person who dies for their cause and becomes a symbol for a movement or a cause

mass religious service held by Catholics, led by a priest

Mau Mau Rebellion military conflict that took place in British Kenya, between 1952 and 1960, between groups that wanted Kenya to become an independent nation and British forces who wished Kenya to remain part of the British Empire

MEP Member of the European Parliament

merchant person who trades and sells goods

miasma name given to what people thought was an 'infectious mist' given off by rotting animals, rubbish and human waste; many believed it caused illness and disease

microbe living organism that is too tiny to be seen without a microscope; includes bacteria, which can cause diseases

migrant person who moves from one place to another

migration the movement of people from one place to another; a person who moves is known as a 'migrant'

militant aggressive and sometimes violent

Model Parliament first parliament that resembles ours today; it had representatives from the Church and the aristocracy as well as those from the counties and boroughs (commoners)

monopoly complete control of the entire supply of goods or of a service in a certain area

mould type of fungus that grows in thin threads, usually in warm, moist conditions

Muslim League political party established in the British Indian Empire; it worked for the establishment of a separate Muslim-majority nation-state, Pakistan

mutineer person who takes part in an open rebellion against authority

National Congress of British West Africa organisation that campaigned to the British government for West Africans to have more control of their own affairs

nationalise when the government takes control or owns an industry or a service

nationalistic having strong patriotic feelings, especially a belief in the superiority of one's own country over others

Native American person that is a member of any of the first groups of people living in North and South America or the Caribbean

Navigation Acts series of laws that restricted the use of foreign ships for trade between every country except Britain

navvy labourer employed in building a road or railway

net migration final change in population after all the people leaving a country (emigrating) and all the people moving into a country (immigrating) have been taken into account

New World name for the territories that Europeans first reached, from the 1400s, such as the Americas

occupy take over another country, town or castle; normally used to describe an invading force who take over a country

orator person who is considered an expert public speaker

pacifist person who is opposed to war and violence

pamphlet small booklet containing information; important during the civil war for spreading ideas and propaganda

pardon act of forgiving a crime

parliament group of people responsible for making laws

partition division of British India into separate independent countries

patron supporter or sponsor

peasant person at the bottom of the social structure in feudalism; normally an agricultural worker

penal colony place of imprisonment and punishment at a remote location

peninsula long stretch of land that is connected to the mainland but bordered by water on three sides

persecution when someone or a group of people are abused or punished, often for their beliefs

petition request to do or change something, normally presented to government; people sign one to show how much support the request has

pharmaceutical industry businesses that develop and produce drugs for use in medicine and health care

philanthropist person who donates their time and money to charitable causes

picket stand outside or near a workplace and try to persuade other workers not to enter the workplace

Pilgrim Fathers group of 102 people, led by English Puritans fleeing religious persecution, who sailed to the 'new world' of America and founded a new colony in 1620

pilgrimage journey, of devotion or of moral significance, to visit a holy place

pilloried when a person is put in a pillory – a wooden frame with spaces for the head and the hands – to be attacked or ridiculed

pious deeply religious, observing religion completely

piracy when sailors steal cargoes from other ships, or even the ships themselves

plantation large farm that specialises in growing usually just one crop

plunder to steal from a place or person, usually using force

pneumonic plague plague spread by breathing in germs from the infected lungs of a bubonic plague victim

pogrom large-scale, targeted, and repeated persecution of an ethnic or religious group, particularly Jews

poll tax tax of a certain amount that all individuals over a certain age had to pay, regardless of income

positive health focus on the prevention of illness and disease rather than the cure

Presbyterian denomination of Protestantism, popular in Scotland

privateer private sea captain given permission to raid and capture enemy ships

privy toilet located in a small shed outside a house or building

pro-European person in favour of Britain's place in the EU

progressive person who is interested in changing politics and modernising society

propaganda literature that is used to promote a point of view; normally used by the government during war

Protestant member of Christian group that protested against the Catholic Church; there are many types or denominations of Protestants, including Quakers and Puritans

providence God's intervention in the world; people who believe that something is divine providence believe that God wants something to happen

public health health of the population as a whole

purgative laxative that makes you go to the toilet

purge physical removal of something or someone; normally carried out violently or abruptly

Puritan hardline Protestant Christian who believes in simple church services and lifestyles; Puritans protested against the practices of the Catholic Church

quack person pretending to have medical ability or fake cures; unqualified, often useless, doctor

Quaker member of Protestant Christian group, also known as the Religious Society of Friends, that believes in equality between members

quarantine confining or stopping people from going in or out of a place

racial profiling when police target an individual for a crime, based purely on their race

racially prejudiced discriminating against someone because of their race

radicalism wanting complete political or religious reform

re-nationalise when the government takes over a previously nationalised industry after a period of private ownership

recession period when the economy of a country or the world is poor; this can mean an increase in unemployment

referendum vote in which all the people eligible to vote in a country or area are asked to give their opinion of or decide on an important political or social issue

Reformation the 'break with Rome' by Henry VIII in 1534, when he made England's official religion Protestantism rather than Catholicism

refugee person who has been forced to leave their country in order to escape war, persecution, or natural disaster

regent person who acts as an adviser to a monarch if they are very young; this person can hold great influence

regicide the killing of a monarch

regulate bring under the control of a law or rule

Renaissance 'rebirth' or revival of European art and literature under the influence of classical ancient Greece and Roman models in the fourteenth to sixteenth centuries

repeal remove or reverse (a law)

republic country with a system of government where an elected President has supreme power, rather than a monarch

Royal African Company monopoly (the only company allowed to invest) in slavery run from Britain in the 1600s

rural relating to the countryside, rather than a town or city

scorched earth military strategy that involves destroying anything that might be useful to the enemy while advancing through or withdrawing from an area

screening checking for the presence of a disease

scutage tax collected during wartime; normally paid by a knight instead of completing military service

second generation people who were born in the UK but whose parents were immigrants

segregation deliberate act of keeping groups or communities separate

Sepoy native Indian soldier

siege military blockade common in medieval battles; usually done to starve out an opponent

single market shared agreement that means that goods, services, money and people can move freely between EU member countries

slave triangle three-part trading journey in which traders traded goods for slaves in Africa; slaves for different goods in the Americas; and these goods for money in Britain

social Darwinism theory that society would be gradually improved as weaker individuals, races and nations were destroyed by fitter (and therefore superior) ones; the theory supported the idea of the 'survival of the fittest'

socialist person believing in the rights of the working class (socialism)

solidarity showing allegiance to a group of people you work with, are the same gender as, or the same class as; working together, not against each other

source country country where immigrants have travelled from

specificity theory that specific germs cause specific diseases

spontaneous generation theory that microbes appear as if by magic, and that germs are the result of disease

spore cell or small organism that can grow into a new organism in the correct conditions

Stamp Act act that imposed a tax on printed materials (such as legal documents, magazines, playing cards and newspapers) paid to Britain and used in the colonies of British America

Star Chamber court where people who had gone against the king were tried; run by supporters of the king

steward person who managed the king's finances and estates; in some cases worked for the king's interests in other countries

strike action stopping work until working conditions improve or demands are met

task force part of a country's armed forces that is given the job of working on a single defined task or activity

temperance moderate intake of, or complete abstinence from, alcohol

tenant person who lived on a lord's land and paid rent and taxes; normally a peasant

tenant farmer person who lives and works on land that they do not own, but rent from a landowner

Tory the Tory Party of the nineteenth century believed in a strong Britain and free trade

trade union organised association of workers or skilled tradespeople; they protect the rights of workers and the conditions they work in

trading station large warehouse at a port where goods were stored and where trading took place

transportation the sending of convicted criminals to a penal colony

trebuchet similar to a catapult; a device used to smash castles and other defences

trepanning drilling holes in the head

tyranny when all power belongs to one ruler and treatment is normally cruel and unfair

Ulster Plantations provinces or areas in the north of Ireland that were colonised by settlers from England and Scotland

urban relating to a town or city

urbanisation process by which large numbers of people move to urban areas, creating larger towns and cities

vaccination using the dead germs of a disease or one similar to it to build up an immunity (resistance) against the stronger form of the disease

vaccine substance that is injected into a person to protect against a particular disease

viceroy someone who rules a country, province or colony on behalf of a sovereign; for example, in the 1850s a viceroy was put in charge of India on behalf of Queen Victoria

Viking Scandinavian pirates and traders who raided and settled in many parts of northern Europe in the eighth to the eleventh centuries

villein similar to a peasant, person at the bottom of the social structure in feudalism; normally a farm worker

Virginia Britain's first colony, set up under time of Elizabeth I (the 'Virgin Queen'), and so named after her

virus/viral infection infection caused by microbes which can be contagious; unlike bacterial infection, most viruses do cause diseases, and antibiotics cannot cure viral infections

visa authorised document that allows a person to enter a country

voluntary migration when migrants move because they choose to leave a particular place of their own free will, rather than being forced to

voluntary repatriation returning to the country of origin and gaining citizenship for that country

welfare state system by which the government looks after the well-being of the nation, particularly those who cannot help themselves, such as the old, children, the sick and the unemployed

Whig political party that believed in the power of parliament; the Whig party was important in reforming parliament

Witan national council or parliament in Anglo-Saxon England

workhouse public institution in which the destitute of a parish received board and lodging in return for work

Index

A

Aboriginal Australians 247
acupuncture 70, 71
Aethelred, King 184–6
Africa
    European colonialism 230–9
    forced migration 140, 246
    Gold Coast 252
    Kenya 168, 253, 255, 259
    railways 246
    slave trade 140
Agincourt, Battle of 196–7
agriculture 22–3, 134, 138–9, 217, 226, 248
Al-Razi (Rhazes) 12, 13
Alfred the Great 182–3
alternative medicine 70–1
American Revolution 126–9, 212
Americas 126–9, 200, 202–13
amputation 14, 28, 42, 46
anaesthetics 14, 42–3, 75
anatomy 15, 24, 26–7, 29, 38–9
Ancient World 8, 10
'Angevin' Empire 190–3
Anglicans 206
Anglo-Saxons 180, 181, 182–5
anti-contagionists 44
Anti-Corn Law League 138–9
anti-slavery movement 140–3
antibiotics 62–5, 70
antiseptic surgery 45, 46–7
archers 196, 199
Argentina 260–1
aristocracy 98
aseptic surgery 48
Asian immigrants 167, 168, 246, 255
Aske, Robert 112, 113, 114
astrology 8
asylum 259
Attwood, Thomas 132, 134
Australia 150–1, 213, 247
autocrats 102, 129
Avicenna (Ibn Sina) 12, 13

B

bacteria 21, 44–7, 49, 50–1, 62
bacteriologists 63
Ball, John 106, 108
ballots 130
Barbados 203
barber-surgeons 8, 14, 27, 32, 39
barons 92–102, 189
    Barons' Wars 97, 101–2
Bazalgette, Joseph 60, 61
Beveridge Report 81
bills (legislation) 141
Black Death 20–3, 104

blood circulation 30–1, 39
blood transfusions 73, 74
bloodletting 8, 14, 32, 33
Boer War 76, 232, 236–9
Booth Report 76
Boston Tea Party 126, 127, 211
Bradshaw, John 122–3
Britain
    emigration 207, 248, 265
    immigration 214–15, 242–5, 254–9, 264–5
    internal migration 248–9
    legal system 227
    population 54, 61, 248–9
British Empire
    African colonies 231–9, 252–3
    American colonies 126–9, 206–13
    celebration of 240–1
    Falklands War 260–1
    independence struggles 225, 250–3
    India 221–9, 251
    loss of 166, 250–3
    migration 246–7
    opinions for/against 228–9
    Rhodes, Cecil 232–3
    Scottish migrants 217
    West Indies 202, 203, 213
Brixton riots 171
bubonic plague 20–3, 104
burgesses 100, 102
Butler, Josephine 147

C

Cabot, John 200
Caliphs 12
Canada 212
Caribbean
    colonies 202, 203, 213
    migration to Britain 166–8, 254, 256–9
catapults 96
catechism 118
Catholics 110, 117–19, 201, 206, 214, 216, 243
cauterisation 14, 28
cavalry 120, 121, 199
cesspits 16, 18
Chadwick, Edwin 56, 57, 146
Chain, Ernest 64, 65
chain migration 169, 245
chancellors 100
Charles I 116–23, 203
Charles II 32, 205
Chartism 134–7
Chauliac, Guy de 15
child mortality 37, 79
children
    employment 144–5, 152
    health 77–80

prostitution 147
Chinese immigrants 255
chloroform 43
cholera 22, 52, 55, 56–60
Church 9, 10–11, 18–19, 23, 92, 110–15
    see also Catholics; Protestants
civil war 94, 101–2, 120–2, 206
Clive, Robert 220, 221
Cnut the Great 186–7
coal industry 144, 160–3, 165
Cobden, Richard 138
Cold War 263
colonies/colonists 126
'colour bar' 258
Commonwealth (British republic) 124–5
Commonwealth migrants 166, 167, 168, 256–7
communism 162
Congress 127, 211, 212
constitution 208
contagionists 45
convicts, transportation of 129, 150–1, 246, 247
Corn Laws 138–9
cotton industry 227
Covenanters 118
Cromwell, Oliver 121, 122, 124–5, 206
Cromwell, Thomas 110, 111, 114, 115
crusades 11, 92, 192
Culpeper, Nicholas 33
Cyprus 254

D

Danegeld 185
Danelaw 182, 183
de Montfort, Simon 98–103
democracy 98, 123, 208
Denmark 186, 187
depression, economic 135
diagnosis of disease 8
diaspora 217
diet 69, 74, 77, 239
    see also famines
diphtheria 53, 75, 79
discrimination 21, 167–71, 240, 258, 259
disease
    cholera 22, 52, 55, 56–60
    colonial spread of 208
    diagnosis of 8
    diphtheria 53, 75, 79
    Germ Theory 45, 46, 48, 50, 51
    housing conditions 55, 243
    infection 15, 40, 44–51, 73, 208
    plague 20–3, 34–5, 104
    rabies 53
    smallpox 40–1
    syphilis 39

typhoid fever 49, 55
typhus 243
Disraeli, Benjamin 234, 244
dissection 13, 15, 24, 26–7, 38, 39
divine right 116
DNA (deoxyribonucleic acid) 66, 67, 68
dockers' strike 153
doctors 8–9, 11, 21, 36, 82
dominions 238
Drake, Francis 201
drugs 62–9, 75
    see also herbal medicine

E

East India Company 219–21
Edict of Nantes 214
education 227
Edward the Confessor 187, 188
Edward I 102–3
Edward III 105, 194–5
Egypt 234–5, 252
Elizabeth I 214
emetics 32
emigrants 208
Emma of Normandy 185, 187
empires 178–80
    see also 'Angevin' Empire; British Empire
employment
    19th century Britain 144–5, 152, 249
    immigrants 166, 168, 243, 244, 256–7, 258
enemas 32
English Civil War 120–2
English identity 199
English Revolution 116–19
epidemics 19, 20–3, 34–5, 44–5, 56–60
Equiano, Olaudah 141
ether 42–3
European Coal and Steel Community (ECSC) 262
European Economic Community (EEC) 262–3
European Union (EU) 263, 264
Eurosceptics 263
Evesham, Battle of 102
exclusion zone 260
exploration 200

F

factory reform 144–7
Falklands War 260–1
famines 139, 227, 229, 242
farming see agriculture
Fawcett, Millicent 154
feudal system 92, 106
First World War 72–3, 158, 160, 228, 250
Fleming, Alexander 63
Florey, Howard 64, 65
forced migration 242, 245, 246–7
foreign competition 160
Forkbeard, Sven 185, 186
France
    'Angevin' Empire 191, 192–3
    Henry III and 99
    Huguenots 214–15
    Hundred Years War 194–9
    Norman Kingdom 189
    Revolution 129
free trade 138
freemen 94
Fry, Elizabeth 147

G

Galen 11, 15, 26, 27, 30, 31
Gandhi, Mohandas 251
general strikes 135, 160–3
genetic screening 66
Germ Theory 45, 46, 48, 50, 51
germs (microbes) 21, 44–7, 49, 50–1, 62
Ghana 252
Godwinson, Harold 188
Gold Coast 252
gong farmers 16
Great Plague 34–5
Great Reform Act 132–3
'Great Stink' 60–1
groats 105
guerrilla tactics 237
guilds 148
Guy's Hospital 36

H

Harold II, King 188
Harthacnut 187
Harvey, William 30–1
Hastings, Warren 221
Hawkins, John 201
health visitors 78
Henry I 190
Henry II 190–1
Henry III 97, 98–103
Henry V 195, 196–7
Henry VIII 110–15
herbal medicine 33, 49, 70
heretics 214
Highland Clearances 216–17
Hong Kong 255
hospitals 10–11, 12, 36–7
housing 54–5, 78, 82, 167, 243
Huguenots 214–15
Human Genome Project 68
'humours' theory 8–9
Hundred Years War 105, 194–9
Hunter, John 38–9
hunter-gatherers 180

I

Ibn Sina (Avicenna) 12, 13
illness see disease
immigration see migration
imperialism 232–3, 240–1
    see also British Empire
indenture system 129, 203, 246
India 218–29
    army 228
    famines 227, 229
    independence struggle 225, 251
    industry 227
    migration to Britain 167, 255
    public health 227
    railways 227, 228
    resources 226
    Sepoy Rebellion 222–5
Indian National Congress 251
industry 227, 249
infantry 120, 121, 224, 237
infection 15, 40, 44–51, 73
inheritance 94
inoculation 40
internal migration 248–9
Ireland
    Cromwell and 125
    famine 139, 242
    Henry II and 190–1
    migration to Britain 242–3, 254
    religious conflict 118, 119
    Ulster Plantations 216
Islamic medicine 12–13, 15
Islas Malvinas (Falkland Islands) 260–1

J

Jacobite Rebellions 216
James I 116, 216
Jenner, Edward 40–1
Jews
    discrimination against 21
    migration to Britain 244–5, 255
jingoism 241
John, King 92–7, 192–3
Jones, Claudia 259
Justices of the Peace 105

K

Kenya 168, 253, 255, 259
Kenya African Union 253
Kenyan Asian immigrants 255, 259
Kenyatta, Jomo 253
keyhole surgery 68, 75
knights 92, 199
Koch, Robert 50–3, 62

L

Labour Party 77, 81, 82, 149, 163
labour shortage 166
Labourers, Statute of 23, 104–5
laissez-faire 58, 145
Langton, Stephen 92
Laudian reforms 117
lavatorium 18
lay people 19
leeches 8
legal system 227
legislation 123, 132–3
Leonardo da Vinci 24
leprosy 11
Levellers 125
Lewes, Battle of 101
Liberal Party 77, 154
life expectancy 82

Lister, Joseph 46–7
Liverpool 205, 243, 248, 249
London 34–5, 59, 60–1, 93, 152–3
Long Parliament 118–19
Louis VII 191
Louis XIV 214
Lovett, William 134, 135, 136
Luther, Martin 110

M

Magna Carta 94–7, 193
Manchester 248, 249
Maroon slaves 142
martyrs 150–1, 156
mass (church service) 92
Massachusetts 208
Matilda 190
Mau Mau Rebellion 253
medicine 6–83
    11th–15th century 8–23
    16th century 26–31
    17th century 32–5
    18th century 36–41
    19th century 42–61
    20th century 62–83
    21st century 83
    alternative medicine 33, 49, 70–1
    herbal remedies 33, 49, 70
    pain relief 42–3
    war wounds 28, 29, 38, 65
Medieval period
    medicine 8–23
    power 92–7, 98, 102–3
mental illness 12, 37, 73
MEPs (Members of European Parliament) 263
merchants 94
miasma 45, 56, 57
microbes 21, 44–7, 49, 50–1, 62
migration
    Asian immigrants 167, 255
    British Empire 246–7
    Caribbean immigrants 254, 256–9
    Chinese immigrants 255
    controls on immigration 168–9
    Cypriot immigrants 254
    emigration, British 207, 248, 265
    EU migration 264
    forced migration 242, 245, 246–7
    government policy 166–71
    Huguenot immigrants 214–15
    immigrant experience 167
    Indian immigrants 167, 255
    internal migration, British 248–9
    Irish immigrants 242–3, 254
    Jewish immigrants 244–5, 255
    Kenyan Asian immigrants 255
    net migration 265
    Pakistani immigrants 255
    Polish immigrants 255, 264
    timeline 180–1
    Ugandan Asian immigrants 255
    West African immigrants 255
militant action 153, 155, 156–7, 158
    see also radicalism
missionaries 230

Model Parliament 102–3
monasteries 18–19, 36, 110–12, 114
monks 18–19
monopolies 210, 219
Montfort, Simon de 98–103
moulds 62
Mughals 220
Muslim League 251
mutineers 224

N

Nantes, Edict of 214
Naseby, Battle of 121
National Congress of British West Africa 252
National Front 170, 171
National Health Service (NHS) 74, 82–3
nationalisation 160, 164
nationalistic 251
Native Americans 126, 208–9
Navigation Acts 210
navvies 242, 243
navy 203, 213
net migration 265
New Model Army 121
New Model Unions 149
New Unionism 149, 152–3
New World 126–9, 200, 202–13
Nkrumah, Kwame 252
Normans 185, 187, 188–9
North America 126–9, 200, 202–13
North Sea Empire 184–7
Notting Hill riots 168, 259

O

occupation of London 93
O'Connor, Feargus 135, 136–7
orators 138
Owen, Robert 146, 148, 151

P

pacifists 146, 158
pain relief 42–3
Pakistan 251, 255
pamphlets 117
Pankhurst, Emmeline 154–5, 156
Paré, Ambroise 28–9
parliament
    and Charles I 116–19, 122–3
    Medieval period 97, 98, 102–3
    reform of 132–3
    unrepresentativeness of 130
partition of India 251
Pasteur, Louis 45, 46, 48, 50, 52–3
patrons 10
peasants 22–3, 95, 104–9
Peasants' Revolt 104–9
Peel, Robert 139
penal colonies 129, 150–1, 246, 247
penicillin 62–5
peninsulas 128
persecution 206, 214, 244
Peterloo Massacre 130–1

petitions 132
pharmaceutical industry 62, 64–5
philanthropists 146
picketing 148
Pilgrim Fathers 208
pilgrimage 10, 112–13, 115
Pilgrimage of Grace 112–13, 115
pilloried 117
pious 98
piracy 201
plague 20–3, 34–5, 104
Plantagenets 191
plantations 129, 140, 202–3
Plassey, Battle of 220
plastic surgery 72, 74
pneumonic plague 20–3
pogroms 244
Poland 255, 264
police 171
poll tax 105, 109
Poor Law 134
Pope 92, 98–9, 110
population 54, 61, 248–9
positive health 70, 71
poverty 75, 76, 78, 239
Powell, Enoch 169, 170
Presbyterians 118
'Pride's Purge' 122
printing press 25
prison reform 147
prisoners, transportation of 129, 150–1, 246, 247
privateers 201
privies 16, 17, 18, 54, 55, 58
pro-Europeans 263
progressive thinkers 146
propaganda 120–1
prostitution 147
Protestants 118, 119, 125, 201, 206, 214–15, 216, 243
providence 125
Provisions of Oxford 100–1
public health
    11th–15th century 16–23
    19th century 56–61
    20th century 76–83
    21st century 83
    epidemics 20–3, 34–5, 44–5, 56–60
    India 227
    Public Health Act 58
    reforms 60–1
    welfare state 80–3
purgatives 32
purges 122
Puritans 117, 206, 208

Q

quacks 31, 32
Quakers 146, 147, 206
quarantine 21, 35, 48

R

rabies 53
Race Relations Acts 170

racial profiling **171**
racism **167–71, 240, 258, 259**
radicalism **125, 130**
    see also militant action
railways **227, 228, 246**
Raleigh, Walter **207**
re-nationalisation **160**
recession **171**
Reformation **110–15, 214**
refugees **214–15, 244**
regents **97**
regicide **122, 123**
regulation, slavery abolition **143**
Renaissance **24–9**
repeal of Corn Laws **138–9**
republics **101, 124–5, 213**
Rhazes (Al-Razi) **12, 13**
Rhodes, Cecil **232–3, 236**
Richard I **192**
Richard II **106–8**
riots **168, 171, 259**
Roanoke **202**
Rochester, Siege of **96**
Romans **180, 181**
Rowntree Report **76**
Royal African Company **205**
Royal Navy **203, 213**
Rump Parliament **122**
rural areas **248**
Russia **244**
    see also USSR

S

sanitation **16–19, 60–1**
Scarman Report **171**
school meals **69, 77**
scientific method **39**
scorched earth policy **238**
Scotland **118, 122, 216–17**
screening, genetic **66**
scutage **93, 94**
second generation immigrants **169**
Second World War **64, 65, 74–5, 250**
segregation **167**
Sepoys **222–5**
servants, indentured **129, 203**
sewer system **60–1**
Shaftesbury, Lord **144–5**
Sharp, Granville **141**
sheep farming **217**
shell shock **73**
Ship Money **117**
sieges **96**
single market **263**
slave rebellions **142**
slave trade/slavery **140–3, 203, 204–5**
slave triangle **204**
slums **55, 82, 243**
smallpox **40–1**
Snow, John **58, 60**
social Darwinism **232**
social reform **78–9, 144–7**
socialists **109, 153**
solidarity **160**
source countries, migration **264**
South Africa **232, 238**

South America **213**
Spain **201**
spontaneous generation **44, 45, 47, 49**
spores **63**
Stamp Act **211**
staphylococcus germ **62–3**
Star Chamber **117**
Statute of Labourers **23, 104–5**
Stephen, King **190**
stewards **98**
Strafford, Earl of **118**
strike action **135, 149, 152–3, 160–5**
Stuart period **200–9, 216**
Sudan **235**
Suez Canal **234–5**
Suez Crisis **252**
suffrage movement, women's **154–9**
Suffragists **154**
surgery
    11th–15th century **14–15**
    16th century **28–9**
    18th century **38–9**
    20th century **66–8, 72–5**
    anaesthetics **42–3**
    antiseptic method **45, 46–7**
    aseptic method **48**
    technology **68, 72–5**
'sus law' **171**
Sydenham, Thomas **33**
syphilis **39**

T

task force **260**
taxation **93, 94, 105, 109, 117, 126, 194, 211**
technology, medicine **68, 72–5**
temperance **136**
tenant farmers **139**
tenants **100**
Thatcher, Margaret **165, 260, 261**
Theodoric of Lucca **15**
tobacco **203, 207**
toilets (privies) **16, 17, 18, 54, 55, 58**
Tolpuddle Martyrs **150–1**
Tories **132**
towns, public health **16–17, 54–5, 58**
trade
    Americas **202–3**
    India **218–19, 226, 228**
    see also slave trade/slavery
trade unions **136, 148–53, 160–5**
Trades Union Congress (TUC) **160–3**
trading stations **219**
transplant surgery **75**
transportation of convicts **129, 150–1, 246, 247**
trebuchets **96**
trepanning **14**
tuberculosis (TB) **52, 55**
Tudor period **200–2, 204–5**
Tyler, Wat **106, 107, 108–9**
Tyndall, John **49, 51**
typhoid fever **49, 55**
typhus **243**
tyranny **116**

U

Ugandan Asian immigrants **255**
Ulster Plantations **216**
urban areas **16–17, 54–5, 58, 248**
urbanisation **248**
USA **252, 261, 263**
USSR **263**
    see also Russia

V

vaccination **40, 41**
vaccines **51, 52–3, 62, 227**
Vesalius, Andreas **26–7, 29**
viceroys **224**
Victoria, Queen **43, 222, 225, 226, 240–1**
Vikings **181–7**
villeins **95**
Virginia **207**
viruses **40, 70**
visas **265**
voluntary migration **242**
voluntary repatriation **169**
voting rights **61, 130–7, 154–9**

W

Wales **135**
war wounds **28, 29, 38, 65**
Washington, George **127, 128**
water supply **16, 18, 58–9**
welfare state **80–3**
Wessex **182**
West Africa **252, 255**
West Indies *see* Caribbean
wheat prices **138–9**
Whigs **132**
Wilberforce, William **141, 142, 143**
William the Conqueror **188–9, 190**
Wilson, Harold **159**
Witan **188**
women
    anti-slavery movement **142**
    rights movement **159**
    suffrage movement **154–9**
Women's Freedom League (WFL) **155, 158**
Women's Social and Political Union (WSPU) **154–5, 156, 158**
workhouses **80, 146**
working-class
    trade unionism **148–53, 160–5**
    voting rights **61, 132–3**

X

X-rays **73**

Y

Yorktown, Battle of **128, 212**

Acknowledgements

The publisher would like to thank the following for permission to use their photographs:

Cover: Print Collector/Getty Images; **p6tl**: Science and Society Picture Library/Getty Images; **p6tr**: Guildhall Library & Art Gallery/Heritage Images/Getty Images; **p6bl**: Iran/France: European depiction of the Persian (Iranian) doctor Al-Razi, in Gerardus Cremonensis 'Recueil des traites de medecine' 1250-1260. A surgeon (left) holds the matula, a vessel for collecting the urine /Pictures from History/ Bridgeman Images; **p6br**: Black Death at Tournai, 1349 (see also 33793), Le Muisit, Gilles (1272-1352)/ Bibliotheque Royale de Belgique, Brussels, Belgium/Bridgeman Images**p7tl**: Granger/Alamy; **p7tr**: Popperfoto/Getty Images; **p7bl**: W.Brown/Otto Herschan/Getty Images; **p7br**: Zephyr/Science Photo Library; **p8**: Iran/France: European depiction of the Persian (Iranian) doctor Al-Razi, in Gerardus Cremonensis 'Recueil des traites de medecine' 1250-1260. A surgeon (left) holds the matula, a vessel for collecting the urine/Pictures from History/ Bridgeman Images; **p9**: Ms Lat 9333 fol.96v Man Vomiting, from 'Tacuinum Sanitatis' (vellum), German School, (15th century)/Bibliotheque Nationale, Paris, France/Archives Charmet/Bridgeman Images; **p10**: A Ward in the Hotel-Dieu, Paris, from 'Science and Literature in the Middle Ages and Renaissance', written and engraved by Paul Lacroix (engraving) (b/w photo), French School, (16th century) (after) /Bibliotheque des Arts Decoratifs, Paris, France / Bridgeman Images; **p11**: World History Archive/AKG; **p13t**: Wellcome Library, London; **p13m**: World History Archive/AKG; **p13b**: Page from the 'Canon of Medicine' by Avicenna (Ibn Sina) (980-1037) (vellum), Islamic School, (14th century) / Biblioteca Estense, Modena, Italy / Bridgeman Images; **p14**: Thaliastock/Mary Evans Picture Library; **p15**: Ms Sup Turc 693 fol.76v Excision of a ranula from under the tongue, 1466 (vellum), Charaf-ed-Din (1404-68) / Bibliotheque Nationale, Paris, France / Archives Charmet / Bridgeman Images; **p16**: Look and Learn History Picture Library; **p19**: Robert Thom/American Pharmacists Association; **p21**: St. Sebastian Interceding for the Plague Stricken, 1497-99 (oil on panel), Lieferinxe, Josse (Master of St. Sebastian) (fl.1493-1508) / © Walters Art Museum, Baltimore, USA / Bridgeman Images; **p22**: Black Death at Tournai, 1349 (see also 33793), Le Muisit, Gilles (1272-1352) / Bibliotheque Royale de Belgique, Brussels, Belgium / Bridgeman Images; **p24l**: The Bodleian Library; **p24r**: Apic/Getty Images; **p25**: akg-images/VISIOARS; **p26**: University of Michigan Museum of Art; **p27**: Wellcome Library, London; **p28**: University of Michigan Museum of Art; **p29l**: Mary Evans Picture Library; **p29r**: Wellcome Library, London; **p30**: Prisma Archivo/Alamy; **p31l**: Science and Society Picture Library/Getty Images; **p31r**: Hulton Archive/Getty Images; **p32**: Liszt Collection/Topfoto; **p33**: Shropshire Museums; **p34**: Bills of mortality: Announcement of death through diseases in London in 1665 during the Great Plague. / Universal History Archive/UIG / Bridgeman Images**p35t**: Henry Guttman/Corbis; **p35b**: Account of the Great Plague of London in 1665 (engraving) (b&w photo), Dunstall, John (d. 1693) / Private Collection / Bridgeman Images; **p36**: Guildhall Library & Art Gallery/Heritage Images/Getty Images; **p37**: Portrait of Captain Coram (c.1668-1751) 1740, Hogarth, William (1697-1764) / © Coram in the care of the Foundling Museum, London / Bridgeman Images; **p38**: National Portrait Gallery; **p40**: Wellcome Library, London; **p42**: Peter Horree/Alamy; **p43**: Sheila Terry/Science Photo Library; **p45**: Everett Historical Collection/Alamy **p46**: Mary Evans Picture Library/Alamy; **p47**: Amaret Tanner/Alamy; **p48**: Wellcome Library, London; **p49**: Mary Evans Picture Library/Alamy; **p50**: Granger/Alamy; **p52**: Hulton Archive/Getty Images; **p53**: BSIP/UIG/Getty Images; **p54**: Mary Evans Picture Library; **p56**: Dudley Board of Health poster announcing the burial procedure for people who have died of Cholera, c.1840's (litho) (b/w photo), English School, (19th century) / Private Collection / Bridgeman Images; **p57t**: awaiit high res from Devon Archives/South West Heritage Trust; **p57b**: Mary Evans Picture Library; **p59t**: A map from 'On the Mode of Communication of Cholera', 1855 (litho), Snow, John (1813-58) (after) / Private Collection / Photo © Christie's Images / Bridgeman Images; **p59b**: Death Dispensary, 1830 (engraving) (b/w photo), English School, (19th century) / Private Collection / Bridgeman Images; **p60**: Father Thames Introduces his Offspring to the Fair City of London, a design for a fresco in the new Houses of Parliament (engraving) (b&w photo), English School, (19th century) / Private Collection / Bridgeman Images; **p61**: W.Brown/Otto Herschan/Getty Images; **p63**: Popperfoto/Getty Images; **p64** & **p65**: BettmanCorbis; **p67l**: India Picture/Corbis; **p67r**: Zephyr/Science Photo Library; **p68**: Corbis; **p69**: Aamir Qureshi/AFP/Getty Images; **p71**: Christopher Pillitz/In Pictures/Corbis; **p74l**: Trinity Mirror/Mirrorpix/Alamy Stock Photo; **p74r**: LH Images/Alamy; **p77**: The National Archives; **p78**: City of London: London Metropolitan Archives/Heritage Images/Getty Images; **p81**: Mary Evans/Everett Collection; **p86**: Ann Ronan Pictures/Getty Images; **p90l**: Print Collector/Getty Images; **p90r**: The British Library Board; **p90b**: Corbis; **p91tl**: The Print Collector/Print Collector/Getty Images; **p91tr**: British Library/Topfoto; **p91bl**: Education Images/UIG via Getty Images; **p91br**: Metropolitan Police Authority/Mary Evans; **p93**: British Library; **p94**: Print Collector/Getty Images; **p95t**: Mary Evans/The National Archives, London. England; **p95b**: G Jackson/Arcaid/Corbis; **p96**: Arcaid/Corbis; **p98**: Mary Evans Picture Library/Alamy Stock Photo; **p99**: Interfoto/Sammlung Rauch/Mary Evans Picture Library; **p100**: Mary Evans Picture Library/Douglas Mccarthy; **p101**: Bibilothèque Nationale de France; **p102**: The British Library Board; **p103** & **p107**: Mary Evans Picture Library; **p108**: The British Library Board; **p109**: Corbis; **p110l**: Mary Evans Picture Library/Imagno; **p110r**: Mary Evans/SZ Photo/Scherl; **p112**: His Grace The Duke of Norfolk, Arundel Castle/Bridgeman Images; **p113**: Mary Evans Picture Library; **p114l**: Bob Skingle/Arcaid/Corbis; **p114r**: Bridgeman Images; **p115**: Mary Evans Picture Library; **p116**: Corbis; **p117**: Hulton Archive/Getty Images; **p118**: British Library, London, UK/Bridgeman Images; **p119** & **p121t**: Mary Evans Picture Library; **p121m**: Bridgeman Images; **p121b**: British Library, London, UK/Bridgeman Images; **p123t**: Mary Evans Picture Library; **p123b**: The Gallery Collection/Corbis; **p124l**: Corbis; **p124r**: British Library Board. All Rights Reserved/Bridgeman Images; **p125**: Rijksmuseum; **p127**: Mary Evans/Library of Congress; **p128**: Corbis; **p130**: Mary Evans Picture Library; **p131b**: Stu/Alamy Stock Photo; **p131t**: The Print Collector/Getty Images; **p131m**: Kaihsui Tai/Wikipedia Commons; **p132**: Birmingham Museum Trust; **p133**: National Portrait Gallery, London; **p135**: CartoonStock; **p136**: Her Majesty Queen Elizabeth II, 2016/Bridgeman Images; **p137**: Punch Limited; **p139**: Illustrated London News Ltd/Mary Evans; **p140l**: Eric James/Alamy Stock Photo; **p140r**: Mary Evans Picture Library/Alamy Stock Photo; **p141**: Mary Evans/Everett Collection; **p142**: Corbis; **p144**: Illustrated London News Ltd/Mary Evans; **p145**: The Print Collector/Corbis; **p149**: Ann Ronan Pictures/Getty Images; **p150**: Print Collector/Getty Images; **p151**: Mary Evans Picture Library; **p152**: Hulton Archive/Getty Images; **p153**: University Of Leicester Special Collection; **p154l**: British Library/Topfoto; **p154r** & **p155l**: Mary Evans Picture Library; **p155**: The March of the Women Collection/Mary Evans Picture Library; **p156**: The National Portrait Gallery; **p157l**: Sean Sexton/Getty Images; **p157r**: Museum of London/Heritage Images/Getty Images; **p158**: Hassall, John (1868-1948)/Bridgeman Images; **p159**: Fred W. McDarrah/Getty Images; **p161t**: Modern Records Office , University of Warwick; **p161b**: TUC Library Collections/London Metropolitan University; **p162l**: Hulton-Deutsch Collection/Corbis; **p162t**: John Frost Newspapers; **p162b**: John Frost Newspapers/Mary Evans Picture Library; **p163**: Punch Limited; **p164**: Graham Wood/Evening Standard/Getty Images; **p166**: London Transport Museum; **p167t**: Irish Studies Centre of London Metropolitan University; **p167b**: Daily Express/Archive Photos/Getty Images; **p169l**: Getty Images; **p169r** & **p170**: Evening Standard/Getty Images; **p171**: Marx Memorial Library/Mary Evans; **p174**: The British Library Board; **p178m**: Mary Evans Picture Library; **p178r**: The Granger Collection/Topfoto; **p179l**: Falkensteinfoto/Alamy Stock Photo; **p179t**: Daily Herald Archive/Getty Images; **p179r**: Bettmann/Corbis; **p178l**: Lovell, Tom (1909-97) / National Geographic Creative/Bridgeman Images; **p180**: Andreas von Einsiedel/Corbis; **p181**: Lovell, Tom (1909-97)/National Geographic Creative/Bridgeman Images;**p183**: Anthony Baggett/Dreamstime.com; **p184**: Mary Evans Picture Library; **p186** - **p188**: British Library Board. All Rights Reserved/Bridgeman Images; **p190**: World History Archive/Alamy Stock Photo; **p192**: GL Archive/Alamy Stock Photo; **p194**: Lebrecht Music and Arts Photo Library/Alamy Stock Photo; **p196** - **p201**: Mary Evans Picture Library; **p202**: The Mariners' Museum, Newport News, VA; **p205**: Mary Evans/Everett Collection; **p207**: GL Archive/Alamy Stock Photo; **p208**: Yale University Art Gallery, New Haven, CT, USA/Bridgeman Images; **p209**: duncan1890/iStockphoto; **p211**: Collection of the New-York Historical Society, USA/Bridgeman Images; **p212**: The Granger Collection/Topfoto; **p214**: Mary Evans Picture Library; **p215**: Mary Evans Picture Library/Alamy Stock Photo; **p217**: The Fleming-Wyfold Art Foundation/Bridgeman Images; **p218**: Mary Evans Picture Library; **p220**: Mary Evans/Pharcide; **p222**: Peter Newark Military Pictures/Bridgeman Images; **p223**: Davie, Howard (fl.1914-44)/Bridgeman Images; **p224**: Falkensteinfoto/Alamy Stock Photo; **p226**: Illustrated London News Ltd/Mary Evans; **p227**: Christophe Boisvieux/Corbis; **p229**: The Print Collector/Alamy Stock Photo; **p232**: Rodger Bosch/Stringer/Getty Images; **p231**: Library of Congress; **p233**: Stock Montage, Inc./Alamy Stock Photo; **p234**: Mary Evans/Grenville Collins Postcard Collection; **p235**: Punch Limited; **p237**: Hulton-Deutsch Collection/Corbis; **p238**: Mary Evans Picture Library; **p240**: Corbis; **p241**: Mary Evans Picture Library; **p242**: Mary Evans /Everett Collection; **p244**: Mary Evans Picture Library; **p245**: Culture Club/Getty Images; **p246**: Mary Evans/Sueddeutsche Zeitung Photo; **p247**: Florilegius/Mary Evans; **p251**: Mary Evans/SZ Photo/Scherl; **p252**: Bettmann/Corbis; **p253**: Hulton-Deutsch Collection/Corbis; **p256l**: Daily Herald Archive/Getty Images; **p256r**: Courtesy of The Cross family; **p257**: Meager /Stringer/Getty Images; **p258l**: Popperfoto/Getty Images; **p258r**: Charles Hewitt/Stringer/Getty Images; **p259**: Hipix/Alamy Stock Photo; **p260**: Bettmann/Corbis; **p268**: The Fleming-Wyfold Art Foundation/Bridgeman Images; **p272**: Punch Limited; **p274**: Museum of London.

We are grateful to the authors and publishers for use of extracts from their titles and in particular to the following:

AQA for practice questions from the AQA GCSE History Paper 2 'Shaping the Nation', copyright © 2015 AQA and its licensors. **Cambridge University Press** for Simon de Montfort by J R Maddicott (Cambridge University Press, 1994). **Curtis Brown Group Ltd**, London on behalf of The Estate of C L R James for The Black Jacobins by C L R James (Secker & Warburg, 1963), copyright © C L: R James 1938. **Guardian News and Media Ltd** for 'Cecil Rhodes colonial legacy must fall - not his statue' by Siya Mnyanda, The Guardian, 25 March 2015, copyright © Guardian News and Media Ltd 2015; and 'Why 492 West Indians came to Britain' by our Special Correspondent, The Guardian, 23 June 1948, copyright © Guardian News and Media Ltd 2016. **Hodder Education** for The British Empire, 1815-1914 by Frank McDonough (Hodder, 1994). **Oxford University Press** for English History 1914-1945 by A J P Taylor (OUP, 1992), first published in The Oxford History of England (1965). **Peters Fraser & Dunlop** (www.petersfraserdunlop.com) on behalf of the Estate of Robert Latham for The Diary of Samuel Pepys: A New and Complete Translation by Robert Latham (Collins, 2010). **United Agents** (www.unitedagents.co.uk) on behalf of the author for Pax Britannica by Jan Morris (Faber, 1968), copyright © James Morris 1968.

We have made every effort to trace and contact all copyright holders before publication, but if notified of any errors or omissions, the publisher will be happy to rectify these at the earliest opportunity.